The Swahili

The Peoples of Africa

General Editor: Parker Shipton

This series is about the African peoples from their origins to the present day. Drawing on archaeological, historical and anthropological evidence, each volume looks at a particular group's culture, society and history.

Approaches will vary according to the subject and the nature of evidence. Volumes concerned mainly with culturally discrete peoples will be complemented by accounts which focus primarily on the historical period, on African nations and contemporary peoples. The overall aim of the series is to offer a comprehensive and up-to-date picture of the African peoples, in books which are at once scholarly and accessible.

Already published

The Shona and their Neighbours*
David Beach

The Berbers*
Michael Brett and Elizabeth Fentress

The Swahili
Mark Horton and John Middleton

The Peoples of the Middle Niger*
Rod McIntosh

The Ethiopians*
Richard Pankhurst

The Egyptians*
Barbara Watterson

In Preparation

The Peoples of Kenya
John Middleton

* Indicates title commissioned under the general editorship of Dr David Phillipson of Gonville and Caius College, Cambridge

The Swahili

The Social Landscape of a Mercantile Society

Mark Horton
and
John Middleton

First published 2000

2 4 6 8 10 9 7 5 3 1

Blackwell Publishers Ltd
108 Cowley Road
Oxford OX4 1JF
UK

Blackwell Publishers Inc.
350 Main Street
Malden, Massachusetts 02148
USA

British Library Cataloguing in Publication Data

A CIP catalogue record for this book is available from the British Library.

Library of Congress Cataloging-in-Publication Data
Horton, Mark (Mark Chatwin)
    The Swahili : the social landscape of a mercantile society / by Mark Horton and John Middleton.
        p. cm. — (The peoples of Africa)
    Includes bibliographical references and index.
    ISBN 0–631–18919–X
    1. Swahili-speaking peoples—History. 2. Swahili-speaking peoples—Commerce. 3. Swahili-speaking peoples—Social life and customs.
4. Merchants—Africa, East—History. 5. Muslims—Africa, East—History. 6. Mercantile system—Africa, East—History. 7. Africa, East—Social life and customs. I. Middleton, John, 1921– II. Title. III. Series.
DT429.5.S94 H67   2001
967.6004'96392—dc21

00-009633

Typeset in 10 on 12 pt. Sabon
by Kolam Information Private Ltd., Pondicherry
Printed in Great Britain by MPG Books Ltd, Bodmin, Cornwall

This book is printed on acid-free paper

Contents

Introduction

This book is about the people known as Swahili, who today live in a string of settlements, from cities to small villages, along the coast and the adjacent islands of eastern Africa. Over the centuries they have been urban-based merchants in long-distance intercontinental commerce: the form of their society and its civilization have largely been shaped by this particular specialization in both precolonial, colonial and postcolonial times. They have been Muslims and a literate society for over a thousand years.

There has been much writing on the Swahili, by both their own scholars and western-trained historians, anthropologists, linguists and archaeologists. Each discipline has looked at a particular type of evidence and has attempted to place it within a wider framework, but it is probably fair to state that a comprehensive 'history' of the Swahili is yet to be written; nor could such easily be undertaken within the modern economics of publishing, the rapid pace of research and postmodern perspectives. Our contribution is neither a history book nor an ethnography, but an attempt to bring together the diverse approaches in Swahili studies as seen from the perspective of an archaeologist and an anthropologist. It is the product of our researches and experiences over several years, and we hope we have made a number of hitherto unnoticed connections and deductions.

Archaeologists tend to work from the past into the present, and observe long-term processes from an origin which they are often all too anxious to locate. Their narrative runs over time and place until a not too distant past, when they have normally handed over to historians and anthropologists. Archaeological information can be all too often of a general nature and so cannot deal in many of the details important to modern anthropology. Anthropologists work mainly in the present, through oral and visual information, helped by documents when they are available. They provide a detailed understanding of the present and can reconstruct the fairly recent past, but further back may lie obscurity. We have found a number of advantages in combining the two approaches. We are dealing with a single society, which, while not remaining static over this long period, has none-theless basic underlying structures that have probably changed little. Our approach has been to use the present, wherever possible, to understand and interpret a past that is visible in the archaeological and historical evidence

The sub-title of this book is *The Social Landscape of a Mercantile Society*, and this summarizes the themes which we have tried to combine. The physical landscape of coast has remained relatively stable over the last two thousand years, with relatively minor changes in sea level, vegetation, coral reef formations and river basins. Onto this the Swahili have built networks to sustain a mercantile economy, involving relationships with hinterland and interior groups to obtain commodities for trade and sub-sistence as well as providing military protection for the vulnerable coastal settlements. The Swahili have built their own settlements whose spatial order and architectural forms have expressed aspects of their social struc-ture. These physical remains can be identified and dated through both excavations and the survey methods of landscape archaeology and provide a direct method to study social relations over long periods of time without recourse to often ambiguous documents and oral traditions.

There have been four main problems in much of the previous writing on the Swahili. One is that historiography and archaeology, as well as more general writing, have assumed, on remarkably little evidence other than wishful thinking, that the Swahili have formed a creole society whose civilization has been implanted on the African coastline by invaders from Asia, mostly from Arabia. This view is widely accepted by many Swahili themselves. A second problem is that much of the historical evidence is external to the Swahili, written by overseas traders, travellers or colonizers. One cannot reject this material, but it may create bias in any narrative, making the Swahili appear as unduly influenced from overseas. The third problem is linked to the second, that many writers have failed to compre-hend the African context of this society. And a fourth issue is the complex nature of Islamic society in eastern Africa.

Swahili civilization has been and remains that of a single group of people and not of a series of distinct settlements; albeit with regional variation the Swahili are quite different from their neighbours. The Swahili speak one language or a cluster of closely related dialects. The ruins of many stone-built towns, including those excavated such as Shanga, Manda, Ungwana, Gedi, Ras Mkumbuu, Kilwa and Songo Mnara, poetry such as *al-Inkishafi* and the Fumo Liongo cycles, and the towns of the present day with their domestic architecture, tombs and mosques, are all elements of this single African civilization. It would appear likely, even if as yet unproven from material evidence, that cultural features such as clothing, cuisine, forms of descent and marriage, the nature of Islamic beliefs and practices, and notions of purity and honour, have been retained over substantial periods of time.

One of the aims of this book is to assess the significance of traditional Swahili mercantilism. This society has been at the centre of an immense trading system that has stretched from the Great Lakes of central Africa to the islands of Indonesia and to China, and from Europe to southern Mozambique. The trade has involved both local coastal exchange and also the intercontinental commerce based upon the role of the Swahili as middlemen acting as commercial and cultural brokers between different countries, nationalities and civilizations, which have only rarely had any direct contact with one another. This type of long-distance exchange has been rare in Africa, and with it have gone certain specific features of this civilization. Thus we have considered problems that have scarcely been posed in past accounts: the prehistoric origins, the adoption of Islam, the local and familial organizations of merchants, their interpersonal ties with trading partners, both within Africa and overseas, the means of exchange, and the social and cultural values given to goods and commodities.

The Swahili were important participants in the economy of the Indian Ocean and the commodities that they traded reached across the Old World and, after the sixteenth century, globally. Their contribution should be discussed in a balanced and informed way, especially emphasizing 'World History' as stemming from the early work of Fernand Braudel. This had as its aim a long-needed change of view of the history of the colonial world as seen from the metropolitan countries and argued that the maritime world provided a uniting linkage between diverse cultures. Almost all of these accounts, after brave statements of intention and insightful analysis of metropolitan aims and achivements, peter out into superficial and colonialist-centred discussions of the peoples at the peripheries of fields of colonialist expansion and exploitation, with little understanding of their own social and economic practices as seen from the viewpoints of the 'peoples without history' themselves.[1]

We think it more valuable to analyse Swahili society as being, in its own view, at the centre and not on any periphery, 'Swahilicentric' and not 'Eurocentric' as has usually been the view of those writing world histories. Our approach sees the Swahili as neither peripheral nor isolated. To write a history of this people with themselves at the centre we have tried to listen to and understand Swahili ideas of their own society as determined by their own views of the past. These views provide rationales for the present and its problems and conflicts: they may be 'accurate' in respect of particular events; they may be total inventions; they may take the form of historical documents, of myths whether written or unwritten, or oral traditions, folk memories, or merely dogmatic statements of facts. All these versions of history are central parts of present knowledge. One of our aims is therefore to relate and analyse that knowledge, which is rarely set out, ordered or explained. Not all Swahili may wish to accept the findings of archaeology, anthropology and history, as some of these run counter to frequent assumptions made about Islam and the past: for example, it is often difficult to accept that many of the coastal towns that have been Swahili for centuries were in fact founded before Islam came to the east African coast; some details of early commerce, such as the slave trade, are held by some best not mentioned as they are thought to run against widely held moral ideas.

These questions lead to a final problem, to define the identity of the Swahili. In a sense the old question 'Who are the Swahili?' is an undiscerning one, based on a misunderstanding of what this mercantile system has been and remains. It is also a question whose answer is dependent upon the situation of the observer – for example as an academic historian or anthropologist, as an active participant in the complexities of coastal society, or even as a casual visitor or tourist. However, there is a sense of a common identity, which has always been important in the past whenever the Swahili were in direct contact with others, and is newly important today when the peoples of the coast have become increasingly marginalized in the affairs and prosperity of their own countries. In many ways, the Swahili have been a global society for millennia, and may survive the impact of present day globalization better than most other African groups. We earnestly hope that this is indeed the case.

We could not have written this, or our earlier books, without the help, advice, friendship and hospitality of many, especially those living on the coast today. We hope that they will approve of a work of which they are, in a very meaningful sense, co-authors. We also have a particular debt of gratitude to various organizations that have supported our fieldwork, especially the National Museums of Kenya; the Zanzibar Museum and Archives; the British Institute in Eastern Africa; the Leverhulme Trust; the British Academy; the Fulbright-Hays Faculty Research Program; the Yale University Program in African Studies; and the Institute of African Studies, University of Cologne. We would also like to thank our many academic colleagues and students, who have helped us over the years understand Swahili culture and society, and the University of Bristol, which employs one of us, and provided a visiting Benjamin-Meaker professorship for the other during which the outline of this book was conceived. Finally, we would like to thank Louise Spencely, managing editor at Blackwell Publishers, and Anthony Grahame, who put our often muddled typescript into order; they have both worked hard to ensure swift publication.

1

The Swahili Coast

The People and their Coast

The Swahili have occupied the two thousand mile-long coast of eastern Africa since the first millennium.[1] Their settlements cling to the coastline, at their greatest extent (about the sixteenth century) from Mogadishu in Somalia in the far north to southern Mozambique in the far south. They also live on the large offshore islands of Zanzibar (Unguja), Pemba, Mafia, the small archipelago of the Comoros and Madagascar, but have never reached the further offshore islands of Mauritius and the Seychelles. Until the nineteenth century few of their settlements could be found more than a mile or two from the coast itself; with the development of the Zanzibar-controlled slave and ivory trades within the interior several new communities were established far inland in Mozambique, western Tanzania and eastern Congo, but these were very much the exception. The Swahili have never formed a single autonomous polity with clearly marked boundaries or an obvious centre or capital, yet they have comprised a single social and cultural entity, Swahili society, with its own unique civilization of which they are deeply proud and possessive.

For well over a thousand years the Swahili have controlled most of the intercontinental commerce between the interior of eastern and southern Africa and the Eurasian world. They form one of a series of mercantile societies located around the rim of the Indian Ocean that have exploited the monsoon wind system to enable long-distance trading across the ocean. These coastal mercantile societies, whatever their individual languages and cultures, have had certain features that have marked them off from other societies of continental Africa and Asia. They have been literate, have depended economically not on themselves being important producers but on being commercial middlemen, cultural brokers and mediators between other peoples who have traded with each other only through them. They have had complex internal social structures and forms of stratification, have

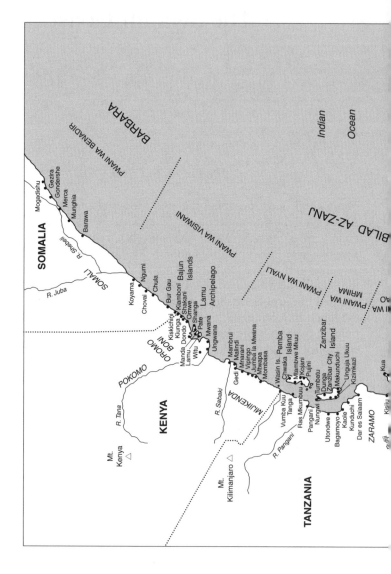

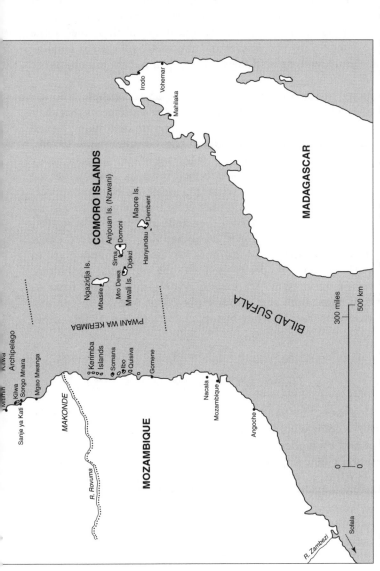

Map 1.1 *The Swahili coast, showing the important settlements and the division of the coastline according to Swahili and Arabic geographical knowledge.*

usually adopted religions and moral values different from those of their neighbours, and have in the end lost wealth and influence to predatory colonial states and empires that conquered them: in the case of the Swahili – Portugal, Oman, Britain, France, Germany and Italy. All these mercantile societies have existed for many centuries and almost all still exist as ongoing societies, even though with little of their former wealth, power, importance and glory.[2]

There are today between about 300,000 and 500,000 people who are known by their neighbours as Swahili, inhabiting the settlements that their ancestors have occupied for many centuries; there are also many ruined sites of abandoned settlements throughout the coastline and islands. Much of the trade on which their society was long based has gone today and the complex system of exchange within their towns is no more, yet the Swahili do not forget their past as merchants. Threatened by what appears to them the intent of the world outside their coastal settlements to destroy them and their cherished way of life, they talk and write about their own past as they perceive and glorify it. Sometimes their perception is supported by less partial analysis, sometimes it is not: the shapes given to the Swahili past are largely determined by the conflicts, ambitions, fears and hopes of the present. We cannot divorce this present from its historical backgrounds, both that as remembered or told by the present Swahili and that constructed from historical, archaeological and other sources.[3]

The Swahili Landscape

The Swahili landscape has largely been shaped by their mercantile role, without which the coast would presumably have been occupied by modest fishing villages and by modern ports and railway termini. It is the people who have shaped the landscape not the landscape the people. Like virtually all landscapes in Africa it is not 'wild' or 'natural' but has been constructed, used, and transformed by those who have lived in it. As with many maritime societies, their landscape includes not just the dry land but the creeks, the mangrove swamps, the shallow waters within the protective reefs and the reefs themselves, all of which are owned by one or other local group. We must include in their landscape the urban and peri-urban settlements, the cultivated lands and plantations, but also what appears to be wild or abandoned land, which is in reality owned but not exploited at a particular moment. In addition a wider landscape stretches far into the mainland – comprising the 'hinterland' lying just behind the immediate coastline, and the 'interior' lying behind the hinterland and extending into the heart of the continent.[4] These are separated in the northern part by semi-arid land occupied by pastoralist and hunting and gathering peoples; to the south of the River Tana the hinterland has been the domain of agricultural peoples, all non-Swahili but speaking closely related Bantu languages. The hinterland and interior groups have been the producers and consumers of most of the long-distance trade goods that have passed through the Swahili coastal settlements themselves.

The East African coastline does not vary greatly throughout its length, in general terms becoming progressively less arid as one sails south. Some parts, especially the offshore islands, are fertile with dense populations, but much of it is almost barren, comprising sand and scrub and little used for farming, although coconut palms grow in sandy soils and grains can be produced in many drier areas behind the coastline itself. The shallow waters within the reefs and creeks are rich in fish and shellfish, and some areas produce valuable mangrove timber.

The coast has many rivers and creeks, many with small islands on most of which have been built settlements; others lie on the creeks themselves, near the sea but protected from the force of the ocean. A few deep rivers are navigable for varying distances, and there are traces of others that have long dried up. The larger rivers extend the narrow coastline inland; the most obvious case has been that of the Zambezi river systems in Mozambique where Swahili traders built towns far inland from the actual river mouths. But other rivers, such as the Tana, Sabaki and Rufiji, have difficult mouths and sea craft were unable to sail far inland. However these river valleys provided caravan corridors into the interior.

The Swahili environment has also extended as a mercantile entity across the Indian Ocean, northwards to Somalia, the Red Sea, and southern Arabia, eastwards to the Persian Gulf, the Malabar coast of India, Sumatra, and Madagascar, and southwards towards the tip of continental Africa. This entire great area has not been controlled from the Swahili coast itself but has been greatly affected by it, by taking its exports and sending it its trade commodities.

A key feature of the ocean is that of its monsoons, known to sailors from at least the Bronze Age (3000–1000 BCE). In brief, the seasonal reversal of monsoon winds, which blow across the Indian Ocean from the south and west between April and September, and from the north and east between November and March, has allowed for both rapid transit and an assured return back to the home port on an annual basis. Navigation has been further assisted by ocean currents which by and large follow the pattern of monsoon winds. The monsoon cycle has not only linked East Africa with Eurasia, but has also provided the means for communication between the Mediterranean, the Red Sea, South Asia and beyond, between the Persian Gulf and South and South-East Asia, and probably South-East Asia and East and southern Africa along a sub-Equatorial route.[5]

On the African side, reliable monsoons extend as far south as Zanzibar, so that the ports northwards have been able to make more immediate use of them, making it possible for ships to make the return voyage to India or western Asia within nine months.[6] Access to the more southerly ports has been less certain, either by using larger and faster sailing ships that probably developed from the thirteenth century onwards or by coastal navigation by Swahili craft with the goods being transhipped in the northern ports.

The Swahili divide the coast into several named stretches based on ports for sailing vessels and termini for caravan routes to and from the interior. This is a social and commercial landscape rather than a geographical one as such: each stretch of coast is given its own mercantile, social, linguistic, and cultural qualities.[7] In the far north is the barren Benadir coast, from Mogadishu as far southward as the Bajun islands near the modern border between Somalia and Kenya. The larger towns of present day Somalia – Mogadishu, Merca, Barawa, Kismayu – were Swahili towns until quite recently[8] (the inhabitants of Barawa still speak a Swahili dialect); this coast is seen as 'lost' by most Swahili today. South of the Benadir lies the green and fertile *Pwani wa Visiwani* (lit. the coast of islands), including the series of Bajun Islands considered by some to have been the original heartland of the Swahili people. It contains the Lamu archipelago with Lamu, Pate and Manda islands each with several large and ancient towns that retain their own version of Swahili civilization. South again is the Nyali Coast, centred on the important towns of Mombasa and Malindi and stretching to the present Kenya–Tanzania border. The Nyali and Visiwani coasts are the best-sited to take advantage of the monsoons between Asia and Africa. Behind them live farming peoples, the Mijikenda and Pokomo, closely related linguistically and historically to the Swahili of the coastline. In northern Tanzania lies the Mrima Coast, opposite the islands of Zanzibar and Pemba, and at one time a trading monopoly of the Sultanate of Zanzibar and the termini of the principal slave and ivory caravan routes. South of the Mrima lies the barren Ngao coast, centred on Kilwa and which was another important region of trade. Farther south, in Mozambique, is the Kerimba Coast, a coastal archipelago occupied by Swahili groups but today mainly by others with connections to the Zimbabwe highlands.

This geography broadly corresponds to that found in the medieval Arab geographies.[9] Here the coast is divided up into Berbara, Bilad az-Zanj and the Bilad Sufala, but these terms were not used with either precision or consistency, making it very difficult to tie down places mentioned in the Arabic documents. The Bilad az-Zanj would seem to cover the Swahili coast from Visiwani to Ngao, while Berbara represents the Benadir, and Sufala the Kerimba coast and beyond.

Towns and Settlements

Swahili society can be followed as a continuous entity in both the historical and archaeological record for over a thousand years. The physical base of this society and its civilization is its settlements, many of which have been inhabited continuously. This is an urban civilization, and the town is the basic unit of social and cultural life, production and government. The Swahili towns form a single category not by their appearance or buildings but because they are so defined by their inhabitants by the single noun *mji* (pl. *miji*): the social and cultural significance of the town, of whatever size, plan or physical appearance, is paramount. We may discern a continuum of settlements known as *miji*, from closely built-up places with mostly stone-built houses set in narrow streets and as clearly urban as anywhere in the world, to what appear more as large villages with mud and palm-leaf dwellings dispersed among overhanging coconut palms. Towns vary in population from a few hundreds to many thousands. No two are precisely alike either in appearance, layout, or ethnic composition, yet all, as 'towns', have long been interlinked into a single mercantile system of considerable complexity.

Plate 1.1 *The traditional Swahili town of Lamu, looking south, from the air. The stone houses lie in the foreground, with the mud houses beyond, while the waterfront was largely created in the early twentieth century (photo Mark Horton).*

Their location and form have been decided by the needs of the commerce and the merchants. The mercantile settlements must possess adequate and safe harbours where ships can rest possibly for long periods while their crews await the change of monsoon. Such harbours may include protected estuaries, channels or islands, where ships can anchor, but in many cases are simply open beaches, where ships can be careened, unloaded and reloaded at low tide.

Harbours must be of easy access from the ocean itself – many indeed lie opposite breaks in the fringing reef – and also for routes into the interior along which have been transported immense quantities of goods for exchange. These sites have had to possess fresh water, able to find adequate foodstuffs not only for their inhabitants but also for what have often been many hundreds of visitors at any one time; they have needed adequate defences against predatory societies from the interior and also from the sea, both their own neighbours and also more dangerous enemies such as the Arab, Turkish, Somali and European 'pirates' who have at various times threatened the Swahili settlements.[10]

These towns have also needed to store and make ready goods for mercantile exchange itself: ivory, gold, all the many objects provided by often distant inland partners, as well as maritime products such as tortoiseshell, ambergris and mangrove poles. No single settlement has been able to rely on its own small population for all these needs, and the mercantile settlements have built up large and complex networks of many kinds of patronage and clientship. Participants have included hunters and gatherers, fishermen, pastoralists, agriculturalists, suppliers of minerals, and those able to supply seasonal labour and occasional military support. Each settlement has had to build up its own portfolio of natural and human resources. Besides these mercantile towns there are many other settlements, all Swahili; their inhabitants are mostly fishermen, farmers, sailors, labourers and craftsmen.

Trade

Commerce has been the driving force behind Swahili civilization and its practice influenced the patterns of settlements, the organization of society and its religious beliefs. It is easy to characterize this commerce as the removal of raw or natural goods from Africa in return for the import of manufactured commodities, but the true situation has always been more complex. Commodities were obtained from an interior stretching from Ethiopia to southern Africa, and during the two millennia covered by this study were subject to fluctuating demands. Thus ivory was in demand for Byzantine art, for bracelets and bangles in Hindu weddings, and for

Table 1.1   Imports and exports from the Swahili coast

Commodity	Exports from the Swahili Coast	Imports from Asia and Europe
1 Clothing and adornment	ivory (elephant, rhinoceros and hippopotamus), animal hides and skins, tortoiseshell and some precious stones	cottons, silks, woollens, glass and stone beads, metal wire, jewellery
2 Perfumes	ambergris, civet	sandalwood, cosmetics, fragrances, kohl
3 Foods	sorghums, millets, sesame (used for oil), cococut oil, vinegar, copra, dried fish	rice, spices (especially pepper, cinnamon, cloves and nutmeg-and-mace), coffee, tea, other foods and flavourings
4 Timber	hardwoods, ebony, mangrove	teak
5 Hardware	boats, sisal, coir, rubber	iron and brass fittings, sailcloth
6 Luxury items	ivory, rock crystal, copal, orchella and other varnishes, tobacco, carved doors and chests	pottery and porcelain, silver, brass, glass, paper, paints, ink, carved wood, books, carved chests
7 Warfare	ivory and rhinoceros horns for sword and dagger handles, forged iron	arms, ammunition, gunpowder, swords and daggers
8 Religion and medicines	incense, myrrh, other gums and resins, rhinoceros horn and many ingredients for 'magic'	religious and aesthetic knowledge and skills
9 Metals	gold, copper, iron	gold, silver, brass and bronze
10 Labour	domestic and field slaves, concubines	religious specialists, craftsmen

American piano keys. Each entailed a distinct set of economic relations between the African interior, the Swahili middlemen and ocean traders.

In broad terms, there was an early period in which the coast and its immediate hinterland was exploited, lasting up to the tenth century. At this time (or possible slightly earlier) longer distance networks also developed with southern Africa, exploiting first ivory and then gold. Other networks may have developed into the Lacustrine area, but there is little evidence at present to document these. By the fourteenth century the Swahili mercantile economy was not limited to any single area or set of towns but extended down the entire coastline and embraced areas of both hinterland and interior. Early observers were struck by the ease and safety with which Swahili merchants could travel up and down the coast. This was also the period of Swahili kingship and the political and cultural power of the patriciates.

The Portuguese changed the nature of the commerce after their arrival in 1498 by introducing armed cargo vessels to the Indian Ocean and by building powerful forts and protected harbours.[11] Their naval, commercial and religious ambitions affected Swahili life and commerce. In the south, in Mozambique, they attempted to take over the gold trade by ousting the Swahili and settling Portuguese in their place, although on the northern coast the Swahili were able to trade much as they had done for centuries. The indirect impact of Portuguese activities within the Indian Ocean was to alter the balance of traditional mercantile activity.

This traditional economy was largely transformed and in places almost destroyed during the rise and political hegemony of the colonial Omani Sultanate of Zanzibar, established by conquest in 1729 by the al-Busaidi dynasty of Oman. From 1832 until 1856 their joint capital was Zanzibar City. The Sultanate was a powerful mercantile enterprise which soon took over control of commerce from the Swahili patricians and reduced them to subsidiary roles. It extended control over not only the coast but also the interior by establishing Zanzibar colonial towns in the interior as far as Maniema in the Congo. The brutal role of Zanzibar and its Swahili partners in the slave trade is still recalled, the cause of much dislike of the Swahili by other peoples of eastern Africa.[12]

This period merged into that of the British and German colonial administrations, the latter of which lasted only until 1918. The British then assumed political monopoly over most of the coast except its extremes, where the Portuguese controlled the far south and the Italians the far north. At first the British favoured the Swahili, using them widely as junior administrative officials, but soon realized the greater potential of the interior and discarded their coastal allies. British overrule lasted until the coming of independence to Kenya and Tanzania in the 1960s, since when the Swahili have seen their political and cultural marginalization as citizens of their own countries.

Swahili Identity

The Swahili are no longer a mercantile society of any importance; but their language has become a *lingua franca* for most of eastern Africa and beyond.[13] They have been used, exploited, and largely discarded by both colonial powers and the independent governments of Kenya and Tanzania, so that the term 'Swahili' has come to refer to a marginalized and internally divided category of people without any obvious sense of single political identity, an 'Other' conceived as a means of self-definition of those who so define them.

Historically the Swahili have had no particular territory around which a boundary could be drawn, they have never had a state centre, or empire, or even a single political authority, yet they have had certain marked features besides their language and their acceptance of Islam that have been unique to them and have distinguished them. One is that they have for many centuries been merchants, commercial middlemen and cultural brokers; another has been that they held and traded in slaves until the end of the nineteenth century; another is that they have had and prided themselves on certain distinguishing cultural features such as house-types, clothing, cuisine, a unique and highly complex poetry, and notions of beauty and purity. One that has not generally been accepted by outside observers is that they have long formed a single society with a structure based upon the reckoning of both patrilineal and cognatic descent, involving the exchange of both goods and marital partners between the constituent settlements.

The often-posed question 'what is Swahili identity' misses the points that the people known as Swahili have now and have had in the past many identities and not just a single one, and that groups and persons can select any one in a given situation and another in another situation.[14] 'Identity' is not an essentialist or generic feature but can be ever-changing, and to be 'Swahili' is only one identity selected from a wide range of names and characteristics. The usual 'Swahili' identities have reflected two views of a postulated history in terms of geographical and ethnic origins.

One is given to them by others, that the Swahili are a culturally broken down people, *Arabisé*, and an 'un-African' cluster of communities, essentially a creole people formed by immigration from Arabia and Persia; an Afro-Arab society in which male Arab merchants took African wives and concubines, but which, culturally, still formed part of the world of western Asia rather than of eastern Africa. As the well-known archaeologist and historian of East Africa, Neville Chittick put it, 'The springs of this civilisation are to be found on the northern seaboard of the Indian Ocean. But it cannot be said to be Arab; the immigrants were probably few in number and there would have been far fewer women than men among them...most Arab men must have married Africans or women of mixed blood and their stock rapidly became integrated with local people.'[15] This view, which is still widely held from school history books to the tourist literature, has also been supported by a narrow reading of the Swahilis' own histories and traditions. These purport to tell of Asiatic origins with founding ancestors and lineages which link them to well-known Middle Eastern groups. As will be explained later, these developed through the process of Islamization, and latterly through the dislocation caused by colonialism, both Arab and European.

The Swahili see their own self-given identity in terms of their claimed ethnic origins, which may include those from outside Africa. Ethnicity refers to actual or claimed places of origin and of descent from them to the present, and has little to do with race. Both external and internal definitions of identity may change and have changed over time, as the criteria alter with developments in local economic, political and cultural conditions and aims. Neither identity or ethnicity are ever static, as may be seen in past censuses: the decennial British censuses of the coast showed often startling changes in numbers of Swahili, Arabs, and other terms, to the bewilderment of the colonial administration.[16] However, whilst accepting these dynamics, outsiders researching Swahili society must respect these local notions of origins from overseas and not reject them completely, in the modern and politically fuelled project to create a totally indigenous African civilisation to balance earlier views of an Asian creole one.

The name 'Swahili' is a Bantu word, rooted in the Arabic word *sahil*, with the meaning of margin or coast, but often in Arab geographies meaning also 'port of trade'.[17] The earliest use of Sawahil (lit. 'lands of the coast') can be found in Ibn Sa'id (1214–75), as the coast close to Qunbalu and other Abyssinian towns.[18] The great traveller Ibn Battuta, who sailed down the coast in 1331, placed the 'country of the Swahili' as two days sailing from Mombasa, but without indicating whether it was north or south.[19] Swahili as an ethnic term was revived by the Omani conquerors who established the Sultanate of Zanzibar in the early nineteenth century so as to make preliminary order in their new colony. They used the word Sawahil as the geographical designation for the East African coast, and the word Swahili for the indigenous population that lived there and the language that they spoke. European travellers followed this usage; for example Lieutenant Smee (in 1820) used the term *Souallie*, in distinction to *Mwarabu*, as somebody of ultimately Arab origin.[20] Non-Muslim subjects were merely 'Africans'.

The name Swahili soon took on a derogatory implication. First, by referring not only to geography but also to the meaning of Swahil as 'margin or edge': the local people were at the edge of both Arabia and the African continent and thus also of Islamic civilization. Although Muslims they were considered heterodox, contaminated in the eyes of the Omani by being Sunni-Shafi'i, unlike the Omani who were Ibadi, and perhaps by their beliefs in many local spirits and adherence to spirit cults. They were thus also considered to be at the border with Black Africa whence came their slaves.

The connection with slavery became even more urgent with its abolition and the need to label those of slave origins living on the coast and increasingly becoming Muslims. These groups of Muslim Africans came also to be known as 'Swahili', especially during the British colonial period when the Christian missionaries and colonial administrators drew 'ethnic' maps of Africa, marked boundaries around groups that appeared to have a single language and some kind of named identity, and then incorrectly assumed that these groups were primordial, stable and unchanging. No African societies have been so and the Swahili are no exception.

Nowadays, the term 'Swahili' is rarely used by those who are the true members of the coastal mercantile society that we shall be describing in this book, and whom we have used as the main source material for our ethno-historical analysis. Instead identification terms derive from their towns or islands (e.g. waAmu, the people of Lamu, waTumbatu, the people of Tumbatu), more limited ethnic terms such as Bajuni or Hadimu, or ones based upon a shared origin myth, such as Shirazi. Kiswahili as the language is used with greater ease, although here also the dialects of the several towns, such as kiUnguja, kiMvita, kiAmu and kiPate have greater everyday importance.[21]

In recent years, especially after independence, 'Swahili' has developed a wider usage, through its adoption by local historians and academics to indicate the indigenous but Muslim identity of coastal society. Those trained or working within the colonial period avoided the term completely,[22] and during a transitional stage, both African and other scholars often used the euphemism, 'Swahili-speaking peoples'.[23] Increasingly, those who used 'Swahili' were those who subscribed to the indigenous nature of coastal society; those who denied this came to use other terms such as 'coastal peoples' or 'East African society'. In the future the term may be revived in the ancient centres such as Lamu and Zanzibar, through local cultural and museum-led education programmes; indeed, there is some evidence that this may already be happening.

The Composition of Swahili Society

Swahili society comprises many ethnically defined elements that together form a single entity basically defined as Muslim and as speaking dialects of Kiswahili.[24] They include groups that may loosely be referred to as indigenous and others whose fairly recent ancestors were immigrants from Arabia. The elements are named, have different and complementary economic and political roles and hold varying places in the overall system of social stratification.[25]

The various groups that inhabit the coast each see their history largely in terms of genealogy, of presumed or claimed descent from a founding ancestor and especially from an original homeland. Some of these claims are historically justified, others are not. Genealogies are not always statements of actual ancestry but are validations of present authority and position: descent and kinship are socially defined and measured for validation of status and may not be biologically or historically true.

Plate 1.2   *A Swahili patrician family observed in 1846–9. Lithograph made from a daguerreotype; from M. Guillain,* Documents sur l'Histoire, la Géographie, et la commerce de l'Afrique Orientale *(Paris, 1856, vol.3).*

It is generally and justifiably considered by all members of Swahili society that the core element is that known in English as patricians,[26] a translation of the Kiswahili term *waungwana*. They have lived generally in the towns, of which they are the *wenyeji* (owners) and are also included as *wananchi* (people of the land or country). They recognize descent in the patrilineal line, and have complex systems of ranking among themselves and with others. They have been the merchants of history, the upholders of *ustaar-abu*, civilization, and *utamaduni*, urbanity, that they hold to be unique to themselves as contrasted to the *ushenzi*, 'barbarism', that surrounds them. Even today, when they have become largely impoverished, they retain their long-standing hegemony as the cultural elite of the coast. The *waungwana* are the possessors of the moral quality of *uungwana*, 'civility' or sometimes defined as 'of gentle birth'. They have formed a closed elite, based on occupation, purity, almost a private religious orthodoxy, and formerly great wealth. They have provided the centre of far-reaching mercantile relations with both Africa and Asia, but were never landed aristocrats; they have remained resolutely urban.[27]

There is no single word in English that correctly describes the *waung-wana*. It is held to refer to qualities such as elegance, good ancestry, gentlemanly behaviour, and we have adopted the word patrician as the closest equivalent, while being fully aware that there remain only broad comparisons with the classical world from where the term derives. It has been used in most previous accounts of Swahili society.

They are members of patrilineal clans, those of its members living in any one town forming a subclan, the clan itself being dispersed. There has been continual movement of patricians up and down the coast, so that the members of a particular subclan may be among the earliest members of one town but among the newest of another. Many patrician subclans have at various times claimed clan ancestry in Arabia, to show an equality with the former elite of the Zanzibar Sultanate and personal kinship with trading partners in Arabia, and to separate themselves by ancestry from their African slaves. Few of these claims can historically be substantiated and most probably date to the nineteenth century.

The words 'clan' and 'subclan' have been used by non-Swahili observers in order to translate several Swahili terms, *taifa*, *kabila*, and *mbari* being the most commonly used for the same types of descent groups. The terms carry the essential significance that the members of such groups claim common ancestry, even though it may be clear that all do not actually do so. Ancestry is the basic quality, rather than ethnicity or locality even though these factors may in fact historically be more accurate. The Swahili privilege ancestry over other factors, and we attempt to follow them in this regard. The division into clans is a means of making consistency and order within a local population whose members may themselves recognize different origins or ethnicities in their personal family histories. The fact that in several of the more ancient towns there are reckoned twelve clans, usually comprising one cluster of nine and the other of three, would argue for the reordering of historical variation for the sake of consistency; but it does not appear possible to prove what can at present only be this surmise.

The patricians comprise three elements. The most numerous are those whose members have often claimed to have originated in Arabia. These are the *waungwana* par excellence, whose urbanity is at the heart of the moral quality of *uungwana* and status of *wenyeji*, who over many centuries have built up this mercantile economy and who often claim themselves to be the most orthodox in Islam (a claim rarely held by others). Their subclans are ranked in any one town, ostensibly in order of coming from Arabia.[28]

There are in the northern towns a few groups who are now considered to be patrician, but were probably historically non-patrician. They are known by the clan names Wayumbili, Kinamte and Famao, often referred to jointly as Makhzumi. They do not claim non-African origins and despite their presumed primordial presence have not acquired political or commercial dominance; they have held ritual duties such as the right to blow the *siwa*, the great brass or ivory horns that are among the towns' insignia, at patrician weddings, and have often been given polluting occupations such as washing of corpses.[29] Today most people whose ancestors bore those names have changed identity and joined other more prestigious patrician subclans.

The third group of patricians are those *sharif* lineages (whose members claim direct descent from the Prophet) whose founders came to Africa about the sixteenth century. They have been referred to as the 'Old Arabs' of the coast,[30] and should be distinguished from those sharif groups who came from the Hadramaut in the late nineteenth century. Although concerned with commerce as much as any other patricians, their assumed high moral qualities from their descent have usually been taken as more important. Their reputation has given them considerable commercial advantages, which they not unexpectedly have used for their own benefit. They also play important jural roles: being attributed Islamic learning and standing apart from the more purely mercantile lineages they can act impartially in secular disputes.[31]

There are several groups, known as Shirazi, claiming an origin in Persia rather than Arabia. For example, the founding myth of Kilwa and some other places refer to merchant princes sailing to the Swahili coast from Shiraz (now in the province of Fars in Iran) and establishing towns among the barbarians.[32] Most known as Shirazi are found on the Mrima coast and the islands of Zanzibar and Pemba, but they are also important in the Comores and around Kilwa. As we shall see, the claimed Persian origin is extremely unlikely. Some may represent early indigenous trading groups which have over time lost much of their mercantile influence and, except in a few centres such as Kilwa Kisiwani, Mafia, and perhaps Tumbatu, do not now consider themselves 'patrician' but rather are farmers and fishermen.

Besides the patricians or former patricians, there are several groups of non-patricians who are always accepted as 'true' Swahili, and who are also known as *wenyeji* and *wananchi*. These are the occupants of the rural settlements, mostly fishermen, farmers and gardeners, whose names typically refer to their location or status (e.g. the waTumbatu, waPemba, waHadimu).[33]

They generally differ from the patricians in not having been merchants, in not formerly owning slaves, and in reckoning cognatic rather than patrilineal descent; if they claim origins from Asia these are ancient and generic, such as Shirazi origins. Some of these claims are, however, invented more recently to establish an earlier but still Muslim origin than the Omani Arabs who wished to oust them from their lands.

On the farther northern coast and islands are the groups known as Bajuni, not merchants but in general reckoning patrilineal descent and often claiming to be *waungwana* (in some colonial censuses claiming to be Arab). Many have recently been driven from their lands by Somali and have moved southwards along the coastline. With the Bajuni may be included the various formerly isolated Swahili-speaking groups of southern

Somalia, some of slave ancestry and others descendants of the original inhabitants of formerly Swahili towns from Mogadishu to Kismayu; in recent years most have moved to north-eastern Tanzania.[34] There are, mostly in Mombasa, a few families of Comorians, who speak a dialect of Kiswahili; their status is ambiguous as although Swahili yet they are of clearly different origin to the mass of coastal Swahili.

There are then the descendants of former slaves, especially those emancipated under European colonialism,[35] known generally (but never addressed) by the somewhat derogatory name *wazalia*, 'those born in the country' and without pretensions to non-African origins. They have typically been given merely African origins, anywhere from Ethiopia to Mozambique: former domestic slaves were given new names and dates of birth by their owners when purchased, so that their original places of origin have long been forgotten. In the mid-nineteenth century slaves formed at least half of the inhabitants of the towns and their descendants continue to form a substantial part of the Swahili population.

The Swahili also include elements in the interior who have come to see themselves as distinct from surrounding peoples by being traders with links to the towns of the Swahili coast; examples are the occupants of the inland Tanganyikan trading centres such as Ujiji or Mto-wa-Mbu, or commercially successful traders among hinterland groups such as the Mijikenda and Zaramo.[36] 'Swahili' here refers essentially to occupation, rather than to any historical actuality of common ethnic origin, even though people have almost invariably claimed it as validation for their belonging to coastal civilization (even if those on the coast may deny any affinity with them).

During the eighteenth century and later there was much immigration of colonists from south-eastern and southern Arabia, the 'New Arabs'. The former were from Oman and so closely identified with the Sultanate of Zanzibar and its rulers, and are generally known as Manga. The latter were from the Hadramaut and generally known as Shihiri (from the Arabian port of el-Shihr), who settled in towns along the coast during the final years of the nineteenth century.[37] In time both categories adopted the Swahili language and have usually been taken by outsiders and visitors as 'Swahili', although this identity is rarely accepted by the patricians proper.[38] The Hadrami, in particular, were part of a diaspora from Arabia to Egypt, India and Indonesia, as well as East Africa, so forming an element in an international mercantile community renowned for its Islamic scholarship. A distinct category of Hadrami immigrants came via the Comoro islands, to settle in Mombasa, Zanzibar City, and Lamu, and have been an important reforming influence in local Islamic practice.[39]

During the early years of the twentieth century there were also many immigrants of labourers from the Hadramaut, who came from social groups of the lowest rank, were barely accepted by the earlier Arab colonists, and who took up menial jobs such as coffee sellers, assistants to higher rank Hadrami retailers, and so on. The members of this last category suffered the most violence in the Zanzibar revolution of 1964 as they were rarely wealthy enough to flee the islands.[40]

The position of these 'New' Arabs, whose ancestors were part of the wave of colonists and settlers under the Sultanate, is ambiguous. Their wealth, education, and high religious authority and scholarship gives them high rank; yet their differences in ancestry and length of settlement in eastern Africa place them as recent intruders and as nouveaux riches. They are also distinguished from patricians and other 'true' Swahili by never being called *wenyeji* or *wananchi*: they remain newcomers despite their wish to belong to Swahili society. It has long been the custom for Omanis to return to Oman in old age to die there; also many left East Africa after the Zanzibar Revolution of 1964 to resettle in Oman and the Gulf States. These factors have been taken by many Swahili as indicating where lie the true loyalties of these 'New' Arabs.

From at least the fifteenth century there have been groups from the Indian sub-continent settled along the coast, mostly Muslims but with some Hindus.[41] They have typically been retailers and money lenders, usually working on their own but in Zanzibar City and Mombasa also representing the Indian finance houses of Bombay and elsewhere. The most important are the Ismaili and Bohora communities. They have never been accepted as Swahili even though there has always been some intermarriage. Those remaining on the coast have diminished in numbers and wealth during the twentieth century, and many of their shops, mosques, schools and even settlements, especially on Zanzibar and Pemba, have been abandoned.

Finally there have been many recent immigrants from the African interior, who have come as labour migrants and plantation squatters; they live as marginal members of the towns and have built their own settlements in places such as rural Pemba island.[42] They have not been accepted as members of the Swahili towns proper and have only rarely accepted Islam, but have played political and economic roles of importance.[43] The Swahili proper often refer to them disparagingly as *waAfrika tu* 'just Africans'. There are small numbers of other non-African immigrant groups: European,[44] Chinese,[45] Malagasy and others. The first have exercised political and economic power in the past as government officials and today as entrepreneurs, hoteliers, representatives of international companies and development agencies.

Swahili society, as we refer to this complex of peoples of various claimed origins, is the subject of this book and we define and discuss its structure and culture – or set of interactive sub-cultures – in later chapters. Its constituent elements are distinguished by claimed origins, by roles played by descent, rank and cultural nuances in this traditionally mercantile society. The list of these elements given in the last pages may imply separateness between them rather than their complementarity and unity. No one element – partrician, non-patrician, Arab, ex-slave or other – can be envisaged and understood without reference to all the others: they live side by side along the coast and they meet, talk, pray and interact with each other in their everyday lives. To distinguish them by generally used names does not distinguish them as though in a census. As with most social identities, their boundaries are there and have meanings, but they are permeable and changeable in many situations, such as cooperative and productive enterprises and religious and recreational participation. Intermarriage, although it does take place, is in general disapproved, with each element properly being endogamous and with its own marital strategies and patterns to maintain its exclusivity; none the less, each element may be recognized by such features as patterns of speech, address and minutiae of clothing, as with patterns of men's embroidered hats or the material and shape of women's veils.

Swahili Society Today

The internal structure remains essentially that of the past, in external form at least, but former patterns of power and authority have changed greatly. Until a century ago, or later, the Swahili towns were controlled by their patricians, the *waungwana*. Their powers have now faded but their traditional way of life is still regarded by virtually all the coastal inhabitants as being that of the 'true Swahili', *uungwana wa haki*, the core of 'civilization', *ustaarabu*. The inhabitants of most rural settlements have changed relatively little in their general social position: those of Zanzibar and Pemba islands probably still live to a remarkable degree much as they have ever done.[46] On the other hand, the Swahili fishermen of the coast and islands of southern Somalia and northern Kenya, the Bajun, have mostly been driven from their homeland by Somali raiders and have dispersed all along the Kenyan and Tanzanian coast. The descendants of slaves, who are also Muslims, today form the lower strata of the towns but are accepted as proper Swahili. The Hadrami are today the most wealthy element, as were many of the Omani who fled Zanzibar at the 1964 revolution; yet both these and other linked urban categories such as Bohora Indians retain something of their liminal status.

The condition of the Swahili Coast and its occupants today appear at first sight to be in a state of some uncertainty, even confusion: ethnic identities that have been at least meaningful, even if always fluid and ill-defined, are under continual attack, doubt and questioning. The past economic and political relationships between its various elements are in a condition of flux. Religious practice and affiliation remain highly controversial. Many of the occupants of the coastal towns, other than very recent immigrants, tend to see a deep gulf between their own concerns and interests and those of the central governments of Kenya and Tanzania, sometimes regarded as the direct colonial successors to the Europeans and Omani Arabs.

Yet much the same could always have been said. We wish to avoid the position taken by so many past observers and by many of the people themselves, that this present time is a meaningful historical point, even a nadir, that is unique and that marks the end of Swahili history as that of a mercantile civilization. A widespread view of the Swahili by outsiders has been that they live in a state of despondency, of nostalgia for a glorious past as means of enhancing the present as a continuation of past greatness, indeed of hopelessness in face of the seeming injustice of the modern world in which they find themselves.

Some Swahili may also see the world like this, but most do not: people tend to see history in the light of their own personal experience and place in its unfolding. We take today as neither a nadir nor a zenith, but as an encapsulation of the past and having within it the future, neither a finite stop in time nor a finite place in space. Swahili civilization has never been at a single level. There have been periods of high wealth, living standards, sense of morality, and the other aspects of its civilization. One might characterize 'golden ages' as the tenth and fourteenth centuries, or perhaps particular places such as eighteenth-century Lamu and nineteenth-century Zanzibar. The low points, from the Swahili interpretation of their history, were when the Portuguese and then the Omani conquered much of the coast from the sixteenth century; or when the Zanzibar Sultanate took over the more profitable parts of their former commerce and then the British took over the Sultanate and abolished slavery.

However, it is fair to say that for the first time for over a millennium, the coast has become economically and politically something of a backwater and to a large extent left alone to cope with the present world as best its inhabitants may. With their economic and commercial decline, the Swahili have long lost their once-favoured position under first the Sultanate and then under early British colonial rule. Today they feel – and have been – regarded as unimportant by their own governments, and subjected to the insults of the tourist trade from which they gain so little.

But that is on the surface. Beneath it coastal society is always changing, as it has done continually over many centuries, in economy, ethnic identities and composition, and in everyday social and cultural life. Much of Swahili wealth has gone, but they continue to live lives of formal elegance and self-esteem. They cling proudly to their traditional forms of clothing, cuisine, and to their code of good and honourable manners and behaviour, *uung-wana*. Their own governments may treat them as marginal citizens,[47] but they are skilled and enterprising people who make their way in this modern world. During the latter part of the twentieth century a Swahili diaspora has resulted in sizeable communities in London and Paris, as well as in the countries bordering the Indian Ocean. This diaspora makes important contributions to global cultural diversity and intellectual life, but also retains close links with the East African homeland.

2

Origins

Two Thousand Years Ago in Eastern Africa

Our knowledge of East Africa in the early centuries of the first millennium is largely based upon the fusion of two types of evidence – archaeological and linguistic. Each tells a slightly different story, but one in which over the last few years there has been a broad convergence of the main outlines. This identifies three main groups living in the region to the east of the Rift Valley. The first were those following a hunter-gatherer way of life, with a technology based on stone and bone, and known to archaeologists as Late Stone Age populations. Secondly were agropastoralists, with a Stone Age technology but maintaining considerable herds of cattle, sheep and goats, and cultivating grasses such as sorghum and millet. Thirdly there were small farming communities, with an iron technology, settled in permanent or semi-permanent villages, with a few stock, either sheep or goats, cultivating sorghum and millets and hunting a wide range of fauna.[1]

These three groups can be identified using the pattern of languages which are still spoken in the region today. The hunter-gatherers have not fared well, and what must have been a complex mosaic of languages survives as isolated examples, such as spoken by the Hadza and Sandawe groups in northern Tanzania. The agropastoralists spoke Cushitic and Nilotic languages, and of these Eastern Cushitic and Eastern Nilotic are still widely spoken, although the commonest language family 2000 years ago was probably Southern Cushitic, which is found nowadays in only isolated pockets, probably the Iraqw of northern Tanzania and the Dahalo of the river Tana delta.[2] The farmers spoke Bantu languages, which today form the most widespread and populous language family in eastern and southern Africa, but at that time was a comparatively recent arrival.

In addition, there were two other groups, for which there is at present only patchy evidence. The first were indigenous coastal peoples, exploiting the rich marine resource of shellfish, fish and sea mammals, using a Late

Stone Age technology. There is no linguistic trace of this population, neither are there any such surviving ethnographically, while the archaeological evidence comprises sites on coastal and island locations (such as on Zanzibar and near Kilwa) that certainly point to the use of boats.[3] Further archaeological work will undoubtedly discover more of these sites, especially where they have been preserved in areas above the sea level rises of the last 2000 years.

The second group is yet more enigmatic, comprising South-East Asian seafarers, who certainly settled on Madagascar – the linguistic evidence linking Malagasy (the language spoken on Madagascar) with South-East Asia is irrefutable – but who may once have spread along the African coast and islands as well. Linguistic reconstructions point to the Austronesian settlement of Madagascar around 2000 years ago, but at present the first trace of human intervention in the pollen record is around 400, and the first archaeological evidence is as late as 800.[4] There is at present no archaeological evidence for South-East Asian settlement on the mainland of East Africa, although an Indonesian role has been suggested in the introduction of maritime and fishing technology, such as outrigger canoes, as well as certain crops, especially bananas and plantains, and domesticated animals such as the chicken.[5]

The Swahili communities of the East African coast developed out of one or more of these groups, and the main direction of the debate at present is to identify exactly which of them contributed to the growth of coastal urban society. The linguistic evidence is clear and unambiguous; Kiswahili forms part of the North-East Coastal Bantu language cluster, and shares many features in common with the Mijikenda and Pokomo languages of the immediate coastal hinterland from the Tana river to northern Tanzania.[6] Simply put, the Swahili of the East African coast represent a specialist coastal adaptation of these more widespread farming societies, through their participation in long-distance trade, the adoption of Islam and the development of urban living.

The two groups which modern scholarship rejects as having anything much to do with Swahili origins, but which played a key part in the narratives of the earlier generation of historians, are those of Arab and Persian colonists. The older literature dwells extensively upon the setting up of colonies for trade with Africa during the early Islamic period, mainly through misreadings of the traditional histories of the Swahili, but despite extensive archaeological investigations no such colonies have yet been found.[7] Several sites are now known to predate the Islamic expansion of trade across the Indian Ocean from the eighth century onwards, while even the settlement of substantial communities of foreign merchants within indigenous towns has little archaeological or linguistic support before the nineteenth century.

The notion of such 'colonies' was a crude (and to a large extent racist) device to explain the development of civilization on the African coast. The rejection of this view has forced a re-examination of the indigenous context for the Swahili. It is equally important to place the Swahili within the Indian Ocean world of trade and exchange, involving not only trade goods but technologies, agricultural innovation, religion, architectural style and ideas. The impact that these had on the development of the Swahili must be balanced by the contribution that these African coastal communities made in their own right to the Indian Ocean world and to the other civilizations that developed along its rim, not just in terms of trade goods but also of African technologies, social organization and aesthetic expression.

Early Indian Ocean Trading Systems

The seasonal patterns of monsoons enabled long-distance maritime trade to develop across the Indian Ocean possibly as early as 5000 years ago, but there remains considerable uncertainty as to the date when East Africa was drawn into the system. An earlier generation of historians tried to link various groups from the ancient world with East Africa, including Egyptians, Sumerians, Phoenicians, Assyrians and even Jewish merchants seeking Ophir.[8] There was very little historical basis for any these links, most of which were generated by a European colonial imagination keen to attribute any African cultural achievement to foreigners.

The evidence for the origins of Indian Ocean seafaring is largely archaeological.[9] The earliest material known at present links the Indus civilization of North-west India with Mesopotamia, c.2500 BCE. While trade between the two areas may have been at least partly undertaken overland, an important port, known as Dilmun, developed on the island of Bahrain, suggesting that maritime trade was particularly important. Excavations at Qal'at al-Bahrain, often identified with ancient Dilmun, includes finds of Indus Valley weights and other Indian artefacts. The presence of both Indus Valley artefacts (including considerable quantities of ceramics) and Mesopotamian material in graves and settlement sites in coastal Arabia points to a maritime trade possibly linked to the mining and exploitation of copper in the mountains of Oman. It seems that boats travelled to this region from both Mesopotamia and the Indus Valley for this copper, possibly setting up the basis for a coastal trade along the northern shores of the Indian Ocean. These contacts seem to have been relatively short lived, and by the beginning of the second millennium BCE had declined.

It is possible that this Bronze Age coastal exchange network extended along the southern coast of Arabia into North-East and East Africa. Here the evidence is botanical, based on finds of early African millets – sorghum, finger millet and pearl millet – in Arabia and northern India. Dates for sorghum in Oman have been claimed as ranging from 2400 BCE to 2000 BCE, with the crops established as domesticates in India from around 2100 BCE onwards. There is no doubt that the wild species on which domestication was based are entirely African, but there is no evidence that these were domesticated in North-East Africa before 500 BCE, and possibly considerably later. Two solutions have been suggested:[10] that the Indian and Omani identifications are wrong, based upon intrusive cereals, or that there was an unexplained trade in wild grasses and cereals out of Africa some 4500 years ago. The source of these cereals could have been either the northern region of the Horn, or perhaps more logically, given the patterns of winds and currents, the East African coast.

One other piece of evidence suggests that there was a trade route down the East African coast during the Bronze Age. An artefact made of copal, a resin collected from hardwood trees, was excavated from a grave at Tell Asmar in ancient Mesopotamia from a context of around 2500 BCE. This proved to be from *Trachylobium*, a tree only found on the East Africa coast, and indeed the main source for the colonial copal industry. Pieces of copal, so far unanalyzed, but probably from *Trachylobium*, have been found on African iron age sites, suggesting that it was exploited at least 2000 years ago, and it is a commodity that could well have been associated with indigenous coastal hunter-gatherers, who used resins as hafting material for stone tools.[11]

Much of the older literature suggests that the Egyptians, by reputation one of the more advanced of the civilizations of the ancient world, sailed to East Africa on a regular basis. This hypothesis rests largely upon the identification of Punt, the destination of a number of expeditions setting out from the Red Sea during the Old, Middle and New Kingdoms.[12]

As early as 5000 BCE, Egyptian trade with the Red Sea region has been suggested through the analytical sourcing of obsidian, which has an Ethiopian or Eritrean origin but is found in Egyptian predynastic graves.[13] Ship depictions in the Egyptian Eastern desert, most of which are predynastic, have been used to reconstruct routes between the Nile Valley and the Red Sea, and it is possible that this trade route extended further, to obtain Asian and North-East African products such as lapis lazuli and resinous incense. But, from the Old Kingdom onwards, and in particular during the New Kingdom, the documented maritime expeditions to Punt to obtain incense, wild animals, gold and skins were almost certainly confined to the Red Sea. Modern scholarship places Punt somewhere inland on the African side of the Red Sea, not beyond the Bab el Mandeb straits into northern Somalia or even on the East African coast.

Indian Ocean seafaring during the Bronze Age, if it was extensive, seems to have largely ceased around 1000 BCE. This may have been linked to the disruption that can be found across the ancient world at this time with the breaking up of centralized states, and a consequent decline in the consumption of high value commodities that formed the basis of the long-distance trade. While archaeological research may reveal traces of this trade extending to East Africa, we can be fairly certain that it had little to do with the origins of the Swahili.

The widespread resumption in Indian Ocean trade around 300 BCE can be associated with Greek interest in the Indian Ocean that may have followed on from the conquests of Alexander the Great and the opening up of eastern Asia to European interest. There are also documented treaty relations between the Persians and Indians at this time, which suggests the presence of maritime links along the Makkran coast. The Ptolemies, a Greek dynasty ruling in Egypt, had a particularly strong maritime policy. They established ports down the Red Sea, initially for collecting war elephants but by the end of the second century BCE as termini for voyages into the Indian Ocean.

While the reconstruction of maritime activity from the historical sources stresses the involvement of the civilizations of the Mediterranean, the Near East and India, it is likely that there was a substratum of local maritime networks, largely unaffected by the rise and fall of the great powers of East and West but based upon exchange of prestigious commodities. Within East Africa, the rare finds of coastal artefacts, including marine shells and a single faience bead (which might have been of Egyptian origin) in the graves of the pastoralists of the interior,[14] dating to the first millennium BCE, could also have been part of a widespread exchange system that embraced coast and interior and may have extended to southern Arabia and the Red Sea.

Such coastal networks are best demonstrated in the Indian sub-continent, where ceramics dating to the late first millennium BCE, including Red Polished and Rouletted wares have a widespread distribution and must have been exchanged along the sea coasts.[15] Classical imports first appear around 250 BCE, but in small quantities, although substantial trade represented by the famous Arretine ware from South Italy as well as amphorae dates from the first century. The growth of Roman-sponsored trade in the Indian Ocean can also be seen from recent excavations of the Red Sea ports, the descendants of the elephant hunting stations of the Ptolemies, the most notable of which are Quseir al-Qadim and Berenice[16] and which must have directly served East Africa. One surprising conclusion from these investigations is that while the classical literature stresses the importance of European and Egyptian sailors in the developing Indian Ocean commerce, the archaeological evidence points to the involvement of Indians sailing westwards, supplying the boats and sails and even establishing communities in the Red Sea ports; it is not impossible that East Africans reached these ports as well.

One means of studying the detail of Roman trade with the East is through the large number of hoards of gold and silver coins struck in the Mediterranean. There are very few such coins from East Africa, but in the Indian sub-continent numerous hoards have been found. These suggest that Roman trade with India (or Indian trade with Rome) may have reached its peak during the first century.[17]

Early Trade with East Africa

The evidence from East Africa is much more fragmented than from the Indian sites but the basic elements of the economics and chronology appear to be the same. In this analysis, long-distance maritime trade with East Africa began about 100 BCE and became particularly important during the first century. This does not deny earlier exchange networks but marks the point at which the coast was drawn into a wider world. Some voyages were direct, between the Red Sea and East Africa, but most of the long distance traders need not have been Egyptians or Greco-Romans: they were more likely Arabians and Indians, carrying East African commodities, especially ivory, northwards to the ports along the sea-lanes linking India, the Persian Gulf and the Red Sea.

Archaeological evidence for early trade with East Africa comes from the excavations conducted some years ago by Neville Chittick in northern Somalia, at two sites at Ras Hafun, one at Daamo, and one at Heis.[18] One of the Hafun sites, that of Hafun West, was occupied during the first century BCE to the early first century, with pottery derived from the Eastern Mediterranean, the Nile Valley, Mesopotamia and India. The site covered less than 0.12 ha, and included a midden of *Murex virginius*, shells collected for their dye. Chittick excavated part of a stone building, possibly a house set around a courtyard. Hafun West may well have been a seasonal site, used by sailors awaiting the change of monsoon, either to cross to India, or to sail southwards down the East African coast. The sites of Heis and Daamo, on the northern coast, seem to be more closely linked with the trade between India and the Red Sea, with occupation in the early first century. Heis is perhaps best known for the large collection of Roman glass, collected in the nineteenth century and brought back to Paris.[19] It was found in burial cairns a short distance from the coast, showing that such imported commodities were exchanged with the local communities and were later used for grave goods.

From the East African perspective, the second Hafun site, known as the Main Site, is of particular importance. This was relatively large, about 1.3 ha in size, with a complex stratigraphy of ash and sand lenses. Post holes were found although no coherent building plan was recovered. Study of the ceramics suggested two periods of occupation in the 2nd/3rd century and 3rd/5th century, with the bulk of its imports coming from the Persian Gulf with a few from India but very little Red Sea or Mediterranean material. Hafun Main Site represents a shift in trade to an axis between the Persian Gulf and the East African coast.

Archaeological evidence for early trade on the African coast further to the south is fragmentary and largely based on coins and occasional other stray finds. There is no pattern of hoards, as have been recognised in India, but rather collections of coins of several different dates and origin, or single coin finds with ill-recorded origins.[20] For example a coin, dated 110–108 BCE of Ptolemy Sotar was being offered for sale in Dar es Salaam in 1901, with the claim that it was found at Msasani, now a suburb of Dar es Salaam. No early occupation has been found here – the site is marked by an eighteenth-century tomb – and the coin could have been a tourist souvenir collected on the journey through the Suez Canal, and somehow lost. A well-known hoard of coins was apparently found at Bur Gau, on the southern Somalia coast, including Ptolemaic coins, but also Roman, Mamluk and even Ottoman coins – the latest dating to the seventeenth century – suggesting that the hoard was buried less than 300 years ago.

Beads and glass provide more secure evidence, as these are less likely to have been gathered by European 'collectors', and they are beginning to be found from excavated East African Iron Age sites.[21] A group of glass fragments from Kivinja, to the north of the Rufiji Delta, have been compared to Greco-Roman glass from the Fayum of the first few centuries while some sherds of an alkaline-glazed ware from this site are very similar to finds from Ras Hafun main site. Kivinja has two radiocarbon dates, spanning the fifth and sixth centuries. On a nearby site a segmented alkaline glass bead of Classical Mediterranean type has also been found. An old find of glass beads near Kisiju and from Dar es Salaam, which were described as 'Frankish' can now be seen to compare to the first century glass found at Heis.[22]

At two sites on Zanzibar, trade can be recognized during later Antiquity. At Unguja Ukuu finds of a few sherds of North African Red Slip pottery point again to a Mediterranean connection, and these are associated with sixth century radiocarbon dates.[23] At the north tip of Zanzibar, at Fukuchani, fragments of amphorae are of the same type as have been found in the upper levels of Ras Hafun main site, possibly of the fifth century. In southern Mozambique, at the coastal site of Chibuene, the lowest levels produced a rim of storage jar with a torpedo shape, probably of Partho-Sasanian origin.[24]

So much can be deduced from archaeology, but there are also two important documentary sources, both written in Greek, which have been much used to understand the origins of East African coastal communities: the *Periplus of the Erythraean Sea*, an anonymous trader's manual of about

40, and the *Geography*, written by the Alexandrian geographer Claudius Ptolemy around 150.[25]

The *Periplus* provides a detailed account of the voyage to East Africa that was taken from the Red Sea, clearly stating that departure took place in the month of July. Chapter 15 of the *Periplus* gives a detailed itinerary from Opone, almost certainly Ras Hafun, listing the runs (a day's sailing) down the Somali coast past the Small and Great Bluffs and Small and Great Beaches (the latter were still called this in the nineteenth century), two place names, Sarapion and Nikon, through the Pyralaoi Islands and the 'channel' later reaching the island of Menouthias. The topography fits closely with the African coastline, with each run working out at a fairly precise 48 nautical miles. Sarapion and Nikon lie on the southern Somali coast (possibly near modern Merca and Barawa), the Pyralaoi islands (or 'islands of fire', possibly so named because they were being cleared for farming) being the Lamu archipelago, and the channel being the passage that can be taken between the islands and mainland, and which provides a safer route than following the coastal reefs that lie some five miles offshore. The first large island to be reached is Pemba, and this fits closely the position given for Menouthias. Menouthias is 300 stadia from the mainland (or around 30 miles), Pemba is 28 miles offshore at its narrowest point. The description of Menouthias, being low and wooded with rivers, fits with Pemba. Menouthias is the first point where inhabitants are mentioned, with their sewn boats, dugout canoes and basket traps for fishing.

In chapter 16 of the *Periplus* the last port of trade along the coast is described. Rhapta, so named because of its sewn boats, was two runs from Menouthias, or using the calculations that fit so well down the coast, approximately 88 miles away. This places it in the vicinity of Bagamoyo, 90 miles distant. A number of observations were made about Rhapta. The inhabitants controlled their own places, but were also under the authority of the governor of Mapharitis and the kingdom of Arabia, 'through an ancient right'. Most of the trade was done by merchants from Muza in southern Arabia, who imported iron implements, glass stones (probably beads), wine and grain; in exchange were ivory, rhinoceros horn, tortoise shell and a commodity whose translation is unclear but may possibly be nautilus shell. The Arab seafarers knew the coast well, who 'through continual intercourse and intermarriage, are familiar with the area and the language'. This suggests that trade between southern Arabia, Rhapta and Menouthias had been going on for some time before 40, almost certainly taking us into the late first millennium BCE.

The text in the *Geography* is more difficult to interpret, and has consequently often been ignored by modern commentators. The purpose of the account was to illustrate a world map, and Ptolemy (c.90–168) worked from earlier accounts of voyages and in particular the geographical treatise

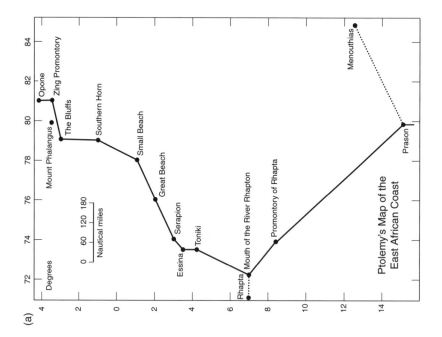

(a)

Ptolemy's Map of the
East African Coast

Opone
Zing Promontory
Mount Phalangus
The Bluffs
Southern Horn
Small Beach
Great Beach
Essina
Serapion
Toniki
Rhapta
Mouth of the River Rhapton
Promontory of Rhapta
Menouthias
Prason

Degrees

Nautical miles
0   60   120   180

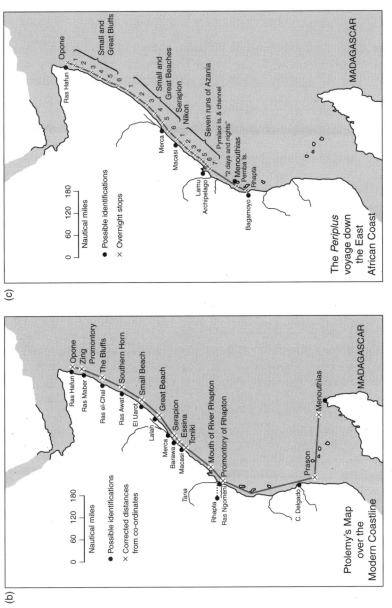

Map 2.1 *The classical topography of East Africa, (a) using the co-ordinates in Ptolemy's Geography; (b) superimposed (and corrected) distances from these co-ordinates placed on the modern coast, (c) the Periplus itinerary superimposed on the coast.*

(c)

Ras Hafun
Opone
Small and
Great Bluffs

1
2
3
4
5
6

Small and
Great Beaches

1
2
3
4
5
6

Serapion
Nikon

Merca
1
2
3
4
5
6
7

Macasi

Seven runs of Azania

Lamu
Archipelago

Pyralaoi Is. & channel

"2 days and nights"

Menouthias
Pemba Is.
Rhapta

Bagamoyo

MADAGASCAR

0   60   120   180
Nautical miles

● Possible identifications
× Overnight stops

The *Periplus*
voyage down
the East
African Coast

(b)

Ras Hafun
Opone
× Zing
Promontory

Ras Maber
× The Bluffs
Ras el-Chal
× Southern Horn
Ras Awat
Small Beach
El Uarot
× Great Beach
Lalah
Merca
Serapion
Barawa
× Essina
Macasi
Toniki
× Mouth of River Rhapton
Tana
× Promontory of Rhapton
Rhapta
Ras Ngomeni
× Prason
C. Delgado
× Menouthias

MADAGASCAR

0   60   120   180
Nautical miles

● Possible identifications
× Corrected distances
  from co-ordinates

Ptolemy's Map
over the
Modern Coastline

of Marinus of Tyre (*c*.70–130) (there is no evidence that Ptolemy knew about the *Periplus*). For the East African sections, he drew particularly on this earlier work, even citing the original sources that Marinus himself used. There were two voyages, accounts of which seem to have ended up in Alexandria and might date to the first century. The first account was of Diogenes, driven off course while sailing to India and ending up at Rhapta after 25 days sailing, and the second of Theophilus, who was 'accustomed to sail to Rhapta' and took 20 days to sail back from Rhapta to Aromata (Cape Guardafui).

Ptolemy (possibly using Marinus) conflated these voyages, to provide an account of topography and distances (in days sailing) down the coast. It is abbreviated and confused, but if read with his lists of places with their co-ordinates (and the main purpose of the *Geography* was to construct a map), it makes some sense. The text suggests that he assumed a daily figure of 400–500 stadia (about 40–50 miles) which if compared to his calculated distances from his co-ordinates gives a range of between 42 and 67 nautical miles a day and the total distance from Opone to Rhapta of around 920 miles, covered in eighteen days sailing. The places passed en route are familiar to the readers of the *Periplus*; the beaches, the bluffs, a new trading place, Essina, then Sarapion and Toniki (probably the same place as Nikon).

At this point the *Periplus* and *Geography* diverge: there are no Pyralaoi islands but rather the mouth of the river Rhapton, Rhapta itself, set back from the sea, and the promontory of Rhapta. This places the river Rhapton where the channel is in the *Periplus*, and which Ptolemy's sailors may have thought was a river. Rhapta might be located at the end of one of the deep creeks at the back of the Lamu archipelago, or possibly up one of the earlier mouths of the river Tana, which reached the sea behind Lamu island itself. Ptolemy provides only the co-ordinates for the island of Menouthias, which is now far to the south, close to the present island of Madagascar, while Cape Prasum, the furthest limit of navigation, 'beyond which the land to the west and south is unknown' would correspond to Cape Delgado.

While both the *Periplus* and the *Geography* provide a convincing fit to the East African coast, there are key areas of difference, in particular in providing two locations for Rhapta, one inland on an estuary, the other on the mainland opposite Zanzibar or Pemba.[26] As Rhapta is yet to be located, we cannot resolve which is the more accurate, but it remains possible that Rhapta, which is not an indigenous name, was where traders were able to meet the local inhabitants with their sewn boats and exchange goods. It may not therefore have been in a fixed position, and possibly moved over time. The account in the *Geography* is possibly a little later than that of the *Periplus* – because Essina is now added, while the trading places were now identified as ports. It is just possible that the terminus of the trade moved northwards during the course of the first century from near to Bagamoyo to the Tana river.

Most of the East African commerce was in the hands of Arabian traders as they could complete the journey within the year. For ships coming from the Red Sea, a full fifteen months was required, effectively blocking out two years of trading time.[27] The extremely profitable voyages to India, while being much more dangerous, only took a year, and it seems likely that few Greek or Roman ships traded with Rhapta on a regular basis. This may explain the confusion, and indeed the general lack of classical finds, along the East African coast.

For most of the classical period no documentary evidence has survived to allude to the continuation of trade. The Ras Hafun evidence suggests that from around the third century trade with East Africa may have been more directly with the Persian Gulf, perhaps reflecting a decline in the Red Sea system but also with the much easier trading links using the monsoons. African products may have been collected en route to and from India, rather than obtained by long voyages from the Red Sea.

By the sixth century, classical knowledge of the area was rudimentary, but there is passing reference to Zingium (almost certainly the East African coast) in a narrative written by Cosmas Indicopleustes and based on a voyage undertaken in 525.[28] This trading pattern may have been temporally reversed during the reign of the Byzantine emperor Justinian (527–65). Within the Mediterranean world there was a boom in the demand for quality ivory – numerous pieces have survived from this period – and this may have resulted in direct trade beginning again with the Red Sea. After *c.*540 the number of ivories in the Byzantine empire dramatically fell, possibly through the collapse of the Mediterranean economy through the spread of the disastrous bubonic plague. Indeed, it is just possible that the plague, which was recorded as coming from Africa at the time, may have been carried by ship rats on board ivory-carrying boats from East Africa.

Early Trading Communities

The *Periplus* provides the only description of the indigenous African communities that participated in the early trade. They clearly had boats, both sewn and dugouts, and were able to inhabit offshore islands. Fishing seems to have been important and basket traps are described in some detail on the island of Menouthias. The imports included iron spears, axes, knives and awls, although this need not mean that they were unable to make their own and so indicating a Stone Age culture, but rather that the imports may have been cheaper or of a different quality. Glass beads, wine and grain were also imported. The most controversial part of the description states that the inhabitants of Rhapta were big-bodied men.[29]

Most historians have doubted that agricultural groups – the early Bantu – had anything much to do with the early trade. Their conclusions have been largely based on the chronology of Bantu settlement, which has been placed on the Kwale and adjacent Usambara and Pare hills, not until the early second century, perhaps 60 years after the *Periplus* was compiled. The conclusion has been that there was little continuity between the *Periplus* period traders and the Bantu-speaking coastal East Africans who seem to be related to the later Swahili communities. The failure to find Rhapta or indeed any other classical trading sites underneath Swahili settlements has further emphasized this discontinuity. The inhabitants of Menouthias may have been different to those living at Rhapta; on the offshore islands, there were groups with a specialized maritime culture, whereas on the coast there were enclaves of pastoralists, who were able to supply the principle trading commodity, ivory.

A reassessment of the evidence and some new discoveries suggests that a Bantu connection is after all possible.[30] The chronology for agricultural settlement had been based on a handful of radiocarbon dates from the type site of Kwale and a few from elsewhere[31] processed in the early days of radiocarbon testing and with a large error margin. The calibrated date range, at one standard deviation, falls within the period 100–500, or, as is now normally quoted, at two standard deviations, 1–600. It is often assumed that these dates represent the 'earliest' date for farming settlements, but new discoveries have produced significantly earlier ones. One of these is the site of Limbo, where two earlier dates calibrated to the first century.[32] Controversially, Felix Chami has reclassified the Early Iron Age ceramics into three phases – called Limbo (1–200), Kwale (200–550) and Mwangia (500–600); in this new sequence, Bantu speaking farmers could have been present on the coast at the time of the *Periplus*.[33]

Recent discoveries from Mafia Island of Early Iron Age pottery clearly indicate that these early farmers had a maritime technology.[34] The voyage to Mafia from the mainland port of Kisiju is over twenty kilometres of open and treacherous ocean. Radiocarbon-dated Early Iron Age material has also been found on Koma and Kwale Islands, lying four and ten kilometres offshore respectively. If these farmers were able to travel to these three islands then they would have also been able to travel by boat along the coast, allowing for the possibility of the rapid spread southwards of the Early Iron Age cultures.[35]

It seems logical to suggest that these Early Iron Age sites were involved in the Indian Ocean trade. Until recently, all the sites which have been excavated contained only local materials, but one site, Kivinja, as mentioned above, has produced Greco-Roman glass and alkaline-glazed pottery with radiocarbon dates in the middle of the first millennium. If these findings are borne out by further excavations and detailed analysis, then at least one early African maritime trading community will have been located.

Ceramics and Swahili Origins

One simple test for Swahili origins relies upon the characterization of their ceramics and a study of the distribution of sites with the same type of pottery. The starting point is those urban and mercantile communities which have a clearly excavated sequence. Study of their ceramics shows that there is a logical progression of types spanning hundreds of years.[36] Sequences dating to the eighth to tenth centuries have been published from coastal sites such as Shanga, Manda, Kilwa, Kisimani Mafia, Ungwana and from the Comores.[37] Of particular interest, however, were the close similarities with pottery found in the coastal hinterland. This was first recognized by David Phillipson, who collected material from Wenje, a village on the middle Tana river, which he then compared to sherds that he found on the beach at Kiunga.[38]

Plate 2.1 *A nearly complete pottery bowl of Tana tradition type showing the typical triangular incised decoration. Excavated from Shanga and dating to around 800 (photo Mark Horton).*

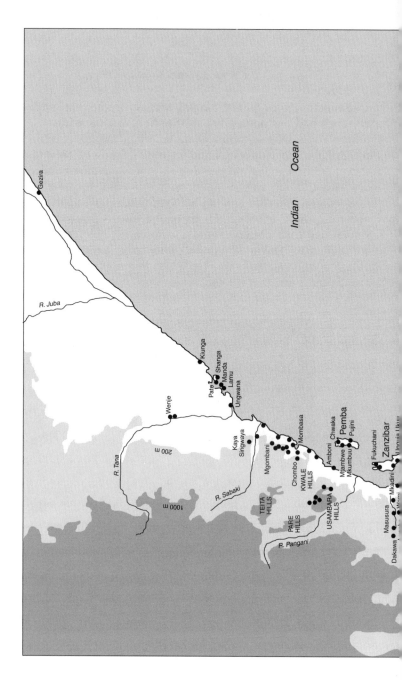

Indian Ocean

Gezira

R. Juba

Kunga
Shanga
Pate Manda
Lamu
Ungwana

Wenje

R. Tana

R. Sabaki

200 m

1000 m

Kaya
Singwaya

TEITA
HILLS

PARE
HILLS

R. Pangani

Mgombani

Chombo
KWALE
HILLS

USAMBARA
HILLS

Mombasa

Amboni
Mjambwe
Mkumbuu

Chwaka
Pemba
Pujini

Fukuchani
Zanzibar
Unguja Ukuu

Mkadini

Masusura

Dakawa

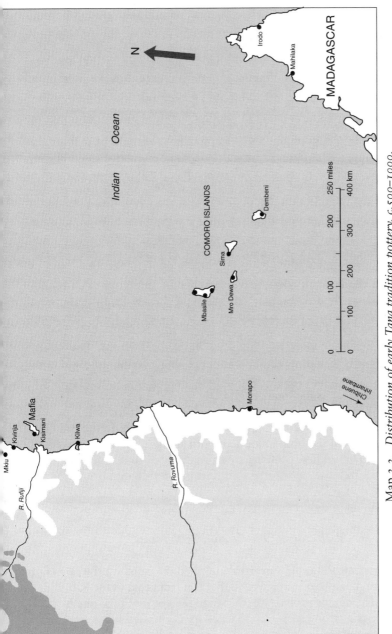

Map 2.2 *Distribution of early Tana tradition pottery, c.500–1000.*

By 1987 it was clear that the pottery of the coast and hinterland belonged to the same ceramic tradition – a simple observation that proved beyond doubt the African nature of early Swahili society. Coincidentally the spatial distribution of this ceramic tradition corresponded closely with that of the North-East Coastal Bantu speakers – that is the Swahili, Mijikenda and Pokomo – and perhaps most convincingly its presence at Kaya Singwaya, one of the early 'traditional' sites of the Mijikenda, further demonstrated this link. However the statistical study of Iron Age ceramics was fairly undeveloped. While the obvious connection between Tana tradition ceramics and Early Iron Age ceramics should have been made at that time, the one serious study, reliant upon statistical analysis of excavated assemblages, concluded that there was no such relationship.[39] Further research, it was hoped, would fill in the gaps and show a logical development from pastoralist pottery instead, with its much longer sequence into the first millennium BCE, into Tana tradition and thus showing a long-term linkage between coast and the interior.[40]

In fact recent research has produced a quite different outcome. First in coastal Tanzania, and most recently in the hinterland of Malindi and Mombasa on the Kenyan coast, a whole range of sites have been found, with good radiocarbon dates, that link the typical early Iron Age farming villages to those with Tana tradition pottery.[41] Crucially these sites were found in lightly wooded environments in which one would expect farming communities to live, while the study of the animal bones show some domestic animals, including cattle, were kept, but that hunting was also important. Rare coastal imports were found, further suggesting participation in long-distance trade. Statistical analysis of the ceramics[42] has now been undertaken to show a seamless development of coastal Iron Age ceramics[43] during the first millennium into the ceramics found on both Swahili sites, as well as those associated with modern groups such as the Mijikenda and Digo. These findings are strongly supported by the linguistic evidence which has always pointed to a north-eastern Bantu origin for the Swahili.[44]

Prehistory of the Coastal Settlements

These early agricultural groups probably reached the coast via the ranges of hills – the Pare, Usambara and Kwale – that run from east of the Rift Valley to the coast. The date is probably earlier than the conventional one of 100–200 and there is a strong suspicion that the users of sewn boats were from these same agricultural communities who successfully settled the coast and offshore islands. They also – as is clear from the ceramics – retained their cultural connections with the hinterland. Over time, these farming/fishing

Plate 2.2   *The early archaeological site of Fukuchani, on the north-west coast of Zanzibar island, showing the beach and sheltered harbour with the middens and habitation layers scattered along the shore for a distance of around 800 metres (photo Mark Horton).*

groups of the East African coast were able to exploit their geographical position and to act as middlemen within a developing Indian Ocean commercial world.

At this stage, there is very little to differentiate the coast and hinterland sites from the point of view of their artefacts. Both have large quantities of locally made pottery, with no typological distinction between the coast and the interior, as well as evidence for iron working and shell-bead making; occasional glass beads have been found, and very rare sherds of imported pottery. The coastal sites are invariably adjacent to protected beaches, onto which small boats can easily be drawn up and which offer fishing grounds and places to collect shells. It is also a characteristic of these beach-line sites that fresh water can invariable be obtained, either actually on the beach itself or at the back of the beach in the area of sand dunes, a phenomenon based on the property that fresh water floats over saline sea water.

Fukuchani, on the north-west coast of Zanzibar, is a typical example of these early coastal sites.[45] The beach is protected by the long island of Tumbatu, and comprises a firm sand surface overlying a coral bed rock. There is a small village still there, and fishing boats use the beach with its local fish market. Water is collected from shallow wells set 50m back from the beach. Middens extend along 1200m of shoreline, and extend to a height of over 2m. There are large quantities of local pottery, but only very rare pieces of imports – less than 1 per cent of the total: they comprise earthenware storage jars, mostly from the Gulf, and dating from the fifth to eighth century. There are also a small number of pieces of Indian origin. It is an assemblage of imports very similar to that found at the Hafun Main site. No post holes were found, but there was a considerable quantity of daub, suggesting timber buildings, as well as shell beads, bead grinders and quantities of iron slag. The diet, from the bones found in middens, had a strong hunter-gatherer component and shows that wild animals were more important as a source of protein than fish. Shellfish were of particular importance and could have been collected at low tide without the need for boats.

Fukuchani was one of a series of contemporary sites fringing the west coast of Zanzibar and the east coast of the mainland spanning the sixth to tenth centuries and seeming to form a distinctive group. They comprise middens and pottery scatters with little evidence for architecture beyond the occasional post hole; some have been eroded away, or built over by later sites – that at Mkokotoni for example has very little of its archaeology left. Most have evidence for iron working, copper working, bead making and contain between 1 and 5 per cent imported pottery. The best known is Unguja Ukuu,[46] geographically extensive (around 10 ha) and spread along a beach and creek well protected from the ocean swell. On the mainland, the centre of Dar es Salaam – only a few metres from the beach, and in one of the best protected harbours on the East African coast – was also important but has been largely built over. Along the coast is Kunduchi, where pottery is eroding along the shoreline; the site itself is covered by an eighteenth-century cemetery and mosque. Close to Bagamoyo there are number of early sites, including Mpiji where the sea is currently over 2 km away, but was much closer when the site was occupied. Kaole (but overlain by later mosques and tombs) lies at the neck of a peninsula, with shelter on either side, depending upon the monsoon, and ranges in date from the seventh to ninth century. Mkadini was found many years ago and was thought to be a salt producing site, but its importance can now be recognized as another coastal settlement.[47] In sum these form a unified group of communities living around the shores of the Zanzibar Channel and may well represent the earliest centre of coastal maritime culture.

A case can also be made out for the early settlement of the Lamu archipelago and adjacent coastline, where beach-line sites are quite common, but none have yet been excavated.[48] Most of the sites became towns and the early levels lie deeply buried below later occupation, and while well preserved are much more difficult to study.[49] At Shanga the first settlement dates to *c.*760 and the site differs in its location from the others in that it is set back behind the sand dunes in a natural depression with a roughly dug well in the centre. There were large trees around the well, growing where the land was damp. There were numerous post holes, some of which formed

Plate 2.3 *Excavations of the deeply stratified site of Shanga in the Lamu archipelago, where four metres of deposit represented occupation c. 750–1425. At the base, cut into the natural sand dunes, were post holes from circular timber buildings, while the first stone buildings appear from around 920. The stone houses seen in the top level, constructed of coral rag and lime mortar, date to around 1320 (photo Mark Horton).*

arcs suggesting circular structures, as well as shell middens. In these early levels there was imported pottery (only 3.8%) and craft activities were mainly iron and copper working and bead making; the diet contained very few domestic animals (occasional chicken, sheep, goat and cattle) but hunted antelopes, turtles, and dugong as well as only those fish species which could be caught inside the reef.

Beyond these two core areas of the Zanzibar Channel and the Lamu archipelago, other early sites have been reported and their distribution is much more scattered. The early levels of Kilwa are known very little, but may date to this early period, as may Dembeni on the Comores and Mahilaka in Madagascar.[50] In Mozambique, two sites, Chibuene (with some sixth-century pottery) and Inhambane, are located among sand dunes, close to the beach, and follow the classic location of the Tanzanian sites.[51] The most northerly site with Tana tradition pottery is Gezira, on the Somali coast.[52] There remain whole areas of the coast for which there is little evidence for occupation prior to the tenth century, but which later become key centres in the development of Swahili culture – including the coast from Malindi southwards to Bagamoyo and much of Pemba and Mafia islands. This may be a genuine absence of sites, or simply due to a lack of survey, which in the past concentrated only on sites with monumental architecture.

There is little to differentiate Iron Age coastal and hinterland communities across a core area from the Rufiji to the Tana rivers during the middle of the first millennium, and there can be now little doubt that these were Bantu-speaking farming and fishing villages. Little is known of the crops that these communities grew, but there was small-scale stock keeping and clearly hunting was also important. Craft activity, especially iron working, was a common theme, and the coastal sites also worked shell beads. One component of this society faced towards the Indian Ocean and developed a number of special features – the exploitation of fish and shell fish (and with it a maritime technology) – and occasional trade with Indian Ocean merchants. As would be expected, most of the imports are found on the coast, but some found their way inland, no doubt as part of a wider exchange system that may have resulted in commodities from the interior (such as ivory and gum copal) reaching the coast. These were not specialized trading communities, but villages content to trade whenever the opportunity presented itself.

The central question remains how did these villages, with their opportunistic trade, come to be transformed into an urban and mercantile society. The archaeological, and to a lesser extent historical evidence, shows that this happened between 500 and 1000, and probably between 750 and 950. It was this transformation which established Swahili society as we can recognize it nowadays and separated culturally (though not economically or linguistically) the coast from its hinterland. If we are to unpack the issue of Swahili origins, we need to look in some detail at the two fundamental changes which affected East Africa, to take place within the context of the Indian Ocean world – the spread of Islam and the development of Islamic-controlled maritime trade.

3

The Acceptance of Islam

The origins of East African Islam is one of the most difficult and controversial issues in coastal history.[1] In the old models of Arab colonization, Islamic origins were synonymous with the arrival of Arab traders. However, the archaeologists working within this paradigm had particular difficulties. Imported pottery from their excavations dated to the ninth and tenth centuries, pointing to the arrival of these supposed traders, but the architectural evidence for Islam was considerably later. The earliest dated inscriptions, from Barawa in southern Somalia and from Kizimkazi Mosque on Zanzibar, date to the beginning of the twelfth century.[2] The great mosque at Kilwa and the early mosque at Kaole also date to the same comparatively late period, while the excavations at Manda, which was claimed as one of these early trading 'colonies', has a mosque dating apparently only from the fifteenth century.[3]

If the architectural evidence was unclear, so too was the documentary. Descriptions by al-Mas'udi, the only early eyewitness account from a voyage undertaken by him in 916, described traditional religious practice as widespread, but only one Muslim community, located on the island of Qanbalu, had a 'mixed population of Muslims and Zanj idolaters'.[4] Buzurg Ibn Shahriyar, a collector of sailor's stories, both accurate and fanciful, recounted how an East African king was captured in 922 and sold into slavery, but managed to escape and return home, now a Muslim; when he confronted his original captors many years later, he was not displeased 'for no other man in the land of the Zanj has obtained a similar favour'.[5] Even as late as the mid-twelfth century Idrisi described Barawa, in southern Somalia, as the last town (i.e. most northerly) in the land of the infidels. By the early thirteenth century the geographer Yaqut described Mogadishu, Pemba, Zanzibar and Tumbatu as Muslim, but another contemporary geographer, Ibn Sa'id, stated that Mombasa and Malindi were not.[6] The first reliable source to provide evidence for the complete conversion of the coast was the eye-witness account of Ibn Battuta, after a voyage that probably took place in 1331.[7]

Those favouring an indigenous origin for the Swahili have consistently discounted the role of Islam in their development by confusing it with ethnic origins. In the recent syntheses, Islam rarely features as an important factor, but as a later layering onto indigenous and well ordered urban communities.[8] Part of the problem has been that to many African and Africanist scholars, Islam = foreignness, and even Islam = Arabs, and thus attempts to identify early African Islam diminish local cultural achievements. We do not accept the architectural and documentary evidence for the lateness of Islam, as there is evidence to show that Islam was practised widely on the East African coast as early as the eighth century. African Islam forms part of the indigenous achievements of coastal civilization; world religions have universal impact, which local societies rework within their own cultural context.

The embracing of Islam by the peoples of the coast represents the point in time when they were differentiated culturally from the peoples of the hinterland. As yet there is no evidence for any permanent Islamic communities inland south of the pastoralist societies of Somalia before the nineteenth century. Without exception, every pre-nineteenth-century mosque or Muslim tomb known is located within 1000 metres of the sea shore. Islam drew a very clear divide through the Iron Age societies of the coast and hinterland, which, as we have seen, enjoyed a substantial degree of cultural unity before the ninth century.

Some have argued that being a Muslim is the absolute minimum requirement to be part of Swahili society. This is indeed the case today, as we have seen in chapter 1, and by this argument, the Swahili, as defined both by themselves and others, can only 'exist' when they become Muslim. However, what is the case today may not have been so in the past, with a more flexible approach to religion. This definition is also restrictive by placing into limbo ancient sites which show obvious affinity in every respect, except religion, to later Swahili communities. Pre-Islamic Swahili communities did exist, but their acceptance of Islam represents a defining moment in their cultural development.

Early Muslim Communities in East Africa

East Africa did not form part of the lands conquered by the Islamic armies[9] and there is no evidence that any consideration was given by the Caliphate to expand into East Africa. Even though the Islamic world was divided, all Muslims viewed the lands beyond these frontiers as *dar al-harb*, literally translated as the 'region of war' in distinction to the *dar al-Islam*. The status of the inhabitants of the *dar al-harb* (which also included India and China) outside the Islamic world was the subject of complex legal and taxation agreements, the *aman* – in the African case because of the importance of the slave trade. In general these rules restricted the early spread of Islam to East Africa and disallowed the actual settlement of Muslims in *dar al-harb* areas.

The early African slave trade was an important factor that restricted the spread of Islam. In general it was not permitted to take slaves from Muslim countries or actually to enslave Muslims, although slaves might in due course become Muslims. The *aman* treaty arrangements allowed merchants to obtain slaves from their African partners in relative security. Once these partners became Muslim, they would become a protected people, liable to a poll tax, and could not be enslaved – although no doubt they could obtain slaves themselves from the non-Muslim areas of the coastal hinterland. It was, therefore, not in the interest of slave traders to allow Islam to spread too freely within Africa.

In spite of this 'official' position, there is now clear archaeological evidence to suggest Muslim communities were in East Africa from the eighth century. At Shanga, excavations investigated the levels below the Friday or Congregational mosque.[10] This building was constructed around 1000 but rested on the remains of earlier structures. One formed an earlier smaller stone mosque, with a mihrab or prayer niche, and dated to the early tenth century. Below were seven separate timber mosques, one over another, most themselves having several phases of rebuilding – indeed the seven mosques spanned twelve constructional phases. The dating of these buildings relied upon radiocarbon tests, stratigraphy and associated imported pottery, with the first dating to the mid-eighth century. The twelve phases, if each represented ten years of use (a figure not uncommon for timber buildings on the coast), would take the first mosque to around 780; fifteen years per phase would move this date to 720.

The identification of these buildings as mosques was conclusive, based upon the form of the buildings, which closely follows that of the later stone mosques, the careful use of the Islamic cubit, and the buildings' alignment, linked to associated burials placed in typical Muslim positions, with an orientation towards Mecca. These early burials are of interest, as they include children and females, while a recent study of their physical characteristic suggests that they were an African population.

Along with these mosques and burials, coins were also found, minted in silver, but minuscule in size.[11] The earliest contained the Arabic inscription in translation 'Muhammad/trusts in Allah', and a slightly later version read 'The kingdom is Allah's/and in Him trusts Abd Allah'. These coins dated to the eighth or ninth centuries. While it is possible that these coins are imports, this is very unlikely. They cannot readily be compared to others in the Islamic world; indeed the right to strike coins was carefully retained by the Caliphate, and these coins certainly do not form any official issue. Comparisons might be made with breakaway Shi'ite groups, such as the

Plate 3.1   *Excavations below the Friday mosque at Shanga between 1986–8 revealed a succession of earlier mosques. The Friday mosque itself dates to around 1000 with an earlier stone mosque of the early tenth century. Below this were found seven earlier timber mosques of post and stake construction, the first dating to the late eighth century. Over time these mosques improved their orientation towards Mecca, the first being some 50 degrees from the correct* qibla *line (photo Mark Horton).*

Fatimids[12] and Zaidites, but no parallels can be found although there are general similarities in the way the coins were made. Another argument for a local origin is that the coins form part of a series which continued in silver issues found on Pemba and copper coins minted at Kilwa and Mafia. These are certainly associated with local rulers.[13] The Muhammad and the Abd Allah coins from Shanga represent an early generation of Muslim leadership, and significantly both names are often associated with Muslim converts. Stylistically the earliest coins are of the highest quality, and this falls over time, suggesting that skills of the first generation of minters were progressively lost.

Taken together, this evidence suggests a small Muslim community living at Shanga, perhaps from the second part of the eighth century. The size of the first mosques was tiny – the first six mosques would have contained fewer than 25 worshippers – and this would suggest a total Muslim population of fewer than 150. The importance of Islam is apparent from the central position of these mosques, adjacent to the main well. From all the excavations there was no convincing evidence for non-Islamic religious activity and it is probable that Shanga was a Muslim settlement from its foundation.[14]

Other sites have evidence for early Islam. Ras Mkumbuu on Pemba island contains a very large early eleventh-century mosque, which contains the remains of an earlier stone mosque in the platform fill beneath the floor.[15] As with Shanga, this was preceded by a timber mosque, evidenced from its post holes and scatters of daub; it was constructed of mangrove poles and probably dates to the early tenth century. The significance of these mosques is that they are on a larger scale than Shanga, indicating a sizeable Muslim population. On Zanzibar, the excavations at Unguja Ukuu have unearthed a large rectangular hall-like building of the tenth century, which may well have been a mosque.[16]

Elsewhere the presence of Muslims can be detected by burials. At Chibuene, on the Mozambique coast, of four burials found in tenth century levels one was certainly buried in the correct Muslim fashion.[17] On Pemba, at Mtambwe Mkuu, a cemetery of twenty burials spread over five phases (perhaps representing 150 years) was excavated, the latest dating to around 1150. These were of particular interest, as most of the bodies were set out at right angles to the regular Muslim orientation and can be interpreted as Shi'ite burials, rather than Sunni or Ibadi.[18] There are also conventionally orientated burials in this cemetery which can be best interpreted as those of a clan or large family group.

More archaeological work is needed but there is now sufficient evidence to suggest that Islam was fairly widespread on the coast by the tenth century, and in certain areas earlier. The archaeological evidence from Shanga favours the conversion of certain indigenous communities so that Islam became a family affair. The advantages for conversion must have been related to the trading advantage that it bestowed and as an insurance policy against enslavement and raiding by overseas merchants. It is probable that there was not a single 'conversion' moment, but that the acceptance of Islam was through a variety of routes, producing a pattern of variation that continued into the historical period.

Some Africans may have reached the Middle East, either as merchants or possibly as slaves, and in the cosmopolitan cities converted to Islam. African merchants could well have sailed to the Gulf ports on a regular basis, as this is clearly allowed for the taxation rules present in ninth-century Oman.[19] Indeed they had preferential taxation, through the *aman* treaties, and thus enjoyed a certain economic advantage over Muslim merchants. But there were other routes for the conversion of the Swahili to Islam, which we can reconstruct through new archaeological evidence and a re-examination of the historical sources which tell stories of the spread of Islamic communities along the coast.

Mixed up with foundation myths, it is often unclear whether these stories are recording the conversion process, or whether the already converted East African Muslims were caught up in the religious politics of their trading partners and of the Middle East in general. There is however a clear relationship between the progress of East African Islam and patterns of overseas trade, and it is certain that Swahili Muslims often changed their affiliations and were fairly tolerant of differences within clans or even family groups, as we have already seen from the burials at Mtambwe Mkuu.

The Shirazi Traditions

The most persistent traditions regarding the conversion of the Swahili to Islam centre around a group of stories that tell of the settlement of Persian merchant-princes from Shiraz in seven towns along the coast. The names of the princes and indeed the list of towns vary according to different accounts, but the basic elements of the story remain unchanged. The oldest version was recorded by De Barros in the sixteenth century, in his paraphrase of the Kilwa Chronicle, *Crónica dos reyes de Quiloa*.[20] This versions tells of Ali, one of seven brothers who came from the Persian city of Shiraz, who had an Abyssinian mother and a father named Hócen (Husain), who embarked at Hormuz and eventually reached Kilwa, where he acquired the island for a quantity of coloured cloth which was sufficient to encircle the island. The Arabic History of Kilwa, surviving in a nineteenth-century manuscript, but also sixteenth century in composition, gives a longer version of the same tradition; there were seven ships from Shiraz, representing the sultan and his six sons.[21] Each stopped at a different place; one ship arrived at Kilwa. Here the new arrivals were met there by a Muslim, Muriri wa Bari; there was already a mosque, called Kibala.[22] The first of the new dynasty is given as Ali bin al-Husain ibn Ali, although his father is named Hasan ibn Ali. The local ruler is named as Muli. In the Swahili version of the *History of Kilwa* (dating to the nineteenth century), the Shirazi prince was Ali bin Sulaiman in one version and Yusuf bin Hasan in another, and the local ruler is named as Mrimba.[23] In several other traditions, the founder is known as Sultan Ali of Shiraz (and sometimes also of Shungwaya), and his name is associated with the *mtepe*, the local variety of sewn boat.[24]

The Shirazi foundation myth observes certain principles. One is that the movement of groups is related as one of individuals. Another is to present relations of power and hierarchy and the making of social and moral boundaries in terms of the superiority of Islam over 'primitive' indigenous religions. Several idioms are used, the most important being the strategic use of marriage and the significance of cloth as a basic object of exchange. The Shirazi merchant-prince found a pagan ruler; the merchant makes proposals to acquire the Island for a gift of cloth and to marry the king's daughter. The king agrees and retires to the mainland in order to hunt, but secretly plans to return to the peninsula at low tide to kill the visitors. The merchants cut a deep channel which created a true island separated from the mainland by Islamic magic and so in an intermediary space between Africa and Asia, where they could legitimately live and where the pagan king could not return. In the Swahili version, the Shirazi defend the island because they had 'the Koran read out as a spell and offered sacrifices'.

The myth makes several oppositions that show the immigrants are morally superior to the indigenes. The most important are between trading and hunting, between urban and rural life, and between Islamic faith and primitive deceit. To acquire legitimate authority the prince married the king's daughter. Having received cloth the indigenous king was now civilized and equal to the newcomers so marriage was possible and as a marriage gift, he gives the town to his daughter's new husband. Finally the prince's son, by the African-born wife, is given the right to the island in perpetuity by his father-in-law, so giving the moral right for patricians to exercise control over commerce.

The Shirazi traditions are extremely widespread[25] in chronicles and traditions, found not just in Kilwa, but from Malindi southwards, on Pemba, Mafia and Zanzibar, as well as in the Comores. The list of ports founded or settled is significant. In the *History of Kilwa* they include Manda, Shanga, Yanbu (?), Mombasa, Pemba island, Kilwa and Anjouan. Another (non-Kilwan) tradition gives the Shirazi prince as Muhammed bin Issa, and the places as Souhaheli (i.e. Swahili coast, possibly here the Lamu archipelago), Zanzibar, Tonguy (?Tunghi), Gongwe (Mombasa), Gazisaz (Ngazija), Anjouan and Bueni.

The Shirazi traditions are much weaker in the northern ports, despite this being the place of the first 'landing'. Chittick suggested this was because the Shirazi settlement was a secondary migration from a northern centre, where Persian culture had been established for some time.[26] He pointed to the archaeological presence of trade goods from Siraf, the outport for Shiraz, in ninth- to tenth-century Manda, as evidence for a close relationship with Persia; indeed he suggested the actual colonization of Manda by Persian merchants.[27] The excavations at Kilwa had recovered a coin series, starting with the coins of Ali bin al-Hasan, whom Chittick identified as the 'founder' of the Shirazi dynasty, whose name, as we have seen, was actually Ali bin al-Husain. According to Chittick, these coins dated to around 1200 on the basis of his excavations at Kilwa, this date therefore being the date of the Shirazis' migration to the southern coast from Manda and adjacent areas. The Kilwa Chronicle does give its own approximate date of 400 years after the Hijra, or c.1009, while the Arabic *History* gives the mid-third century (c.864); these dates were dismissed as being far too early.

Attempts to write history from these Shirazi traditions have foundered upon a misunderstanding of their nature. Instead of being a literal narrative of past events, they represent myths or foundation charters for the southern

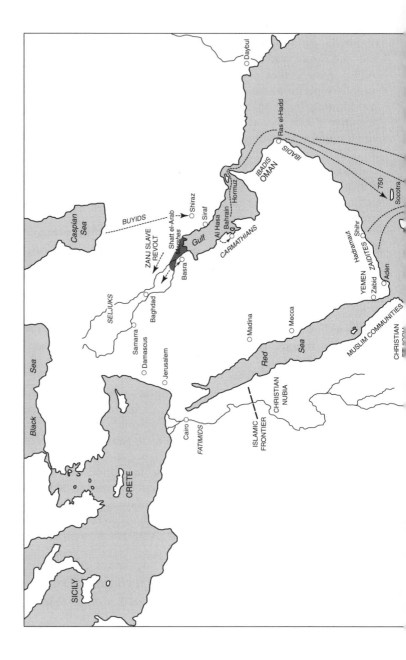

Daybul

Ras el-Hadd

IBADIS

Socotra

IBADI
OMAN

750

Shiraz

Siraf
Hormuz

Bahrain

BUYIDS

Al Hasa

Hadramaut
Shihr

Shatt el-Arab

CARMATHIANS

ZANJ SLAVE
REVOLT

Marshes

Gulf

Caspian
Sea

Basra

YEMEN
ZAIDITES

Zabid

Aden

SELJUKS

Baghdad

Samarra

Madina

Mecca

MUSLIM COMMUNITIES

Damascus

CHRISTIAN

Jerusalem

Red

Sea

Black

Sea

CHRISTIAN
NUBIA

Cairo

ISLAMIC
FRONTIER

FATIMIDS

CRETE

SICILY

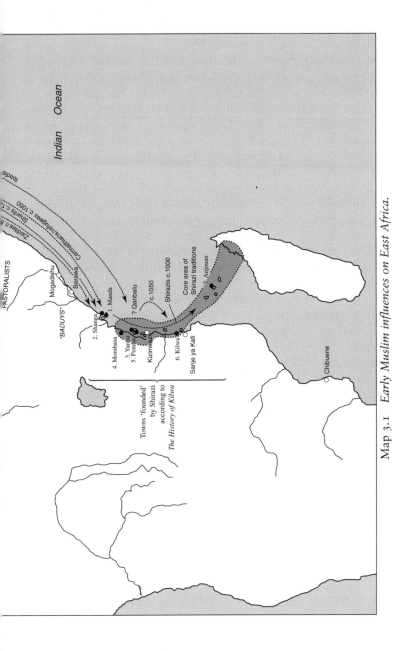

Indian Ocean

Ibadis

Zaidis c.?
Sharifs c.?
Sharifs refugees c.1050
Carmathians/refugees c.1050

PASTORALISTS

Mogadishu

"BADUYS"

Barawa

2. Shanga

1. Manda

? Qanbalu

c. 1050

4. Mombasa
3. Yambu
5. Pemba

Kizimkazi

Shirazis c.1000

Core area of
Shirazi traditions

7. Anjouan

6. Kilwa

Sanje ya Kati

Chibuene

Towns 'founded'
by Shirazi
according to
The History of Kilwa

Map 3.1   *Early Muslim influences on East Africa.*

coastal dynasties. Thus the descent from a noble Islamic family and an Abyssinian slave 'explains' why the rulers were both black but also with royal Muslim descent; the giving of cloth to the ruler made him 'civilized' and so his daughter became marriageable. This marriage to the local ruler's daughter sanctioned local authority. The 'purchase' of the town and island legitimated their presence, while the presence of a Muslim and a mosque already on the island is to show that their claims were not because they were the first Muslims, but through the validity of this transaction. In sum, the Shiraz traditions were part of a foundation myth for a particular group of African Muslim leaders and merchants. We need not see them as 'coming from Shiraz' but their choice of Shiraz as their supposed origin is instructive.

Shiraz was a relatively minor provincial town in the province of Fars, in what is now Iran, except for a brief period between 945 and 1055, when it was the capital of the Buyids. The Buyids were mercenary troops who seized control of the Caliphate and reduced the Caliph to little more than a puppet. They were nominally Shi'ite and may have descended from a branch of the Zaidites who had set up a small state on the shores of the Caspian Sea. During their ascendancy the Buyids controlled much of the Middle East from the Gulf to the Black and Caspian Seas. The wealth that this empire generated was partly used to beautify Shiraz with splendid mosques and palaces; its fame spread widely across the Islamic world. In 1055 the Buyids were defeated and the Caliphate fell under the control of Sunni Seljuks. After 1055 Shiraz returned to its provincial status, although religious learning continued there.

It may be that some African Muslims on the Swahili coast chose to associate themselves with the Buyids, the choice of Shiraz as a perceived place of origin should tie into the chronology of these events and we should seek the beginnings of the Shirazi traditions during the period 945–1055. It is likely that it was the prestige of the Buyid court which they wished to copy and the use of the Buyid court title, *amir-i-amiran*, in court ritual in East Africa at this time is particularly significant.[28] The East African Shirazis in their choice of 'origin' were reflecting contemporary Middle Eastern politics and may therefore have been opposed to the Buyids' rivals who might have set up communities in East Africa, such as the Carmathians and Ibadis and indeed even Sunni Muslims.

A case can be made for the historical reconstruction of these African Muslims through the indigenous coinage, a link that was first made by Neville Chittick during his investigations at Kilwa, but new archaeological discoveries have thrown considerable new light on the matter. A hoard of silver and gold coins was discovered in 1984 at Mtambwe Mkuu on Pemba Island, buried under the floor of a merchant's house in a cloth pouch after 1066, the date of the latest of ten Fatimid dinars found in the hoard.[29] Of over 2600 silver coins there were ten named rulers/minters; most can be ordered into four generations through the study of overstriking and stylistic attributes, while two names seem to come from a second related dynasty. The head of the first dynasty was Ali bin al-Hasan, almost certainly the same ruler/minter whose copper and a few rare silver coins were found at Kilwa and also in another hoard at Kisimani Mafia, in this case found in a pot dating to *c*.1050.[30] To fit in four generations, with a deposition date after 1066 (and given the fresh state of the gold coins, not that much later), the Mtambwe coin sequence must span the eleventh century, placing Ali bin al-Hasan around 1000, rather than 1200, as originally suggested by Chittick. In this new computation, his lifetime lies within the period of Buyid control of the Caliphate and of the fame and prosperity of Shiraz itself.

The origin of these minters can be suggested from the second dynasty. The Mtambwe coins contain two names, Khalid bin Ahmed and a successor (using his epithet) Ahmed bin Khalid. Khalid bin Ahmed may be one of three brothers; al-Husain bin Ahmed whose coins are only known from Zanzibar in copper, but which are very similar to the coins of Ali bin al-Hasan, and Ali bin Ahmed, whose single silver coin is known from Shanga. This piece is very significant as it is intermediate between the earlier Shanga silver coins of Mohammed and Abd Allah, and the Mtambwe series. It was found in a sealed layer dating to *c*.1050, but is probably earlier in date. This provides the first direct archaeological evidence that the coin producers of the southern coast may have moved south from the Lamu archipelago during the late tenth or early eleventh century.

The Mtambwe coins supplied many new names, which can be added to other minters on Kilwa, Mafia and Zanzibar, making a total of twelve names before the late thirteenth-century issues of al-Hasan bin Talut, a ruler identified in the *History of Kilwa*. By taking these names together and in studying their distribution across the different islands it is possible to suggest familial relationships between rulers/minters in the island towns of Pemba, Zanzibar, Mafia and Kilwa, suggesting that a closely related dynasty may have lived on these islands from *c*.1000–1150, a date not that different to the one given by De Barros for the arrival of the Shirazi. More information can be gleaned from some of the names used in the coins. Several are of Old Testament origin, an indicator of Shi'ite associations, while on one of the early Kilwa coins, a couplet translates as 'trusts in the Lieutenant of God' with its clear Shi'ite meaning. As we have seen, the cemetery at Mtambwe Mkuu, which is contemporary to the coins almost certainly issued there, had a predominantly Shi'ite population. One of the names, Bahram, is very unusual, and points to a Persian derivation.

However there is a difficulty as none of these twelve names can be identified among the rulers of Chittick's 'Shirazi dynasty'; indeed, as we have seen, the founder of this dynasty in the *History of Kilwa* was given as Ali bin al-Husain, a quite different person to that found on the coins.[31] Ali's

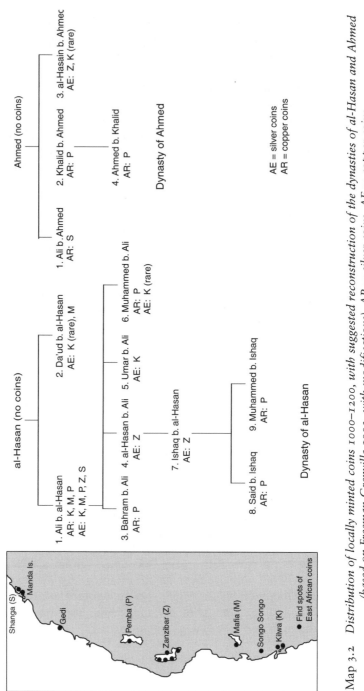

Map 3.2 *Distribution of locally minted coins 1000–1200, with suggested reconstruction of the dynasties of al-Hasan and Ahmed (based on Freeman-Grenville 1993, with modifications). AR = silver coins, AE = copper coins.*

named five successors also minted no coins. Indeed, given the regnal lengths of the dynasty of Ali bin al-Husain, and that his grandson acceded immediately before the dated Mahdali dynasty of al-Hasan bin Talut, in c.1280, this places these rulers in the period 1150–1280, much too late for the coins. The most likely explanation is that the Shirazi myth was embellished at the front of the Kilwa histories, maybe as late as the fifteenth to early sixteenth centuries, when Kilwa came under strong Shi'ite influences from Malindi, a town where St Francis Xavier, who stopped in there in 1542, was told by the Qadi that 'if in three years Muhammed did not come to visit them, he would not believe any more in him or his sect' – a reference to the disappeared twelfth Imam rather than the Prophet.[32] The opening section of the *Arabic History of Kilwa* is a theological disquisition, whose author was most probably an Ithna'ashari (i.e. twelver) Shi'ite.[33] We will examine below the possibility that the dynasty of Ali bin al-Husain was most likely a non-coin producing Ibadi one, and that the later author of the *History* deliberately confused Hasan and Husain in order to provide a longer ancestry for the fifteenth-century Shi'ites at Kilwa.

The probable basis for the Shirazi traditions is that some of the Muslim inhabitants of the Lamu archipelago (including Shanga) moved south around 1000, with their coining tradition and a distinctive local form of Islam. The Shirazi traditions start the list of 'founded' settlements with Shanga and Manda and this provides further clue that it was from the Lamu archipelago that the 'Shirazi' originally came. They may not have seen themselves as Shirazi in the Lamu archipelago,[34] but developed this notion of their origin as they moved southwards, probably to Malindi and Mombasa, along the Mrima coast, and as far as Mafia, Kilwa and the Comores. In essence, the Shirazi traditions represent the arrival of Islam into many of these areas, explaining their strength and persistence.

There is architectural evidence to support this reconstruction. These Shirazi Muslims seem to have built mosques with a distinctive plan of a free-standing rectangular prayer hall, with a raised floor, often on a platform of white sand, with four internal columns and pilasters on the side walls which probably terminated in squat pillars to support a thatched roof. Each side had three doorways, with external steps to the thresholds. The mihrab was normally deeply recessed and much decorated. The model for this architectural form can be found at Shanga, although here the mosque also had a southern room, possibly for ablutions.

The exemplar of this type of mosque on the south coast is that at Kizimkazi, on Zanzibar island, which survives largely intact and is still in use, although restored in the eighteenth century and again in the early 1960s. Its mihrab, an extraordinary survival, comprises a trifoliate arch and complex panels and recesses of carved coral. The inscriptions remain *in situ* on both the mihrab and along the north wall, carved in floriate Kufic,

Plate 3.2   *The mosque at Kizimkazi (Zanzibar island) with an inscription dating its construction to AH 500 (1107). The mihrab is largely intact from this date, with its extraordinary trefoliate arch and decorated recess. The associated inscription used floriate Kufic lettering in a style identical to that employed on tombstones carved at Siraf, a major trading port with East Africa on the Gulf. The Kizimkazi inscriptions and mihrab use local coral showing that the carving was undertaken locally (photo Mark Horton).*

giving a date of AH 500 (1107), and recording the foundation of the mosque by Sheikh es Sayyid Musa al-Hassan bin Mohammed el Amrani.[35] The style of lettering employed is that of the Siraf workshops – Siraf being the outport for Shiraz – but carved using local *Porites* coral and presumably by local craftsmen. A second, similar mihrab was found in 1989 on Tumbatu island, again using a trifoliate arch and Kufic inscriptions, while a third piece of inscription is known from Kioni (near Kilifi).[36]

The mosques and coins provide the archaeological evidence for the spread of the Shirazi, not as Middle Eastern immigrants, but as northern Swahili Muslims directly descended from the earliest converts, moving south, founding mosques, introducing coinage and elaborately carved inscriptions and mihrabs. They converted non-Muslims or displaced Muslim of other sects. They should be interpreted as indigenous African Muslims who played the politics of the Middle East to their advantage, and still used a foundation myth a millennium later to assert their authority, even though the context of this myth had long been forgotten. African Islam must have been diverse and fluid, and the particular communities held no particular loyalty to one sect or another but were content to change their religious orientation as part of their wider political action.

The Early Muslims of the Northern Coast.

The Shirazi Muslims of the south coast derived from a long-standing Islamic community, which we have argued developed in the Lamu archipelago and adjacent region, and for which we have direct archaeological evidence from the excavations at Shanga. Again the traditional sources allows us to examine the more detailed nature of this community. The earliest of these comes again from De Barros, who recorded a second tradition concerning a Shi'ite group known as Zaidites,[37] or here the Umma Zaidi (literally the followers of Zaid).

> The first foreign people whom the fame of this gold attracted to settlement in the land of the Zanj was a tribe of Arabs – as Arabia is very close – banished from their country after receiving the creed of Muhammed. This tribe was called Emozaydy, as we have learned from a Chronicle of the kings of Kilwa... The cause of their exile was because they followed the doctrine of a Moor named Zaide, who was grandson of Hócem son of Ali, nephew of Muhammed, married to his daughter Axa. This Zaide held various opinions contrary to the Koran... As they were the first people to come from outside to inhabit this land, they did not found any celebrated towns, but only collected in places where they could live in security from the Kaffirs. From their entrance, like a slow plague they worked their way along the coast, occupying new towns...[38]

As they are described as a 'tribe of Arabs', these Zaidites were most likely those living in the Yemen from the late eighth century onwards and subject to periodic persecutions by the Abbasids. During the ninth century, Zaidites, as the least radical of the Shi'ites, enjoyed a certain rapprochement with the Caliphate so that by early tenth century a Zaidite state was established in the Yemen with other communities along the northern Somali coast of East Africa. In the chequered history of the movement, it is difficult to identify whether any particular persecution might have resulted in their flight to East Africa, or to separate the suppression the religious aspects of Zaidism (where the term was often used to describe a catch-all of numerous Shi'ite revolts) and the political which resulted in the creation of an Islamic state that threatened the authority of the Caliphate.

It is just possible that the early Muslim community at Shanga comprised Zaidite refugees who converted the local population, but more likely it was formed by local Swahili converts who had come under Zaidite influence further north.[39] The early coins from Shanga, which date on stylistic grounds to between 700–850, and were found in archaeological levels dating to before 900, bear a strong resemblance to the coins being minted by the early Zaidi Imams from the mid-ninth century, especially in the method of coining using coin moulds.[40] By the tenth century there was commercial contact between East Africa, southern Arabia and the Red Sea, developing a trade in luxuries, in particular ivory, crystal and gold – corresponding to the heyday of the Zaidite state of the Yemen. The early tenth century also sees the adoption of *Porites* coral stone architecture in East Africa, a technique derived from the Red Sea, for mosques and ceremonial buildings and found first in the Lamu archipelago, spreading southwards in the eleventh century. The development of trade links may have resulted in religious as well as technological connections that built upon existing traditions. As the Kilwa tradition stated, the Zaidites did not found towns but came to areas where they could live in security in settlements that already participated in trade, presumably within the *aman* treaty framework.

De Barros goes on to report that Zaidite influence was displaced by another group, this time from the Persian Gulf:

> three ships came there with a great number of Arabs under the leadership of seven brothers, who belonged to a tribe living close to the town of Laçah (al-Hasa)...The cause of their coming was that they were greatly persecuted by the King of Laçah. The first town that they built in this land of Ajan was Magadoxo (Mogadishu) and the next Brava (Barawa), which even at the present time is governed by twelve chiefs, descendants of these brothers in the manner of a republic. The town of Magadoxo gained such power and state, that it became the sovereign, and head of all the Moors on the coast, but as the first tribe who came here, called Emozaydy, held different opinions from the Arabs with regard to their creed, they would not submit to them and retreated into the interior, where they joined the Kaffirs, intermarrying with

them and adopting their customs so that in every way they became *mestizes*. These are the people whom the Moors of the seaboard call Baduys...[41]

This second 'arrival' has often been given little historical weight, as it seems to be an alternative ('Arab') version of the Shirazi myth with seven brothers, coming this time from al-Hasa, a medium size trading centre on the Arabian mainland adjacent to Bahrain. Archaeological evidence provides a suggestion that it may have some historical basis. The mosque sequence at Shanga is one of continuous development, from timber to stone and of enlargement, with the present surviving mosque constructed around 1000. The one discontinuity is around 1050–75, when not only is the mosque burnt down and rebuilt on a different plan, but the adjacent public buildings are demolished and robbed, their valuable coral and teak used to fuel a lime kiln.[42]

One possibility is that this point marks the arrival of Carmathians, who had a small state on the island of Bahrain from 899–1076. The origins of the Carmathians is somewhat obscure, but they were 'seveners'[43] – Ismaili Shi'ites, who emerged near Kufa during the late ninth century and thus belonged to a different Shi'ite tradition to the Zaidites. The Carmathians set up an independent state with its capital on the island of Bahrain in 899, very close to al-Hasa, which was located on the mainland. They were particularly radical, with secret societies and guilds based upon equality of not just rank but caste and race. The Carmathian state was destroyed in 1076 after two centuries of bloody conflict with the Caliphate, and it is not impossible that in the aftermath some Carmathians fled to East Africa. Indeed the radical origins of the Carmathian movement may have resulted in the aftermath of the suppression of the Zanj revolt in 889,[44] and some of the Carmathians might have looked to their African roots as a place of refuge when their state was destroyed in 1076. A hint of Carmathian influence comes from the reference to seven brothers, which reflects the sevener tradition, and the republican government noted at Barawa,[45] and which survived there, as well as in the Lamu archipelago, until the early twentieth century.

However the Kilwa tradition, as recounted by De Barros, is specific in observing that those who fled the Gulf were oppressed by the King of al-Hasa, suggesting that the refugees were in fact fleeing from the Carmathians. Carmathians were intolerant of other Muslims, held a strong missionary tradition, and would have forced out any that did not submit to their new theology. Thus those coming to East African might have been of any group, displaced by Carmathian expansion and presumably prior to 1076.[46] One nineteenth-century East African tradition identified them as the Sunni Harthi, who were forced out by the Carmathians from Bahrain in 924 (a traditional rather than an accurate date), and 'founded' Mogadishu and Barawa.[47] On balance, it is more likely that there was an arrival of a small number of Sunni Muslims to reconvert the northern Swahili during the mid-eleventh century, not least because there is no remnant of Shi'ite traditions in the area today.

Of particular interest is the disappearance of the Zaidite Swahili in the face of these new arrivals. According to De Barros, they retreated into the interior where they mixed with pastoral groups, known as Baduys or Bedouin. This may be indeed the case, as some such as the Rendille retain Islamic clan names[48] and could once have been partly Muslim. The reference to Baduys may also link to the origins of the term Bajuni, Swahili living along the northern Kenyan and southern Somali coast, in the same location as this early Zaidite influence. As we have seen, Musa bin Amrani, a founder of Kilwa, was also described as a Baduys, and if he is the same as the builder of the Kizimkazi mosque, was living around 1100, approximately the same time as we have suggested that the Zaidite Swahili were forced out of their towns. The Shirazis, who may have moved south from the Lamu archipelago around 1000, may also have been broadly Zaidite, but by this stage with African Islamic traditions, but who decided to adopt a stronger Shi'ite identity, linked to the Persian side of the Gulf.

Kharijites and Ibadi Islam

The northern Swahili, as they moved south during the eleventh century would have encountered non-Muslim communities as well as those following Ibadi Islam. The Ibadis were probably localized on the islands, and may have been as long-standing as the Islamic communities of the north, but because these Ibadi communities did not survive after the thirteenth century there is much less traditional evidence for them.

Kharijite-Ibadi merchants were major participants in the early Indian Ocean trade and there is evidence that their influence spread to East Africa at an early date.[49] A community of moderate Kharijites flourished in Basra during the late seventh century, at that time one of the most important trading towns of the Gulf, who came to be known as the Ibadiyya, the practitioners being known as Ibadi. The Ibadiyya was favoured by close-knit groups, often living within tribal areas, especially within Arabia but also in North Africa. To them the Caliphate was seen as remote from the original revelations, and as they were against central authority they opposed any form of leadership that went beyond that gained through the consensus of the community. The Imam, or religious leader, was chosen solely for his religious knowledge and military skills, irrespective of tribe or race. The Ibadi were persecuted under the Caliphate, although from time to time established their own independent states in particular in Oman. The

Omani Ibadiyya survive as a religious community today and were important as the colonial rulers of the Zanzibar Sultanate.

The earliest evidence for Kharijite interest in East Africa dates to the early eighth century. Unfortunately this is only recorded in a late eighteenth-century Omani source and is not found in any East African account. According to this tradition, two brothers, Sa'id and Sulaiman, leaders of the Ma'wali Julanda family, fled Oman to East Africa after their defeat by the Umayyad army.[50] While this story has been dismissed as a later invention, the clan name Julanda is recorded in East Africa in circumstances which cannot be fully explained, because by this stage the Julanda were no longer of any prominence in Oman and survived as a few herdsmen in the Omani interior. In the *Book of Zeng*, the Julanda are linked with the Kilindini clan living in and around Mombasa, while a land deed for the ownership of Ras Mkumbuu on Pemba island, surviving as a colonial document, but giving the date of AH 910 (1504), names the original purchaser of the land as Mwijaa bin Mgwame al-Jilindi.[51]

The connection with Ras Mkumbuu is of interest, as this place seems to be linked phonetically with Qanbalu, an early port which was visited in 916 by al-Mas'udi, and which as we have seen was the only place where he noted a small Muslim population. While there, he recorded a tradition concerning its origins which throws further light on a possible Ibadi connection:

> Among the inhabitants of the island is a community of Muslims, now speaking Zahjiyya, who conquered this island and subjected all the Zanj on it in the same manner as the Muslim conquest of the island of Crete in the Mediterranean. This event took place around the period of the changeover from the Umayyad and Abbasid dynasty.[52]

These comments show that the Muslims on Qanbalu had abandoned Arabic in favour of the local language – presumably an early form of Swahili – and the date he gives for the 'conquest' of *c*.750, would be time enough until his visit in 916 for Arabic to have been forgotten in everyday speech. His comparison with the Arab conquest of Crete (undertaken by Andulusian refugees and free-booters under ibn Hafs Umar al-Balluti in around 821–6[53]) compares closely with the Ibadis in Oman, who too were victims of Umayyad oppression but managed to set up a short-lived Ibadi state in the mid-eighth century, lasting until around 790.[54] They were successful merchants, who developed the Indian Ocean trade in collaboration with the Kharijite community in Basra; they were particularly important in the Zanj slave trade. But this trade was short-lived and after the Zanj revolt of 868 collapsed, so that by 916, during his visit to Qanbalu, al-Mas'udi did not even mention it.

The Ibadis of Oman developed a navy during the eighth and ninth centuries. During the career of al-Julanda b. Mas'ud a successful expedition was mounted around 750 to take the island of Socotra. This documented expedition, typical of the military activity sanctioned in the *dar al-harb* where the pretext may have been that the Christian inhabitants were interfering with the Indian Ocean trade, seems to be of the kind that al Mas'udi may have been referring to during his visit to Qanbalu.[55] It is quite possible that a similar but undocumented campaign was launched against Qanbalu at exactly the same time to secure a base for the African slave trade, installing a small Ibadi community on the island through the conversion of the local Swahili.

There has been considerable debate about the location of the island of Qanbalu, although a town of this name was located by the Arabic geographer Yaqut on Pemba island in the thirteenth century, probably referring to the extensive archaeological site (with the phonetically related name) of Ras Mkumbuu.[56] The archaeological evidence from Pemba has so far identified tenth-century occupation at Ras Mkumbuu itself, at Mtambwe Mkuu and an important series of eighth-century sites near Churaka and Pujini;[57] al-Mas'udi's reference suggests that Qanbalu refers to the entire island, rather than a single town, and that Ras Mkumbuu is one of the most prominent headlands. However, the tenth-century stone mosque at Ras Mkumbuu is of Ibadi type, as the mihrab recess was probably set within the thickness of the north wall[58] providing an interesting confirmation of this historical reconstruction. Below this mosque, like at Shanga, there was a predecessor of timber. The second (stone) mosque was replaced around 1050 by a much larger third mosque of Sunni or Shi'ite type, and it is possible that the Ibadis left Mkumbuu at this time, leaving little historical record of their former presence. It is tempting to link these changes with the arrival of the northern Muslims, who seem to also have settled Mtambwe Mkuu in the (?later) tenth century, building there a typical 'Shirazi' mosque with its deep mihrab recess and minting their characteristic coins.[59]

The Ibadi community of Pemba island may have moved south to the Kilwa archipelago and for this there is both historical and archaeological evidence. The 'Awtabi *sirah* is an Ibadi polemic written around 1116 to two brothers living at Kilwa, named Ali ibn Ali and Hasan ibn Ali, suggesting that they were actively propagating Ibadi Islam in the Kilwa area at this time.[60] Unfortunately Chittick's excavations did not investigate in any detail the mosque lying beneath the Great Mosque at Kilwa (maybe built around 1200), but a mosque does survive on the nearby island of Sanje ya Kati, where, while unexcavated, surface pottery suggests occupation from around 1000. This mosque[61] is identical to that found at Ras Mkumbuu in dimensions and plan, with a typical Ibadi style mihrab set within a double-thickness wall.

Sanje ya Kati[62] features in the Kilwa histories as a place of conflict with Kilwa. According to the Arabic *History*, there were two periods in which the people of Shanga (i.e. Sanje ya Kati) took over Kilwa, one with the appointment of Khalid bin Bakr, who ruled for two-and-a-half years, and a second twelve years later when they set up Muhammed bin Husain al-Mundhir, who came from a family named as the Matamandalin and who ruled for a further twelve years while the fifth ruler of Kilwa, Hasan bin Sulaiman, fled to Zanzibar. A document, *al-Maqama al Kilwiyya*, recently discovered in Oman[63] and written around 1200 gives details of a mission to reconvert Kilwa to Ibadism, as it had recently been effected by the extremist Shi'ite Ghurabiyya doctrine from southern Iraq,[64] and names the apostate (i.e. former Ibadi) as al-Munghirah, a name temptingly close to the usurper from Sanje ya Kati. Ibn al-Mujawir, writing about 1232, remarked that 'Kilwa reverted from the Shafiyya to the Kharijiyya and remain attached to this legal school until the present day', suggesting that the Ibadis were victorious in this conflict during the second quarter of the thirteenth century. The surviving northern section of the Great Mosque at Kilwa may have been built during the usurpation period, covering some 26 years (?c.1200–1230), with its projecting mihrab. Also significant for this historical reconstruction is the discovery of a side aisle in the Friday Mosque on Tumbatu, an island lying off Zanzibar. This was added to the mosque in the early thirteenth century and has its own mihrab set within the thickness of the wall, in the Ibadi style. It is tempting to see this special structure as having been put up for the refugee ruler of Kilwa, Hasan bin Sulaiman, during his sojourn in the 'land of Zanzibar'.

This account is a radical reinterpretation of the accounts of Chittick and of Freeman-Grenville,[65] but has both historical and archaeological support in its favour. It suggests that the Shirazi traditions have been 'written in' at a much later date, and that Kilwa had a longer and unrecognized Ibadi history, which has gone largely unrecorded, that dates from broadly 1050–1250. The dynasty of Ali bin al-Husain began around 1150, and before this there may have been earlier rulers, quite possibly the nine additional names given by De Barros, but out of order. Two of these are brothers, Ali bin Ali and Hasan bin Ali, who could well be the same brothers mentioned in the 'Awtabi *sirah* in c.1116.

These followers of Kharijite-Ibadi doctrines, present on the coast until the mid-thirteenth century, disappear by the fourteenth century. The doctrines were reintroduced by Omani Arabs, first in Mombasa and then in Zanzibar, with an impact upon the entire coastline in the late eighteenth century. By the nineteenth century, there were again Ibadi mosques in Lamu, Mombasa, Pemba and Zanzibar.

Plate 3.3   *The Friday mosque on the island of Tumbatu, excavated in 1991, and
dating to the twelfth century. In the thirteenth century an aisle was added to the east
side of the prayer hall with its own mihrab set within the thickness of the wall, which
may have been intended for an Ibadi community that was resident in the town
(photo Mark Horton).*

Sunni-Shafiʻi Islam

When Ibn Battuta visited the Kilwans in 1331, he commented that their
qualities were devotion and piety and that they followed the Shafiʻi school
of Sunni Islam; nowadays, Swahili Islam remains Sunni-Shafiʻi and must
have been largely so since Ibn Battuta's times. This was the mainstream
practice of most Muslims, followed by the Umayyad and Abbasid Cali-
phates, and by the majority of the population even in trading cities such as
Fustat, Siraf and Basra. The northern Swahili coast was most likely Sunni
from the tenth or eleventh centuries, but, as we have seen, Shi'ite and Ibadi
Islam was also present. There were also pockets of non-Muslims living
within towns and rural areas.

To Swahili Muslims, sayyids and sharifs,[66] direct descendants of the
Prophet from the Arabian peninsula, represented something new. The
sharif tradition, based upon the widespread Arab practice of maintaining
accurate genealogies, enabled descent to be documented, through Ali, to the
Prophet. Through this descent the sharifs could claim *baraka*, which literally meant charisma but took on a wider meaning of religious power –
linked to miracles and a range of religious skills (such as the writing of

charms and amulets), as well as mediation between God and ordinary Muslims. They also became scholars of Islamic theology, linked to the Shafi'i school of Sunni Islam, as well as having Sufi connections. The sharif movement developed in the Yemen during the eleventh century and the period of the consolidation of Sunni Islam that followed the disintegration of the Caliphate. The established trading links with the Yemen made the East African coast an obvious place to extend sharifian activity. These developed in particular during the mid-thirteenth century, when trade with southern Yemen replaced that with the Gulf, as is evidenced by the frequent finds of Yemeni pottery on Swahili sites.

With their *baraka* the Yemeni sharifs were readily accepted as religious specialists and could expect to enjoy a relatively high status with the community. They were particularly successful in already established Muslim communities but did not act as missionaries to non-converted groups. In the early period it is very difficult to track particular sharif families, as they did not arrive at a single 'historical' time but as a long-term process. However their impact was to ensure that within a relatively short time the various sects and religious groups of East Africa became strongly Sunni in outlook.

In general, there was a north to south movement in this process, with the earliest evidence in the north. According to traditions, the Qahtani Wa'il clan was present in Mogadishu and were experts in the judicial and religious matters, and became the qadis of the town, and khatibs of the mosque.[67] Their influence was interrupted by another Arabian group, one of whose leaders, Abu Bakr b. Fakhr ad-Din, became the ruler, although Qahtani influence survived as hereditary religious leaders as late as the nineteenth century. The Fakhr ad-Din group were established in the mid-thirteenth century and the Qahtani may have arrived in the period 1150–1250. The Fakhr ad-Din Mosque in Mogadishu dates to around 1300.

Another widespread tradition concerns the Mahdali.[68] In some traditions this family are linked with the Amrani,[69] whom we have already met in connection with the Shirazi traditions, but this may be through later intermarriage. What is clear is that the Mahdali are the first genuine sharifian lineage to have arrived on the main part of the Swahili coast and appear as a new dynasty at Kilwa in *c.* 1280, with Hasan ibn Talut using the Mahdali *nisba*. This family can be traced back to Yemen as a small sayyid clan, descended via Ahmed ibn Isa (living in the early tenth century) living in the Wadi Surdad near to Zabid. How they became rulers of Kilwa remains obscure, or indeed whether they came directly to Kilwa from the Yemen or via the northern coast. While their political success was dramatic at Kilwa, there is evidence that the Mahdali also reached Barawa, Lamu, Pate and Mombasa. It is probable that the Mahdalis were responsible for the widespread adoption of Sunni Islam at Kilwa, and it is also interesting that they resume the production of coins at Kilwa, after a gap of 150 years.[70]

The migration of sharifs to East Africa is much better documented from the sixteenth century onwards.[71] One important lineage descends from the Hadrami saint, Abu Bakr bin Salim (1514–84), whose two sons were invited to Pate sometime during the late sixteenth century. While they returned to the Yemen, they left descendants behind who lived in Pate; some moved to Lamu, while others went to the Comores where they became rulers of small sultanates in the eighteenth century. In Lamu they became important literary figures, one member being the author of *al-Inkishafi*, the famous Swahili epic poem. Another lineage was the Jamal al-Layl, of which Ahmed b. Harum traditionally reached Pate in 1543 and his descendants members spread from there into the major urban centres. A member of this lineage was Habib Saleh, the famous Lamu saint and Islamic reformer who arrived in Lamu in the late nineteenth century from the Comores. Other important lineages are the Qadri and Husayni. Their founders arrived in the seventeenth and eighteenth centuries, and their descendants moved into many of the urban centres.

The sharif movement should not be seen as a large-scale migration of Arabs to East Africa, as in most cases the lineages were founded by a single individual although the descendants are now numerous. Some of the sharifs saw themselves as reformers and were responsible for the ending of traditional sectarian and non-Islamic practices in coastal religion; others were integrated into the local religious scene and had little long-term impact. They did contribute to the development of the coast as an area of Islamic learning with their connections with the central Islamic lands. Through the sharif movement, Swahili communities developed as centres of *umma* or sanctity.[72] Umma was a major contributor to ideas of coastal urbanism. The community supported a learned elite who maintained the ritual purity of the town and the efficiency of rituals, as well as Islamic learning, which included the production of books.

Bantu Islam?

The historical evidence for the development of Islam is complex and often contradictory and thus difficult to understand. What is now clear is that Islam has a very long pedigree in East Africa, and that it should not be seen as something foreign but as linked closely to indigenous practice. The 'external sources' suggest a bewildering range of different conversion and migration processes. However, the situation on the ground may well have been simpler. This is evident from the architecture, which shows very little variety in the plans or mosques, in the form of mihrabs, or in the presence of foreign-inspired buildings such as minarets or madrasas, which are extremely rare. The mosques of present day East African Islam are direct descendants of the flimsy timber structures excavated at Shanga built over 1000 years ago. The many changing alliances should be seen as a veneer over a long-term continuity of religious practice.

Alongside this continuity there is surprisingly little evidence for non-Muslim religious activities, or even for syncretism of African religious practices within coastal Islam. The most sensitive indicator is that of burials, and where they have been properly recorded from excavations the majority are found to have been of Muslims. However, there have been several burials found close to mosques but clearly in a non-Muslim position, where it has been claimed that the commemorated may have lived as Muslims, but at death were 'laid to rest in a manner acceptable to ancestors'.[73] At Ras Mkumbuu, one such burial was found over the abandoned early mosque but was of relatively high status, as it was buried within a stone tomb.

The importance of spirits in contemporary Swahili society is often cited as evidence for syncretism, but both the archaeological and historical evidence points to their importance only during later centuries and especially after the ending of slavery. The choice of ancient sites where the spirits dwell is because these are perceived as ancient and sacred places in the landscape.[74] The ruined mosques and tombs are constructed of stone and so survive in the tropical environment, while their use has been abandoned and their original owners long since disappeared. There are numerous cases of incense burners found in the remains of tombs and mihrabs, but it is almost impossible to date their deposition.[75]

What this consideration of the archaeological and historical evidence shows is that Islam was long established among the Bantu-speaking inhabitants of the coast and that there have been local Muslims communities in this part of Africa for as long as in many of the more 'central' areas of the Islamic world. Over this very considerable period of time, a distinctive regional character developed which should now be recognized as a distinctively African contribution to the Islamic world.

4

The Swahili Coast and the Indian Ocean World

Swahili society has been a mercantile one as far back as evidence goes; virtually all the early sites described in chapter 2 contain imported pottery in their deposits. Not all Swahili people have themselves been merchants – only a minority has been so at any given period – but their society has been organized to engage in a particular kind of economy and its culture has been based on mercantile values. In addition it has been at the core of a wider coastal economic system engaged in the same commerce, its members, both Swahili and non-Swahili, playing different but necessary and complementary roles. The Swahili have been the ultimate suppliers and consumers of the many trade goods coming from and going to Africa, Europe and Asia, the whole comprising an immense trading system covering the coastal lands of the Indian Ocean and their interiors.

Pre-Islamic Trade

During the late sixth century the classical and Mediterranean trade within the Indian Ocean declined, through the economic collapse associated with the ending of the Roman empire in the west and the emergence of Byzantium as an inward-looking eastern Mediterranean polity. For example, the working of elephant ivory ceased, except for re-using earlier pieces, until the tenth century, and was replaced in the Mediterranean and Europe by bone, walrus or even fossilized mammoth ivory. This decline not only effected the Swahili coast, but also trading states such as Aksum in Ethiopia, which played a vital part in the revival of classical trade during the time of the Emperor Justinian.

The axis of trade may in reality have already shifted to the Persian Gulf, and it is now recognized that the Sasanians were important maritime traders as well as maintaining a successful Persian empire.[1] The Sasanians and Aksumites were competing for trade in sixth-century Ceylon, and it is very likely that Sasanian trade with East Africa became important at this time. The ceramics found at sites such as Ras Hafun, Fukuchani and Unguja Ukuu illustrate the importance of this connection, although documentary evidence is very slight. In addition to ivory, the Sasanian traders may have been after slaves, as it is during this period that Zanj slaves are first mentioned. The two ports in the Gulf which played a pivotal role in East African trade in the Islamic period, Siraf and Sohar, both have significant Sasanian levels at their base.[2]

Early Islam

With the rise of Islam in the seventh century, Indian Ocean trade was within a common legal framework which permitted a certain degree of security, at least for the merchants operating between North-West India and the Red Sea. But the Umayyad Caliphate was focused on Syria and the Mediterranean, and it was left to dissident Muslim groups to develop the Indian Ocean commerce. The most notable were the Kharijite merchants living in Basra, at the head of the Gulf, which became an extremely wealthy and active centre. A late ninth-century document, the *Jami'* of Ibn Ja'far, gives an Ibadi-Kharijite perspective on the status of African communities, of particular importance because of the scale of their trade with East Africa at this time.[3] According to Ibn Ja'far, within the *dar al-harb* (lit. 'the region of war'), where occupants were defined by Muslim law as polytheistic, only temporary treaties could be concluded, in contrast to those with monotheism, such as Christian Nubia and Ethiopia, where there could be a permanent peace, the *sulh*. Temporary treaties were made because in the future the Muslims might become powerful enough to conquer these areas, whereas within the Christian areas the frontiers were respected. During the term of these treaties, good faith, *aman*, was expected between the Muslims and polytheists; if this broke down, Muslims were allowed to take booty, *ghanima*, but in general were not allowed to carry arms into these areas except to protect themselves from piracy. Taxation was due on goods from polytheistic areas that were brought to Oman by Muslim merchants at the rate of 2.5 per cent, but polytheist merchants (i.e. Africans) arriving in Oman were only taxed at the rate that Muslim merchants were taxed in their own lands, as regulated in any *aman* treaty. Merchants were not allowed to reside permanently in polytheistic areas and were still liable to taxation back in Oman.

The Basra merchants seem to have played a key role in the development of the East African slave trade and, as we have suggested in chapter 3, used their Ibadi allies from Oman to take control of Qanbalu around 750. These merchants, making substantial fortunes from the Indian Ocean trade, reinvested their funds in draining the marshland of lower Iraq. This required

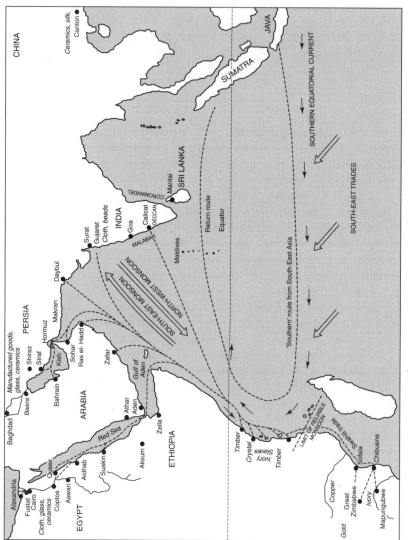

Map 4:1 *The oceanic trading world of the Swahili, 800–1500.*

labour, and the most obvious source was East Africa.[4] By the early ninth century substantial numbers of East Africans, or Zanj as they were known, were being imported and the size of labour units employed in the many drainage works varied from 500 to 15,000 slaves. The trade must have been on a very substantial scale as it seems that only male slaves were imported, requiring their constant replenishment. The conditions in the swamps of Iraq were so atrocious that these slave communities rebelled in 868, forming a substantial army that first sacked Basra itself (and appalling cruelties were visited upon the inhabitants) and then laid waste most of southern Iraq, reaching the gates of Baghdad and threatening the survival of the Caliphate itself. The revolt was finally put down in 883, and it is likely that the Zanj army was massacred. From 868 until the nineteenth century, the demand for East African slaves in the Middle East was on a much smaller scale, largely for domestic servants and concubines.

The most useful source in locating the slaving centres on the East African coast during the eighth and ninth centuries is al-Jahiz[5] who identifies their origin as Qanbalu and Lanjuya (the islands of Pemba and Zanzibar); these islands could not have supported sufficient populations of their own, and the slaves must have come from the adjacent African mainland. Archaeological evidence includes a chain link and two possible irons from Shanga and three rings from Manda.[6]

In 749 the Caliphate passed to the Abbasids who shifted their capital to Baghdad in 762. One consequence was a change in focus with the development of an eastern court and its demand for luxuries that did much to encourage long-distance maritime trade. This was partly funded through new supplies of silver from Panjshir in Khorasan and Ilaq in Transoxiana, that created a stable currency, the dirham. From Baghdad and the ports of the Gulf complex trade routes were developed. One for example, extended overland through Russia to the Baltic, and beyond to the North Sea and Ireland, and was at least partly in the hands of Viking traders.[7] Another involved direct maritime trade with South-East Asia and southern China, where there is clear documentary evidence for single ships making this 8000 mile voyage. Siraf, the port on the Gulf from which these China voyages were undertaken, has been excavated, and Chinese ceramics first appear there from around 780, but in quantity from around 800.[8]

In comparison the maritime trade with East Africa was relatively straightforward and has much documentary as well as archaeological evidence.[9] The two main Gulf ports were Sohar, still largely in the hands of the Ibadi merchants, and Siraf, which had a more mixed but probably largely Sunni community. Ivory, in addition to slaves, seems to have been the key commodity. The best account is that of al-Ma'sudi, who makes much of the importance of ivory, especially as India was a major consumer (as well as producer), as ivory was used for handles of daggers and sword scabbards, and indicates that much African ivory went on to China.[10] The Abbasid ships were keen to obtain ivory for their China trade rather than for consumption in the Islamic world itself.

The other vital East African commodity was timber. There are references that Siraf was built with *saj* and other kinds of wood from East Africa during the ninth and tenth centuries.[11] Saj is normally translated as teak, and while true teak does not occur in East Africa there is a wide range of hardwoods of very similar character. Mangrove poles were also important. This very hard, dense, and termite resistant wood was sent to the Gulf until the 1980s for building purposes in a region in which there are few trees. Mangrove poles are cut to a standard length which produces a room width of around 2.6 metres. Not only is this found in East Africa but also in Siraf, where mortared impressions have been found confirming that mangrove poles were the standard roofing material. It is probable that the new cities of Baghdad and Samarra also made extensive use of these versatile poles, making parts of the coast, such the Lamu archipelago and the Rufiji delta, enormous 'lumber yards' for these Middle Eastern building projects.

Plate 4.1   *Mangrove poles stacked on the waterfront at Lamu. This versatile building material, which is heavier than water and resistant to termites, is found in the swamps of the archipelago and was cut in lengths of 2.6 metres. It was used in building along the coast, but was also a major trade item to the Middle East, at least from the tenth century. It was one of the last remaining commodities of the traditional dhow trade, and its export ceased in the 1980s largely through environmental concerns. However poles are still cut for local buildings (photo Mark Horton).*

Plate 4.2   *A complete glazed jar, of the type known as 'Sasanian-Islamic', and dating to the eighth or ninth century. The jar (in Lamu Museum) was found by sports divers off the important trading town of Manda and may be from a wreck site. These jars came from the Gulf region, and were used to export a variety of commodities to the Swahili coast, of which date syrup may have been of particular importance (photo Mark Horton, courtesy of Lamu Museum).*

There was also a range of luxury items which were obtained during the ninth and tenth centuries, mentioned in the sources although there is little archaeological evidence. These include rhinoceros horn which was popular in China, but may also have had a market in the Middle East for knife and dagger handles. Ambergris, the waxy secretion from sperm whales, although found throughout the Indian Ocean, was common on the East African beaches due to the pattern of currents; it was used as a fixative for perfume. Tortoise shell, according to al-Ma'sudi, was used for making combs. The shell comes from the hawksbill turtle, *Eretmochelys imbricata*, which has East African breeding colonies; it is mentioned as an export as far back as the *Periplus* and was used especially for inlay work.

Archaeological evidence supports the notion of this developing trade between East Africa with the Gulf under the Abbasids. Assemblages of pottery and glass found on Swahili sites contain a characteristic range of material, including alkaline-glazed jars (sometimes referred to as Sasanian-Islamic), to pitch-lined earthenware jars, fine wares such as white-glazed, lead-glazed and lustre wares, and even small quantities of Chinese pottery such as painted stonewares, olive green jars and early greenwares. The earthenware jars are known to have been made in Siraf, as the actual kilns have been excavated there.[12] The other finds are almost precisely replicated from Siraf's merchant houses. East African pottery, a generally poor quality earthenware, has been found in the Gulf at this date, at the site of Ras el-Hadd.[13] These pots were probably used as water jars; Ras el-Hadd was the first landfall in Arabia, where broken vessels may have been cleared out from the voyage. A cache of Islamic pottery, also broken on the voyage, was found on the beach at Manda in the Lamu archipelago. The voyage between the Gulf and East Africa during the ninth and tenth centuries was regular, profitable and almost routine.

Egypt

During the tenth century a new energy developed in Egypt, under the Fatimids, with the consequent revival of long-distance trade through the Red Sea with the Indian Ocean. Due to the pattern of monsoon winds, this trade was orientated more towards India than East Africa. It is possible to reach India in a single season from the Egyptian Red Sea ports, but extremely difficult to reach East Africa. As a result, direct voyages between Egypt and East Africa must have been infrequent and remain largely undocumented. The archaeological evidence for bulky commodities such as ceramics is also very rare; not a single sherd of Fatimid pottery has yet been found in East Africa, although some painted glass has been found at Manda.[14]

Trade between the Red Sea and East Africa during the tenth and eleventh centuries can be suggested on a number of grounds.[15] The first is the coin evidence. The Mtambwe hoard, containing locally minted silver coins, also had ten gold Fatimid dinars, or imitation dinars, the latest dating to 1066, while miniscule silver coins come from excavations on Manda, Shanga and from a hoard near Tanga.[16] Gulf coins during this period are absent. The other piece of evidence is architectural. The first use of *Porites* coral as a building material is recorded in East Africa about 920. This is undersea coral which is collected by divers and can be shaped into ashlar blocks while still soft and wet. It was also used for carving, a technique found generally in the Red Sea and not in the Gulf. While the use of *Porites* coral may have diffused to East Africa, it is most likely that it did so on the back of an existing trade route.

Egyptian trade with East Africa was to acquire three luxury items; gold, ivory and rock crystal. Gold was the foundation of Fatimid economic success, as silver was to the Abbasids, and they were able to obtain reliable supplies through the trans-Saharan trade with West Africa via Almoravid sources. The purity of the Fatimid dinar, which came to be the gold standard of the medieval world, resulted in Cairo (and adjacent city of Fustat) becoming the commercial and artistic centre of the eastern Mediterranean. The Fatimids sought out alternative supplies to help fund their trading activities in the Indian Ocean. Part of this came from Nubia, where gold mines were reopened, but other African sources were also important. This African gold was apparently minted at the Yemeni port of Athar. The Athar dinar was famous in the tenth and eleventh centuries for its quality and reliability.

The sources of southern African gold were located in Zimbabwe and northern Transvaal, where it was extracted from placer deposits as well as adit mines.[17] Unfortunately the latter, of which many hundreds were known, have been destroyed by later mining, and there are no firm radio-carbon dates. Gold is known from burials,[18] for which the twelfth century site of Mapungubwe is the most famous, which suggests that indigenous gold working had begun by this date. Crucibles for purifying gold have been found on the coastal Mozambique site of Chibuene.[19] The mid-tenth-century account of Buzurg ibn Shahriyar tells how at the farthest point in the land of the Zanj, 'men dig for gold there, and excavate galleries like ants', but 30 years earlier al-Mas'udi makes only the most cursory reference to gold from this region.[20] Gold remained an important commodity for Swahili merchants until the sixteenth century, after which its trade was taken over by the Portugese.

The history of ivory is more difficult to pin down as it was a commodity that also formed part of the Gulf trading network. However, from the late tenth century into the eleventh century there was an extraordinary expansion of ivory carving in the Mediterranean world, in Islamic Cairo, North Africa, Sicily and Andalusia, as well as in the courts of Christian Europe, both western and Byzantine. The Andalusian ivories are particularly remarkable for their size and skill, and while a West African source is possible (and is generally assumed to be the case), East African ivory is generally of better size and quality. The evidence of surviving pieces indicates that during the 960s a major new source of ivory became available in Europe, and this can be best explained through the opening up of this Red Sea route with East Africa.

The third luxury item, rock crystal, illustrates how much we rely upon a single historical reference to understand these complex trade routes. Until a few years ago, rock crystal was not considered to have been an East African export at all, despite a published remark by the eleventh century Nasr-i Khusrau, who saw crystal vessels in the Cairo market in 1046 and 1050 and remarked that the material came from East Africa.[21] Al-Biruni also noted the export of rock crystal from East Africa at around the same time. A number of pieces from the Fatimid workshops have survived and are extraordinary skilled pieces of craftsmanship. All belong to the late tenth to mid-eleventh century, after which the supply of crystal seems to have stopped.

The archaeological evidence from East Africa confirms this. Waste pieces of exceptionally clear crystal have been found; the clarity of the crystal is the particular feature of the Fatimid pieces. These may have been 'off-cuts' from larger lumps sent to Cairo and used to make beads. Waster beads, where the drilling went wrong, have also been found in eleventh-century levels at Shanga. The actual source of the crystal on the African mainland might have been Tsavo, where recent archaeological survey has recovered examples of this very pure type occurring naturally, together with evidence for trade with the coast at this period.[22]

The Later Islamic World

From the eleventh century onwards maritime trade patterns within the western Indian Ocean become confused, in part due to the decline of centralized authority, whether that of the Abbasids who became puppets of their military patrons, the Buyids and Seljuks, or the Fatimids whose control of Egypt became very uncertain. Natural disasters also had their impact, such as the earthquake that devastated Siraf in 977 and from which it never fully recovered. Long oceanic voyages were replaced by regional networks with the emergence of entrepôts at the points of intersection. Many different groups, not only Muslims, participated in the maritime trade, and we see the emergence of important transnational groups (of which the Jewish are the best documented[23]) and mercantile centres with their own rulers or governance.

This confusing picture was exploited in East Africa by the Swahili. Their entrepôts might expect a range of visitors arriving on the monsoon from many different places, and they were in a position to play one group off against another. The archaeological evidence suggests variation between towns, as can be gauged from the imported ceramics, with particular ports favouring Gulf, Indian or southern Arabian merchants.[24] The Swahili may themselves have ventured overseas in their own ships, as was recorded by Ibn al-Mujawir in *c*.1232, who saw East African outrigger boats in Aden which had sailed from Mogadishu, Kilwa and Madagascar.[25]

A number of developments that affected East Africa can be suggested. The Gulf trade continued through the twelfth century (the type fossil is lead-glazed sgraffiato pottery), though now conducted at ports at the mouth of the Gulf (where they could be more easily linked into the Red Sea–India trade) such as Sohar, Ras el-Hadd, Hormuz and Kish. According to al-Idrisi, the ruler of Kish actually raided East Africa for slaves in the twelfth century. These ports were very cosmopolitan places and there were certainly Indian merchants living in Kish in 1170.[26] It is from around this time that Indian as well as Chinese pottery is found in quantity in East Africa, and these assemblages closely match the ceramics found at Kish and Hormuz. Indian trade may have been developing with East Africa, but via the Gulf.[27]

A rival network was based in southern Arabia – and most importantly at Aden, with links to the Red Sea and Mameluk Egypt; indeed there were conflicts between Aden and Kish over access to the Swahili coast. There is a clear ceramic indicator, a type of pottery known as 'black-on-yellow' ware, which was made in kilns outside Aden and reached East Africa between 1250 and 1350. Aden lay on the trade route to India and China, and may well have been the source of much Indian and Chinese material, especially Lonquan (Celadon) wares. By the fourteenth century some Mameluk pottery was reaching East Africa, while there are a few pieces of East African earthenware known to be from the Red Sea port of Quseir el-Qadim.

The Aden merchant community was mainly interested in two commodities. The first was ivory, which was certainly dealt with by the Jewish merchants mentioned in the Geniza archive. It is interesting that as in the tenth century so in the mid-thirteenth century there was an explosion in the use of ivory in Europe – the Gothic ivories – at the same date as we see the development of trade between Aden and East Africa.[28]

The second commodity was gold, and here there has been a great deal of discussion centered on Kilwa, which, according to the Portuguese version of the Kilwa Chronicle, took over from Mogadishu and 'became absolute masters of the gold trade'; the internal chronology of the *Chronicle* suggests this took place in the early part of the twelfth century.[29] It is likely that the Kilwa gold trade actually reached its height in the early fourteenth century, a chronology that closely matches the rise of Great Zimbabwe, the southern African polity that may have controlled the gold trade of the Zimbabwe plateau. A Kilwa coin has been found at Great Zimbabwe, while the same Mahdali ruler of Kilwa, Hasan ibn Sulaiman, was minting his own gold coins in the early fourteenth century, styled in a similar way to that of the Rasulids of Yemen.[30]

In the emergence of world-trading systems, 1348–50 was an important period, with the spread from the East of the bubonic plague pandemic. While it effected medieval Europe (where it is known as the Black Death), it also spread throughout the Middle East and the Indian Ocean world via ships' rats.[31] In East Africa the town of Tumbatu may have been abandoned as the result of the plague while there is evidence of decline and dereliction at Kilwa. The rapid reduction in population levels resulted in economic collapse in Europe and with this there was a period of deflation and shortage of bullion, perhaps linked to disruption in the West African gold trade. Great Zimbabwe was abandoned by the fifteenth century for unknown reasons. Kilwa continued the gold trade on a reduced scale, possibly with the emerging polity at Mutapa, but other Swahili towns entered the gold trade, including Mombasa and Malindi if early Portuguese sources can be relied upon. When the Portuguese came to Kilwa in 1498, they were able to carry away enough gold to make a monstrance which still survives at Belém near Lisbon.[32] They noted special structures at Kilwa, known as *caracenas*, 'with some arches where they are said to weigh the gold that comes from Sofala in ingots.'[33]

The fifteenth century saw a decline of Islamic trade with East Africa and its replacement by Indian trade.[34] This was probably conducted directly across the ocean: Vasco da Gama had no difficulty finding a pilot to take him from Malindi to India in 1498. The early Portuguese saw Indian trading communities living in Malindi, Mombasa, Kilwa and Pate. Duarte Barbosa described the great profits made by the merchants from Cambay; Tomas Pires noted that the Cambay merchants took rice, wheat, soap, indigo, butter, oils, carnelians, coarse pottery and all kinds of cloth to trade with. Cloth was the most important import, and the virtual industrial production of textiles in western India, many printed, was set to alter the balance of the commercial system. The Swahili gave up making their own cloth (evidenced by the disappearance of spindle whorls in the archaeological record), and used Indian cloth for trading with the interior. What is surprising about Pires' list is that it is very ordinary, with little there of interest to Swahili merchants. Archaeology suggests Chinese pottery was also important, with greenwares and in the fifteenth century blue-on-white porcelain.

The Portuguese Intervention, 1498–1728

The Portuguese blundered in 1498 into a commercial system in decline.[35] The economic imperative for European expansion was the need to solve the shortage of bullion within Europe, created by the continual outflow of gold from the Mediterranean into the Indian Ocean world to pay for spices.[36] There were two solutions: to find a direct maritime route to the spices to avoid the Mameluk and Levantine intermediaries, or to find alternative sources of bullion. Spanish and English expeditions (the latter under the Genoese John Cabot) attempted to find a westerly sea route to China and the East, while the Portuguese sailed east, following the expeditions into the eastern Atlantic begun under Henry the Navigator. The bullion crisis was solved in an unexpected way, first through the looting of gold of the conquered central and south American civilizations and then when this ran out through the mining of rich silver deposits in south America.

The first part of the sixteenth century was dominated by the Portuguese looking for spices and gold; it was in south-eastern Africa, in the region known as Sofala, that they believed that gold could be obtained, and all their early accounts are dominated by references to this promised wealth. But at the point of their arrival the gold trade seems to have been in relative decline and the inland groups unwilling to work the gold, possibly because they were already well supplied with Indian cloth and beads. The producers were very scattered and from official Portuguese figures production rarely exceeded one ton a year.

Ivory was a more important export, not least because the hunting of elephant produced meat as well as ivory and thus produced additional benefits. The Swahili were heavily involved in the ivory trade with Sofala, shipping the ivory back to Malindi and Pate in particular for onward trade across the Indian Ocean, especially to India. The Portuguese hoped to take over this gold and ivory trade by sacking or developing treaties with the Swahili towns (in the case of Malindi, they even set up a short-lived customs house) and building forts at Kilwa, Mozambique and Sofala, thus blocking Swahili exports. That on Mozambique was massively fortified and a new fortress was later built in Mombasa and named Fort Jesus in 1593. They then attempted to trade on their own with the inland groups, using Indian cloth and beads, and trading outposts were established along the Zambezi and on the Zimbabwe plateau.

The Portuguese never fully succeeded in monopolizing either the ivory or gold trade, as the Swahili were very experienced in sailing these waters and the Portuguese officials themselves were often corrupt, enriching themselves through illegal trade. Official interest in gold was renewed in the mid-seventeenth century when the Portuguese lost control of the Spice Islands to the Dutch and had to buy their own spices using Sofala gold. However, in the 1690s they were expelled from the Zimbabwe plateau and in 1698 they lost Fort Jesus to the Omani Arabs; although they did reoccupy it briefly in 1728–9.

The Portuguese period provides a documented account of Swahili trade with the interior, especially in the south.[37] It is unclear how representative

Plate 4.3   *Zanzibar from the sea, c.1857, from R. F. Burton,* Zanzibar; City, Island, and Coast *(London, 1872, plate facing p. 145). The details of the waterfront can be clearly seen, with the European consulates to the right, the Omani fort (and former church) in the centre and royal palaces to the left. The main trading shore lay in front of the fort, where there was also a market.*

the situation in the sixteenth to eighteenth centuries was of earlier centuries, especially with the growth of the Indian mercantile economy in the fifteenth century. But it is remarkable how little impact the Portuguese actually had on the Swahili coast proper. The towns continued to prosper and there are numerous mosques, houses and tombs dating to this period. If ivory and gold were restricted the Swahili still traded in timber, shell, ambergris, skins, copal, orchella, slaves and foods such as sorghums, millets, sesame, coconut oil, vinegar and copra; they were able to maintain a respectable mercantile economy. The Portuguese merit only passing mention in their chronicles, whenever they intervened in internal affairs in a particularly outrageous way.

Colonization and Aftermath, 1729–1998

Omani political interest in East Africa developed with the beginning of the Yarubi dynasty in Oman in 1624, which first moved against the Portuguese holdings at Sohar and Muscat – their fort falling in 1650 – and then continued as an Indian Ocean naval force against East Africa, culminating in the siege and capture of Fort Jesus in 1696–8.[38] While initially welcomed as fellow Muslims, in a very short time the Omanis were resented as much as the Portuguese, and a complex of Swahili alliances enabled the Portuguese briefly to capture Fort Jesus in 1728–9. Finally it fell to the Omanis and governors were appointed from the important Omani Mazrui family (who may already have settled in Mombasa), who developed close relations with the Swahili patriciate and were able to acquire extensive land holdings around Mombasa and on Pemba.[39] The Mazrui became effectively independent of Oman and for this reason, the Busaidi (who replaced the Yarubi in 1749) developed Zanzibar as an alternative political focus for their East African empire. The Portuguese factory and church, located on the seafront of Zanzibar, was converted into a fortress, which still survives, and during the course of the eighteenth century suffered a series of attacks. One impact of these struggles was that the Swahili towns allied with these different protagonists, to help them in their own internal disputes. The watershed Battle of Shela in 1812 put an end to Pate's aspirations as the leading Swahili port of the north, after its defeat by Lamu with Busaidi help.

But in many ways the eighteenth century was a Golden Age for the Swahili, as it was a period that saw the removal of the Portuguese and of internal conflict between the Omani successors. It is to this century that many of the elaborate stone houses of Lamu and Pate belong, and much of the famous Swahili poetry such as *al-Inkishafi*.[40] The Swahili were able to develop a successful ivory and slave trade largely outside the colonial control and taxation systems. What little evidence there is suggests an annual demand of slaves by Oman of around 500, mainly to tend the date plantations.[41] Lamu and Pate developed a sizable ivory trade both with Mozambique (where they still had to pay duties) and their own coastal hinterland. Kilwa also enjoyed a second period of prosperity in the 1780s as a slave trading centre under French encouragement, to supply the sugar plantations of the Mascarene islands and Madagascar. Mombasa, under the Mazruis, developed plantations along the coast. Mangrove poles remained another important and valuable coastal export.[42]

In the early nineteenth century East Africa became an important resource for products in demand in Europe and America, changing the nature of the trade from an Indian Ocean to a world trade.[43] By the early nineteenth century cloves were being cultivated (the French claimed to have first introduced them to Kilwa in the 1780s) on Zanzibar. After the capture of Pemba by the Busaidis from the Mazruis in 1823, Pemba became the main centre of clove production because of its soils and climate, involving the introduction of slave plantations and the clearance of the interior of the island. Another product which came to be important was copal, a vital ingredient in varnishes and polishes, which was collected from the hinterland. There was a new demand for ivory and ebony, led largely by the fashion for pianos which needed ivory and ebony keys. To take advantage of this trade,[44] European powers set up consulates in Zanzibar, and American or British merchant ships were now as common as Arabian dhows.

In 1832 Said bin Sultan moved his capital from Oman to Zanzibar. This was followed by the settlement of Omani merchants, keen to join the new prosperity. The Sultanate extended its authority along the coast, building and renovating powerful forts strategically placed to subdue local populations as much as outside enemies, and, in the major towns, establishing local governors, *liwali*, all of them Omani from Zanzibar and in many cases kin of the sultans'. They were backed by contingents of mercenary Baluchi troops whose officers, the *jemadars*, acquired considerable power and reputation for brutality; military outposts were established along the major caravan routes to maintain Zanzibar's monopoly over the ivory and slave commerce. The sultans' army was controlled by the British General Lloyd Matthews, also a mercenary but of a rather superior kind, who ended as First Minister of the Sultanate. With all such actions came the effects of changing forms of religious reformation, innovation and education; fashion in housing, clothing and cuisine; of relations between old and young, between men and women, and between free and servile, of individual aims to acquire wealth and increase social standing. Behind all were the ever-changing patterns of commerce and exchange, of relations between the coast, hinterland and interior, of relations between coast and Asia.

The rise of the Sultanate had far deeper effects than had the Portuguese occupation, finally gaining cohesion and strength under Sultan Seyyid Barghash ibn Said al-Busaidi, who between 1870 and his death in 1888 achieved political and commercial unification of and control over the coast. The British helped him through their strong military, naval, and especially financial presence in India; after many years of vying with other European powers the British took the lead, its consuls and residents becoming *de facto* governors under the titular sovereignty of the sultans.

Barghash's problems were less military than economic. He and his Omani followers,[45] who included immigrant settlers owning the Zanzibar and Pemba plantations, lacked the mercantile skills, experience and organization that the Swahili had perfected over centuries. The Swahili realized this and were determined to retain the commerce for themselves. They refused the continual offers to marry their daughters to the Omani rulers and officials, knowing that to do so would very soon lead to their losing control over their towns and property: a political governor was one thing, an all-powerful son-in-law was quite another.[46] The non-patrician Swahili did the same, except in some cases, such as Pemba, where they lost control of their own lands in consequence.[47] They could do less about the authority of

Omani Muslim judges, but here the Sultanate proved wise and rarely enforced its own Ibadi law onto its Shafi'i subjects, judges of both schools acting together in the larger towns; later, the British-appointed judges were competent in both Islamic and British civil law.[48]

The Swahili lost in the end. First the sultans declared the Mrima coast, opposite the islands of Zanzibar and Pemba and the centre of the coastline, a monopoly in which only their own agents could engage in the interior-ocean commerce; and Zanzibar had the advantage of controlling the new issuance of Indian coinage and of having local agents of the major Indian finance houses living in Zanzibar City and able to finance the interior caravan trade.

Sultan Barghash opened up the Tanganyika and Nyasa regions to his own Omani traders (usefully helped by Swahili who had prior knowledge of the interior) as far as the distant lands of Maniema in the Congo where he established his own satraps, such as Tippu Tip,[49] and there traded with the Belgians coming from the west. Most major caravan routes ended at the ports of the Mrima coast, where the goods were easily shipped across to the markets in Zanzibar for export.[50] This effectively cut out the Swahili merchants along most of the coast engaged in this lucrative commerce, leaving them only less important commodities. The northern Swahili towns had traditionally acted as trans-shipment ports between Zanzibar and the south and the ports of Asia;[51] but by the end of the nineteenth century larger sailing vessels and steamships took over most of the ocean traffic, sailing directly between Zanzibar and Asian ports by being able largely to ignore the constraints of the monsoons.

The crucial economic factors at the heart of the disasters of the period for the Swahili were first the abolition in 1873 of the export of slaves and then that of slave holding itself, in 1897 in Zanzibar and Tanganyika and in 1907 in Kenya. These measures had severe repercussions for the Swahili merchants in their own towns and indirectly for the non-slave-owning occupants of the countryside. It destroyed most of the local productive system of the merchants, who could no longer use their slave labour for growing of grains on their plantations nor the cutting of mangroves from the coastal swamps, both products providing the basis for the coastal trade with southern Arabia. Abolition did not all that greatly affect the interior trades in ivory and other goods, as slaves were not an essential element in caravan transport, but it did affect their carriage and storage within the towns themselves. The impoverishment of the merchants contributed to that of the countryside whose local trade with the towns quickly faded from what it had been for centuries.[52]

The freeing of slaves, at the time as much as half the coastal population, had an immense social impact as well as a directly economic one. One problem was what to do with them once freed according to British law.

By the Islamic shari'a law only an owner can free his or her slaves, and since the British did not own them their emancipation was somewhat shallow. Many slaves did not regard themselves as emancipated, and their owners were only rarely about to free them themselves. Some sold their slaves to the British, as they saw it; the British saw it as awarding compensation for the loss of domestic and field labourers. But in any case slaves were given no lands of their own. In the north, behind Malindi and Lamu, many of the wealthier and more enterprising claimed unused and forest land, cleared it, planted crops for export to Arabia and Mombasa and some became wealthy and powerful. Among them were women, and for them emancipation was a blessing, although for most women it was little of the kind. In the north ex-slaves were for a time protected by being in the vaguely defined territory of the German-backed 'Sultanate of Witu', which lasted from 1856 until 1890. The Witu rulers kept slaves themselves but could not greatly control the ex-slaves in the remote hinterland area north of the town.[53]

During the twentieth century slave labour was replaced by that of squatters, free persons who entered into contracts with landowning employers to do so many days work a week, month or season in return for a plot of land on which to live and grow their own crops. This system continued on the plantations of Zanzibar, Pemba and the Mrima coast until the 1964 Zanzibar Revolution. With it, mainly after the building of railways in both Kenya and Tanganyika, was the appearance and marked growth of labour migration from inland to the plantations and especially to the rapidly growing coastal towns, particularly Mombasa: the main immigrant groups were Luo, Kikuyu, Kamba and Makonde/Makua, most of whom became permanent residents but not, of course, Swahili, with marked consequences as far as political representation and the development of trades unions were concerned.[54]

While the brutal effects of the colonization process created major dislocations within traditional society, aspects of oceanic trade continued, and was controlled by the Swahili patricians, although Indian and Arab merchants took an increasing share. The 'dhow trade' as it is often referred to (the ships are more correctly termed *jahazi*), continued between the Gulf and East Africa, supplying natural African products, especially mangrove poles, and the customs books in places such as Lamu and Mombasa meticulously recorded the boats and their cargoes.[55] The dhow trade with the Gulf ceased in the 1980s not least because of environmental concerns for the mangrove forests that were being cut down. *Jahazi* still sail in East African waters, and are even built. They are used for coastal trade especially to the islands and more distant coastal regions such as Somalia and Mozambique, and still have an important role in smuggling across national boundaries. They also carry passengers as when Lamu was cut-off for several months during the heavy rains in 1998, or refugees escaping the conflict in Somalia.

5

The Trading System of the Swahili Coast

The Mercantile System

The Swahili-controlled trading region has comprised the extreme western parts of the Indian Ocean and has drawn in the many peoples of the immediate hinterland and the interior, from the Nile and Great Lakes to Zimbabwe. The Swahili merchants have been the brokers between these diverse peoples, with differing goods to export and differing demands for what they have imported, and with different languages, cultures, religions and degrees of literacy; they have been not only mercantile but also cultural brokers between these African societies and the wider mercantile community of the Indian Ocean. Exchange has taken place for a series of reasons, to cement social relationships, to enable the acquisition of commodities which are required by some or all societies but which are unequally distributed (salt being the best example), or to provide luxury items which can confer status; the Swahili have participated in all these.

In general communities have been prepared to deal with outsiders, only if they were getting a good return. This view has depended upon notions of 'value', and value has been socially embedded. To the Islamic societies of the Middle East, items such as cloth and glass beads have had a much lower value than ivory and gold, while to the societies of the interior of Africa the reverse has been very much the case, ivory and gold being comparatively useless items. The Swahili, as brokers, have been able to bring these two value systems together, as they have belonged to both the Islamic world and to Africa and so have been the real beneficiaries.

The long-term success of such a system has depended upon the notion of value not becoming universally held, as for example happens with the introduction of currency, or of a single legal or religious system. It is for this reason that Islam may have been restricted to the coast, as we have seen in chapter 3, until the development of commodity exchange in the nineteenth century, when it spread inland. Swahili ability to act as middlemen would have been limited if their inland partners were Muslim as well. They may have realized this and actively kept Islam as a coastal monopoly.

In fact the early Swahili went further and restricted the supply of many items, to which they had access through their Indian Ocean trading partnerships, that would have been in demand inland. Archaeologically visible items such as glass and ceramics are very rarely found on sites inland and were retained in the coastal towns, where they are found in quantity. These towns were extremely active in craft production, such as shell and stone bead making, iron working, copper working and cloth and leather working and it was these items that were traded inland, using local raw materials that had little to do with the Indian Ocean trade. For the various craft activities they were able to exploit the technological advantage gained through their wide-ranging contacts, and possibly by the actual settlement of overseas craftsmen within the towns.

While external sources stress the connections between the Swahili coast and the outside world, this was only one part of a complex network of relationships which can only be understood fully for the nineteenth century. Before this period there are fragments of historical evidence which can help us to understand the now ever-increasing archaeological evidence, from both the coast and the interior. For these earlier periods the nineteenth-century evidence is of uncertain help in understanding the mercantile system.

The oceanic traders – wherever they came from, and this varied much over time and place – arrived on the monsoon, carrying their trade goods, hoping to obtain return cargoes on which their prosperity relied. It is very unlikely that they left with a single commodity, but rather with a wide range of items of varying bulk and value. The traders sought out known ports, and the geographies are full of the terrible fate awaiting lost ships in hostile lands. It was not a case of arriving on an unknown beach, unwrapping the trade goods, and expecting local Africans to emerge from the bush carrying loads of ivory and gold to trade with. For example the tenth-century writer, Buzurg ibn Shahriyar, describes how sailors, driven off course, realized they were going to perish as they were 'falling among cannibal negroes' and repeated the profession of faith.[1]

The mercantile system worked because the exchange was embedded within the social structure of the coastal communities. The crucial element was trust between the traders and the Swahili, and this could only be maintained by making the traders quasi-kin of the coastal inhabitants. A ninth-century Chinese source, describing trading practices, illustrates this clearly, 'if Persian merchants wish to go into the country, they collect around them several thousand men and present them with strips of cloth. All, whether young or old, draw blood and swear an oath and only then do they trade their goods.'[2] These were blood brotherhood rituals in which the traders became quasi-kin of lineage groups. Blood brotherhood rituals like this have survived into the twentieth century. When linked to trading practice they provided considerable protection, as the potential murder of the trader would be considered in the same way as the murder of a full member of the lineage.

A variation on this was the sponsorship of traders by the local communities: Buzurg wrote in the tenth century that 'when merchants go to Berbera, they take escorts with them for fear that a native will seize them and geld them. The natives collect the testicles of foreigners'.[3] Sponsors were described in early thirteenth-century Mogadishu, where 'they have no kings, but their affairs are regulated by elders, according to their customs. When a merchant goes to them, he must stay with one of them who will sponsor him in their dealings'.[4] When Ibn Battuta visited Mogadishu in 1331, he describes the same system in detail. As Ibn Battuta was a lawyer, he was looked after by the qadi and provided lodgings in his house. For visiting traders, there were strict rules:

> When a ship comes into port, it is boarded from sanbuqs, that is to say little boats. Each sanbuq carries a crowd of young men, each carrying a covered dish, containing food. Each one of them presents his dish to a merchant on board and calls out: 'this man is my guest.' And his fellows do the same. Not one of the merchants disembarks except to go to the house of his host among the young men, save frequent visitors to the country. In such case they go where they like. When a merchant has settled in his host's house, the latter sells for him what he has brought, and makes his purchase for him. Buying anything from a merchant below its market price or selling him anything except in his host's presence is disapproved of by the people of Mogadishu.[5]

By the fourteenth century, the surviving architecture provides traces of specially constructed guest rooms which are found in the outer courtyards of stone houses.[6] They have their own washing facilities and latrines enabling the privacy of the household to be respected. In the eighteenth-century stone houses of Lamu[7] these rooms are common and are known as *sabule*.

We can probe into the relationship between the overseas trader and the local sponsor. It is often assumed, as a result of archaeological investigations, that the main commodities to be traded were ceramics and glass. These are ubiquitous on early sites, but curiously are rarely mentioned in the external sources as trade goods. Ceramics and glass vessels (but not beads) are rarely found inland; even from major inland sites such as Great Zimbabwe[8] there is little more than a handful of sherds of imported pottery, including only four of Chinese celadon. In fact, while ceramics are common on the coast, it is possible to calculate the rate of loss from controlled excavations. This was done at Shanga where for the first hundred years less than five pots per year were lost, rising to twenty per year in the tenth century and around 140 per year in the fourteenth century – or less than one pot per household per year.[9] As the ceramics do not seem to have been traded inland this represents closely the rate of exchange especially as it includes both fine wares and jars containing oils and syrups. The trade in ceramics and glass cannot have been on a large scale, and was more likely to have been gift exchange to cement relationships between overseas traders and local merchants. The manner in which these commodities were displayed in specially constructed niches within the stone houses further demonstrates their special character.

Until recently it was assumed that exchange along the Swahili coast was based on a system of barter until the arrival of colonial coinage in the nineteenth century. While locally minted copper coins were known from Mogadishu, Kilwa, Mafia and Zanzibar, these were considered little more than symbolic tokens that played no part in the mercantile system.[10] Part of the problem was that on some sites coins were indeed very common but along other areas of the coast (in particular the Kenyan coast) no coins were found. There have been two new archaeological discoveries to challenge this view. First, by the use of sieving during excavations, coins are found more widely, including along the Kenyan coast.[11] These include not only copper coins, but minuscule silver coins, as thin as foil, and only 6–8mm in diameter. Secondly, three minted gold coins have been identified, produced in the name of a well-known early fourteenth-century Kilwa ruler, Hasan ibn Sulaiman.[12] Local coins were issued in gold, silver and copper, confirming an eleventh-century Chinese description that coins were made by officials of the government using three metals, gold, silver and copper.[13]

At present, the archaeological evidence is sporadic. Small silver coins of local issue date from the ninth century, where they were found in sand, filling the platform of the mosque at Shanga. Their origin may actually have been the beach, where they were dropped during trading, and not recovered but incorporated in fill that was then taken up to the mosque.[14] Sporadic numbers of silver coins were also found in the settlement levels, but here losses could be more easily recovered. The eleventh-century merchant's hoard of coins found at Mtambwe Mkuu on Pemba island contained over 2600 locally produced silver coins and probably ten dinars mostly from the Fatimid world. From this hoard, the coins of Ali bin al-Hasan are known in silver and from Kilwa and other places in copper, showing that both metals were used at one time.[15] We do not know if by the eleventh century the gold coinage comprised only imported Fatimid coins or whether there were also locally minted gold coins, possibly at first imitations of Fatimid coins[16] and then later, official issues of the kings of Kilwa. However the evidence suggests that a trimetallic system of coinage was in operation at certain times.

Confirmation that this was the case comes from early Portuguese sources. There was an agreed system of value, based upon the local mithqal, and the Portuguese recorded their tribute extracted from the Swahili as well as the accounts of their factories at Sofala and Malindi in this currency. The mithqal was noted by Ibn Battuta during his visit to Kilwa in 1331 and the Sultan of Kilwa gave 1000 mithqals towards the rebuilding of the great Mosque at Kilwa during the fifteenth century.[17] The three gold coins from Kilwa, while of variable weights, average together precisely 4.20g, exactly that of the Cairo dinar, which became the standard weight for Islamic coinage in the Indian Ocean. Mithqals and dinars were interchangeable terms, and the gold issued on the coast must have been tied into the Islamic system. The Portuguese confirm this by providing an exchange rate for the reis; 390 reis were worth a gold Portuguese cruzado (which weighed 3.58 g) and 460 reis in 1505, for the local mithqal working out at the weight at 4.18g.[18] De Barros recorded that 500 Kilwan mithqals minted 584 cruzados working out at a weight of 4.28g.

The Portuguese allow us to value the silver and copper coins as well. According to Fra Monclaro, silver coins, looking like the scales of fish (a very accurate description of the Mtambwe coins) were still in use in Mombasa in 1569. He estimated that they were each worth four Portuguese reis.[19] No sixteenth-century coins are known from Mombasa, but the earlier Mtambwe coins did show a marked consistency in weight, at 0.04g, 0.12g and 0.18g. At 115 silver coins to the mithqal, the bimetallic rate would be 1.1, 3.3 and 4.9 if these represent Monclaro's coins, making East African gold cheaper (or silver more expensive) than was the case in the Mediterranean, where the rate ranged between to 10 and 15.[20] Rates of around 6 can be suggested for East Africa from the valuation of the Portuguese silver pardau (which weighed 22g) at 400 reis in Pate in 1637.[21] Hans Mayr described the copper coins on the coast as 'like our ceptis' valued at four to the reis, so that sixteen would equate to a silver coin and approximately 1600 to a mithqal.[22] The copper coins weigh a fairly consistent 2.6g, making a bimetallic rate for copper to gold of 1000. It is tempting to conclude that the Swahili coinage operated on trimetallic rate of 1:10:1000, for gold, silver and copper, using a weight system that fitted into that of the Islamic world. This is surely a monetary system of some complexity.

These coins must have been used for trade, although their distribution was very limited. Thus only one coin (a copper issue of Hasan ibn Sulaiman) has ever been found inland, significantly at Great Zimbabwe. Some copper coins are known from overseas, including a small hoard in the Northern Territories of Australia, from Oman and Julfar;[23] each represents a rare or exceptional find. The use of these coins was confined to the coast itself and must have been to facilitate business dealings between the coastal merchants themselves, operating over substantial distances. Ibn Battuta suggests that while exchange was monopolized by coastal merchants, a fair price had to be achieved in their dealing with overseas traders, and such transactions were assisted by a common system of value, backed by coins, using metals coined at known weights. As two of the three metals, gold and copper[24] were readily available, the minting of coins within an Islamic system enabled the Swahili merchants to participate within the Islamic economy and accumulate high value goods but without the need for the coins actually to leave the coast. In fact there is good evidence to suggest that the coins were recycled over centuries, given their often extremely worn condition and their discovery in layers laid down 400 years after they were minted. The system lasted from the ninth century until the sixteenth century, when the Portuguese interferred with gold production in southern Africa and drained the Swahili towns of coinage through incessant demands for tribute. Between the seventeenth and nineteenth centuries, the Swahili coast reverted to a system of barter and gift exchange, reverting to the use of coinage under colonial influence during the 1850s.

The Swahili Corridor

A key element of the trading system was the Swahilis' ability to sail along the coast with comparative ease from the Horn of Africa to southern Mozambique, Madagascar and the Comores. This was facilitated by an indigenous tradition of boat and ship building, using local materials, and the seasonal shifts in wind direction and currents which mirrored those of the monsoon system as a whole. This navigation has been termed the 'Swahili corridor' and it enabled commodities to be obtained along the entire coastline, and concentrated at certain centres – entrepôts – for exchange into the Indian Ocean commercial world.[25]

The evidence for traditional boats is both ethnographic and historical. The best-known type is the *mtepe*, a sewn boat (pegged and stitched), with a characteristic hull shape that includes a projecting bow post (carved apparently to imitate a camel's head) and a square matting sail; one measured in 1928 was 16.8m long and 4.5m beam, drawing 1.7m.[26] A variant is known as *dau la mtepe*, which has a different bow and stern arrangement using bresthooks, and seems to have been a little smaller. No example of either craft survives, but there are several photographs and accurate ship models from the late nineteenth century. They were important cargo vessels, especially for the carriage of heavy materials such as mangrove poles, while their matting sails were suitable for sailing with the wind, and apparently into it as well. The flexible hulls enabled the boats to sail faster than a rigid hull, while they were able to run ashore or over shoals without too much difficulty. These boats were certainly the normal form of coastal transport in the sixteenth century, when they were described by the Portuguese,[27] as comparable in size to their caravels of 50 tons and able to sail to Sofala from as far north as Malindi and Lamu. Those encountered by Vasco da Gama in 1498 were described as 'large, without decks; they are not nailed and sail tightly bound with esparto cord; and their boats the same. Their sails are of palm matting and their mariners have Genoese needles by which to steer, and quadrants and sea charts'.[28]

Before the sixteenth century there are no comparable descriptions of indigenous boats, and we certainly cannot claim there to be a direct link with the sewn boats of the *Periplus*, which must have been much smaller in scale; the sewn hull construction was a common feature of Indian Ocean maritime technology. However the archaeological evidence can be used to show that there was a regular maritime connection along the coast; this is clear from local earthenware pottery with distinctive fabric and decoration which can be found widely distributed from its source.[29] The trade in raw materials such as schist from Madagascar, for reworking in the northern towns, is also suggestive of indigenous coastal trade. In general terms, the parallel cultural developments in architecture and ceramics over a millennium suggests a regular connection between the Swahili communities along the 2000 mile coastline and beyond.

The Hinterland

The earliest evidence for exchange between the coast and the interior comes from archaeological evidence from the coastal hinterland.[30] As was explained in chapter 2, we can identify a single Iron Age farming society, represented by coastal and inland settlements. Where these inland sites have been excavated, items of Indian Ocean origin have been found. These may be local (such as sea shells) or imports from more distant areas, such as glass and stone beads, and more rarely, glazed pottery and copper artefacts.[31] These are found on the Tanzanian and Kenyan coastal hinterland, and are dated from the fifth to the fifteenth centuries.

Whilst this material forms a persistent pattern, it cannot be described as frequent and is normally represented by single sherds or beads from excavated settlement sites and middens. It may be that if burial sites were investigated in this region (as they have been in southern Africa) a very different picture might emerge of exotic items being used for grave goods. It is also probable that this material is a very imprecise indicator of the exchange network, and that cloth, which does not survive, may have been the most commonly traded item.

The exchange networks at this date did not include caravans, but more traditional systems of patron–client exchange. We know about this in more detail in the nineteenth century, but it seems likely that the hinterland agricultural communities established relationships with both the hunter-gatherers and pastoralist groups, and set up a series of exchanges, which included not only agricultural produce and wild resources such as honey, but also iron, cloth and access to resources (such as the river Tana). The Swahili exchange was probably largely (but not exclusively) focused on their agricultural clients, but in some areas, such as the Lamu archipelago, they also dealt with Oromo pastoralists, who largely controlled the supply of ivory, which was in turn collected by their clients, the Boni and Waata hunter-gatherers.[32] Historical linguistic research, through loan words and borrowing, allows us to suggest a very complex series of economic relationships along the coast during this period.

Over the centuries the presence of the coast as a place of supply of certain items became known and then increased. This led to the demand from the coast for new commodities, in particular minerals, ivory and slaves. Change in indigenous items and modes of production was brought about by that demand, especially when previously produced items became more easily obtainable from the coast (such as textiles and beads in the early period and arms in the later period). The consequence was the centralization of production of items and the rise of more powerful economic and political leaders in the interior, who were later on to include men from the coast itself, particularly from Zanzibar. These were typically clients of Swahili or later Zanzibari merchants, who also controlled the ocean trade, who established many long-distance networks, each based on a merchant town.

The Swahili relied upon these networks not only to supply commodities, but also for their own protection. Before the sixteenth century, town walls or defensive perimeters are absent from coastal towns, even those located on the mainland. After this date, walls were built (although never of any great substance) partly because of the destabilization of the coastal polities by the Portuguese, but mainly because the arrival of Oromo pastoralists from southern Ethiopia upset the status quo. Another episode of wall building dates to the eighteenth century, along the southern Kenyan and northern Tanzanian coast, when fortified enclosures were built complete with gate houses. Local traditions attribute these to be defence against the Maasai, who moved into this area around this time.

A more effective protection was to use clients in the hinterland to protect them in times of crisis. The Portuguese described Malindi's use of the Mossegejos in 1593, who by their account were particularly brutal pastoralists, who 'to prevent them from spoiling their crops and making war upon them, they buy them off with cloth and other things, but their usual dress is made of skins.',[33] while as late as the nineteenth century the town of Siyu called upon an army of Katwa pastoralists to drive off the army of Sayyid Said from Zanzibar.[34]

It is easy to characterize the hinterland as an area of long-term stable relationships between different groups, and to an extent the archaeology of areas such as that occupied by the Mijikenda shows continuity from the eighth century to the present day. There were also periods of disruption, such as the arrival of the Oromo and Maasai,[35] but which also offered new possibilities for long-distance trade into the interior. Earlier episodes may have been caused by Somali migrations into the northern section of the coast. One group in particular can be identified only from their pottery, which was decorated by wavy lines. They settled as far south as Gedi during the tenth to twelfth centuries, and judging by the location of their sites had a strong pastoralist component. Sherds have also been found at Shanga, suggesting that they reached the islands as well. They may have also introduced the camel from the north into the coastal settlements, as these bones appear at the same time as their pottery. The 'wavy-line' pottery people cannot be directly identified in either the linguistic or historical record,[36] although it is possible that they were the proto Segeju/Mossegejos. They must have been an important factor in the development of coastal culture.

One early export that one would expect to find in the archaeological record is slaves. It has been suggested in the previous chapter that for a period up to 868 there was a considerable trade in slaves, with many thousands reaching the Gulf region, probably being exported through the islands of Zanzibar and Pemba. The adjacent coastal hinterland, in particular including the well-watered Kwale, Pare and Usambara hills, was an area of early Iron Age settlement, with a relatively dense population. Surveys[37] indicate a reduction in the overall number of sites, the development of rudimentary fortifications around village sites and some reafforestation at around this date.

It is difficult to judge how far the 'hinterland' extended. Certainly the old-fashioned notions of the Nyika, a semi-desert 50 or so miles back from the coast, beyond which any contact ceased, is overstated even by modern historians, as the rivers provided corridors, and the landscape was not particularly inhospitable. Survey now being undertaken in Tsavo shows that this was populated in the past and early sites are being found with coastal imports. Much further inland, glass beads have been found at Hyrax Hill, but are thought to date from after 1800, while the majority of glass beads from the Lacustrine area also date from this period. But modern excavations are now beginning to recover glass beads from thirteenth- and fourteenth-century contexts, from sites such as Ntusi. At Kibiro, a salt producing site on the east shore of Lake Albert, a female burial was excavated with 238 shell beads and 16 glass beads, the latter of typical Indian Ocean type, from a radiocarbon dated level of around 1400.[38] The Kibiro and Ntusi finds open up the possibility that trade networks extended much further inland at an earlier date than has hitherto been assumed, and with it the implication that Indian Ocean trade may have been a factor in the development of the Lacustrine states.

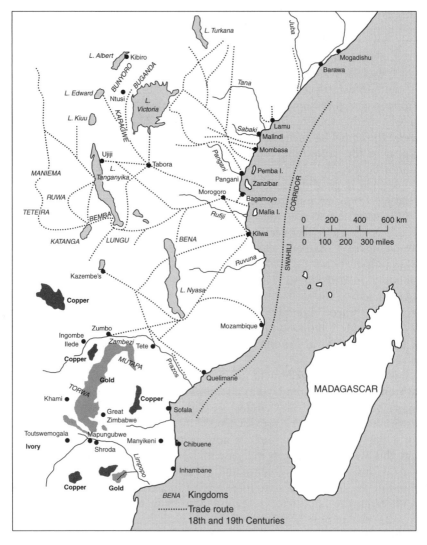

Map 5.1   *The Swahili coast and the interior, 800–1850.*

Trade with the Indigenous Polities in the African Interior

It has generally been held that the Swahili and Zanzibari merchants sent caravans into the interior, hitherto untouched by trade, during the nineteenth century and so 'opened up' that interior to the outside world, there having been until this time very little connection between the coast and the interior.[39] This view is exaggerated, and for many areas wrong. What did happen was that the nature of the trade changed during the nineteenth century, with the development of formal caravans of traders and porters, protected by firearms, a changed emphasis on particular trade objects and the commoditization of the goods exchanged. From the view of the interior peoples, the Swahili traders were newcomers to be used by them. This system replaced more traditional methods of exchange, such as 'down-the-line' and patron–client exchange and trade organized by specialist groups who enjoyed a degree of protected status. Nonetheless, the Swahili were still the beneficiaries of this more indirect trade during the pre-nineteenth-century period, while Indian Ocean and coastal commodities reached the interior, albeit in somewhat smaller quantities.

The three main items of long-distance trade throughout eastern and central Africa had always been iron, salt and copper. The centres of production of these resources were geographically dispersed; an area possessing one of them could use its monopoly to acquire wealth and influence over a wide area, yet was also under a perennial threat from more powerful neighbours. To the communities on the coast, none of these three commodities were needed. There was ample salt in the sea which could be obtained by evaporation, while there were sources of iron ore close by; copper (or rather better brass and bronze alloys) was in wide circulation within the Indian Ocean. In contrast, what were needed for the Indian Ocean trade were ivory, gold and slaves, all commodities of little use in the interior, and it was this demand and availability that brought the Swahili into the trade networks of the interior.

The best evidence for the scale of the Indian Ocean trade within the interior is found in southern Africa, surprisingly distant from the Swahili towns themselves. The control of the sea lanes by the Swahili extended as far south as the Mozambique channel, and the 'Swahili corridor' was a mechanism to concentrate commodities at ports accessible to the trans-oceanic trade. Given the nature of the monsoon winds and the available maritime technology, a voyage to the southern African coast was no longer more hazardous than trade into the coastal hinterland.

There is very early evidence that southern Africa was important. The tenth- and fourteenth-century site of Chibuene in southern Mozambique is as typically 'Swahili' as sites on the Tanzanian or Kenyan coast, with Tana tradition pottery, imported Islamic white-glaze pottery and Muslim burials. Chibuene is not alone, and other early coastal sites with evidence for imported pottery include Inhambane and Dundo.[40] It is likely that coastal trade reached as far south as Cape Correntes. From there the Limpopo valley was relatively accessible, and it is there that the first evidence for long-distance trade can be located, at sites such as Shroda and Pont Drift, which were occupied from around 800. Substantial quantities of glass beads and cowrie shells were found, along with the evidence for the processing of ivory and skins.[41] The faunal evidence from these sites suggests the importance of cattle, sheep and goats in their economy, a significant development for the early Iron Age farming communities of the south.

The next phase of development comes from the site of K2, dating to the late tenth century, where there were frequent finds of glass beads and fragments of ivory in virtually every level. K2 was a very large village site, with huge middens,[42] and clearly had a substantial population. Evidence for emerging stratification comes in the early twelfth century, when the adjacent Mapungubwe Hill was occupied.[43] It is likely that this was taken over as an area of royal residence, with richly furnished burials. These include the use of gold wire and golden objects made of foil, including the famous rhinoceros. Indigenous cloth production (possibly using cotton) and the making of ivory bracelets[44] are evident.

Farther inland, in the river catchment areas of the Limpopo adjacent to the eastern edge of the Kalahari, a similar sequence is known as part of the Toutswe tradition. These date from around 700 onwards and have a distinct settlement hierarchy, dominated by three very large hilltop sites, Bosutswe, Shoshong and Toutswemogala.[45] These sites are dominated by evidence for cattle-keeping, with much rarer evidence for trade or ivory working, and the social complexity may have developed through the accumulation of surplus through cattle rather than trade. It is significant that both the Toutswe sites and Mapungubwe decline at the same time, both ending around 1300, suggesting an economic interconnection, and one could postulate a complex network of exotic items, cattle and the hunting of elephants on the Kalahari margin by specialist hunter-gatherers. It is now widely accepted that the Indian Ocean trade, operated by the Swahili towns, was one significant factor in the development of stratified societies in the Limpopo valley between 800 and 1300.

The organization of the exchange between the coast and the developing states of the interior is not known but it was likely to have involved specialist groups, who may have enjoyed special protection.[46] It is very likely that trade was closely linked with the establishment of trust between the parties, as the early eleventh-century writer al-Biruni makes clear:

For instance it is the custom of seagoing merchants in their dealings with the Zabaj and the Zanj that they do not trust them in their contracts, so their chiefs and elders come and give themselves as hostages so that they are even held by fetters. Then the goods which their people desire are handed over to them for them to take to their land and there divided among them. After that they go out to the deserts to seek the price and each one of them finds in those mountains only as much gold as is proportionate to the goods which have fallen to his share . . . they bring it to their ships and deliver it to their ships and their hostages so as to pay for it. They remove the fetters from them and let them go with honours and gifts. The merchants wash this gold or heat it in the fire as a precaution, for they relate of one of them that he put a piece of this gold into his mouth and died on the spot.[47]

The archaeological evidence suggests that long-distance trade was substantial between the Swahili and the southern African Iron Age communities, and it must be assumed that the emerging states on the Limpopo controlled the route to the sea. Ivory must have been the foremost commodity, and its availability in this region (as well as hunter-gatherers to collect it) may have led to the early developments of trade routes and states, but in time, gold became as important. The sources of this gold lie to the north in the basement complex of the Zimbabwe plateau, and it is here that the next stage in state-formation and Indian Ocean trade can be seen.

The rise of Great Zimbabwe mirrors the decline of Mapungubwe and Toutswe; it is possible that the emerging state moved north but more likely that Great Zimbabwe was a rival, able to develop on the eastern edge of the gold-bearing reefs found on the plateau, with a relatively convenient route to the coast along the Save river. Whilst there are early Iron Age levels, the site seems to have been reoccupied around 1100 until the late fifteenth century, with the period of greatest prosperity c.1250–1350.[48] This coincides with the importance of Kilwa, and its control of the gold trade which has led some to conclude that Kilwa and Great Zimbabwe's economic fortunes were closely linked, a conclusion supported by the discovery of the single copper Kilwan coin at Great Zimbabwe.[49] This may be overstated, as there is no direct historical evidence for this link, neither is the quantity of imported pottery or glass found at Great Zimbabwe particularly large and comes mostly from hoards, rather than occupation deposits.[50] As with the sites further south, cattle, rather than the Indian Ocean trade, may have been a causal factor behind the development of this complex society.

One 'Zimbabwe' type site is located off the plateau, on the Mozambique coastal plain, some 75 km inland of Chibuene, on a route that links to the Save river. Manyikeni might be interpreted as a trading post between the coast and interior, with frequent finds of beads and sea shells, and a single sherd of celadon pottery.[51] The site of Chibuene was also reoccupied at this date with evidence for the processing of gold. No fourteenth-century site equivalent to Manyikeni is yet known further north in the region of Sofala, where the Kilwan merchants might have more logically traded with the Great Zimbabweans.[52]

The cycle of state-formation in the region resulted in two successor states developing in the fifteenth century: Torwa, in south-west Zimbabwe[53] and Mutapa[54] on the Zambezi. Both were closely involved in long-distance trade. Torwa, with its capital at Khami (or possibly Danangombe) had buildings in the Great Zimbabwe style, and when the sites were robbed by Europeans huge quantities of gold were found and melted down. Less is known about the imports, although beads and pottery (especially celadon and blue-on-white porcelains) have been found. Torwa continued into the seventeenth century but is missed by the Portuguese sources, and may well have continued to trade with the Swahili beyond the Portuguese blockade of coastal trade. Mutapa is better known through historical sources than archaeology, as the early Portuguese were keen to develop the gold and ivory trade on the Zambezi. One site on the Zambezi, but further inland, Ingombe Ilede,[55] contained a cemetery dating to the fifteenth century with glass beads and possibly Indian textiles included in the graves, as well as copper ingots, bangles and trade wire. This shows that international trade goods were reaching at least 850 km inland by the fifteenth century.

The pattern of trade between the coast and the southern interior between 700 and 1600 is contrary to what might be expected. Rather than trade routes moving further down the coast, it appears that the earliest ones are the most southerly, based on the Limpopo, and that successor states developed routes based on the Save and Zambezi rivers. Internal dynamics linked to cattle may have been more important in developing social stratification than international trade. A consequence of these emerging states was a demand for higher status objects that could be obtained from the Indian Ocean, thus establishing the trading networks which supplied the Swahili with their vital commodities on which their own prosperity depended.

The trading relationship between the coast and the interior has always been asymmetrical – one of exploitation of Africa by the outside world. Typically, the interior has exchanged its natural and raw materials for manufactured commodities, at first from Asia and later from all the world, and profit has gone to the non-African partners while the African ones have lost their natural wealth. This was the basic imperial and colonial pattern everywhere and certainly in eastern Africa.[56] The acquisition of commodities was until comparatively recently organized and controlled by Swahili patrician lineages that have acted as brokerage houses. These lineages have acted independently but in concert with the quondam rulers of the towns, with other houses of the same town, with those of their own sub-clans elsewhere along the coast; and they have worked together with non-Swahili traders and partners behind the Swahili towns both in the coastal hinterland and in the more distant interior.

This system was severely weakened and in many ways brought to an end from the sixteenth century onwards, when the Swahili merchants had their earlier control taken from them first by the Portuguese, then by the colonial Arab state of Zanzibar with its Omani and Hadrami colonists, and finally by European companies and settlers and emerging nation-states. Yet they still consider themselves to be the rightful and most skilled entrepreneurs involved over the centuries, and only they possess the quality of *uungwana*, of rightfully belonging to the patriciate and of possessing its commercial skills and observing its moral tenets that validate those skills as being approved by God.

Interior Trade during the Nineteenth Century

In the late eighteenth century, the more informal trading patterns with the interior had been transformed into a caravan trade, although the reasons behind this transformation remain unclear. Most Swahili towns which arranged the caravan trades are on islands just off the coast. The commodities brought down to the coast by inland caravans ended at places such as Pangani, Bagamoyo and Changamwe, and were then shipped across to the towns which organized the onward shipment across the Indian Ocean. Imports from Asia followed the same routes in reverse. In some areas, such as the mainland opposite Pate and Lamu islands, the final caravan stations were controlled directly by partician lineages from the island towns themselves, with their representatives living on or near the large grain plantations that they owned on the mainland.

There were five main regions from which commodities came and to which others were sent. These were, from north to south, Ethiopia; the eastern African highlands and the northern Lakes of Victoria and Baringo; the region of Lakes Nyasa, Tanganyika, and Mweru; Maniema and the Upper Congo; and the region of Zambezia, Mozambique, Zimbabwe and the Transvaal. As might be expected, these large areas merged into one another, but in general there was a congruence between north and south on the coast and north and south among the five regions, in the sense that each region was linked by trade to a particular part of the coast. The guiding factors included the distribution of resources and of routes, and that ocean shipping was easier, quicker and safer from the more northerly ports, the areas of the south being dependent upon coastal trans-shipment to the north.

The locations and the 'ownership' of the early main areas producing iron, salt, copper and cloth were widely known, and the owners themselves in most cases assumed monopolies of supply to other groups, often from great distances.[57] These monopolies seem often to have been accompanied by the development of politically centralized groups. The most important politically and commercially were the several Lacustrine kingdoms to the north and west of Lake Victoria, the most important being Buganda.[58]

These polities existed before the trade but developed as a direct consequence of it. Their rulers and attendant bureaucracies needed constant supplies of cattle, women and often servile labour; from the nineteenth century, arms and ammunition were also in increasing demand. Trade goods were taken from politically uncentralized peoples on the fringes of the states with certain valuable resources, especially human beings and ivory. The most widespread pattern of exchange within the state was of political tribute from subjects to their rulers and the expected return of protection from rulers to subjects, the whole being part of political relationships and measured in those terms. Exchanges were of goods required by rulers for defence, for example iron, copper or hides for shields, in return for immaterial things such as military or ritual protection. Goods given as tribute included enclaved items of symbolic power such as lion skins, feathers of predatory birds, and legs or horns of powerful animals. Tribute of this kind was of ritual and political rather than economic value.

These kingdoms shared common structural problems, in particular that of reliable supply of tribute and labour to enable the central administrations to function peacefully, and that of the orderly succession to kingly office. The latter typically involved a fraternal struggle for the office, in which brothers were killed, sent into exile, or delegated to remote and junior posts. Royal internecine struggles meant that when guns, ammunition and gunpowder became available from the eighteenth century they were eagerly seized upon as not only desirable but also politically essential commodities. The main exception was Buganda where fraternal struggles were avoided because there was no royal patrilineal clan (kings belonged to their clans and were selected without infighting). Buganda also had a prolific and reliable food supply with the plantain as the staple and so could devote most of its resources into the conquest of neighbouring groups and their incorporation into the Buganda state. It therefore needed even more guns than the other Lacustrine kingdoms. By the latter part of the nineteenth century, the sources of guns were Zanzibar, Egypt and the Congo Free State; each area competed to send their traders to the Lacustrine region, and to obtain the valuable supplies that were available there.

The general impact of the Swahili commerce inland was largely to change forms of tribute given to chiefs by subjects from objects of largely political and ritual value to those of mainly economic value. The most widespread of these over the interior as a whole were ivory and slaves. The collection of these commodities was not made by individual hunters or small groups of kin, but required large-scale organization not only for collection but for storage and later carriage to the coast. In return the rulers distributed trade goods received from the coast such as cloth, beads and wire. The process often required the near-abandonment of small-scale production of foodcrops, hunting and fishing, and the substitution of large-scale collection of ivory, involving the slaughter of elephants, hippopotamus and rhinoceros, non-productive activities in any direct sense although there was some game meat as a by-product. The collection of human beings demanded the division of local populations into the collectors and the collected and the depopulation of human beings over large areas. All this required forms of commercial and political authority in order to organize and control the collection, storage, packaging, carrying and later redistribution of commodities received in exchange from the coast.

Another factor was that of porterage. Good roads and railways did not exist until the beginning of the twentieth century, and the prevalence of tsetse fly ruled out the use of draught animals.[59] Human porters provided the only means of carriage, but although adequate for local purposes its use

Plate 5.1   *An ivory caravan approaches Morogoro around 1885 (Rhodes House Library, University of Oxford). A. Leroy and Bauer, A Travers le Zanguebar: Voyage dans l'Oudoe, l'Ouzigoua, l'Oukwere, l'Oukami et l'Ousagara (Lyon 1884, facing p. 83). This caravan station lay 100 miles inland from the coast and the terminus at Bagamoyo, and comprised a defended settlement with mostly timber huts, but also at least one rectangular 'Swahili' type house, visible at one end of the settlement.*

in long-distance commerce was slow, expensive, dependent on lack of heavy rain or drought, and made difficult by the virtual monopoly held by local entrepreneurs and traders from only a few agricultural groups.[60] These became the first migrant labourers in eastern and central Africa, skilled workers who also traded profitably on their own account, and were immune from enslavement. They included many who became rich and powerful, and they transported not only trade goods to and from the coast but also new ideas and moralities. It is clear that inland caravan entrepreneurs could, and often did, hold the merchants to ransom.

The entire system was one of fine balance between all the groups involved, all trying to maximize their own control, security and wealth, not powerful enough militarily nor in control of a total economic monopoly in any place except the more powerful Swahili coastal towns. *Biashara ni vita*, 'Trade is war', a war that had to be waged delicately and diplomatically by careful, judicious, and at least seemingly honest dealing and exchange.

Until the late nineteenth century exchanges with partners in the interior were by patronage and clientship, joking relationships, blood brotherhood, and concubinage or marriage between representative members of coastal merchant lineages and the daughters of their trading partners.[61] Children of concubines were legitimate and took the subclan membership of their fathers. This concubinage and marriage produced large numbers of 'Swahili' living in the interior who acted as agents and caravan organizers for the coastal merchants and who thereby organized much of the system of commerce. Most interior rulers and mercantile satraps kept such people as their own agents who besides the essential kinship ties with the coast had knowledge of events and useful persons in the towns.[62] These intermediaries were valuable in passing information to the coastal merchants, their kin, of the demands of interior groups as to kinds and colours of cloth, wire and other goods, so that the merchants could pass them on to their Asian partners who could order them for export to Africa. They were renowned for their mastery of both Islamic magic (they were Muslims) as well as 'African' magic from their local mothers. They also often acted as organizers and leaders of caravans, a highly responsible, dangerous, and respected occupation.

Behind the immediate system of carriage and exchange of goods has been that of patronage and clientship, the patrons being the Swahili coastal merchants and the latter those working for them in the towns, the hinterland and the interior. The usual Swahili word for 'patron' is *mtajiri*, pl. *watajiri* (lit. 'a wealthy person') can also be used for a successful merchant and professional entrepreneur. *Mtajiri* is a man – it can be used of a woman but merchants have typically been men – who has used his own personal ability to become a recognized patron; and he can lose the status, whereas he cannot lose that of being a patrician.

Rights in the labour and support of other persons are seen as forms of mercantile wealth, to be used, exchanged and transformed; they are not bought, sold or bartered commercially as their clients would thereby be defined as slaves. A patron acquires certain rights in the support or labour of clients in return for forms of protection, aid in finding employment or in selling crops the client has grown. The patron is a member of higher and wider networks than is a client, whose social world is smaller and depends upon a patron to enter, under conditions of the patron's control, the latter's wider social world.

Patrons wish to become *watajiri* in order both to have wealth and power and also to possess the reputation of successful *wangwana* of high degree. It is largely in this situation that we may talk of the permeability of Swahili identity. In brief, patrons already possess it or can acquire it by becoming *watajiri*; clients hope both to acquire wealth by becoming members of new and wider networks by a 'trickle-down' process, and if successful can move to the boundaries of Swahili identity and perhaps even cross them.[63]

Many early accounts by European travellers into the interior mention both 'Arabs' and 'Swahili' traders in the interior acting as agents for coastal merchants and especially for Zanzibari trading houses. The 'Arabs' were certainly Omani from Zanzibar, often representatives of the sultans; the 'Swahili' may well have been those we have just mentioned. Swahili patrician merchants rarely if ever went inland very far but sent agents, some Swahili (including trusted slaves) and others not. Their own children would presumably have been considered more reliable than others.[64]

Links with Arab trading partners in Asia were typically, or at least very often, by marriage between a visiting trader and a younger daughter of the particular patrician with whom he traded regularly and in whose house he stayed as a son-in-law when in Africa.[65] Marriages with Indian partners were rare, as Muslim and non-Muslim Indian firms used Arabs as their representatives, most of whom were Omani from Zanzibar. This pattern of mercantile kinship is still used today in traffic between the coast and the Gulf States.

At the end of the nineteenth century most of the former kinship links we have described were abandoned in favour of guns, which the Omani held to be more effective as they took over virtually the entire interior commerce. Also kinship became increasingly unimportant with the growing presence of Indian representatives of both the Zanzibar and Bombay Indian finance houses, which by then controlled most of the Zanzibar and Mombasa commerce and economy.

The Omani merchants from Zanzibar gradually took over most of the interior trade from Swahili patricians. They added greatly to the number of Arabs in the interior, who were related by descent to Omani lineages in Zanzibar, and also married or took as concubines daughters of local African rulers. Their children were therefore Omani Arabs and their local brothers-in-law more easily able to acquire coastal commodities, especially guns and ammunition from their Zanzibari affines. Some of these Omani and some local African chiefs became economically and politically powerful rulers in the interior: men like Mirambo, Kazembe, Tippu Tip, Mumia and many others were linked to Zanzibar in these ways. The Swahili proper found themselves left in the cold as of little importance as they lacked Omani wealth and ability to provide weapons. Many new trading towns were founded or became more important by the later part of the nineteenth century, such as Ujiji and Tabora, with permanent Omani residents.[66]

A peripheral subsystem of exchange was that of commodities acquired from individual sailors who were allowed to carry small amounts of goods for their own personal trading. In return the sailors acquired commodities on which they could make profit on their return to Asia. The point here is that the close interpersonal ties of commercial partners were linked to the trust between kin and affines, however distant or fictive, who were considered equal in rank. This meant that sailors on dhows exchanged their goods with those of equal rank on the coast, and patricians would have been unlikely to have been involved unless the sailors were linked with them as personal dependents.

Indian traders also moved inland, especially after the establishment of British and German rule and after the building of the Uganda Railway. The large and wealthy Indian financial houses were also family companies. They sent younger members inland, each main religious group – Bohora, Khuja and others – maintaining its own network of small stores engaged in collecting ivory in return for cloth, beads and petty consumer goods that were in increasing demand everywhere. Trade routes were necessarily based on earlier caravan routes and on the early colonial administrative posts.[67]

After the transfer of the sultans' forts along the coast to the British the situation with regard to the ivory trade changed somewhat. The forts and other military posts had been manned largely by Baluchi and other mercenaries, each post commanded by a *jemadar*. After the transfer many Baluchi soldiers turned to elephant hunting on their own, and were soon scattered throughout the interior.[68] Hunting, travelling, and selling and buying of ivory were controlled by the British 'collectors' at administrative posts who issued passes and receipts for the various fees demanded. Ivory brought into the Indian outposts by Baluchi (and many European) hunters, with locally recruited bodies of aides and porters, was transported by train to Mombasa.

Until the mid-nineteenth century money was not used for the exchange controlled by the Swahili merchants on the African side of the commerce. There coastal coinage was useless until the late nineteenth century, and exchange was by barter and gift exchange between quasi-kin, patrons and clients. This was an important distinction between the western and eastern sides of the mercantile system, in which notions of profit, interest, and of the trader himself, were very different.

From around 1850 the use of coinage became at first occasionally useful and then essential for exchanges of goods at the intercontinental level. With it were introduced a certain type of market, that in which prices were determined on grounds of an impartial cost and value rather than on those of kinship and similar interpersonal relationships. Coinage and the new impersonal markets were intimately related, based on a process of the impersonalization of exchange, the breakdown by the colonial powers of traditional forms of tribute and redistribution by local rulers, changes in means of transportation from human caravans to steam trains, automobiles and steamships, and changes in the relationships between time and profit brought about by the last two of these factors.[69] The introduction of Indian metal coinage to Zanzibar at mid-century by necessity brought local forms of exchange into line with wider colonial systems, with concomitant changes in the personal quality of market dealings. The Zanzibar slave market was built by mid-century, at which slaves were sold to the highest bidders. Sellers and buyers in that market and between buyers and original producers and ultimate buyers overseas were not always linked.[70] The Zanzibar slave market seems to have been the first impersonal market in coastal history, although we do not know to what extent the earlier Portuguese took on roles of both seller and buyer.[71]

There are a few references in Swahili material that might refer to markets and that have been accepted as being markets for the exchange of intercontinental commodities. The best known of these is that made by el-Zein who stated that the ward in Lamu known as Otukuni, 'at the market place', refers to the former existence of a large market on the Zanzibari model.[72] He was mistaken: it was the place for the exchange of petty local produce, mainly food and local handicrafts. The more important long-distance commodities were not exchanged there but within the safe walls of the patrician merchants' houses.[73] Local exchanges of this kind have been universal throughout Africa, have rarely been based on money except in recent years, have often been seasonal, and degrees of kinship and friendship between sellers and buyers have always been relevant.[74]

The Twentieth Century

With the abolition of slavery and the construction first of railways and then of roads into the interior, the nature of the relationship between the coast and the interior changed, but did not disappear. There have always been problems about the production, carriage and exchange of foodstuffs and the availability of seasonal labour. These difficulties increased markedly after the abolition of slavery, and the use of squatters on plantations in place of slaves never resolved them. A man who could acquire a network of food producers and labourers was economically and socially at an advantage, especially in the new and growing places such as Mombasa. Whereas in the smaller and more traditional settlements the changes after the abolition of slavery may not have been as onerous for the bigger merchants and entre- preneurs, they were certainly so among lesser people in the larger centres. Here the impact of imperialist capitalism was the most marked, with steady increase in needs for foodstuffs for both local subsistence and export and for unskilled labourers as in the docks and streets of Mombasa, Dar es Salaam and Tanga.

Mombasa is the largest and most mixed of all Swahili towns, and has been an important port for many centuries. Mombasa harbour was at Old Town, but since the First World War its steamship harbour has been at the opposite side of the island, at Kilindini and linked to the railway system. Most of its population is and has been for a century non-Swahili, and it contains a greater proportion of Arabs, Indians and others to the Swahili patriciate than any other coastal town. Mombasa was the place most affected by the post-slavery changes and difficulties, perhaps made more difficult of solution by the diminution of the Swahili population relative to the growth of dense populations both within and around the city. A patron, or a man wishing to make rapid name and fortune, had to make bonds of clientship with many non-Swahili. The Swahili or other patrons attracted food-growers, coconut-tappers, fishermen and other clients for Mombasa markets, which the patrons usually controlled, as well as labourers for the Kilindini harbour and railways. The clients were only rarely other Swahili, nor were they upcountry immigrants (Luo and Gikuyu), but were rather from the neighbouring Mijikenda groups whose own elders could become subordinate patrons working with the bigger *watajiri*. These sub-patrons had as an immediate aim to become accepted as Swahili (often by becoming Muslims) and as a longer-term one to build status in their home groups for their old age.[75]

Commodities and their Meanings

The changes from what may be called personal to impersonal exchange and from barter and gift exchange to that made by money contain another dimension, that of the social and cultural meanings of the commodities exchanged by the Swahili acting on behalf of their African and Asian partners but also very much to their own advantage.

The many goods exchanged have never been mere objects in a purely economic sense, if there should ever be such a thing. The trade goods imported and exported through the Swahili ports-of-trade, and in time exchanged in both the interiors of Africa and Asia, were of several kinds irrespective of their utilitarian or innate qualities. Some were natural and unprocessed; others were commodities deliberately intended for exchange by barter, gift or money, depending on many factors; others were non-commodities and yet others were immaterial. These various qualities were usually not those innate to the objects themselves but were given to them by their producers and consumers, and in particular by the Swahili brokers, one of whose functions was to turn them into various kinds of commodities and often to change them from one kind to another. All the these objects were given 'life-histories' or 'biographies'[76] mainly by the Swahili merchants, and placed into certain relationships with the merchants and those who received the objects from them. The qualities and relationships could be changed at different times in the objects' histories. In them were embodied and symbolized the ambitions and social positions of those who handled and possessed them.[77]

The main exports from Africa over many centuries were originally natural objects, lacking any other than innate qualities and to which no others had yet been given,[78] except that they were obtained knowing they would be exported. They had value only in terms of what would, immediately or later, be gained by the return of other objects from the Swahili coast, trade commodities that would be given a higher value on account of their later decommoditization by the rulers who would receive them. The same process took place on the other side of the Indian Ocean. In the centre were the Swahili brokers whose roles were both to make possible changes in the moral qualities of commodities as they passed through their hands by determining the particular modes of exchange, and also to detain and decommoditize them as 'enclaved' for their own use in order to sustain and symbolize their own places with their own society.

The most important objects in this regard included textiles, slaves and porcelain. Cloth was an ambiguous substance once woven and its innate qualities removed. It was used as a medium of barter, as a means of bestowing moral and social qualities, of marking both high and low status. It was not merely body covering but an object to which were attached social and cultural significances. As we have already seen, the Swahili *History of Kilwa* provides an example. By acquiring imported cloth the indigenous and 'barbaric' king became 'civilized' and so equal in rank to the immigrant Swahili merchant who may then 'correctly' marry his daughter (Swahili marriages must be between equals). The covering of the peninsula of Kilwa with cloth by the merchant made the area of land 'urban' and it could then safely be transformed into an island and into a Swahili Muslim town. Different coloured cloths were worn by persons of different rank, from the scarlet of kings to the black of slave women. Cloth was no longer a mere commodity but was given social and political significance.[79]

Slaves were objects captured in the interior by both participants in warfare and specialist hunters who found that their rulers and coastal traders would buy them. They became commodities once taken to the coast by caravans and paid for by Swahili and Arab traders: until the Zanzibar slave market was established, payment was by barter between kin and quasi-kin, with the new market cash was used by Arab traders who shipped the slaves onward to Arabia and elsewhere in Asia.[80] Those shipped remained commodities, to be treated as things or at best animals. Others remained on the coast as plantation field slaves, and some as domestic slaves. The former became redefined as responsible human beings in that they could be punished for failure to work, the latter became decommoditized in that they were given Muslim names, if male were circumcised so as not to pollute the houses in which they worked, could become trusted humans, given responsibilities as though family members, might take on 'outside' work as semi-independent entrepreneurs, could become mothers of lineage members, could become poets and Muslim scholars and so quasi-patricians. It was then difficult if not impossible to re-commoditize them: they could not easily be resold, physically punished or mistreated, and if they were their owners were considered guilty and could themselves be punished either by public opinion or by the sultans. Slaves could be freed by their owners, a voluntary act that gave the manumitter social and religious credit and removed all quality of commodity from the manumitted other than the faint one of tainted ancestry.[81]

Porcelain was owned in eastern Africa almost entirely by Swahili patricians and became an important symbol of status. Its use goes back to the imported Chinese and Islamic ceramics of the ninth century which were clearly intended for display, and from the thirteenth century onwards it was used to decorate the tombs of patricians. In the eighteenth century imported porcelain, generally Chinese blue-and-white wares, obtained through Dutch VOC trade, and later Japanese and then mass produced shallow bowls from Maastrict (the Netherlands) which were decorated in gilt and red. It is uncertain how the patrician merchants obtained them – by barter or by gift, probably the former – but they decommoditized them and removed them from further trading. The plates (the great majority of these items) were either given as gifts to their own sub-clan fellow-merchants, to other people with whom they wanted a better personal relationship, occasionally to partners in the interior, or kept for their own uses. They were displayed in the *zidaka* niches in the walls of patrician houses, or mortared onto the outside of their tombs. In either case they lost any commercial value but became representations of *uungwana* status and civilization.

Plate 5.2 *Tombs at Siyu (Pate Island), one with a date of AH 1270 (1853–4), which illustrate the split identity of nineteenth-century Swahili patricians, and copy an African vernacular architecture, but were also covered with hundreds of inset Chinese porcelain plates. Unfortunately most of these have now been robbed and only tiny pieces are left behind (photo Mark Horton).*

Another important class of display objects for which we have only archaeological evidence is textiles and tapestries. In ruined houses the front rooms often have regularly spaced dowel holes from which to suspend cloths, which must have been highly ornate and decorated. The elaborate *zidaka* niches of eighteenth-century houses are developments of this earlier scheme of expressive decoration.

Other objects as well were treated as treasures that would in time become heirlooms and placed in the wall niches. They included manuscripts and copies of Islamic sacred books, rare silks, jewels, personal arms such as ornamented daggers, and accoutrements of gold and silver such as containers and silver used for sandals and bed-ladders. These were typically objects of geographically remote provenance and denied use by non-patricians. They were used to bestow high personal social and moral status and were associated with Islam. An important decommoditized gift between patricians was that of trained slaves from the giver's domestic servants: males would be given who could look and dress well as personal retainers, and women might include trusted nursemaids and concubines. The exception were gifts given to inland trading partners, not objects of Islamic significance but usually clothing, arms and objects of magical significance that could protect caravan leaders from the mystical and physical dangers of the interior. Gifts given to *watani* and blood brothers were of the same kind, although we have been told by the elders of Lamu that gifts of Muslim value would be used at times to cement these shaky bonds.

6

The Urban Landscape

The Swahili have their own concept of urbanism, which bears little resemblance to universal definitions.[1] They refer to *utamaduni* as the characteristic of those living in towns; it has been literally translated as urbanity and refinement, but implies those who share a common view of the essential qualities of civilization in contrast to outsiders, or *washenzi* (lit. barbarians).[2] The qualities are Islamic (but not exclusively so, as Muslim outsiders from overseas or from converted areas of the coastland cannot possess them), but also linked to concepts of purity, behaviour and ultimately to the possession of a reputable ancestry.

Swahili towns are known by their inhabitants as *miji* (sing. *mji* or *mui*). The sites are often very long lasting, with deep archaeological stratigraphy and often tombs and ruins from several periods. Even those now completely abandoned sites, when investigated in detail, can be shown to have an extremely long and detailed history. We can observe towns nowadays and obtain an idealized view of how they should work or of how they may have worked in the past. This oral information is probably directly relevant to as far back as the eighteenth century; beyond there is only archaeological and fragmentary historical evidence, but which, given the evident continuities in coastal societies, can be more readily understood within the ethnohistorical context.

Swahili society has certain interlinked principles of organization. These include spatial organization of towns and clusters of towns and settlements; a system of descent and kinship; a structure of social ranks; forms of both religious and non-religious associations; and forms of kingship and political authority. Whatever the reliability of present-day knowledge of the Swahili past, it is clear that urbanism was always an important feature, with certain characteristics also found in many other mercantile societies. They include a large service economy, a politically and militarily weak government, a complex system of social stratification, and elaborate notions of purity and pollution with rituals to order and control them.

The Process of Urbanization

In chapter 2 we identified a pattern of small coastal settlements, with a mixed farming economy including fishing, hunting and gathering, which were also able to exploit their position as intermediaries in the Indian Ocean trade. By the mid-eighth century, these communities included Muslims, almost certainly local converts. How, when and why were these humble villages transformed into the urban centres of the Swahili coast, with its developed mercantile culture? In many ways this transformation represents the defining point at which the Swahili communities became distinctive from the farming villages of the hinterland.

Surprisingly little attention has been given to this key question by arch-aeologists and historians, who have concentrated upon the search for the 'origins' of the Swahili. To the older generation, this was a non-question, as quite simply, the Arab and Persian merchants brought Islamic urban culture with them from the Middle East, and any indigenous culture was merely swamped by this more advanced civilization. However the archaeological evidence shows no discontinuity but rather a steady development over time. Sensitive indicators such as local pottery styles continue to develop and change but in a continuous fashion, while the proportion of imported to local pottery stays static at around 5 per cent over the many centuries: large numbers of Muslim colonists would not have been satisfied with crude earthenware vessels for cooking and eating. Another measure is diet, which does change over time, but again in an even manner, without serious dislocation.

Along the East African coast it can be estimated that there are around 500 known sites which contain evidence for habitation prior to the nineteenth century; further survey will uncover more. Many of these sites are little more than scatters of pottery indicating occupation, but surviving stone architecture is also a common feature. Recognition is often much easier where there are ruins, and for this reason the present knowledge of site distribution is skewed towards sites with architecture. Where survey is undertaken on a systematic basis, non-architectural sites of different periods are discovered, changing our perception of Swahili culture as not confined to stone houses and large urban complexes but also including rural settlements.

The construction of 'stone houses' – an essential feature of patrician identity – dates from around 1320–50. This is when walls are first made of coral rag bonded with lime mortar and has been found wherever sites have been excavated in detail, such as Shanga, Manda, Kilwa or Gedi. Ibn Battuta's observation that both Kilwa and Mombasa were built of wood at the time of his visit in 1331 may not be entirely inaccurate. The rapid

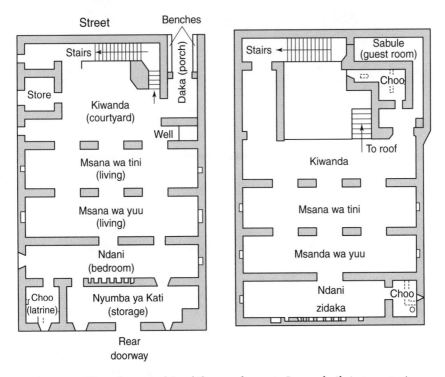

Ground floor

First floor

Plan 6.1 *Plan of a typical Swahili stone house in Lamu, built in two stories, the earliest part being the ground floor, dating to the eighteenth century, the second storey being nineteenth century.*

change in building technique during the first half of the fourteenth century is surprising as both coral rag and lime had been already in use for tomb and mosque construction for at least 200 years, but the essential new element was the use of lime as a mortar to bond the stones for these houses. The result was robust walls that survive to this day, unless they have been destroyed or robbed for their building materials for later buildings.[3]

It is possible to trace in some detail the development of the stone house from *c.*1320 until the present day. When they first appear in stone, these houses already contained many of the elements found in later houses. They were entered through a courtyard, with rooms set back in rows. Unlike later Swahili houses, sometimes the outer rooms were divided; store rooms were frequently found in the centre of the houses, strongly indicating their mercantile function. The houses had porches with benches, entering onto the street, and often guest rooms within the courtyard for visiting merchants.

Plate 6.1   Zidaka *niches in a partly restored Lamu stone house which date to the nineteenth century and are made from stucco. They would have been used for the display of luxury items acquired through foreign trade (such as porcelains, glass, and perfumes) and formed an important part of the decoration of the patrician house during wedding ceremonies (photo Mark Horton).*

Excavations in the courtyards suggest multiple functions, especially cooking and food preparation. There were pit latrines and washing areas, as are found in later houses, as well as niches set in the walls. Decorated niches, clearly related to the later *zidaka* found in Lamu and Pate houses, date to *c.*1350 at Shanga and *c.*1500 on the mainland sites of Ungwana and

Mwana Mchama, although they were positioned slightly differently to those found in later houses. Doorways were often with pointed arches, although flat topped openings were also normal. No early doors have survived, but they were unlikely to have been the heavily carved doors of Lamu, Mombasa and Zanzibar which date to the nineteenth century, and more like the delicately carved and painted doors that survived until recently in Siyu.[4]

The houses ranged in size from a courtyard and two to six rows, and as far as we can tell were only of a single storey, although the Portuguese described two storied houses in Kilwa and Mombasa. The distribution of these early Swahili houses ranges from the northern Kenyan coast and the Lamu archipelago to Gedi, Jumba la Mtwana and Mtwapa, Pemba and Tumbatu islands, Kilwa and Songo Mnara and the Kerimba islands – effectively covering the entire coast.[5] There were some small variations until the eighteenth century, when the well-known and very formalized patrician house plan fully emerged on the northern Kenyan coast.

Only at Shanga has it so far been possible to trace the origins of this architecture. It is based on an earlier but very similar house plan, first in timber (from *c*.1050) and later in mud and coral walls (from *c*.1150). The archaeological sequence shows that these houses were rebuilt with the same plan, one over another, but using more permanent wall materials. By *c*.1200, the houses were built of stone, bonded with mud rather than lime, and then given a plaster face to preserve the wall fabric. When most of the houses at Shanga were rebuilt using lime around 1325, some remained in the more old fashioned mode, and it is possible that this reflected patrician/ non-patrician status, although to the casual onlooker there would have been little difference in the external appearance of the houses, except perhaps in the flat roof, that could now be supported on the more solid stone walls; the mud and coral walls would only have carried thatch.[6] There is nothing particularly Arab or oriental in the plan or form of these stone houses and they can be explained entirely as an indigenous development of a local vernacular architecture.[7]

The houses are found either individually or in groups. Normally they were attached, forming either terraces or complexes enclosed within a compound wall; up to five houses could be linked in this way as a block or ward. When these complexes of houses have been excavated in detail, as at Gedi, Songo Mnara, Mtwapa, Takwa and Shanga, they have been shown to have had several phases, presumably representing the fission and fusion of family groups over time. The houses may originally have been standing in open spaces, but over time these were filled up with additions, leaving narrow streets with frequent dog-legs between the blocks. The houses generally followed a common alignment, which may reflect that of the mosque, the shoreline or some other feature. Courtyards were generally

Plate 6.2   *A typical late eighteenth- or early nineteenth-century stone house in Lamu, built on two stories, showing the internal courtyard and rooms. This house is 'unrestored', and gives a good impression of how patricians' houses must have looked in reality (photo Mark Horton).*

located (as they were in later houses) on the north side, followed by westerly courtyards, apparently providing protection for the living rooms from the monsoon winds and rain as well as facing towards Mecca.[8]

Many of the towns which have been studied have several surviving mosques, in addition to the actual Friday mosque. The latter can sometimes be identified for certain by the stone pulpit from which the Friday sermon was delivered. Broadly this mosque tends to be the oldest, but from the fourteenth century onwards the towns acquired additional mosques – Gedi for example has at least six, which must have served as neighbourhood mosques as they did in later towns. The Friday mosque tended to be in the middle of the town, and often had open space (and burials) around it. When the town plan is well preserved, it is sometimes possible to suggest a moiety division represented by an axial street, as is the case in later towns such as Siyu. From the sixteenth century onwards some towns, especially on the mainland, were given perimeter walls with gateways. These were never particularly elaborate, and often follow an ill-defined course, as if avoiding or incorporating buildings which are no longer visible. These ruined stone towns may incorporate considerable areas of mud and thatch houses around the periphery, but so far this has only been demonstrated for Shanga.

Planned Urban Landscapes

Certain Swahili clan groups express their social relationships in spatial terms. The expression *mlango moja* (lit. of the same gate) has a wider meaning as belonging to the same descent groups,[9] suggesting a common ownership of a physical gateway. This meaning can be understood in the Comores, where the village communities have an enclosure in their centre termed a *fumboni*. Here communal activities take place, including marriage, rituals, funerals, dancing, poetry competitions and the meetings of elders; there is often also a well, mosque and tombs. Entry to the *fumboni* is through a number of gates, each of which is the property of a single descent group. In Comoran society, *mlango moja* is an expression implying that a particular group shares an entry into the communal *fumboni* and thus by implication, belongs to the same clan.

These enclosures are more difficult to find on the northern Swahili coast. An enclosure with its gates is clearly seen in a nineteenth-century illustration of Mogadishu, and one of the names of the moieties is Hamarweyn, mean-

Plate 6.3   *Mogadishu in 1882–3, from C. Révoil,* Voyages chez les Benadirs *(1885). This view is typical of many towns on the coast, with a large open area reserved for communal activities and trading (note for example the kiosks). There is also a mosque (the late thirteenth-century Fakhr ad-Din mosque), a monumental gateway into the Hamarweyn moiety of the town, and the large multistoried stone houses beyond.*

ing 'stone enclosure'. At Mombasa there is also a traditional moiety name, Haram el Khedima, or ancient enclosure. The best archaeological evidence is from Takwa, a seventeenth to eighteenth century site, where there is a central walled area with north and south gateways, linking to a north–south axial street.[10] It contains the mosque but also enough space for other activities. There may have been enclosures on other sites, but these have been destroyed. There are possible examples at Pate, Siyu and Matandoni, where the Friday mosques are placed in the centre of open spaces dividing the two moieties of the town.

The earliest evidence for deliberate spatial planning of settlements comes from Shanga, where a sufficiently large area of early deposits has been uncovered, to recover two boundary lines, marked initially by a row of posts, and later by walls, on either side, east and west, of the main well of the settlement, about 73m apart. Two gateways were excavated which cut through the boundaries, and in one case, had an elaborate arrangement of posts. In the zone between the boundaries there was little evidence of settlement, but instead of ceremonial buildings, a timber mosque, burials and temporary kiosk-like structures. This arrangement dated to around 750–800, but continued to be respected through the life of the settlement, so that the gates and paths became streets, the ceremonial buildings and mosque were replaced in stone around 920, and the whole area was kept clean by spreading a special kind of shelly beach sand. Outside the boundary were located the houses. Overall, the original plan included a rectangular enclosure, with seven gateways, centred on the well, and an outer square enclosure with four gateways. Settlement was found between these two enclosures, and could be divided into seven areas around each gateway. There may have been seven clans which founded Shanga. It is impossible to know the names of these clans, but the evidence suggests that there was variation across the site to suggest patterns in diet, craft activity and trade to indicate that the clans may have been occupational.

This model does enable us to make some sense of otherwise perplexing town plans. At Gedi, there is an inner and outer wall, which reflects the early plan of Shanga, but this may be a considerable modification of an earlier double enclosure, with the original central enclosure with its large (newly-discovered) ruined mosque, tombs and wells. The so-called inner walled city was originally a quarter of a much larger settlement. When the town walls came to be built, only the most important part – that probably inhabited by the patricians – was enclosed. At Ungwana, the Friday mosque is located against the town wall, suggesting that here too only half the settlement was enclosed, with an open central enclosure containing only tombs. The Friday mosque is an unusual double structure, possibly reflecting two moieties. At Mtambwe Mkuu, the entire island is used for the settlement; a roughly rectangular plateau has walls defining its perimeter and the interior comprises a mosque, tombs and a possible ceremonial building. The houses, mostly of timber, are all found in the lowlying areas, below the plateau, adjacent to the beach.

When Swahili towns were provided with town walls from the sixteenth century, the idea of gateways into the central enclosure moved to the outer perimeter. Thus for example, Pate was provided with seven gates for its seven clans, while nearby Siyu was given twelve gates reflecting the twelve clans, when its town wall was built, probably in the nineteenth century.[11]

Patricians' Towns

Two types of town are recognized nowadays by the Swahili; these may be called patricians' towns and commoners' towns.[12] They should be seen as ideal types at opposite ends of a continuum rather than totally distinct types. Every town is in certain ways unique – in size, plan, ethnic and rank composition, main occupations, wealth and poverty, and so on, but all may be placed on this single continuum, which is based on internal spatial and descent patterns and on degree of involvement in the African–Asian commerce.

The patricians' towns have been gateway communities, the foci for the international commerce controlled by the patrician merchants. As entrepôts they have had many functions and have had to supply many kinds of services. They have had to deal with incoming shipping from across the Indian Ocean; they have also had to cope with trade and caravans from the interior, although where the towns were on islands the caravans did not cross onto them but stayed opposite in satellite settlements, often those of mainland groups linked symbiotically to the towns themselves on their islands. They have also been engaged in local exchanges of foodstuffs, labour and patronage. Most of their mercantile functions have fallen into desuetude, but some towns still recognize the offices connected with them even if today they have no real duties. These towns have always been the homes of the patricians, and formerly of their slaves and today the descendants of those slaves.

Patricians' towns are compact settlements of densely built-up streets and alleys. The houses (of one or two storeys) are constructed in coral rag, bonded in lime mortar (although sometimes with mud added), with mangrove poles supporting flat stone ceilings and roofs. If properly whitewashed and kept in repair (including the replacement of the ceiling beams every thirty years or so) such a house can last for many generations. There are some houses still occupied in Lamu which date to the eighteenth century. These houses are far from being mere shelters; they are symbolically complex structures, centres of urban living and moral purity set apart from the dirt and impurity of the town outside.[13]

These houses are set along narrow streets, each house sited so that its living rooms, which occupy half the internal space, face north; the other half contains the open courtyard, the whole is generally enclosed by high walls. Their internal plan is of parallel rows of rooms, up to six deep. There are no external windows other than a few small ornamented apertures. The only entrance is by a large main and usually double door set in a small entrance porch. The houses have elaborate systems of external and internal drains that take water to the street. In most towns, like Lamu, gutters run down to the sea as the rains are heavy, and adequate drainage has always been a necessary and often difficult task. Towns are typically located along the seafront, or adjacent to an estuary and streets are set back at right angles, an alignment that can cause problems with mosque orientations.

A town is the seat of an *umma*, a community of Muslim believers,[14] and as such is centred on religious buildings, the most important of which has always been the central or congregational mosque, usually referred to as the 'Friday mosque', *msikiti wa ijumaa*, attended by all males on Fridays, irrespective of rank or wealth, and properly on all five occasions of public prayer (women do not attend mosques, although may have done so in the past). The congregational mosque is a Sunni mosque (even in Zanzibar City), members of other schools of Islam having their own mosques but not in the central position. Most towns dating to after the fifteenth century have several mosques, in addition to the Friday mosque which is generally the largest, which are used for daily prayer and are often known as neighborhood mosques. In some communities there are two Friday mosques, a situation that arises through theological dispute, such as whether the sermon should be delivered in Arabic or Swahili. Membership of these factions normally reflects social ranking.

A town also has tombs of holy men of the past and typically built of stone, often with thatched roofs. Many are those of saints and former religious innovators of fame from not only the coast itself but also from Arabia and the Comoro Islands who came to settle in East Africa, and are the objects of regular pilgrimages from great distances, which demand complicated local arrangements for hospitality. There are also scattered tombs within the settlements (and normally a few around mosques); these generally have particular status as founders of mosques, holy men or past rulers, but often their identities have long been forgotten. Towns also have cemeteries, usually one at each end, outside the town proper; each is divided into areas for different ranks, ethnic groups and neighbourhoods.[15]

Waterfronts, harbours and jetties tend to be twentieth-century innovations, often undertaken under colonial direction. In Lamu, an additional fifty yards was added to the width of the frontage through reclamation, and the present main shopping street was the waterfront until the late nineteenth century. In Zanzibar city, the Fort was originally close to the waterfront, but nowadays there is a large area in front of it laid out as gardens during the colonial period. However, reclamation of the beach has been found on a number of archaeological sites, dating from the tenth century at Manda, eleventh century at Mtambwe Mkuu and fourteenth century at Shanga (and probably also at Pate), and involving the construction of stone walls and mangrove palisades, behind which rubbish was dumped. Over these new areas mosques and houses were built, and the walls may have formed a frontage to the sea and anchorage.

Within the towns there are various informal open public spaces in vacant plots for rope making, dancing and other functions, and small gardens for betel, jasmine, roses and herbs. There are also market places for the selling of foodstuffs, although most of these are probably recent innovations. Some towns have their stone defensive walls and gatehouses, or if they are ruined their lines can be pointed out. Where they have been investigated they can be shown to date to the fifteenth century or later.

Around virtually every town there are areas of mud and thatch houses, which are spatially distinct from the stone houses. In these live non-patricians, ranging from the families of ex-slaves, to high status *masharifu* of recent arrival,[16] and those who have lived in the town for a very long time but never gained patrician status. These houses tend to have a different plan to the stone houses, incorporating a central passage with rooms leading off on either side. They are often termed Bajuni or Swahili houses, and the plan may well date back to the sixteenth century.[17]

The traditional 'owners', *wenyeji*, of these towns have been patricians, and continue to be considered so today except that other categories may also live in them and the concept 'owners' has become rather more widely used. Most stone-built houses are still owned by patricians despite their impoverishment during the twentieth century. In some cases, such as in Siyu, the patricians moved out of their stone houses in the early part of the twentieth century, but left them standing as proof of their ownership and status.

Some patricians' towns do not have extensive stone architecture, yet have played similar commercial roles and present many similarities of symbolism and sense of urbanity. Examples are Bagamoyo and Pangani, formerly termini of many caravan routes into the interior, and there are others along the Mrima coast as far north as Vanga and Wasin. The Mrima towns were more deeply subjected to close Zanzibar control from the eighteenth century onwards, and much of their independent mercantile role was taken from them: these processes may well account for their singularities.[18] In those patricians' towns that lack stone-built houses, their house and town plans remain those of stone-built towns, and retain the same significance. To build or inherit such a house is a sign of full patrician membership of the town, of creditworthiness as member of a business house that lasts for many generations, and of honour and piety. This last quality can be augmented by the building or contributing to the upkeep of a neighbourhood mosque, by Muslim learning, giving of charity and orthodox Islamic behaviour. The wealth is not often shown openly, nor should it be: it is represented by the houses themselves, by their interior displays of heirlooms and treasures, and by their purity amidst the bustle and pollution of surrounding streets.

Commoners' Towns

The commoners' towns have been, and remain, different in both their composition and roles in trade, although always reckoned as being Swahili settlements.[19] They have had neither patrician nor slave residents. Their inhabitants are mostly fishermen who also grow subsistence and market food crops for themselves and neighbouring patricians' towns. Some also are known for canoe and ship building, palm frond weaving, and other crafts, and they also supply seasonal labour. Despite their many variations, commoners' towns have long been permanent settlements each with its strong sense of local Swahili identity within the wider coastal system, and are very different from the economically and visibly often rather similar non-Swahili settlements along the coastal hinterland.

The commoners' towns, also known as *miji*, physically resemble rural villages rather than towns. Nevertheless, they are not mere clusters of houses and have a degree of spatial organization. The larger ones are typically dispersed over a wide stretch of land, and composed of several constituent units known as *kijiji* (pl. *vijiji*)), the diminutive form of *mji* and so translatable as 'village': a *kijiji* is not a truly independent settlement, merely a spatially discrete part of a town. The commoners' towns often reflect their rural location by facing the land rather than the sea. Even those which are close to the sea are often 500m or so away, with paths leading to the beach, where the fishing boats are kept, boatbuilding is undertaken, or a fish market located.[20]

The houses of commoners' towns are normally made of impermanent materials. The walls are made of mud and coral mixed together, often around a frame of mangrove poles. There are sometimes stone walls at foundation level to provide secure footings and protection from erosion. Some houses have walls of mainly palm leaf matting. The houses are single storied, thatched with a pitched roof, sometimes hipped or nowadays roofed with corrugated iron. They normally follow the 'Bajuni' plan, even on Zanzibar and Pemba, with rear courtyards for cooking and keeping animals, and a front bench or baraza, set either side of the main door.

These towns are often spread out over considerable distances; the town of Makunduchi, in south-eastern Zanzibar, is well over a mile or more in width. These towns may often have only a single mosque – the only building in stone – located close to the middle of the community. Walking around these communities, there is less of a sense of urban planning and they can seem haphazard. The spaces between the houses can be wide or narrow and cannot be described as streets, and different alignments are quite frequently employed. There are gardens occupying open spaces, and if one is a stranger it is very easy to get lost. Some towns, especially in areas where there is little wood but available stone, such as Nungwi in northern Zanzibar, or Uroa on the east coast of the island, build in stone but retain the same informality while the house plan is of the 'Bajuni' type.[21]

Settlement Patterns

The ethnohistorical distinction between patricians' and commoners' towns is less clearly drawn in the archaeological record, although there is clear evidence for ranking between settlements, and this is reflected in their architecture.[22] Certainly there are sites, especially in the Lamu archipelago, which contain many stone houses, set together within a compact street system, which possess the elements of the later patricians' towns: examples might include Shanga (fourteenth century), Manda (fifteenth century), Takwa (sixteenth century), Pate (seventeenth to eighteenth century).

Along the mainland northern Kenyan coast, opposite to the Lamu archipelago, there are sites covering large areas without domestic architecture or only occasional stone houses, but with numerous tombs and large and elaborate mosques. Examples include Ishakani, Mwana Mchama, Uchi Juu, Omwe, Dondo, and Luziwa, Ungwana, Mwana and Shaka.[23] Ornate tombs are a feature of these sites, which were occupied during the fourteenth to sixteenth centuries, at a time in which patricians' stone built towns are a feature of the islands. Many of these sites were given defensive walls in the sixteenth century and can be described as urban; they also possessed many of the features of the commoners' towns in terms of their large size and lack of overall spatial order. Some of the sites cover very large areas indeed, and even with the higher rate of destruction of ruins on the mainland as a result of large animals, cannot have been as densely settled as the island towns but must have included extensive stock enclosures, gardens and shambas. Whilst these places were politically independent of each other (or in some cases forming small confederations) there was nonetheless a close economic relationship whereby these mainland towns were supplying foodstuffs, as well as commodities such as ivory, to the island towns. Study of the faunal evidence from sites such as Shanga suggests that hunted game was consumed in some quantity, and this could only have been obtained from the mainland. However, the island towns also consumed huge quantities of fish from the adjacent reefs and lagoons.[24]

Further down the coast we do not have much detailed evidence for the larger towns such as Malindi and Mombasa, but there is a similar pattern of communities set within their hinterlands. Around Malindi, there were Mambrui, Gedi and numerous small sites around Mida Creek, while between Kilifi and Mombasa there were Mnarani, Jumba la Mtwana and Mtwapa. At Jumba, where the plan is preserved, there were about ten stone houses (and four mosques) fairly widely spaced out with large enclosures that may have been for keeping stock or for growing garden produce. Mtwapa, only 2 km away, is more typically a patricians' town, with an estimated 77 houses, five mosques and a town wall, and a plan that shows the buildings to be tightly organized in blocks with narrow streets between them.[25]

South of Mombasa, along the Mrima coast, the sites contain only stone mosques and tombs. These mosques are often very elaborate – with ornate mihrabs or the use of domes – while the tombs often include complexes of pillar tombs or large enclosures. It may well be that there were once stone houses at these sites, but surface indications does not suggest extensive stone scatters. In a few cases, there is a single stone house, for example at Kaole, which may have had a special function. These may have been largely agricultural and fishing communities, linked through an economic relationship to the ports-of-trade.

A number of sites do not fall into this catagorization. Tumbatu, located on the south-east tip of a waterless island, had very little agricultural potential, and its relatively well preserved plan shows little similarity to the northern towns.[26] There were some 40 stone houses (and three mosques), many with large courtyards, arranged along nearly 1000m of coastline. The houses were built in open spaces, and took a whole range of alignments, suggesting that town developed in an *ad hoc* fashion over time, and must have looked very much like modern Nungwi. Tumbatu was clearly an important trading centre, judging from the range and quality of the imports found, including numerous copper coins. A similar site may be Songo Mnara, where again there are large houses with enclosures set in an open area without narrow streets or densely built stone houses.

A wider dynamic in the archaeological record may explain this diversity. Towns which once were important trading communities may revert to an agricultural function if the commercial activities decline. Nowadays this is visible on Pate island, where the once important towns of Pate and Siyu are little more than villages, and have not directly participated in the Indian Ocean trade since the late nineteenth century. However these towns still retain their traditional social structures; in the case of Siyu, the patricians' have moved out of their stone houses into mud and thatch houses but in Pate new stone houses are still built in the traditional manner and plan, but using mud rather than lime mortar. This pattern may explain the anomalies of other sites, such as at Ras Mkumbuu on Pemba, which in the tenth century was a very important 'town' which is visible as a series of house platforms and mounds. In the thirteenth century, the town moved from a plateau overlooking the beach to the waterfront, where new mosques were built and numerous tombs were constructed, but only a small number of stone houses were constructed along the waterfront on either side of the mosque. By this date the community was largely agricultural, exploiting the rich hinterland of the Mkumbuu peninsula. When the Portuguese arrived, Pemba island was noted for its importance in supplying grains and food-stuffs to Mombasa and Malindi, rather than as a trading centre. Its patricians' may not, however, have totally abandoned their aspirations to their former mercantile role within Swahili society.

Internal Organization

The possession of a central mosque, cemeteries, and perhaps a modicum of important tombs to which pilgrims come define a proper town. A Swahili town is not merely a settlement. It must be 'founded', -*buni*, by having a mosque built at its centre. A settlement without a mosque is not considered a 'town' in the sense of being a place of 'civilization', *ustaarabu*, and especially of 'urbanity', *utamaduni*, the two qualities considered to be at the base of proper Swahili society. This implies that there were no proper towns before the coming of Islam, as we have mentioned, a point of con-siderable discussion and disagreement at the present time in the light of recent excavations of pre-Islamic settlements over which have later been built the Swahili towns of today.

All towns, even the smallest, are divided into various levels of spatial units, each with its own function. There has been much confusion in past records and accounts over the composition and roles of the constituent units of a town, whether patricians' or commoners' town. The people themselves use sets of terms that refer to many kinds of social units and social action, the reference being clearly defined according to particular situations in which the usage has many referents and locally understood meanings. Some of these units are spatial, others are defined by the relations between their members that are based on claimed and accepted descent and rank. Definition of these various units, so important to the people themselves, lies at the heart of any understanding of the working of Swahili society.[27]

The congregational mosque is, or has been, typically set in a central street, often the only street with its own name.[28] In many towns this street is merely a wide open space of sand or grass, without other buildings, as in Pate, Matandoni or Makunduchi. The mosque and this street or space divide the town into two spatially and socially opposed named halves, for which the term 'moiety' has typically been used in English.[29] The Swahili word translated as moiety is *mtaa*, (pl. *mitaa*), used only in the sense of a constituent unit of a town, either a moiety or a ward.[30]

The division of towns into moieties is not merely a superficial formality. They unite by formal opposition. In some towns the members of these units fight each other, literally or not, on many occasions and especially at the New Year, *mwaka* or *nairuz*. Today traditional conflict in most places no longer involves open fighting but continues in the forms of poetry competitions.[31] football matches, 'band' competitions and the like. In the northern town of Lamu they are linked to the traditional Swahili New Year cleansing of the town by the killing of a bull.[32] One of us (JM) witnessed the rite in Lamu in 1990 but it was greatly reduced by lack of support by younger people; he also witnessed the *mwaka* in Makunduchi in 1958 when it was still flourishing and the young men of the moieties fought each other with swords; today it has become merely a tourist attraction. In both cases he was told that the rites 'cleanse the town'.[33]

Moieties may change location and names for various reasons. In Lamu, for example, there were until the mid-nineteenth century two moieties, Mtamuini and Mkomani; as the town grew by immigration of Hadrami and by freed slaves who no longer lived in their former owners' houses, the boundary was moved, the former moieties were amalgamated into a single one, Mkomani, and a new moiety, Langoni ('at the gate') came into existence occupied by non-patricians while the patricians themselves remained in Mkomani, the name Mtamuini being dropped. With moving of the boundary another mosque was selected as the congregational mosque for the town.[34] However the moiety organization itself persists, of central importance as throwing into relief both the town's origins, internal history, and the unity and cohesion of the population of the entire town. Whatever the locally claimed origins or processes of formation, the system of moieties found in both patricians' towns and commoners' towns is a basic defining feature of all Swahili towns and has the structural function of making unity through opposition, which prevents the holding and abuse of power by any single unit and thereby stresses the formal equality of all the town's members and domestic groups.[35]

The word *mtaa* is most widely used for a ward or quarter, a territorial unit occupied by the members of a local group as their primary place of residence. Wards are territorially defined, bounded and named units; however their functions vary among the towns along the coast. The ward is a local unit composed of buildings and streets, and the word is also used for the group or cluster of people who live in it. Such a residential unit has two aspects, that of shared space and that of shared kinship, the one or the other being emphasized by whether or not in any particular town it is or is not corporate. In the past, they may also have represented occupational areas within towns, and this is sometimes reflected in *mtaa* names. Their size varies greatly, but an approximate average size of a ward may be about 150 to 250 persons, some having only a few dozen and others three or four hundred.

There may be anything from some half-dozen to several dozen wards in a town. Their names typically refer to assumed or claimed places of origin in Asia or the northern coast of Kenya and Somalia (they seem rarely if ever to refer to places on the southern Swahili coast); to original clans of the northern towns from which members claim to have moved southward in early centuries retaining their original clan names; to assumed original occupations; or to the names of heroes in Swahili history.[36] Many, perhaps most, of these names are found in several towns up and down the coast. Many efforts have been made to write a coastal history using these names as evidence of origins and population movements. It seems obvious that something of this kind would be possible, but apart from offering putative evidence of past population movements along the coast, little has yet come of these attempts.

The Uses of Land

Besides those named territorial units, Swahili towns comprise various categories of residential and productive land which may briefly be mentioned insofar as they have social and cultural connotations. This landscape includes coastal lands, the shore, estuaries and swamps, and the waters between the shore and the reefs. Their soils vary in fertility, from those of irrigated gardens to stretches of sand, scrub, bush and forest. All land is subject to various rights, each vested in particular descent groups, different rights in the same piece of land often being held by different groups and persons at the same time. *Viwanda* (sing. *kiwanda*) is the word used for any productive working spaces that are owned by social groups and so not for unused or uncultivated space.[37] For example *viwanda* has been used to refer to the demarcated stretches of mangrove swamp used for cutting of building poles, and then even further to stretches of bush and forest yielding many resins and gums as well as ivory, collected by non-Swahili groups such as Dahalo and Boni who have been clients of individual Swahili lineages.

The part of any settlement with houses built in it is generally known as *majengo* (lit. places of building)[38] as opposed to unbuilt land. *Majengo* include streets, wards, houses, palaces, mosques, tombs and wells, and any small unbuilt stretches of land between them, especially if the town has surrounding walls. Beyond the *majengo* are the townlands, *ardhi*, for the town's own use, that extend through settlement, farms, plantations, bush, forest, and sea between beach and reef up to the townlands of neighbouring towns.[39] The 'owners', *wenyeji*, of a town hold rights in its townlands against members of other towns. As forming a single corporation they may extend rights of tenancy to other people, almost invariably kin of some of the townspeople, but this is not permanent alienation. There is a great number of types of productive land and variant names for them. The most widespread – although not found in every part of the coast – are *kiambo, konde, kiwanda* and *bustani*, all forming parts of a single town's townlands.

In commoners' towns the term *kiambo* is used widely and loosely, and led in the colonial period to some confusion to officials trying to codify land law. *Kiambo* is an area of residence and of crop-growing in permanent plots and gardens,[40] rights which belong to the constituent local and descent groups of the town. A *kiambo* contains house-sites, known as *vitongo* (sing. *kitongo*), growing plots (*mashamba*, sing. *shamba*)[41] and gardens (*bustani*, sing. *bustani*), both of which are cultivated permanently, ferti- lized and irrigated (as distinct from fields, *makonde*, which are used for only one or two seasons). Both *viambo* and *vitongo* are given names associated with the descent groups whose members hold or have in the past held rights in them. They may be used by members of other kin groups for planting coconut palms, planting being by agreement with the 'owning' kingroup and carrying no rights in the land in which the palms grow.[42]

Since the rise of the Sultanate of Zanzibar, the Swahili rules and conven- tions to do with rights in land have existed side by side with the then introduced rules under Islamic law. There have been many important differ- ences between 'Swahili' or 'Arab' law. The main difference is respectively that between forms of communal law and private or personal law, the former allocating rights to kin groups and the latter doing so to individuals, and the former prohibiting sale of rights in property and the latter permit- ting it. Here has lain one distinction between patricians' towns and com- moners' towns: the former has recognized both forms, the latter recognizing only traditional Swahili practice.[43]

The principles of Swahili land tenure are, in general, that there is no land, tidewater, bushland or forest that is not subject to permanent rights held by descent groups; that rights of many kinds are vested in these groups; and that land rights can be alienated only in certain situations, and usually then only temporarily.

Exploitation of the Landscape

The economy of the Swahili towns has always been complex. The coast is ecologically mixed, with only a few places of high fertility. And the crucial importance of the international commerce and the 'trickle down' process, with the low living standards of most of its former slaves and their descendants, have tended to conceal the details of local production and distribution. The members of the Swahili elite have always lived well, marked by differences of the staple being rice rather than sorghum,[44] in the proportion of protein (fish, meat and hunted game), and in the use of spices and condiments. Swahili patrician food is and has always been of high quality, as is evident from descriptions by travellers such as Ibn Battuta, or from the study of faunal residues from archaeological excavations.

The settlements of almost all African subsistence and peasant societies possess their own productive lands, whether cultivated or not, and their inhabitants are responsible for their exploitation. They typically produce enough surplus for local exchange and for sale for cash with which to buy domestic supplies that they cannot produce themselves. The Swahili situation is and has probably always been very different. For one thing, the coastal economy has been, and remains, divided between three sectors, those of the patricians' towns themselves producing little but obtaining footstuffs from the other sectors; of the commoners' towns dependent mainly on fishing and gardening and supporting both themselves and supplying other towns; and those of neighbouring non-Swahili farming peoples such as the Mijikenda and Zaramo, pastoralists such as Oromo and Somali, and hunting and gathering peoples. Resettlement schemes of upcountry farmers on the coast now make a significant contribution. Commoners' towns have never held slaves and have relied upon their own labour to produce foods, from both the sea and their own fields.[45] All towns produce from their own gardens a few crops such as tamarind and mango fruit, herbs, and flowers used on ritual occasions such as bourbon roses and jasmine.

The agricultural production of towns is further confused by the situation that developed during the nineteenth century, when plantation slavery enabled the coastlands to produce a wide range of commodities that entered into the Indian Ocean trading system. These plantations, which prior to the nineteenth century were not of importance, were owned by both Omani Arabs, in particular on Zanzibar and Pemba, and by Swahili patricians along the more distant parts of the coast. They produced grains, oil plants such as sesame, by-products of coconut such as copra and coir, spices (especially cloves), sisal, sugar and rubber. Some of these commodities survived the abolition of slavery, in particular cloves on Pemba island, and sisal, which was taken over by European concessionary companies in Tanganyika.

Prior to the introduction of plantation slavery, patricians' towns did produce some of their own food, using their own labour. On Pate island, the townsmen of Pate, Siyu and Faza would cross over to their farms on the mainland, generally around the Wange and Dodori Creeks, together with their slaves. They would appoint a farm leader, or *jumbe ya wakulima*, who was chosen for his skill and good fortune in farming, whatever his rank in society. Work was communal, including clearing, burning and harvesting, and all would live together in the same temporary settlement and eat the same food. There was a large *ngoma* or dance before the townsmen crossed over, and prior to burning the fields a series of very ancient songs known as *vave* were sung.[46] Pate subsisted on sorghum (and still does) as their stable carbohydrate, rather than rice symbolic of an Asian origin, and this may explain why the more ancient methods of cultivation survived into the nineteenth century.[47] While this has been confined to Pate and its mainland it is likely that similar practice was widespread on the coast before the nineteenth-century boom in slaves and the preference for rice, which was cultivated in more limited irrigated locations, such as the Tana delta and on Pemba and Zanzibar islands.

Livestock is often kept in towns in small enclosures, hand fed or taken out into the countryside on a daily basis to graze. Considerable numbers of goats and even cattle are reared in this way in Pate and Mambrui as well as on Pemba, and the archaeological evidence for stock compounds suggests this to be an ancient and well established practice. Fishermen are generally of non-patrician status and act as specialists with an extensive knowledge of the reefs and sailing. Some may come from the commoners' towns (the Bajuni and waTumbatu are especially well known), but land and sell their catches in the patricians' towns, as fresh fish has a very short life.

In commoners' towns there is often a marked gender division in production. Women are normally involved in agricultural activity, which may take place on individual plots, or communally in dry land swidden cultivation n the coral bedrock. Roots (especially cassava), sesame and tobacco are grown on individual plots, sorghum tends to be farmed communally. Women also collect shell fish which they dry and store. The men undertake fishing, the rearing of stock and craftwork, such as boat building or leatherworking.

Slavery

In order to produce food and other goods settlements have required labour, which appears always to have been in short supply. During the nineteenth century, the patricians owned slaves[48] and their labour was basic to the new plantation economy. Before this date there is very little information about the scale of slave ownership, and whilst domestic slavery may have been widespread, the use of slaves for agricultural production was less substantial.

The plantations founded in the nineteenth century for new export crops required large amounts of dependable (that is, controllable) labour and that could not be found among free inhabitants of the coast and hinterland. The patricians' towns seem always to have relied upon domestic slave labour for their enjoyment of urban life and for merchants' ability to devote time and effort to mercantile operations; without the supply of lower-ranking labourers and means to pay them, and with the moral support of Islamic practice, slavery was both feasible and sanctioned. But it seems likely that until the nineteenth century and the rise of the Zanzibar Sultanate the numbers of human beings enslaved by the Swahili (and their local agents) was never as great as has often been considered.

An economy with unfree labour is deeply different from one whose entrepreneurs have to pay for their labour. The patricians produced goods at a far lower cost and in far greater amounts than could non-patricians, whether Swahili or not. Admittedly they had first to purchase slaves, but the price was minimal in contrast to the profits made possible. In addition, their urban culture was utterly dependent on slave labour, male and female. After abolition there arose the institution of so-called 'squatters', being ex-slaves or independent labourers allowed to live on patrician- and Arab-owned land, mainly plantations, in return for so many days of labour a year, a system that continued until the Zanzibar Revolution of 1964.[49] The use of squatter labour on clove and other plantations was consistent with the fact that labour, although necessary for weeding throughout the year, was needed mainly for picking and preparation for export at times of clove harvest: squatters obviated much of the need to recruit seasonal labour, and cost nothing. In Zanzibar, at least, it was linked to the existence of urban casual labourers or porters, *wapagazi*, who could be employed for short periods when crops had to be taken to warehouses for storage until shipment.

There were several categories of slaves in and attached to the patricians' towns. Most were field slaves, *watwana*, the majority being men. Field slaves were allowed small plots to grow their own food but most of their labour was agricultural on behalf of the owners, especially for rice for domestic use and crops, mostly sorghum, for export to Arabia; many worked at the hard and unpleasant task of cutting and preparing mangrove poles.

Another category was *watumwa* 'those who are sent or used'. This included male and female domestic slaves, those with long experience and of personal reliability or allotted special tasks such as plantation supervisors, caravan leaders, sailors and even soldiers, and the personal confidants of their owners. Domestic slaves were chosen for their good appearance and behaviour, received some Islamic education and new Muslim personal names.[50] Female slaves in particular might easily be given intimate tasks such as acting as trusted nursemaids (*somo*, pl. *masomo*) for the patrician daughters, remaining with them throughout their lives.[51] A household of wife, husband and five or six children might easily have at least a dozen female slaves who slept in the house, whereas most male slaves had to sleep outside it – in some towns even outside the town walls.

Female slaves were available as sexual objects but sexual relations with them by their owners had properly to be outside the house itself, the only sexual activity permitted within it being between married patricians.[52] Trusted male slaves acted as personal guards and assistants and held positions of recognized importance. Many male and female trusted slaves could work outside the house and fields as craftsmen, sailors, caravaners, prostitutes, and paid their owners a rent, *ijara*, equivalent to the wages of a free person. Such slaves often saved money and purchased both their freedom and also slaves of their own.

The status of any category of slave was never as straightforward as the few terms for them might imply. Much depended on the identities of those who owned and traded in them. The undoubted brutalities associated with East African slavery were found mainly in their treatment by nineteenth century Omani of Zanzibar, for whom the slaves were virtually animals caught in the wastelands of the interior. For Swahili patricians and others the slaves were more ambiguous, being essentially human and linked to them by their common African origins, by close domestic interaction and shared dislike of Omani colonists.

Conurbations

The effective social and economic unit as far as everyday production is concerned has always been larger than any single town, a cluster of neighbouring towns and settlements which may be considered as forming a single complex of linked communities. No town has ever been self-sufficient in either food or trade items and all have relied on their relationships with other settlements in order to exist. The economy has been based on complementary production by exchange between three categories of settlements: the patricians' towns, (which in the nineteenth century used slave labour), the commoners' towns, using only their own free labour; and non-Swahili settlements of many kinds. This grouping, centred on a particular patricians' town, may be termed a conurbation.[53]

Each conurbation has been tied together into a single unit by various bonds of neighbourhood, kinship, political and religious authority, and by some expression of shared or complementary ethnicities. It has not been limited to only those groups generally known as 'Swahili' but has typically included non-Swahili groups as well. Their geographical extent has at times been very considerable (for example, the linking at various periods of Mombasa with Pemba, as its main supplier of foodstuffs, which came to include political contral as well). Most sets of relations of fictive kinship used in trade have been within the same conurbation.

The composition of the different elements of these conurbations has changed over time, changes that may be seen to have been accompanied by several kinds of conflicts, from open warfare to religious revival. Many of the more obscure episodes in the traditional Swahili chronicles and histories can best be interpreted in this light.

On the ground several conurbations may be recognized.[54] The Lamu Archipelago comprised five, two based on Pate Island, and including parts of the Benadir coast and the mainland opposite the island. The Pate conurbation included at certain times the towns at the mouth of the Tana, with interests on Pemba and along the Mrima coast. The Lamu conurbation included the islands of Lamu and Manda, and the mainland opposite the island, including places such as Luziwa. Another seems to have centred on Malindi, including Mambrui to the north and Gedi and the Mida Creek and Watamu sites to the south. The region centred on Mombasa included Mtwapa and Jumba, but also extended southwards, and at times included the island of Pemba. Another grouping occurs at Vumba/Vanga and Wasin island and the associated Shirazi settlements on Mafia and in the Kilwa archipelago. Zanzibar and the adjacent Mrima coast were closely linked politically before the development of the caravan trade, but during the nineteenth century these regions either side of the Zanzibar channel became economically interdependent.[55]

In all these cases both Swahili and non-Swahili have played complementary roles over history, including much competition and even conflict between neighbouring conurbations over political and mercantile supremacy in terms of trade, commodity resources, mercantile services, food production and craft construction. But each has contained wide variations in terms of ethnicity, language and details of religious practice and behaviour, which have provided each of them with its own cultural as well as geographical identity.

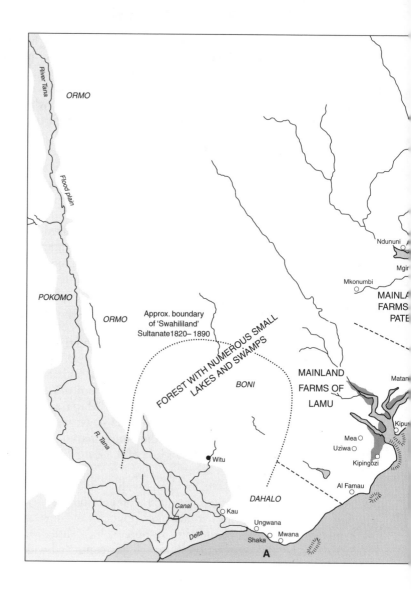

ORMO

River Tana

Flood plain

POKOMO

ORMO

Approx. boundary
of 'Swahililand'
Sultanate1820– 1890

FOREST WITH NUMEROUS SMALL
LAKES AND SWAMPS

BONI

R. Tana

Witu

Ndununi

Mgir

Mkonumbi

MAINLA
FARMS
PATE

MAINLAND
FARMS OF
LAMU

Matan

Kipu

Mea

Uziwa

Kipingozi

DAHALO

Al Famau

Canal

Kau

Ungwana

Mwana

Delta

Shaka

A

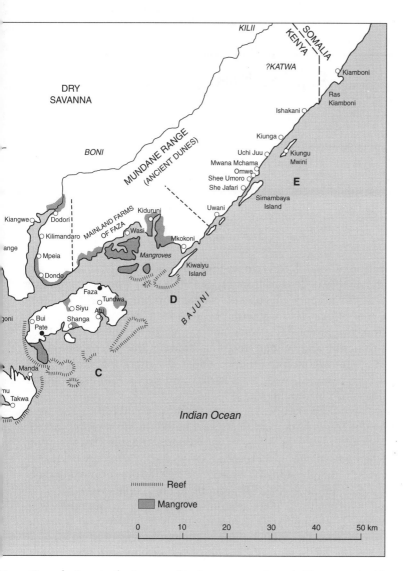

6.1   *Conurbations in the Lamu archipelago, 1400–1850. A: Tana, acquired by*
from Malindi during the sixteenth century, re-established in the 1820s by the
[W]hanis from Pate, first at Kau and then Witu; B: Lamu, including west side of
[Man]da island and adjacent mainland; C: Pate, including Siyu and Shanga and the
[west] side of Pate island and adjacent mainland; D: Faza and the east side of Pate
[islan]d and adjacent mainland; E: Omwe and adjacent sites, mostly abandoned in the
sixteenth century.

7

Social Networks

Ancestry and Social Position

The organization of Swahili towns over time has been conceptualized by the use of history, myth and descent from original ancestors whether beyond or within Africa. We discuss the use of claimed origins in various places throughout this book; here we wish to consider the notion of descent from ancestors to present-day people and the ways in which it has been and is used to define and validate relations between the latter themselves. The Swahili usage of concepts grouped under the rubric of 'descent and kinship' has been complex, with great variety and variance of usage, much ambiguity and much uncertainty.[1]

The towns have been occupied by groups whose members see the links between them in terms of descent. Relations based upon space are largely expressed and sanctioned in terms of genealogical relations based upon time, and when genealogies are claimed that go back to origins in Arabia a sacred element is thereby added. Descent and kinship are social constructs which may or may not be historically accurate but in people's views are so at any one time. The members of these groups enjoy rights in land and other property, material or immaterial, by virtue of their ancestry; a desirable ancestry may be claimed precisely so as to validate enjoyment of rights, and may by no means be historically accurate by reference to documents, archaeological excavation or claims made by other groups. Rights in property may in fact determine ancestry although local theory holds that it is ancestry that determines the allocation of property and the possession of wealth. The situation found among Hadrami sayyid families in the Hadramaut may be paralleled in many Swahili towns: sharif (sayyid) lineages are given the spiritual quality of moral probity that ensures them commercial success, but in historical actuality it is the latter that may confer the former.[2]

In order to live where they do or wish to do, people have claimed membership of descent groups, for which there are many terms. There has been frequent confusion among observers between residential and domestic groups and the descent groups that provide a frame or skeleton to them. Incorporation and amalgamation of descent groups have occured with consequent adjustments to their histories, composition and previous relations, and after the abolition of slavery various segments of the population underwent many changes in composition and social position. Almost every town has had its own forms and rules of kinship, descent and forms of marriage, and conclusions made for one town may not be applicable to others.[3]

The Organization of Descent

There are several categories of descent and kinship units in Swahili towns. One comprises those based on patrilineal descent; the second and most widespread comprises various clusters of cognatic kin; a third comprises categories of quasi-kin, fictive kin, and clients who assume certain obligations and expectations of kinship. To suggest that any one is more 'basically' Swahili other than others would be fraught with uncertainty and conjecture.

Several Swahili words denote descent groups and clusters. Some refer to the criterion of settlement or space, others to that of descent irrespective of space. Some have Arabic roots and others Bantu roots, the former having higher prestige or propriety in speech than the latter. The complexities in their usage may well reflect those of past population movements and amalgamations as well as historical changes in the social importance of units linked to particular local economic, political and social factors. Only one or two terms have specific reference to clearly defined or bounded units; others may be used to varying degrees for groups or clusters of people whose sizes, compositions and identities vary over time. None of these terms are very clearly defined, and they are given meanings that refer to both territoriality and descent, emphasis being assumed by speakers' and listeners' definitions of a particular situation. Every term refers both to a spatially defined unit and also to the group that lives in it, irrespective of kinship relationships. They may be set out as follows:

	from *Arabic roots*	from *Bantu roots*
Territorial	taifa	mji, nyumba, mlango
Descent	kabila	ukoo, tumbo, mbari, ufungu

A detailed analysis of the usages of these terms would be beyond the scope of this account. They are used in varying ways among the different towns of the coast, in the sense that the same term when used in different towns may refer to different groups, due to slight differences and nuances of reference from one town to another; also the same group may be referred to by different terms according to stages reached in its cycle of development.

The patricians recognize patrilineal descent from ancestors claimed to have originated in Arabia or Persia, with a few from Shungwaya, the mythical homeland on the far northern coast. By recognition of patriliny a person may claim Arabian ancestry by descent from a single Arabian merchant who has married a patrician's daughter at any time over recent centuries. Certain families, especially well-known being the Mazrui of Mombasa and the Nabahani of Pate, can most certainly claim 'full' origins in Arabia; but this does not invalidate the statement that the 'true' patricians, those known as the owners, *wenyeji*, of the towns, are essentially African in origin. We know of patrician descent lines in which the last Arab from Arabia itself married into the family probably about 1750, and all later members have claimed to be Arab. Many of the women in this and other lines have been concubines of direct African ancestry whose children are counted as Swahili or Arab. The same applies to descent lines among Omani and Hadrami immigrants of the late nineteenth century, where direct ancestry to Arabia may legitimately be claimed whatever the ethnic origins of their wives and concubines. The process of claiming Arab ancestry may reflect no actual distant origin in Arabia but rather the desire by a group resident in Africa to acquire a socially more acceptable or useful history.

The depth of genealogies[4] varies greatly, and they are only rarely historically accurate for more than five or six generations back from the present. As statements for the allocation of status and authority, the higher the latter the deeper the genealogy. Ten to twelve generations are the average for patrician lineages; those of Omani and Hadrami tend to be longer and those of sharif lineages certainly so, as they have to show links back to their founder, the Prophet. Those of non-patrician Swahili lineages average some four or six generations; those of slaves two or three only.[5] As well as reflecting social position and the ownership of property, they also reflect moral distance. The shorter are from Africa only, the longer extend to Arabia and the longest to Mecca itself: the longer the genealogy the higher the rank and the greater the moral purity.

The basic patrilineal units of the patricians may be called, in English, clans, segmented into subclans, and these into lineages.[6] There has been much argument as to whether or not the Swahili have 'clans', a term often misused and misunderstood. Clans are named patrilineal descent groups, usually called *kabila* (pl. *makabila*) or *taifa* (pl. *mataifa*), both terms with Arabic roots, the latter usually being larger than the former and referring to locality rather than to descent and often translated as town. There are at least 50 patrician Swahili clans,[7] each large enough so that actual interpersonal kinship ties may not be traceable between all the members, and dispersed throughout the various towns, although not all. In most cases they claim origins in Arabia and close relationships with the clans found in Oman and Yemen; the names used by patricians are not always those also found in Arabia, but that does not affect their claims. The localized members in any town may be referred to as forming a subclan. Members of a particular subclan thus recognize presumed patrilineal kin both elsewhere along the coast and in southern Arabia, kin who in the past acted as trading partners and between whom marriages should be made (patrician marriages are clan-endogamous and between those of equal rank). The subclans of any particular town are ranked relative to other subclans of the same town. The head of the senior lineage of a subclan is the recognized head of that subclan, although without very clearly defined authority other than that of merely having genealogical seniority.

Subclans are segmented into lineages, for which many terms are used: *mbari*, *ufungu*, *tumbo* and *nyumba* being the most common. A lineage is a corporate segment of a clan or subclan, with a single head with authority, and is presumed to be permanent over the generations. Lineages have acted as the actual business houses in the international trade, as the possessors of the stone houses that symbolize the success and creditworthiness of their owners. They are the everyday patrician family groups of town life, invested with mercantile and other property, and the greater their membership the higher may be their social position.

The process of segmentation, dependent mainly on size and on movement of small segments between towns, has not been that of the well-known segmentary lineage systems of societies like the Nuer and Somali.[8] Incorporation of new segments, whether from elsewhere on the coast or beyond, has been and remains a basic feature of Swahili social organization; and the transfer of individuals and their families from one clan to another has been an endemic pattern, usually made to increase social standing by belonging to a higher ranking group. A commonly stated reason is to escape persistent illness, witchcraft or commercial failure. It is therefore considered impolite to ask too clearly for personal reasons for moving and claiming the relationship of 'brothers' to a resident lineage. So long as incoming residents are not notorious for anti-social or sacrilegious behaviour they are likely to be accepted and welcomed as strengthening the host group. In addition, due to complexities of past marriages and divorces, incomers and hosts may often find existing but hitherto unused ties of kinship that can provide a link and so reason for incorporation. But in general, incorporation by claimed common origin, however vague, is more usual than actual shared descent, a process that makes interpretation of family histories, which are typically recounted in terms of presumed actual descent, extremely problematic.

In some towns the situation is complex, the best-known example being Mombasa. Some writers have denied the local recognition of patrilineal descent groups in that city, stating that the only local groups are cognatic descent groups.[9] The Mombasa patricians have a more complex and confused history than those of other towns, have had most of their traditional residential areas taken from them, and seen their main area, today known as 'Old Town', inhabited by immigrants from Arabia and India. They have been divided in past centuries into the Twelve Tribes comprising the Nine Tribes and the Three Tribes, which were distinct patrilineal groups engaged in both ocean and local commerce. It is often said that these units no longer exist; it is true that they have not played commercial roles for a long time, but patrician friends have told us that they are all quite aware of them even if they no longer use affiliation to them except when arranging marriages. In addition, city commerce has long been taken over by immigrants – Indians, Hadrami, Omani, and descendants of slaves from other towns. The Nine and the Three Tribes are still known, and their constituent local residential groups, known as *mbari*, provide the framework for the cognatic families important and visible in everyday affairs.[10] Even if a local settlement is composed of families of many different ancestries, there is always a core or skeleton provided by an 'owning' patrilineal descent group, originally a segment of one of the Twelve Tribes.

The second category of descent groups comprises those that are not patrilineal but cognatic; these are more widely dispersed along the coast. They are found in the commoners' towns, where perhaps typically the largest cognatic group is known as *ukoo* (pl. *koo*) whose members form the majority of the population of a town but are also dispersed throughout a wide area occupied by a set of ultimately related *koo*; an example is that of the Hadimu of southern Zanzibar island: but the same term is used on Mafia Island for a different group.[11] The Hadimu *ukoo* is divided into smaller groups known as *tumbo*, *mlango* or *ufungu*, terms also used for the lineages of patrilineal subclans.

Tumbo, 'womb' or 'stomach', is generally used to refer to the smallest family group, the people descended from a single grandmaternal womb;[12] *mlango* 'gate' or 'door', is said to 'show the way' into or from the wider cognatic group that may be dispersed over many towns; it is therefore the largest local domestic cognatic kin group and the 'owner' of a residential or gardening plot; the *ufungu*, from the verb *kufunga*, 'to close', generally refers to the short patrifocal line that provides the core for the actual residential group and in which rights in use of a *kiambo* tend to be vested. The *ufungu* is patrifocal, as the *upande wa mume*, 'side of the male' is given privilege over the *upande wa kiike*, 'side of the female'. These various small groups are composed of close kin who share the right of use of a small piece of land for residence or gardening. There is no single pattern of membership but the composition of each is a consequence of the particular histories of its members. The very frequent divorces in commoners' towns lead to wide scattering of former spouses and their children and affines, and local domestic groups tend to be unstable and short-lived; immediate domestic authority is perhaps more generally held by women than by men, as they are the more stable members over time. The terms used vary greatly between settlements, depending mainly on types of productive land held, degrees of recognition of cognative ties over wide areas, densities of population, rates and histories of divorce, and the wealth of particular settlements.

Cognatic groups are found also in the patricians' towns among non-patrician families, although those of recent Omani or Hadrami ancestry reckon patrilineal descent. As in the commoners' towns, most of these groups have lacked important heritable property of houses and other items and have not engaged in the ocean trade.

These two modes of descent are nowhere totally opposed, and indeed a given group may change from one to the other. The main factor is the possession or lack of possession of rights in particular forms of property, in particular that of lands or resources that produce items for long-distance trade. For example, many formally cognatic groups on Pemba Island whose members have acquired clove trees by enterprise or marriage now recognize patrilineal descent as owners of commodities for export.[13] In some places (including Mombasa) patrilineal groups have become so impoverished and landless that their members today form clusters of small cognatic groups only.

All Swahili, male and female, old and young, are members of several descent groups, and they also recognize interpersonal kin ties based upon their genealogical interrelationships. The terms used for categories, levels and degrees of interpersonal kinship are many, and there are some variations in the sets of kin terms found in different parts of the coast, the main distinction being between those north of Mombasa and those of Mombasa and the towns to its south.[14]

Interpersonal kinship bonds, based upon modes of descent, are used to limit conflicts and competition in business matters; they ensure wide networks of trust and lack of intrigue (*fitina*); they place individuals into positions of power and influence relative to one another. Kinship relations act as effective idioms for those of power and authority that are determined by other criteria, and they provide validation for those relations.

Fictive and Quasi-Descent

Other categories include both patrilineal and cognatic ties as well as those with neighbours and others not related by kinship. The most important is the *jamaa* (pl. *majamaa*), usually misleadingly translated as 'family'. The *jamaa* is not a descent group nor is it restricted to kin, but is an ego-centered network of kin, neighbours, clients and friends of ever-changing composition, and includes both men and women. Its members may be called upon for financial and other help at any time, and expect reciprocity when they require it. These groups are formed especially around powerful and wealthy people, both men and women; young and unimportant people try to belong to the *majamaa* of the powerful who act as patrons with their personal clienteles, and in time hope to become patrons themselves. The memberships of these groups is constantly changing. At a patrician wedding there are appointed women and men of the two families concerned, known as *waalishi* (lit. inviters), whose role is to invite others to contribute to any particular wedding in various ways, and who by so doing in fact define the effective *jamaa* for that occasion.[15] *Majamaa* of other compositions may later be formed specifically for other occasions. A person's *jamaa* is non-corporate, volatile in membership from one situation to another, and called into operation in only specific situations. It is, however, the most often called-upon social unit outside the immediate lineage or domestic family, and its membership may include persons related by descent, affinity, rank, neighbourhood and even ethnicity, without privileging any of them: every *jamaa* is *sui generis*.

A second category is that of *mtani* (pl. *watani*). *Watani* are those linked by the quality or tie known as *utani*, usually translated as 'joking relationship'.[16] *Utani* refers to a relationship that is ambiguous in the sense that the rights and obligations denoted by it are potential and the parties to it are not as yet in a long-lasting socially or ritually validated relationship. This structural ambiguity is expressed culturally by 'joking', teasing or unconventional behaviour. Those who can and are likely to marry are referred to as *watani*, as were those leaders of caravans in contact with inland political authorities through whose territories they hoped to pass in peace.[17] This latter relationship was less effective than the fictive kin tie of blood-brotherhood, perhaps usually made between those who were already *watani* and also used in trade exchanges; it created a longer-lasting and closer relationship more akin to that of 'true' kinship in that it was subject to moral and even jural sanctions. In both cases the relationship was accompanied by the formal exchanges of gifts between the parties and most interior exchange was in the form of gifts between them. *Watani* were linked to a potential marriage, whereas blood brothers became fictive consanguineous kin who never marry. There is a reflection of the process of marriage itself and the distinction between cross- and parallel-cousins, who may marry, and full siblings, who may not, the former relationship temporary and endable by divorce, the latter permanent and unchangeable.[18]

The Strategies of Marriage

Descent groups are perpetuated by marriage and the procreation and birth of legitimate children, and Swahili marriages are strategies to this end. They vary, therefore, with variations in the composition and purpose of different patterns of descent. The basic principle is that patricians, especially those of higher rank and greater wealth, reckon kin ties as widely as they can within their own clans and subclans whose members are dispersed among the patricians' towns along the coast. Ties of marriage or affinity are not extended outside these clans and subclans. Patrician marriages, especially, should be between those of exact equality of rank, known as *wakufu*; since clans are ranked relative to one another, it follows that the marriages must be endogamous. The patrician subclans and lineages are rigorously exclusive, with the limitation of and so control over the rights in their various forms of property. Conversely the cognatic descent groups of the commoners' towns are inclusive, with the extension by marriage of rights, as widely as possible within the largest cognatic groups recognized in a particular locality.[19] Patrician marriages are properly between paternal parallel- and cross-cousins only, a pattern that ensures that the business house, the lineage, continues as a close-knit corporate group, and also demonstrates the extreme importance of purity and honour in these lineages. Neither aim is of prime importance to non-patrician groups, except among Omani and Hadrami Arab lineages, although there the cultural idioms are rather different.

All Swahili marriages should be – although the practice is today falling into disuse – arranged by betrothal when the couple are children and even before one or both may yet be born. Or future spouses may be adopted as infants from among kin, in order to make a useful betrothal possible. Arranged marriages are also used to express close friendship and trust between the respective sets of parents, and among Hadimu, at least, are often made as a means of joining two small enterprises into a single larger one.

Other forms of marriages and near-marriages exist, especially by patricians who fear the ending of a lineage by its failure to produce sons; a lone daughter may informally be regarded as though male as far as exercising lineage authority and business acumen is concerned, and the adoption of trustworthy slaves as sons certainly took place. There are also the factors of demonstrating worldly success and appeasing sexual appetites. These are marriages with 'secret' wives, *mabibi wa siri*, and unions with concubines. Secret marriages are legal unions but without permission of parents or transfers of marriage payments; their children are legitimate. Concubinage is a union of a patrician and (formerly) a female slave, known by the title of *suria*;[20] any children are legitimate but the union is not formally recognized by ritual or marriage payments.

Rank and Class

There have been two perceptions of Swahili stratification. One is that high status has been associated with and is the consequence of pure patrilineal genealogy; this is the view accepted by most Swahili themselves. The other is that it and genealogical purity are the consequences of the acquisition of mercantile profit and wealth. The factors relevant to the distinction include the nature and allocation of rights in both material and immaterial property; the pattern of corporate and non-corporate groups; the competition for commercial success both between one town and another and also within each of them; enjoyment of allocated political, religious and other authority; and the introduction by the Zanzibar Sultanate of an overall coastal hierarchy based upon its own wealth and power, an hierarchy that was to a large extent taken over by the British within their Protectorate.

The word for 'rank' is *daraja*, a step on a ladder or staircase, with the implication of ascending and descending. Swahili patricians, at least, hold that rank is based either upon birth into a particular descent group that is itself placed in terms of superiority or juniority to others, or upon the acquisition of God's blessing to become a holy man or woman or even a saint. All Swahili are well aware that descent groups are permeable, and that a person may move out of one and become accepted into another. We must, as always with Swahili terms, be careful not to portray the system as too rigid: the word *daraja* can refer to many kinds of informal and marginal status as well as that by birth.

Ranked units within a town are the patrilineal descent groups we have mentioned: clans, subclans and lineages. Cognatic descent groups, whether in patricians' towns or in commoners' towns, are not ranked in any strict sense: within them only individual rank differences are recognized, based upon achievement rather than ascription. The Swahili pattern of ranking appears rigid and unchangeable but is in actuality everchanging with persistent competition, ambition, geographical mobility and acquisition of Islamic learning. In this mercantile society status achievement is recognized as well as that by ascription, and both have permeable boundaries.

The Swahili usually consider and express hierarchical differences as arising from ethnic origins. This is a rationale except in the broad sense that slaves were taken from the African interior and the elite has usually claimed origins in Arabia or Persia. A basic contradiction within Swahili society is that between claimed ancestry in Arabia or elsewhere in Asia on the one hand and in Africa on the other, the former in the past and largely today being considered the 'better' origin and associated with higher rank. However, it may well be argued that rank differences essentially reflect wealth and power, which enable persons and groups to act at the centres of interpersonal networks of patronage and clientship; this process is certainly more common today than in the past, with easier personal rank movement by new forms of achievement.

Ranking among patricians on the southern coast was more complex than can be found in Lamu or Pate, where patricians were ranked according to the seniority of their lineages. Here, especially along the Mrima coast, there were a series of grades through which a male patrician would pass, accompanied on each occasion by gift giving and feasting.[21] For example at Vumba, after circumcision, he would be known as *kijani*, youth; after marriage, known as *harusi ya ada*, 'marriage by fee' he became a *mwole*. If cattle were slaughtered at the wedding feast, it was known as *harusi ya ngombe*, 'marriage by cattle' and he would gain even more status. If he could not afford to give a feast, he was termed *mondo*, and lacked respect. If having married, and paid his marriage fee or *ada*, he could then become *mtenzi*, 'active or mature person', after another feast, while there was further promotion after the birth of his son.[22] These various grades were marked by practical proscriptions; youths, *vijani*, were not allowed to eat with *watenzi*; a *mondo* had to follow the orders of a *mwale* or *mtenzi* without question, while a *mtenzi* could demand an invitation to any feast that was held in the town.

Similar ranking can be found on the Comores, associated with the great marriage, *harusi kuu*, where only after this has been passed does the groom become an adult, or *mtu mzima*, 'whole' or 'full person' sometimes also termed *mafaume ya mji*, (lit. rulers of the town). Because these marriages are enormously expensive, Comoran males often undertake them later in life, as they need not be their first marriage, or often not at all.[23]

We could use the term 'status' in place of 'rank', but prefer the latter because Swahili society is both extremely highly stratified in its formality of address and references and also highly competitive and, just as merchants have competed over trade commodities, so have they competed over rank. The various social categories have behaved differently: Omani and Hadrami colonists have perhaps tended to place more emphasis on rights in material rather than on immaterial property; whereas the patricians have tended to do the opposite – at least in the past hundred or so years when they have in any case lost much of their former material wealth to members of Omani and Hadrami lineages. The inhabitants of commoners' towns have competed over rather different but mainly immaterial forms of property, and most of those of slave ancestry have had little to compete about other than over relatively small possessions.

Some recent historiography has depended largely on Marxist categories of 'class', categories that have been forced onto a far more complex situation than they were designed to illuminate.[24] Swahili society before the eighteenth century probably lacked differences that might usefully be called those of class. It may be argued that class relations developed in some parts of the coast with the development of European colonial rule and the appearance of employers and employees in capitalist companies. The British colonial hierarchy was typically expressed in terms of ethnicity, the three main 'classes' of local society, upper, middle and lower, being described as 'European', 'Asian and Arab,' and 'African' respectively. This simplistic classification, for which the term 'caste' would more correctly be used, had the advantage for the rulers of denying possibility of vertical mobility by anyone else, but the disadvantage for the ruled of ensuring uncertainty of the status of those Swahili patricians who claimed Arabian ancestry.

Another suggestion has been that ranking is a remnant of a system of age-sets through which a person passes. J. de V. Allen has argued that originally these rituals and feasts would have been held communally, so that a group of males would pass each set at a time, and a set would act together to defend its members or support a particular political or military cause. The basis of this is a somewhat speculative reading of the Arabic *History of Kilwa*, but in the ethnographic record there is only notice of individuals achieving particular status through their acquisition of personal wealth through trade.[25]

Property

At the basis of differences and interrelations in the Swahili system of hierarchy has been the allocation of rights in property. In addition, those of gender may be analysed in terms of the allocation of similar rights, and ideas of both have changed radically over the recent two centuries.[26] We may distinguish rights of physical possession, of user, of inheritance, of trust, of gift, of sale, of loan, of occupation, of abandonment, of destruction. These, and there are others, may be held in any item of property by the same person or group or by different persons or groups.[27] The items of property may be material (e.g. a house) or immaterial (e.g. the right to live in it, precedence in religious or civic processions, positions of rank and gender, even moral purity and knowledge), and as far as we know there is no item of property in which some person or group does not own some right or other. Before the coming of Islam there may have been few rights in land, but since then there is no land in which rights are not held, beginning with rights over a piece of land held first by whoever vivicates it.[28] Rights in property may be held both by living persons and by spirits; there are or have been uncertain and borderline situations, such as those rights held by slaves *qua* slaves or by slaves *qua* agents of their owners. Finally it is held that all rights in everything are held by God, so that all rights held by persons or spirits are held by His favour.[29]

Rights in property and in wealth may be held by an individual person, by a corporation, by a social group of any size and any composition. Rights may be inherited or otherwise acquired, and the property may be owned in trust.

The most important items of property are permanent and heritable objects, whether material or immaterial. The more costly of the former include stone houses, plantations and ocean-going ships; slaves were also costly but more easily replaceable. The latter include publicly accepted ancestry, religious knowledge, moral purity and probity, and commercial trustworthiness, all of which are represented by possession of particular material items. All have been in one way or other obtainable by direct and indirect acquisition, have been heritable, and have been transferable by marriage.

The high cost of building and maintaining the merchants' traditional stone houses and of the plots on which they are built demonstrate mercantile wealth and standing, creditworthiness, and the permanence of the owning lineage and family, especially when that lineage is also one of ancient ancestry. Today, when patricians have lost much wealth and position in the society at large, they have largely lost the money needed to build and maintain these houses, but they refuse to sell them to non-patrician Swahili or to Hadrami, who therefore build new concrete houses.[30] The greatest buildings are the mosques, mostly built and owned by patrician lineages. Houses in commoners' towns lack the quality of showing social position: they are impermanent and not costly to build or maintain.

Centrally important in this context has been the institution known as *waqf*,[31] which surprisingly has been largely ignored in most writings on the Swahili. There are two types of *waqf*, which may best be translated as 'trust':[32] one is *waqf ahli*, used for houses and similar property 'for the maintenance and support, either wholly or partly, of any persons including the family, children, descendants or kindred of the maker';[33] the other is *waqf khayri*, used for religious or charitable purposes such as upkeep of a mosque. Here we are discussing the former.

Waqf used with regard to houses and similar properties is declared on them by the owner: the property is then withdrawn or 'detained' from disposal by sale, inheritance, or by any other method, and rights in it are vested in whatever categories of kin or other persons stated by the owner, although a descending line of kin is the most frequent. They may not sell or dispose of it nor rent it for money – money may not be put into *waqf* trust. The usual *waqf* group is the patrilineal lineage of the trustees (men often left such trust to their slaves, and the patrilineal descendants of those slaves only could enjoy it). The trustees enjoying a *waqf* are referred to as *shirika*, a property-owning corporation of associates or shareholders, often today a business company. A *waqf ahli* has no time of ending other than the dying out of the members of the *shirika*. Certainly a high proportion of stone houses in a town such as Lamu are subject to *waqf*, and often in a state of near-ruin as the *waqf* is not wealthy enough to pay for maintenance. Property left by normal testament, known as *walii*, is different and not under the supervision of the Waqf Commissioners in Zanzibar and Mombasa,[34] who have the ultimate power to dispose of a *waqf* for charitable purposes if the *waqf* group dies out some time in the future.

A factor that is also centrally important with regard to property is that of the moral quality of objects and persons. The patrician stone houses are more than merely large and costly buildings; if they are properly maintained they are places of purity and give high moral status to their owners; this is not so in the case of other dwelling houses. High personal rank, as distinct from that of a lineage or subclan, can also be acquired by possession of certain moral competencies and qualities. The most important are those of understanding Muslim theology and knowledge, and composing poetry and music. Lesser competencies include carpentry, pottery and other abilities to transform raw materials into those approved by God. These competencies have been open to women as well as to men: the latter depend more on the ranking of their subclans and lineages, whereas women may acquire higher status by their individual abilities and qualities, provided they are acceptable to God. Formerly high moral status could be granted to those slaves, male and female, who acquired these moral abilities and might then be granted what may be called the honorary rank of patrician insofar as they would then be so treated in everyday behaviour. It should be stressed that change in rank and reputation of these kinds were for many centuries controlled by the patricians of a given town; these thereby retained their cultural and religious hegemony. In the twentieth century this control has been weakened with the loss of much of their religious authority to non-patricians, especially to Hadrami religious innovators.[35]

A persistent problem in respect of lineage property is that although women inherit only half the share of their brothers, if they marry into lineages other than their own they take a share of the lineage wealth with them to their husbands and children. The patricians avoid this by enjoining clan-endogamous marriages, and those of first-born daughters in particular should be with a paternal parallel cousin; marriages in commoners' towns are also properly between cross-cousins and paternal parallel cousins. Otherwise a great deal of the group's wealth can soon be dissipated even though wives will bring in wealth with them from their natal groups. A daughter who marries her patrilineal parallel cousin will also benefit from his share in any rights he may possess in *waqf* property.[36]

Gender

Status defined in terms of gender has usually been considered in terms of situations of cultural and legal dependence, independence and autonomy, as well as crudely defined factors such as religious belief and practice, and of course in terms of the nomenclature of the many different but named offices of authority, whether in family or state, and the many possessors of moral qualities.[37] In many cases the analysis has been in terms of unchangeable gender; but, as with too many analyses of rank, radical events and processes such as the abolition of slavery and the introduction of money have been ignored. The effects of colonial rule have indeed been considered, although usually without much attention to detail; but this has often been vitiated by limiting colonial rule to that of the European powers and omitting rule by the Zanzibar Sultanate, the local representative of Omani colonialism.[38]

There are several variant patterns in the definition and relationships of gender, the principal being those of patricians, of non-patricians, of persons of slave ancestry and of Arabs of recent immigration. One of the weaknesses of many studies of Swahili gender has been a misleading amalgamation of these differing levels of society, so that figures for marriage and divorce, for example, may lump together all the social ranks of a town whose members have extremely different modes of marriage and rates of divorce: the amalgamated figures are worthless. Within each category there are many variations dependent mainly upon wealth, age, and personal achievement and reputation.

There are many words that may refer to gender, almost all in specific contexts. There are the terms *mwanamume* and *mwanamke*, literally 'male person' and 'female person';[39] there are words such as *mngwana*, *mwenyeji* and *mwananchi*, which refer to rank and legal position; there are terms such as *mfalme*, *malkia* and *mtumwa*, usually translated king, queen and slave; and there are words that refer to phases in a woman's life cycle, such as *msichana* and *mwanamali*, a girl past first menstruation but uninitiated and unbetrothed. Certain unities and differences between these several categories are discernible largely in the context of their rights in property of various kinds.

Many writers have referred to *mngwana*, *mwenyeji* and *mwananchi*, using the first in particular as referring to males, the patrician-merchants and members of the lineages that own the stone-built houses and other items of property of great value. But these terms refer as equally to women as to men. The situation is frequently misunderstood, the most common example being in the statement that stone-built houses of the patricians' towns are 'owned' by the patrician wives who live in them. A first-born patrician daughter is given rights of residence in a house at her wedding, and she and her husband (properly a paternal parallel cousin or paternal cross-cousin) live in the house by uxorilocal residence. The wife cannot dispose of the house, and since almost always it is owned by the patrilineal lineage under trust, no one may do so either unless the lineage dies out when the building's ownership passes to the Waqf Commissioners in Zanzibar City or Mombasa. We stress this, since so many accounts of Swahili gender have held that a stone house is 'owned' by the wife who resides in it, so that accounts claim the existence of patrician matrilineal descent groups, which do not in fact exist.[40]

Patrician women do however own rights in many kinds of property, both material and immaterial – it is only the patrician stone houses that are the exception. They have held rights in plantations, ships, and especially slaves; and they may become recognized as learned scholars and poets in their own right even if they may not enter mosques. Patrician women of both free and slave ancestry may also fully own houses which they purchase or build with profits from commercial activity such as the retail trade. Among groups such as the Hadimu of Zanzibar many non-stone and so impermanent houses and gardens are owned by female heads of small kin groups whose members work them. Also among the Hadimu every town has its ritual leaders, *mwyale* or *mzale*, most of whom are women.

An often mentioned factor is that of dependence/independence or autonomy of women. Caplan has contrasted patrician women who are, as a category, 'dependent' with non-patrician women who possess 'autonomy', the latter presumably being women since the abolition of slavery.[41] The contrast is crude: patrician women certainly have very great domestic autonomy (although greatly lessened by the loss of their slaves), and that has continued since the abolition of slavery; non-patrician women, and especially those of slave ancestry, have legal autonomy but usually little worth derived from economic or social freedom.

Incorporation

The skeleton of Swahili society has been the network of relations between these various corporate groups. The accepted criteria for a group's being corporate include its having a name, usually a single territory or residential space, an internal structure of authority, and a sense and expectation of perpetuity and unchangeability of members' descent over the generations. There are in the Swahili towns two main levels of corporate group. One is the town itself, each having its own name, sense of perpetuity, a bounded location, and in the past at least a formal internal government. The other level is that of one or another type of residential group, and here there is a crucial distinction between patricians' towns and commoners' towns.

Among the patricians, the corporate group is the patrilineal lineage that acts as a business house and owns its own stone built houses and treasury, *hazina*. Their wards are not corporate today, although by their names that refer to occupations and clan origins they might once have been so. Wards today are places, areas of occupation, but they act as little more than addresses for which their occupants have loyalty and pride based on long habitation by a lineage's forebears.[42] However in the commoners' towns the wards are indeed corporate groups, with its own names, territories, holders of internal authority, and each with their own 'purse', *mkoba*. The cognatic kin groups are not corporate – they cannot be so, by definition, since their memberships overlap and change in composition at every generation.[43]

All societies recognize at the local level both territorial bonds and kinship ties. Which they choose as a basis to make corporate groups is significant in several ways. The main one is that of recognition of rights in material property and their inheritance, and succession to rights in immaterial property. Tenure of some Swahili positions and offices is either by lineage succession or by forms of election in terms of personal prestige, wealth or personality. Examples of the first include the status of patrician merchant and head of a commercial business house, some of the town's offices, and membership of sharif lineages; examples of the latter include the membership of town councils and ritual officials in those commoners' towns where these are found, membership of most offices in the southern patricians' towns such as Bagamoyo and Pangani, and very often the offices associated with mosques and Islamic law throughout the coast, although these may be hereditary.

The systems of authority within the domestic group and family are central to operation of the formal system of local and genealogical ties that we have mentioned. They vary greatly between the main kinds of corporate groups. In general the senior person in a domestic group, whether lineage based or cognatic, has overall authority and control over its members. This is frequently more formal than real, much depending on the stage reached in a group's normal cycle of development. The person exercising authority in a patrician lineage is properly a senior brother but which of them does so is determined according to his potential for achievement considered by his predecessor and other kin of the superior generation.[44] The choice is typically made before the brothers reach adolescence and are married, as it is he who should marry his predecessor's first born daughter; the ideal marriage of a firstborn patrician daughter is with one of her paternal parallel cousins who is typically of the same lineage as herself.

Since the group in question is the lineage, and a lineage typically has several small segments within it, the successor lineage head is rarely the son of the previous head but is one of the latter's brothers: succession to lineage headship is by rotation between segments. If there should be only a single son in a generation, and in cases where there are several sons one of whom clearly has greater ability than the others, but no daughter of any reputation,[45] then the bride is typically another cousin who is adopted for the purpose by the head of the lineage. The adoption of children, especially when the lineage segments are jointly trying to select a future head, is frequent; marriages may even be planned between children not yet born. These stratagems are logical within a system of corporate patrilineal lineages.

Several points may be considered here: that authority depends on both ability but also on wealth or its expected inheritance; that the factors of personal ability and lineage continuity are equally important and that many stratagems may be used to ensure them; should the factor of outstanding ability be achievable only by the lineage's head being a woman, we know of two cases in recent history where this has been satisfied by the 'daughter' later becoming a _de facto_ head, even if not the _de jure_ one;[46] and that as might be expected there is an important distinction between authority within the lineage as a business house, and within the family based upon it as a domestic group, a male usually at least formally exercising the former and a female informally exercising the latter. There is finally the distinction between mercantile competence within the subclan and lineage and the group's continuity, perpetuation and moral purity, the former being the responsibility of the males and the latter that of the females.

Authority within Omani and Hadrami lineages would appear as in most ways similar,[47] with the difference that although their patrilineal lineages have, at least in the past, largely been engaged in commercial activities outside the long-distance ocean trade, the emphasis placed by the patricians on lineage and house purity, which affects their marriage strategies and the form of weddings, is clearly closely linked to their own mercantile role.

The locus of domestic authority in commoners' towns is dependent upon the great variation in local kin-based groups. The wide distribution of kin groups to take up dispersed plots of farming and residential land and a high divorce rate lead to the sharing of authority between men, who hold legal rights to property, and women, who hold authority in probably 50 per cent of families.[48] Although often formally declared that the 'side of the male' is stronger than the 'side of the female', in practice commoners' town women exercise much authority in domestic and kin group matters.

8

Governance

For much of Swahili history the most striking political figures were the kings (and occasionally queens), known generally as *mfalme* in the northern half of the coast and as *maliki* in the southern part. Their power and grandeur varied and were probably never as great as recent myths and local histories might claim. Despite many tales of vast Swahili empires, ruled from Pate, Kilwa and elsewhere, these rulers rarely if ever reigned over more than a single town. In general they headed, perhaps more in name than in everyday practice, local bureaucracies; they represented their own towns when dealing with others and with the successive colonial overlords whom they suffered for so much of their history; and they acted as sacred figures who represented the towns in dealing with spirits and other mystical powers. With them there have been various levels of town officials and of representative councils.

The political domain of Swahili society lay at the interface of the African and the Indian Ocean world. It is possible to approach the study of Swahili kings and their courts as parodies of the great medieval Islamic courts, who were infinitely richer and whose activities were luxurious and opulent, but such was the fragmented nature of Swahili society that political authority resided within each town or small group of towns. Thus, for example, when the Portuguese came to deal with the inhabitants of the Lamu archipelago, they had to deal with no less than five 'kings' (or in some cases queens), three of whom resided on Pate Island, little more than twelve miles in length and five miles wide. These Swahili courts could hardly be expected to measure up to the wealth of the Caliphate, or indeed to the wealth of other Islamic African kingdoms such as in Ethiopia or West Africa. Nonetheless they borrowed elements from the central Islamic world, in particular from Buyid, Fatimid and Mamluk court rituals.

These Swahili royal courts form a central part of the understanding of coastal society. While they used Islamic court ritual and procedures, these were superficial; Swahili kings were essentially African kings, and many of the underlying structures reflect African practice, recorded and well documented across the continent. Our account of kingship is based on early eyewitness descriptions, surviving monuments and royal regalia, as unfortunately there is no living tradition of kingship on the coast: the last indigenous kings died out in the early twentieth century during colonial expansion.[1]

The many Swahili chronicles form a much neglected source of information about kingship; indeed this is really what they are about, and contain little else of social or economic importance.[2] Modern historical accounts which have relied upon these chronicles and histories have done much to reconstruct dates, names and lineages. However the nature of the institution itself is a key factor in understanding the historical narrative; for example why descent passed in particular ways, the process of royal election and legitimization of new rulers or how new dynasties began. As earlier contact between the Swahili and colonial outsiders, such as the Omani Arabs, the Portuguese and the British, was normally conducted through these rulers, their accounts also deal in some detail about the local kings. The deep misconceptions that arose between the colonial rulers and the Swahili were in many cases due to a failure to understand the nature and authority of local systems of kingship, with the inevitable tragic consequences.

These royal courts formed one part of the governance of a community, and were by no means essential, as several Swahili towns did not have kings through much of their history, and others had long interregnums. When new rulers were required (when for example an old dynasty 'died out'), they were often obtained from outside the community or its patrician groups; members of sharif lineages or immigrants from Arabia or from elsewhere on the coast often became kings. The true economic and political power of these kings was often no more than that of the patrician merchants; their role was as the embodiment of the sacred and magical qualities of the town which were especially useful for its protection and for trade with non-Muslim African groups of the interior.

Town Government

As we have seen, towns were corporate units, each with its own form of internal government and administration *vis-à-vis* other towns and overall colonial and postcolonial rulers and agencies. No one town's pattern of administration has been the same as that of others. The local governments and their leaders have had many but basically the same functions: the variation is in the means by which they have been performed and in the identities of those selected by a town's inhabitants to do so. We may discern several governmental functions at the town level, essentially those to do with internal administration and settlement of disputes between the town's constituent groups, and those to do with representation of the town to external units and its relations with the colonial power ruling over it at a given period.

Historically, virtually every patricians' town has had what is often described as a 'Council of Elders', and this has most probably comprised the heads of the patrician lineage groups. Even when the town had a king, this council seems to have had particular importance, especially in relation to economic activity and in dealing with disputes over succession. In some towns, the influence of the patrician lineage heads was such that kings were not deemed necessary. This was the case for much of the history of Lamu, Siyu, Faza, Barawa, Merca and Mogadishu, but may well also have been so for many of the towns that are known only archaeologically and about which nothing survives of their governance. At many of these sites there is no trace of a royal palace or other indicators of kingship, even though most of the stone buildings survive. Republican government was probably wide-spread; this may explain the general lack of chronicles from many Swahili towns, which were by and large written to record and legitimize ruling dynasties.

The mechanisms of republican government are only known in detail from Lamu, but there are hints that this was a representative pattern. There is a tendency for all towns to have been divided into moieties, *mitaa*, and these had some political functions, as we have already seen. In Lamu the moieties are found in conjunction with slightly different groups that may be called demes, which provided the structure of town government. A deme[3] is known as *mkao*, 'a community of joint residence', and sometimes as *chama*, 'association': reference is thus to a group or category of people, and not, as with the term *mtaa*, to a residential area or space. The town's patricians were divided into the two demes known as Zena and Suudi, names still known and frequently referred to in everyday talk.

Each deme included members of the patrician subclans of the town, with its own sheikh. Details are few but it seems that the members of Zena and Suudi did not live each in one moiety or the other, which are territorial, but were dispersed throughout both of them – which means that all the members of a particular subclan did not necessarily live in the same ward. If all members of a deme lived in the same moiety then there would be no distinction between moiety and deme, yet the distinction is clearly made. The two leading patricians of the demes were known as Bwana Zena and Bwana Suudi, and they together chose a town leader, the *mwenye mui*, 'owner of the town', to act as head of the town's government for a four year period, the *mwenye mui* coming from Zena and Suudi in turn. These may have been the 'kings' of Lamu to whom the Portuguese documents refer.

The *mwenye mui* presided over the *yumbe* or 'government' for his period of office (there are indications that some such leaders held on to power for longer periods); the exact composition of the council is uncertain, but certainly the *mwenye mui* alternated between the two demes.[4] There was a council chamber, the *nyumba ya ezi*, 'house of power', whose location is still pointed out – it is in ruins but efforts are being made to restore it. The council itself was sometimes called *diwani*. The army of Lamu consisted of two regiments, under two amirs, again reflecting the didemic structure. This system came to an end with the formation by the British of a ruling council whose members were selected on ethnic grounds to represent the population.

While Lamu did not have kings, it did apparently have regalia items which along with ceremonies such as the New Year ritual emphasised the town's identity and sacred nature. The copper alloy *siwa*, or side-blown horn, now in Lamu Museum, and probably dating to the fifteenth or sixteenth century, is a survival of such items.[5] The right to have the *siwa* blown at marriages and circumcisions was strictly controlled by the patricians.

The important town of Pate also had a strong republican tradition, even though there is a chronicle which purports to recount the town's history from the arrival of the Nabahani rulers, in (1204) AH 600.[6] The Nabahani were an important tribe in Oman, who effectively ruled Oman until they were ousted by the Yarubi in 1624, an event that the *History of Pate* attributes to their settlement in Pate.[7] There are other glaring historical inaccuracies, such as the arrival of the Portuguese which is dated to the fifteenth century, as was the construction of Fort Jesus (in fact built in 1593).[8] The 'foundation' date of AH 600 is also very suspicious and is a date shared by two other towns, Vumba and Tumbatu; it must have some mythical basis but one that remains unresolved. There are several versions of the *History*, but all seem to derive from one written down during the reign of Fumo Madi, who died in 1807; all the modern versions can be traced back to Bwana Kitini, a prominent Nabahani living at the beginning of the twentieth century, who embellished and paraphrased the original, extending the text until 1908. While there are real problems in accepting the literal historicity of the *History*, there is material here which helps illuminate the governance of an important northern town over a considerable period of time.[9]

The *History of Pate* is largely a piece of Nabahani propaganda. The early rulers listed as Nabahani very likely came from other patrician groups and were perhaps elected. The first genuine 'Nabahani' ruler was probably Abubakar bin Muhammed, who married the daughter of the previous sultan, Ahmed bin Muhammed, and who ruled during the first part of the eighteenth century. From then onwards, the sultanate descended within the

Nabahani family, from father to son or between brothers, until the late nineteenth century; a Nabahani family council decided upon succession. However, there were other institutions in the town that seem to be a survival of an earlier system, and were in many ways similar to those found in Lamu. This included the *wakulu wa Pate* ('great men's council') and the *nyumba ya ufalume* ('house of the kingship'). The former comprised of 40 members,[10] and the latter, the ruler, a three-membered state council, and hereditary office bearers such as the wazir and amir. The Nabahanis came to use fairly brutal methods to achieve their political dominance including the massacre of the entire *wakulu wa Pate* by Sultan Fumomadi because, as the *History* put it, 'if you leave these people they will make trouble again directly they have gained strength'. By the nineteenth century the state came to be dominated by the Nabahanis, hiding the earlier influence of the patrician lineages.

By tracing the *isnads* (names) of the rulers mentioned in the *History of Pate*, the earlier pattern of succession can be reconstructed in some detail. There seem to be three dynastic lines, with considerable confusion between rival lineages as to succession; the three-membered state council may have been a relic of this earlier arrangement.[11] The *History* records complex politics, as for example when Mwana Darini, who was married to a deposed (and later executed by the Portuguese) Sultan Abubaker bin Fumo Omari, attempted to have the *siwa* blown at the circumcision of her son but was denied the right. According to the *History*, she then had another *siwa* made for the ceremony, displacing the original, thus conferring legitimacy onto her own family's descent. The surviving ivory *siwa* from Pate (now in the Lamu Museum) may be that which dates from this episode around 1690, or more likely, is an earlier *siwa*, dating to around the sixteenth century, and the account is pure historical invention. Another item of Pate royal regalia, the royal chair or throne survives in the Natal Museum in South Africa, having been seized by the British in 1890. Recently part of another *siwa*, probably one of the five seized by the Portuguese in 1683, has turned up in a museum collection in France.

The Nabahanis may have come to Pate several centuries before their accession as rulers, and came to be accepted as patricians. A possible date for their arrival is during the later fifteenth century; the *History* gives the founder of the Nabahani clan as Sulaiman bin Sulaiman bin Muzaffar, who may be the same as a prominent Nabahani who died around 1500. While in Oman they must have been Ibadi, and it is interesting that there is no trace of Ibadism in Pate, suggesting that they soon became assimilated as Sunni-Shafi'i. Their familial connections with Oman provided a commercial advantage during the turbulent period of Portuguese rule, and it was probably this that eventually allowed them to secure the throne at the very end of the period of Portuguese control. The Nabahani Sultans and their Swahili predecessors were first and foremost merchants who accumulated much wealth, in the form of ships, slaves and cattle, and at times maintained their own private army. There is very little evidence for elaborate court rituals or of particular sacredness associated with the royal personage or clan. For example when Fr Gaspar de S. Bernadino had an audience with the Sultan in 1606, he was seated on the ground, on costly carpets, robed in white, 'as in the Moorish fashion'. The Portuguese were given chairs and cushions to sit on.[12]

Pate, according to its *History*, came to dominate the coast during the fifteenth and sixteenth centuries, but for this there is no independent evidence. It may have been locally important; destroying and burning towns such as Shanga[13] and Manda and for a period controlling Lamu, Faza, Siyu and the towns at the mouth of the river Tana. The claims in the *History* that Pate went on to conquer Malindi, the Mrima coast, Kilwa and Kerimba would seem to have been fabricated and were certainly not noticed by the Portuguese. Their dominance of the coast was more commercial than political, and Pate seems to have been able to benefit from being outside the direct area of Portuguese control and traded with Sofala as well as its own hinterland.[14] This was certainly how the Portuguese saw the town when they tried unsuccessfully to set up a customs house there in 1633.

Neither Pate nor Lamu had 'kings' in the traditional sense and this seems to be the case for the Lamu archipelago in general, from the archaeological evidence. There is no clear evidence for royal palaces in the surviving architecture, although some houses are larger than others. Where we know that there were rulers, such as at Kilwa, the palace can be identified as the only building with its own private mosque, while the Friday mosque itself has its own enclosure for the ruler; none of these features are found on the northern coast. The absence of coinage (after the tenth century) may also be an indicator of the lack of royal authority. In the very early period it is possible that there were kings – the lion figurine from Shanga could have been a regalia item[15] – but of the nature of this kingship we know virtually nothing.

J. de V. Allen described these northern towns as operating an 'Arab-Wangwana mode of dominance', by which he meant that the patricians used their privileged access to Islam, through their purity and perceived Arabian origins, to establish their rank within the society.[16] Islam had central symbolic importance for the patricians, and this was expressed in the numerous Qur'an that they kept in their houses (often in the decorated *zidaka* niches), and the numerous mosques used by the patricians for their private use, which were generally fairly restrained in their decoration. Sharifs were welcomed, because of the *baraka* they carried that contributed to the community. While, as we have seen, Swahili society was deeply ranked, this ranking was not so evident among the patricians, who developed a strong aversion to any individual ruler who was ranked over them, and they certainly understood the ambivalent Islamic attitude towards authority. While Allen suggested that these ideas arrived in the early fifteenth century through Ibadi influence, the evidence from Shanga indicates that they were much older, possibly arriving in c.1050, when the central enclosure wall disappeared and houses, initially built of timber, can be traced directly through the archaeological record to the typically stone houses of the Swahili patricians, from around 1320.[17] The two large neighbourhood mosques at Shanga (dating to around 1300) provide evidence for loosening of the influence of Friday mosque which may have retained old fashioned notions of Islamic practice.

An important aspect of the government of most towns has been the participation of its client groups living elsewhere in the conurbation of which the town government is at the centre. This may be seen in many places, the best-documented being Mombasa. We know little of the centuries before the Portuguese, but after them a dual system was established that has lasted until the present. The two territorial halves or moieties were properly called Gavana and Haram el Khedima but appear to have had little significance, at least after the Portuguese occupation.[18] More important have been two clusters usually known in the literature as confederations, each of which comprises several patrilineal clans (in the literature here usually called *mataifa* or 'towns' or 'tribes'). As with all Swahili clans they and their internal subdivisions are linked not by common ancestry but rather by neighbourhood, intermarriage and incorporation of groups sharing commercial interests.

The Mombasa confederations are the Nine (Mataifa Tisa) and the Three (Mataifa Thelatha), the former, known as the waMvita (those of Mombasa) living in the northern part of the island, and the latter, known as waKilindini (those of the deep harbour) living in the southern part of the island and the immediate mainland. Each sub-group of the Nine and the Three has its own sheikh responsible for its internal affairs. Each confederation contains segments known as *mbari*, a word used for descent groups of all sizes and of both patrilineal and cognatic descent, the latter typically formed around a patrilineal core that today is of little functional importance. As elsewhere along the coast, the Twelve patrilineal clans were almost certainly in earlier centuries the main mercantile groups; as the intercontinental trade has faded so has the importance of their particular reckoning of descent.[19]

Each confederation has had and retains its own head, known as *tamim*, and its own court for settlement of internal disputes. Their histories of rise and fall in power and influence need not be recounted here: they are part of the long history of the rivalries and alliances of the Omani rulers of Zanzibar and the local Omani rulers of the Mazrui clans.

Each confederation also has close political, commercial and social links with the neighbouring groups collectively known as Mijikenda.[20] In the case of the Nine, the links are controlled by the various sheikhs of each clan; in that of the Three they are controlled by the single *tamim* of the confederation. This system is found elsewhere along the coast, forming the pattern of patron–client conurbations, with commercial and political functions. The patricians both controlled a wide network of trade; they also acquired labour and political support when needed. The clients entered into the profitable system of long-distance exchange and obtained protection from the urban centre to which they are attached. The whole has made Mombasa into a remarkably powerful centre, and of course also a desirable possession by the various Arab and European powers of the region who have competed for its control over many centuries.[21]

The Nine patron clans	*Mainland client groups*
Mvita	
Mtwapa	
Kilifi	Giryama
Jomvu & Malindi	Chonyi and Jibana
Pate	Kauma, Kambe, Ribe
Shaka	Rabai
Paza	
Katwa	
Bajun (recent addition)	

The Three patron clans

Kilindi ⎫	
Changamwe ⎬	Digo and Duruma
Tangana ⎭	

Mombasa used to have kings. There are vague accounts of an early 'Shirazi' dynasty, one of whose rulers was known as Shehe Mvita, or according to the *History of Mombasa*, Shehe Mahaham ibn Misham. The site of his tomb is still known and New Year ceremonies are still performed there. This dynasty seems to have died out some time in the sixteenth century. In 1592, the Portuguese imposed the king of Malindi, forming a condominium of the two towns; the king moved to Mombasa and was granted at first only the interior of the island, then the area of Kilindini in 1596, as well as a third of customs revenues.[22] The relationship between the imposed ruler and the Mombasa patricians was not particularly close, as is apparent by the events in the early seventeenth century. Relations between the king and Portuguese deteriorated, initially over the payment of rice tribute from Pemba (of which Mombasa had taken control) in 1610. The king fled to Kilifi, and used his mainland allies, whom the Portuguese called the Muzungulos,[23] most likely the Mijikenda, to raid Mombasa. There followed a period of Portuguese interventions including the baptism of Yusuf b. al Hasan, the heir to the throne, his marriage to a Portuguese noblewoman and coronation in Goa, and his return in 1626. In 1631, he reverted to Islam, and led the so-called Mombasa rising, in which the Captain and 250 others were killed and Fort Jesus taken. Crucially, his support for this rising came not from the Mombasa patricians (he could count on only ten Muslims during his initial assault on the Portuguese), but again from the Muzungulos, who burnt the town down, and left it empty and in ruins. The rising was short-lived and the Portuguese and patricians returned in 1632, but the sultanate was never properly re-established.[24] During the later Portuguese period, and then under the Mazrui and Busaidi, the relations between the two *matamim*, as the representatives of the Swahili patricians and the Liwali (or governor), a Zanzibari colonial appointment, have always been complex but need not be discussed here.[25]

Towns with Kings

Contemporary with these developing systems of town government on the northern coast, there is some evidence for kingship in the adjacent mainland towns. The best known surrounds a semi-mythical figure, Fumo Liongo, who probably lived in the late fifteenth century, as he is named in the *History of Pate* as a genuine historical ruler of the town of Ozi, in the Tana delta, which was attacked and defeated by Pate[26]. However, around the historical Liongo have developed numerous myths and legends, as well as a considerable quantity of poetry, much attributed to Liongo himself. He is often claimed as a 'culture hero' of the Swahili people living in the area vaguely known as 'Shungwaya'.[27]

Fumo Liongo[28] is said to have been born either in the town of Shanga on Pate island or more likely of Shaka (the site, known archaeologically as Ungwana) on the mainland north of the river Tana. He was a son of the ruler's sister – in some versions the son of a concubine – and so ineligible to succeed. In either case his status was ambiguous in the patrilineal system. He was driven out by the ruler's son, his successor, and captured by a hunting group on the mainland; he escaped and married a woman of a pastoralist group farther inland by whom he had a child. Thus he had everywhere an anomalous or ambiguous status: sister's son or concubine's son; a captive farmer and town dweller among nomadic hunters where he none the less became a famous hunter; a stranger among transhumant pastoralists who had there a child, who by rule of patrilineal descent was a member of the town of Shanga or Shaka. Finally he returned to Pate island, led the defence against invading Arabs and became a truly Swahili and African king.

This myth, here given in short outline only, has many variants and even more interpretations.[29] It states and resolves the basic paradoxes of Swahili history: the relationships between Africa (Swahili) and Asia (Arabs), between urban and rural, settled farmers and urban merchants on one hand and hunters and pastoralists who provided ivory and other trade goods on the other, and in social organization the networks linking urban mercantile Swahili patrons and their mainland clients of different economies, languages, cultures and religions. As king, Fumo Liongo is shown at the hub of trading networks, as were all other Swahili rulers.

The historical Fumo Liongo belonged to the same clan as the rulers of Malindi, the Bauri, who according to an early Portuguese account claimed to have descended from the kings of Kitau, one of the Tana delta sites.[30] The Portuguese attacked another of the Tana delta sites, Hoja (probably meaning the town of Ozi) in 1507, at the behest of the Malindi king, and this might have been because it had been taken a short while earlier by Pate, as is suggested in the *History of Pate*; it is more likely that these Tana delta sites formed part of the Malindi conurbation, which had been annexed by Pate.

The king of Malindi, while anonymous, was described in some detail by the early Portuguese explorers as lavishly dressed with turban and robe of damask. He was shaded by a canopy of satin, and was accompanied by players on two siwas and many oboes.[31] Another feature of the Malindi polity was their alliances with the hinterland groups such as the Mosseque-jos (?the modern Segeju), who could be relied upon to help defend the town, and with whom cloth and other commodities were exchanged.

We can examine the role of kings as the hub of these networks of relationships in the case of the diwans of Vumba,[32] as the office survived into the late nineteenth century. Along the southern Kenyan coast there are a number of settlements, which according to tradition numbered eight. They were linked together into a single polity, sharing a Shirazi tradition of origin and ruled by a single king. The remains of these sites, including a place known as Shirazi and another known as Munge, comprise fifteenth-century mosques and tombs but no stone houses: today the settlements could be described as commoners' towns. At the south end of this polity, the town of Vumba was developing in prosperity, and in building its alliances with mainland non-Muslims including the Segeju and the Digo, with whom its members had *watani* relationships. In the early seventeenth century, the Vumba defeated the Shirazi, and imposed historically significant surrender terms, including that they were forbidden for ever to wear either sandals or turbans, to use umbrellas, to allow their women to veil their faces, to have solid wooden doors or to possess any drum other than a very

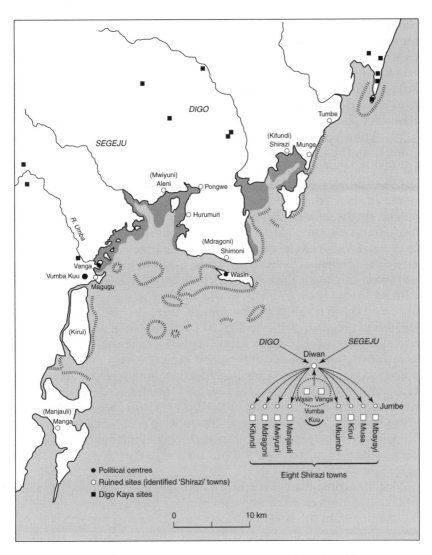

Map 8.1   *The Vumba polity on the southern Kenyan and northern Tanzanian coast*
(after Prins 1967, p. 95, with modifications).

small hand drum. These items were the essential components of high rank, that used dress and regalia to signify its status.

The Vumba took over these symbols of power and during the eighteenth and nineteenth centuries were able to operate an independent polity along the southern Kenyan coast. The patricians lived within a ranked society, based upon the ability to proceed with a series of increasingly expensive ceremonies with large feasts, from circumcision, to marriage to a virgin of the correct lineage, to another feast and becoming a *mtenzi*. The ruler, the diwan, had to be chosen from the ba-Alawi, a descent group of sharifs (who may have been the earlier rulers of Tumbatu), generally the son or close relative of the previous diwan and with the status of *mtenzi*. The election of the diwan involved yet another feast and present giving among the patricians of Vumba; he was then allowed to wear wooden sandals and a silver chain around his knee. His enthronement of the diwan then took place in the forest at Vumba Kuu (the original town had been abandoned) near the grave of the founder. His feet were washed, he was given a turban, and he announces his chosen throne-name, at which point he was carried on a bedstead, shaded by an umbrella, to where a large feast was prepared and to which the Digo and Segeju, *watani* partners, were also present and swore to defend him; in return they were given large quantities of cloth. Presents were also given to the Shirazi towns, as well as the tribes of Mombasa. There then followed music and dancing using a *siwa*[33] and large drums (which still survive) and cymbals. Thereafter the life of the diwan was accompanied by rituals; he was always accompanied by slaves carrying an umbrella, seated on a chair and proceeded by a *siwa*, but probably rarely left his house.[34] At one point, rival diwans were established in Wasin and Vanga, but by the end of the nineteenth century the diwanate fell into abeyance because nobody could afford any longer the gift giving and feasting that the elections entailed.

Along the Mrima coast of northern Tanzania similar small polities existed until the late nineteenth century, with similar systems of patrician ranking and kingship.[35] In this area, the rulers were known as *jumbe, shomvi* or *diwani*, and were at the head of a highly ranked society, in which the patricians held a bewildering number of public offices, including *waziri* (chief minister), *amiri* (head of the army), *mwenye mkuu* (chief elder), *shaha* (the *jumbe*'s 'double'), *akida* (war leader), *tajiri* (treasurer), *makata* (judge) and *mwinyi mtwana* (controller of slaves).[36] Elevation to these offices involved public feasting and were reserved for individuals of particular rank. The election of the *jumbe* was particularly elaborate, with gift giving and pilgrimages to the tombs of former *jumbes*, the placement of turbans and the processions of beds around the village. Regalia items included the *ngoma kuu* (lit. great drum), while only the *jumbe* could use the state umbrella and wear wooden shoes. Funerals of these rulers were also elaborate, with long periods of mourning, prohibitions on wearing hats or even shaving. The tombs of the Shomwi of Kunduchi are a very good example of the elaborate marking of graves, with several pillar tombs, decorated with Chinese blue on white plates and surmounted by what appear to be turbans, as well as numerous huts and enclosures. Inscriptions on these tombs date this use of this royal cemetery from 1670 to 1848, giving an indication of the span of this dynasty.[37] It is probably incorrect to class these *jumbes* as kings, although this is how the Portuguese refer to them, but as local rulers, surrounded by great ceremony, of what were little more than a few villages.

There were also diwanis on Pemba island, but much less is known about them. Pemba, like the adjacent mainland, seem to have operated a ranked system, with leaders, known as *masheha*, in each town or district, with a single paramount chief or diwan. There is some evidence that the ruling dynasty changed around 1750, possibly to sharifs from Wasin island, and the names of the last diwans are known as they were involved in the struggles first against the Portuguese and then between the Mazrui and Busaidi Arabs for control of Pemba.[38] Traditions provide information on an earlier Swahili ruler, Muhammed bin Abdulrahman, who took the nickname Mkame Mdume; apparently he was living during the late fifteenth century and claimed Shirazi as well as Segeju and waDiba origins. The site of Pujini is normally attributed to him, and recent archaeological research has shown this to be a very rare example of a royal fortress. He is still remembered in vivid terms on Pemba as a ruler adept in magic and of exceptional strength and cruelty, and at Pujini have been found not only shrines (one of which was decorated with a *siwa*) but also buried *fingo* pots, thought to contain magic. His son was Haruni, whose pillar tomb still survives at Chwaka, decorated with a *siwa* made of plaster stucco on one wall. While the traditions associated with the legendary Mkame Mdume have been greatly embellished, they provide evidence for a highly ranked society in which the ruler was able to do whatever he liked as a sign of his sacred power, backed up largely by magic rather than military force.

On Zanzibar, the ruler of the Hadimu was known as the *mwenye mkuu* in the nineteenth century; a term generally used as a subsidiary title on the mainland, and possibly adopted on Zanzibar after the arrival of Busaidis, the last *mfalme* being Hasan who died around 1845.[39] The dynasty seems to have come from the mainland; the first real evidence for a ruler on Zanzibar comes from the Portuguese, who identified a queen of Zanzibar and her son, the king of Otondo (Utondwe, on the mainland) in 1653. Later another queen of Zanzibar, known as Fatima (recorded in a Portuguese source of 1699) married the king of Otondo, presumably a cousin. Barely the names of the ruler survive through the eighteenth and early nineteenth centuries, living in various locations, including Zanzibar city, Bweni and Ozi island.

The last important ruler was Muhammed bin Ahmed, the son (or possibly brother) of the last *mfalme* Hasan who had married the queen of Tumbatu.[40] The Busaidis accepted the continuation of traditional leadership of the Hadimu, and the *mwenye mkuu* was allowed to build a palace around 1845 in the centre of the island at Dunga, as well as collect a poll tax on his subjects, half of which he transmitted the Sultan.

The Palace at Dunga survives largely intact and while built in an Arab style, is laid out in a traditional manner, with a central audience chamber with a dais at one end for the royal chair, reached by an offset step. To the right there was a similar chamber, with a dais, and presumably reserved for the senior wife. The kitchen area lay on the wife's side, while on the king's side there was a separate room with windows and niches, that may have been intended as a council chamber. At the back of the palace there was a large raised *baraza*, at which the ruler greeted his subjects. There was a separate room that may well have been used to store the carved wooden drums and *siwas* (which survive today in the Zanzibar Museum). This seems to have been very much a ceremonial palace as nearby there are the remains of another group of buildings, including a mosque and domestic accommodation. In an echo of Mkame Mdume, he was thought to be cruel, according to traditions killing and walling up slaves inside his new palace.

Muhammed bin Ahmed ruled from around 1845 to 1865, and like other rulers was surrounded by ceremony; he could only be approached on knees and with uncovered heads, and nobody was allowed to be higher than him whenever he went out. He was credited with supernatural powers and when at one point was imprisoned by the Sultan, no rains fell until he was allowed to return to Dunga. He operated a well-organized system of government, in which the island was divided into a number of *shehia*, each headed by a *sheha* or headman whom he appointed. In most areas the *masheha* were hereditary, but the *mwenye mkuu* often appointed his own nominees. A *sheha* was given a special turban and was expected to provide a large feast on his appointment; he was able to claim part of inheritances in his *shehia*. At Muhammed's death his young son, Ahmed, became *mwenye mkuu*; he died of smallpox in 1873 and the dynasty died out, the appointment of *masheha* passing to the Zanzibar government.[41]

In addition to the *masheha*, responsible for the relations between the town and higher government authority,[42] each town had its own council of representatives of the constituent wards, known as the *Watu Wanne*, 'Four Men', or merely *Wazee*, 'elders', chosen from the major sub-groups of the town. They met regularly and in the past possessed a town 'purse', *mkoba*, made up of moneys given by tenants living in townlands and related to particular wards whose elders, *wakubwa wa mtaa*, 'big men of the ward', gave them permission to take up land. Each ward had its own head, the *mkubwa* or 'big man' who attended the meetings of the council of the town

Plate 8.1   *The Palace at Dunga (Zanzibar island), showing the raised dais for the 'throne' of the mwenye mkuu, with the step set off the main axis and a second lower dais for the senior royal wife. The palace was built in the 1850s, using the styles of Arab and Indian influenced architecture, but retaining the spatial planning of a traditional Swahili royal palace. The building has been recently conserved by the Zanzibar Museum and Archives (photo Mark Horton).*

if the ward's interests were being discussed and also various mosque officials whose power depended mainly on the size and wealth of the town itself and its mosque. There was also a ritual expert, known as *mvyale, mzale* or similar terms, whose role was to introduce tenants to the local spirits of the town; tenants paid money known as *ubani*, 'incense', which should go to appease the spirits so that they accepted new tenants peaceably. This official was usually a woman, succeeding an earlier woman of her kinship group. The authority of these officials from the town itself has long waned, and they have typically lost financial power with the abolition of town 'purses'. However, their identities are usually still known and they play organizational roles at the various Islamic festivals held during the year; the *wavyale* were still active in the late 1950s.

Early Towns and their Rulers

There is a strong supposition that some elements at least of this highly ranked system of government found on the Mrima coast and adjacent islands has its origin in a much earlier system of kingship. When Ibn Battuta visited Mogadishu in 1331, he observed very similar court procedures to those for example of the Vumba diwans.[43] There were numerous ranks of wazirs, amirs and court officials. The Sheikh prayed in his own enclosure, known as a *maqsura*, inside the Friday mosque. After Friday prayers, the Sheikh went in procession with his officials, wearing sandals, with a silk canopy over his head, wearing lavish clothes and preceded by drums and musical instruments, including most probably *siwa* and *nzumari* (translated as oboe). Ibn Battuta also describes an audience hall, the destination for this procession, as well as the place for legal proceedings on the following day, in which the Sheikh did not normally take part.

Kilwa is the best known of the early polities of the coast, not least because of the survival of at least three versions of its *History*, and because the site has been extensively excavated by Neville Chittick.[44] By the fifteenth century it had a similar system of governance, and the *History* mentions court officials such as wazirs and amirs, as existed at Mogadishu during the fourteenth century. However in 1331 Ibn Battuta did not describe endless court processions but a more humble kingship, at which he almost casually met the Sultan in the street coming back from prayers, and at which the Sultan freely gave away his clothes to a passing beggar.

This sultan was Hasan ibn Sulaiman and the archaeological evidence indicates that he was ruling during a period of great prosperity; he is the only ruler known to have minted gold coins and was the fourth ruler and the grandson of the founder of a new dynasty of southern Arabian sharifs, the Mahdali, who took over the sultanate in the late thirteenth century. During his reign, or that of his grandfather, there was a period of substantial building, including the extension to the Friday mosque and the complex to the east of the town known as Husuni Kubwa. The extension to the mosque (which actually fell down during his reign, to be rebuilt only in the fifteenth century) included a domed enclosed area, presumably a *maqsura* as Ibn Battuta described at Mogadishu, but which was also mentioned in the *History of Kilwa* as the place where the Sultan prayed and which Chittick identified as part of the original extension to the mosque.

Husuni Kubwa is an extraordinary structure, conceived as a huge royal palace, and including an octagonal water basin in one of its four inner courtyards. Attached to the palace is another courtyard with a series of rooms, store rooms with apartments above surmounted by conical domes (of a type otherwise found at the Fakhr ad-Din mosque in Mogadishu), which may have been intended for visiting merchants, who presumably were 'sponsored' in the traditional manner, and thus indicating an attempt to monopolize foreign trade by the Sultan. Attached to the palace there is another house that may have been intended for a royal official such as a *wazir* or *qadi*.[45] The palace was not completed and only partly occupied for a short period at the beginning of the fourteenth century. Both Ibn Battuta and the *History of Kilwa* are silent on this building, and we can only speculate that it represented an investment in royal power and mercantile activity that was resented by the Kilwa patricians and was abandoned half finished during the lifetime of Hasan bin Sulaiman. Another candidate for a royal palace was excavated in the centre of the town and known as the 'House of the Mosque', which included vaulted rooms and an integral small mosque dating to the fourteenth century; this may well have replaced Husuni Kubwa.

The period prior to the accession of the Mahdali dynasty around 1280 remains difficult to reconstruct on the basis of the surviving historical and numismatic evidence. The two longest accounts, recorded by De Barros and the Arabic *History*, cannot be easily reconciled, especially for a large group of rulers (generally numbered 9–17) which are only found in the Portuguese version. The discussion has been further confused by the coins found at Kilwa and whether they can be identified with named rulers. Those named coins issued by the Mahdali dynasty can be identified readily with historical records. However three issues found at Kilwa, of Ali bi al-Hasan, Daud bin al-Hasan and Umar b. Ali, have been claimed as issues of the earlier 'Shirazi' dynasty, even though their names cannot be found in either version of the Kilwa histories.[46] We can now identify, as a result of the coins discovered at Mtambwe Mkuu, at least nine names who were minting coins from a dynasty connected with Ali bin al-Hasan and dating from around 1000, but not a single one of these names occurs in any versions of the Kilwa histories.

The origins of the Shirazi traditions are most likely contemporary with the early coin-producing dynasties of the southern coast, a point that we have argued in chapter 3. But whoever the early Shirazi rulers of Kilwa were (and they may not have even existed) they were omitted from the Kilwa histories. In fact, in both versions, the Shirazi myth leads directly onto the non-coin-producing dynasty of Ali bin al-Husain, who must have been living in the mid-twelfth century. While coins are common at Kilwa, none of this dynasty apparently minted coins for a period between approximately 1140 and 1280, but simply reused earlier coins which became increasingly worn down. This reuse of coins explains the otherwise problematical occurrence of copper coins throughout the Kilwa stratigraphy. One possible explanation why the Kilwa sultans stopped minting coins is that the new dynasty was Ibadi, a suggestion that that we have already made in chapter 3, and reluctant to mint coins for theological reasons. The takeover by the Sunni Mahdali dynasty around 1280 was also marked by a resumption of coin production, using the earlier coins as the model for their new issues.[47]

The Mahdali dynasty survived at Kilwa until the sixteenth century, although there is much confusion during the fifteenth century within the ruling house, especially in the period around 1430 when Muhammed bin Sulaiman, surnamed al-Adil, becomes Sultan. It is during this period that we see the numerous patrician office holders, such as wazirs and amirs, to emerge to challenge the authority of the Sultan. The Adil branch rebuilt the Friday mosque which had collapsed (there is archaeological evidence to support this). Part of the confusion may be reflected in the introduction of court ceremonial from Malindi, and the Shi'ite influences (and even the Shirazi traditions themselves) found in the Arabic *History* may have been reintroduced at this much later date.

Another town for which there is some evidence is Tumbatu, which was abandoned in *c.*1350 leaving a very poor historical record,[48] but where a ruling dynasty survived into the nineteenth century in the small town of Gomani in the northern part of the island. The early rulers of Tumbatu seem to have been a group of Yemeni sayyids, the Awali/Ahdali,[49] and who are also linked with Barawa, Pate and Vumba. The archaeological evidence from Tumbatu, a town abandoned in the fourteenth century, includes a building specifically associated with the Ahdali.[50] This large house (known locally as the ruler's palace) began as a modest mud and stone house on the extreme edge of the town. Over several phases (approximately 1250–1300) it grew into a large complex, with additional courtyards, and a separate house added to one side. In the final phase, about 1300, what can be interpreted as a council chamber was added. This has three doorways, one from the main 'palace', one from the separate house (reserved for the *qadi*?) and one from the outside; this later was reached via a wide flight of steps. Inside, the room was divided two-thirds down its length, providing a reserved area at one end. One interpretation is that the Ahdali sharifs were at first marginalized within the community – as happened in the late nineteenth century with the arrival of Comorian sharifs in Lamu – but were able to use their *baraka* to move over time into positions of influence, eventually

Plate 8.2 *A large complex of stone buildings on Tumbatu island, excavated in 1991, which may be the remains on a fourteenth-century royal palace. The rectangular room in the centre may be a council chamber, accessible from the outside, from within the palace and from an ancillary house, possibly that of the Qadi.*

becoming sultans for a brief period of time. They may even have minted coins (like the Mahdalis at Kilwa), as large numbers have been found on the site, but all are illegible.

One striking feature of Swahili history is the number of queens mentioned. The term used is *malkia*, derived from *maliki* (lit. rule or power) and normally translated as 'queen'. Twenty-five queens are mentioned by various sources[51] but most are little more than names and in most cases with only an approximate indication of the centuries in which they lived. Some may be mythical 'mother founders' of towns in the distant past, some may have been regents or widows of kings, while others may have been, using English terminology, 'queen mothers' rather than queens.[52] But it is also probable that there were genuine regnant queens following the traditional rule of marrying cousins. It is possible, as in the case of the headship of patrician lineages, a daughter may occasionally be recognized as effective head over incompetent brothers.[53]

The Origins of Swahili Kingship

Ethnographically, coastal East Africa differs from many other areas of the continent by the absence of highly developed systems of kingship – as for example can be found in southern Africa, the Great Lakes region or Ethiopia. In southern Africa in particular there has been much archaeological research into the development of sacred kingship and associated state centres such as Mapungubwe and Great Zimbabwe.[54] The evidence from Swahili history suggests that similar kingship systems may have existed on the coast, and were then given an Islamic interpretation.

The fullest description of the pre-Islamic coastal peoples is contained in al-Mas'udi's eyewitness account,[55] and this has been much used by historians, but there are specific difficulties in its interpretation. He describes the capital of the Zanj (or *dar mamlaka*, which has more of a meaning of a 'state centre') as lying far to the south on the Sofala coast, probably in the area of Mozambique. The Zanj he describes have armies apparently on mounted cattle, and were cannibals who filed their teeth – the practice of teeth filing is found nowadays widely in South-East Africa, especially in the Makonde, Yao and Luvale areas. In these descriptions of indigenous practices it may well be that he is not referring to the Swahili coast proper, but the area at the far southern end.

He includes two words in the local language,[56] which he provides a translation – *waflîmî* 'which signifies son of the Great Lord' and *mkulu njulu* 'which has the meaning of Great Lord'. The latter word can be recognized as the southern Bantu word *unkulu-nkulu*, which has precisely the same meaning nowadays, but *waflîmî* has presented more problems, with some comparing it to *mfalme* (pl. *wafalme*), meaning king; al-Mas'udi confused the single and plural forms of the word. J. de V. Allen[57] has suggested alternatively that it relates to the Cushitic term for the sky god, *wag/waga*, and the eastern Cushitic *ilman*, with the meaning of son, thus conveying the same meaning as provided by al-Mas'udi.

Al-Mas'udi recorded that a Zanj king could forfeit his position as son of the *mkulu njulu* (thus *unkulu-nkulu*) if he were tyrannical or acted incorrectly; he was killed and the succession excluded from his family. Important figures in this society were the travelling holy men (*zihad*) who expressed themselves with eloquence in their own language. On occasions one of these holy men

> addressed a large crowd of them exhorting them to draw near to God and render him obedience, frightening them with his punishment and authority, recalling them to the example of their former kings and ancestors. They have no revealed law to turn to but the customs of their kings.

Another tenth-century geographer, Abu Zaid al-Hasan, gives a similar account:

> Religious discourse is engaged in front of the people. One finds at each nation sorcerers of the people in that language. In the country there are men devoted

to religious life who are covered in leopard skins or monkey skins. They carry a stick in their hand and come towards the houses. The inhabitants are also seduced; the devout sometimes stay all day until evening on their knees occupied by their preacher and recalling the memory of God (whom they exult). He showed them the fate which those of their nation would experience when they died.[58]

Al-Idrisi refers, in the twelfth century, to the sorcerers, or more properly doctors, in Mulanda (? Malindi) by their still used Swahili term *mganga*, while Bazawa (? Barawa) was

the last in the land of the infidels, who have no religious creed, but take standing stones, anoint them with fish oil and bow down before them. Their worship and their depraved beliefs consist of this and similar absurdities but they are steadfast in them.[59]

A number of observations can be made from these descriptions. The first is the reference to former kings and ancestors, suggesting that ancestor cults were important. The anointing of standing stones with fish oil may not be part of some Cushitic ritual, as some have argued, but part of the control of ancestors – the standing stones marking the graves of the ancestors. There were ritual specialists, who preached and wore leopard skins, who were distinct from kings, – and indeed partly regulated their activities. In modern ethnography, we would recognize these as spirit mediums, who could assume considerable authority and provided a threat to the authority of the sacred king himself. They were of particular importance in southern Africa during the nineteenth century, when they even assume their own territories, but in the earlier period did not have such territories, but were itinerant, just as the sources imply. At a more general level, these descriptions fit well with practices associated with Bantu groups in eastern and southern Africa.

Along the Islamized coast, elements of earlier practices seem to have survived for two reasons. Because the Swahili towns were militarily weak, they needed their hinterland clients for their protection, and kingship was a method to bind these groups into the coastal polities without having to convert them to Islam. Thus elaborate rituals, social ranking and the importance of ancestors are found in those areas where the hinterland was the most dangerous – from the Tana delta southwards along the Mrima coast. Here governance looks more African in character, even though it was translated into Islamic practice and terminology, and the rulers were often of sharifian origin. These rituals and ceremonies signified sacred qualities in the ruler, who controlled both Muslims and non-Muslims within the kingdom. On the island locations – such as the Kilwa and Lamu archipelagoes, Mombasa, Zanzibar, Pemba and on the Benadir coast – traditions of kingship are much less strong, and were often more 'Islamic' in their nature, with in some cases no kings at all.

But the hinterland groups were also partners in the trading system, in which the goods from the coast were exchanged for items such as ivory, and coastal kingships were central for the maintenance of the security in this trade. Those towns without elaborate kingships were at a particular disadvantage, although they tried to use their access to Islamic knowledge as an alternative strategy for their trade in the hinterland. It is likely that most of their commercial dealings were with other Swahili towns, or with much more distant areas such as the Sofala coast.

Historical processes can be observed which have rather confused this general pattern. Most obviously, the intervention of the Portuguese into Swahili affairs led to new alliances at Mombasa with the Mijikenda, or in the case of Pate and Siyu with the Katwa of the mainland, and with this the strengthening of local kings and sultans, who may have taken on a dual nature of Islamic patricians at home and sacred rulers when on the mainland. Fifteenth-century Kilwa may have undergone a similar transformation, possibly because of changes in the ethnic structure of its hinterland. The cases of Zanzibar and Pemba are of some interest, as here mainland kingships seem to have spread onto the islands as late as the fifteenth centuries, possibly displacing the earlier town governments, with possibly nominal sharifian rulers at their head, as can be inferred from Tumbatu island.

The gap in time between the accounts of al-Mas'udi and Idrisi, and those of Ibn Battuta and the Portuguese is not so long to rule out the survival of elements of traditional kingship in those areas where it was beneficial in economic and military terms – especially around Malindi and to the south – but it is also clear that from the sixteenth century, possibly in response to external colonial pressures, there was a revival in these traditional systems of kingship, and it would be unwise to imply this as universal in earlier centuries.

9

Knowledge, Purity and Power

For many centuries the Swahili patricians controlled the international trade. They lacked the means to exercise overt political power but maintained control through their carefully defined and sanctioned religious and cultural hegemony: their moral superiority concealed their underlying economic power. This was threatened by the establishment of the Zanzibar Sultanate, against which they fought tenaciously, not militarily but by using their ethnicity and 'civilization'. Thus they were able to retain their cultural hegemony on the East African coast despite the loss of their former economic and political position. This does not mean that they thereby have been popular – the memory of Swahili slavery remains too vivid, and their frequent disapproval of policies of the newly independent countries leads to resentment by others; but their civilization and its skills remain respected and even feared. In recent years, their cultural hegemony has not been enough to maintain their overall superiority and it has been fading throughout the twentieth century.

The main cultural factor for defining their identity is generally accepted to be adherence to Islam. Swahili Islam, different in subtle ways from the many forms of the faith in other parts of the world, has varied over the centuries and along the coast in details of belief, practice and organization. The last 150 years or so have been a time of radical organizational changes linked to continual pressures both to introduce new religious elements from elsewhere in Islam and also to counter them by local religious scholars and leaders.

Swahili 'civilization', *ustaarabu* ('the possession of long residence in a single place') and 'urbanity', *utamaduni*, two essentially moral qualities, have provided the basis for their society and have marked it off from others of eastern Africa. Their opposite, *ushenzi*, 'barbarism', is a quality against which civilization and urbanity can be defined and measured. The three terms refer basically to aspects of the presence or the absence of Islam at the heart of Swahili religion that is largely concerned with the possession and exercise of knowledge and power under God.

Plate 9.1   *An incense burner on the tomb reputed to be that of Sh. Fakihi Mansuru, dated to AH 1094 (1682–3) at Takwa, on Manda island. This tomb remains an important place of pilgrimage (both for Muslims and non-Muslims) from Shela and the mainland and is visited biannually to pray for rain (photo Mark Horton).*

The Anatomy of Swahili Religion

'Swahili religion', as a single body of beliefs and practices, includes not only 'orthodox' Islamic beliefs and rites but also many often deemed to be marginal to it.[1] The Swahili distinguish the former of these as *dini* (usually translated as 'religion') and the latter as *mila* (usually translated as 'custom').

The essential distinction is that *dini* comprises matters discussed in the Qu'ran, the Hadith of the Prophet and the writings of learned Islamic scholars, many of whom have been Swahili themselves, and that its message is written in Arabic, the sacred language of Islam. *Mila* is concerned mainly with ties to the many forms of local spirits. Some writers have separated *dini* and *mila* to posit a cultural boundary between orthodox and less orthodox and between Asian and African.[2] It is at times held that the elements of *mila* to have 'African' origins were linked to female slaves and to free women who had been taught by slaves in childhood; this hypothesis is doubtful.

The *dini* has always been based upon worship in the mosques. As we have mentioned earlier, the larger patricians' towns have had several mosques, one being the Friday mosque and other lesser ones built by and mainly attended by patricians. Commoners' towns generally have had only a single Friday mosque, although there are exceptions. By the middle of the nineteenth century each patrician subclan had come to have its own forms of sermons, *maulidi*, and other rites, and emphasis was given not only to the teachings of the Prophet but also to the acts of their own subclan forebears.[3] They have always been highly exclusive, as have been their weddings, funerals and other rites; however, Friday attendance at a town's congregational mosque and the various annual New Year rites in which all groups of the town, free and slave, have participated to demonstrate their single identity and unity, have involved them as joint members of an entire town. The exclusivity persists although the New Year rites are rarely observed today.

Divine Knowledge

The beliefs and practices of Swahili religion refer to power and the knowledge that Swahili maintain must stand behind it. Power over others can only be bestowed by God; without that bestowal, which includes knowledge, power is illegitimate. Mere belief in God is not enough to define one as a proper Muslim: one must also have a degree of knowledge about God's works and laws. That knowledge may be – indeed should be – the means to acquire wealth, moral status, authority and power. Knowledge (the usual translation of the word *elimu*) is of two kinds. One is that of the world, *dunia*, gained mainly by study of cosmology and astrology, the interpretation of divine signs and the use of medicines, spells and oblations which are often put together as 'magic'.[4] The other is that gained by theological and sacred learning based upon the Qu'ran, and which may also be directly given by God through revelation. Both forms contain good and danger: it is good for the living to learn of the world and make proper use of it, but to attempt to equal God in knowledge is hubris and leads to damnation, as it did to Iblis or Satan.

Learning in local Islamic law is considered by Swahili patricians to provide acceptable knowledge, although only with explicit approval of local judges and mosque leaders.[5] Each town has its own body of Muslim officials, from the imam of its congregational mosque and the town's judge downward. These form an elite on grounds both of Muslim knowledge and also of subclan descent and standing. They may be referred to as *waongozi*, 'people guided by God', *watukufu*, 'exalted ones', and other terms. They have been remembered as ancestors and even as saints, and until the reforms of the late nineteenth century their names were mentioned in prayers and sermons perhaps as often as that of the Prophet, a sign of what the reformers considered lack of orthodoxy. Many have been given the power of intercession with God for forgiveness of sin, and they may even acquire something of the Prophet's quality of *baraka*, 'the power of blessing'.

The work of East African Muslim scholars has been important in the history of local society.[6] Many have been Hadrami and Omani immigrants and it is likely that their work has been recorded in writing more than that of local thinkers, especially in the nineteenth and twentieth centuries, as many were linked to the Zanzibar Sultanate and were given more recognition than local figures. The former generally supported the power of Zanzibar and weakened the traditional authority of local scholars, many of whom were devoted to the retention of traditional Swahili culture. There was also, as elsewhere, the importance of reformers' coming from outside the society.

Knowledge is concerned not only with the essence of Divinity and humanity, but with the occasions and methods by which God and spirits affect and influence living people. It is a matter of pragmatics as much as of theology, and knowledge of the world includes skills of all kinds. To know how to build a dhow that will sail well is to understand how God has ordered kinds of wood and rope, the winds, waves, depths of the sea and the directions shown by the compass.[7] For patricians, knowledge includes the skills needed to practice mercantile exchange, to overcome envy and intrigue, to perceive the tricks of one's competitors.

In Swahili society the roles of men are relatively clearly defined whereas those of women are not, being ambiguous and less certain as to role. Almost all men seek knowledge of the actions of God, everlasting, ubiquitous, never totally comprehensible or foreseeable, and limited in neither time nor space. Many women tend in addition to seek that of the actions of spirits, like themselves ambiguous and uncertain, and although dangerous, permitted by God and immediate in both time and space. This mirrors a main distinction between the roles of men and women; and in the case of women of slave ancestry, whose lives generally remain those of poverty and uncertainty, it is the immediate that matters.

Purity

Swahili thought holds that civilization is based upon knowledge in thought and purity in behaviour. Knowledge requires scholarship and intellectual work, and purity requires the work needed to make it manifest. Knowledge is particularly linked to men and purity to women, and much of the traditional qualities expected of each reflect this sharing of human responsibility to God. It is still generally considered to be more difficult for patricians to carry out their work than it used to be for slaves, but a slave who acquired deep knowledge, and even a concubine who could acquire a degree of purity and learning, would often be given the honorary status of 'patrician' and much of the respect that went with it.

Purity, *usafi*, is a quality held by women, and certainly in the past by free women. It, or more precisely its potentiality, is bestowed by God, but was rarely held by slave women who were essentially impure. Potential or innate purity is made overt in free women at marriage, but to differing degrees. The most pure is typically a firstborn patrician daughter, and only if she and also her house (residential rights in which are given to her by her father at her marriage) both undergo rites of cleansing and she is shown to be a virgin at her wedding. She should then properly live a life of seclusion, purity and piety, in which her own understanding of God and the Prophet are central. Her life will endow her husband with *heshima*, reputation. Firstborn patrician daughters should marry their father's brother's sons, both members of the same lineage, which is also thereby given mercantile probity and credit-worthiness. A bride's purity is linked to and essentially part of the quality of her 'beauty', *uzuri* (which also means goodness), which is ritually made manifest during her pre-bridal preparation. Men are given *heshima* by their female kin, as wives, so that women give men the main moral quality of being trustworthy merchants and thus form both the rungs in the 'ladder' of descent and rank are also morally the essential members of a mercantile lineage or business house.[8]

Purity is also a quality of a patrician house, a mosque, and a tomb. These buildings are places of purity set in the midst of the pollution of the towns, and are kept pure by cleansing, whitewashing, and prayer and ritual observance.[9] This appears a very ancient idea: many of the excavated stone houses have sumps incorporated into their plaster floors so that they can be properly washed with water.

A quality also associated with women, certainly more so than with men, is shame, *aibu* or *haya*, which in addition connotes modesty. Fear of personal or moral shame is a powerful incentive for the modes of behaviour that lead to the public recognition of a woman's purity; it can also motivate men to behave according to the expectations of their particular statuses in society. In general these qualities are part of the status of *mngwana*, which can never be lost even if a person's behaviour brings shame to herself or himself. Shame is felt by free and patrician women: formerly slaves could rarely feel shame as they were in their very nature impure and shameless.

The linked notions of knowledge, purity, shame and beauty are traditionally linked to the moral qualities of patrician women. Patrician men can have knowledge but not the other qualities, and knowledge held by men is acquired differently from that of women. It is by scholarship and devout religious behaviour, whereas that of women comes rather with their purity,[10] and all these qualities are less important the lower the rank or class: they are essentially aspects of *uungwana*.

Social and Moral Order

Linked to purity and knowledge is what in English might be called 'order', 'certainty' and perhaps 'propriety', of both persons, material possessions, and descent groups that possess 'good' origins and histories and so the quality of *uungwana*. Order pertains to the entire society and its way of life, and to its passage from the past to the present and indeed the future. It concerns and affects the entire Swahili society and to a considerable extent the non-Swahili groups in a client relationship to Swahili mercantile patrons.

This merchant society is filled with conflict, competition and intrigue (*fitina*). People of different ranks and descent groups compete not only with material but also with immaterial qualities. This last includes the purity of patrician women, honour of men, knowledge of God's will, and communication with both good and evil spirits. Behind the seeming order of house and mosque and the disorder of the streets lies what outsiders may see as a half-hidden world of danger, poverty, lack of firm or 'good' ancestry, ignorance and evil. But for the Swahili it is not half-hidden but part of everyday experience, to be controlled by knowledge and purity.

As purity is important, so is pollution. Situations of pollution are especially those in which ordered relations of rank become threatened. Pollution is brought largely by evil spirits, that try to harm the living at situations of sickness and death (when the distinction between free and slave became confused, since these came to both), when venturing into the bushland behind the coastal settlements (caravans went through much mystical as well as physical danger), and when a patrician house is opened to outsiders. Pollution is dealt with by ritual practitioners: the *mwalimu* or 'teacher', who essentially deals with Islam and knowledge of God's will and is typically male, and the *mganga* or 'doctor' (often called *fundi* or 'person of skill'), who works more directly with spirits and who is either male or female.

There are two main types of purificatory ritual. *Sadaka*, which involves beseeching God or saints, often requesting prayers from children (who are pure), or giving charity in order to prevent pollution by purifying the immediate surroundings; and *kafara*, the offering of food and other objects to remove pollution once acquired, pollution then taken by the food which is either thrown away into the bush or the sea (places of powerful spirits), or given to the poor, who formerly as non-domestic slaves were in any case impure. *Sadaka* is performed by teachers and *kafara* by doctors, who generally use different forms of divination, teachers basing theirs on astrology and doctors on forms of divining board. But the distinction is not clear-cut, as most doctors like to call themselves teachers. This again is a situation for the playing out of the contradictions between Islamic civilization and barbarism, between Asia and Africa, and between higher and lower ranks.[11]

Swahili Society under Zanzibar and Britain

Some responses to the more important recent economic, demographic and political developments were brought about by the rise of the Zanzibar Sultanate and the abolition of slavery. Other responses were military, such as the Abushiri and other revolts against German rule in Tanganyika.[12] Others were in a broad sense religious, concerned with matters of justice, morality and theological understanding. Swahili Islam had always claimed divine validation for the ethnic and hierarchical organization of Swahili society; it provided a rationale for patrician superiority over and control of others, the low placement of slaves, the positions of free and slave women, and the relationshisp of non-Swahili clients to Swahili patrons. As these changed, especially when radically so in the second half of the nineteenth century and later, so did the forms of validating them, bringing into the open previously hidden and potential conflicts.

A factor that gravely affected the position and the identity of the Swahili was that of renewed immigration from Arabia during the last third of the nineteenth century. The Zanzibar Sultanate had long encouraged the influx of immigrant colonists from southern Arabia. Those from Oman had mostly gone to Zanzibar itself, where they were under the direct protection of the sultans who reserved clove growing and plantations for them. Now immigration came rather from the poorer areas of south-western Arabia, especially the Hadramaut, and large numbers of Hadrami settled along the coast. They were not accepted as patricians nor would patricians intermarry with them – just as they had earlier refused to marry their daughters to Omani immigrants, however socially exalted. The Hadrami did what was open to them, mainly retailing everyday consumer goods. They were unexpectedly fortunate in that the abolition of slavery was occurring at the same time – it was a process and not a sudden event, except for the passing of the actual decrees. Slaves and ex-slaves, however poor, required consumer goods and the Hadrami were there to supply them. They had the necessary kinship and so commercial links with other Hadrami along the coast and with southern Arabia itself, and unlike the patricians were perfectly willing to sell to slaves and ex-slaves. They were also fortunate in that this period saw the introduction of more imports from India, Europe and America. This trade partly replaced the import of textiles and other items that had so largely featured in the earlier interior trade that was at the time fading. Within a few years the Hadrami had replaced the patricians as wealthy retailers, although only in local merchandise and not in intercontinental commerce; but that was dying in any case.[13]

Some Hadrami were sharifs, direct descendants of the Prophet, healers able to bless those who came to them; many had come via the Comores, never under Zanzibar control and renowned for their healing traditions. They established themselves as healers and retailers of spices and drugs, and soon prospered. The most famous came about 1880 to Lamu, where after some time as a healer he became an influential reformer of the traditional form of religion, bringing in new *maulidi* and other forms of worship, including drumming and dancing, both disapproved by patrician religious leaders, and catering mainly to the poor and illiterate ex-slaves of the town. This was Seyyid Saleh ibn Alwy ibn Abdullah Jamal al-Layl, usually known today as Sheikh Habib Saleh. He founded a school, *madrasa*, for ex-slaves and the poor, and also the great mosque of Ribat ar-Riyadh, 'the Hospice of the Sacred Meadows', the largest mosque of the town. His grave is the site of annual pilgrimages from far afield in the Muslim world.[14]

In the later years of the nineteenth and the early years of the twentieth centuries there was much confusion of identities of those living in or coming from Zanzibar City and the lesser towns on the Mrima coast. Zanzibar City was a small place before the coming of the Omani sultans, and so was essentially an Arab and Indian town, its architecture owing little to pre-existing Swahili models[15] and its other inhabitants comprising slaves and remnants of the indigenous Hadimu who stayed after their ruler had set up his court at Dunga. At the top of local society were the court Omani, those of the 'great' Omani clans linked closely to the Busaidi. They used Arabic as a domestic as well as a public language for some decades, but by the twentieth century most used Swahili and many of their members knew no or little Arabic, learning it only by rote as part of *madrasa* education. Beneath them it was frequently uncertain as to whether individual men were 'Arab' or 'Swahili'.[16] The situation with regard to women was rather different, due to the prevalence of concubinage and multiple marriages in which the ethnicity of wives of an Arab or Swahili man (except for the patricians of the 'old' subclans) was often genealogically irrelevant. Early accounts by visitors typically confuse Arab and Swahili; non-Omani and non-Hadrami Swahili might become recognized as Arab if they had acquired enough money, wore formal Arab dress, and became close to powerful Arab patrons.

There came about a marked differentiation between those of patrician and those of slave ancestry, which for men was to a large extent reflected in religious attendance at mosques, the former preferring to attend at their own 'private' mosques and the latter at the town's Friday mosque. Women could not worship at mosques and their position was different. During the twentieth century the patricians have become impoverished and politically weakened, whereas those of Hadrami and Omani ancestry have become both wealthier and politically more powerful from their affinity with the rulers of Zanzibar and the British as these took over power from the sultans.[17]

Those of slave ancestry in most cases have remained at the bottom of society, although the stigma of slave ancestry has lessened and the main distinction within Swahili society has changed from that between free and slave to that between patricians, on the one hand, and non-patricians of Hadrami and Omani ancestry who are closely tied to the scholarly and commercial elite on the other. Non-patricians side mostly with the patricians, while those of slave ancestry are divided, some still siding with the houses of their former owners, the majority not. Recently fundamentalist Islam, mainly Shi'ite, has gained much popular support and this too seems to reflect earlier allegiances.

For all men and women, far more for those in the patricians' towns than those in the commoners' towns, the former more or less stable order of society has changed radically during the past hundred years; the 'natural' order of hierarchy in both social and moral terms has lost importance and with this have gone changes in religious ritual and belief. The traditional interdependence between the *dini* and the *mila* had to some extent reflected the earlier hierarchical structure, but this has largely vanished, and it would appear that rites and beliefs associated with the *mila* have gained in importance, and certainly in visibility. It has been conventional among many writers that the *dini* has been mainly associated with men and the *mila* with women; but it has rather been a matter of rank and more importantly of uncertainty in the placement of persons and groups within the overall schema of superiority and inferiority.

The social positions of ex-slaves and their descendants since abolition have become central to the internal organization of Swahili society. There were different categories of slaves and there have been different categories of *wazalia*, 'those born in the country', those of slave ancestry. There were in any event no slaves in the commoners' towns, so their descendants are found only in the patricians' towns and those places where some settled in unused land along the coast as grain-farmers. Slaves could in some circumstances purchase their own freedom. By moving to an important patron, perhaps typically their former owner or one of his lineage, such men, and a few women who had made money in petty trade or prostitution and so also purchased their freedom, could become generally accepted as though genealogically junior members of their patrons' descent groups: there might be gossip but an honourable patrician would not shame such a dependant.

It has been since the abolition of slavery, and especially with the steady movement of people from the smaller coastal towns to the modern cities such as Mombasa and Dar es Salaam, that we can talk properly of the development of a system of class. Also the continual immigration of unskilled labourers to the cities from the inland areas of East Africa has been directly relevant, in situations where ethnicity has lost its importance and another mode of organization has become more relevant with the growth of trades unions and cross-tribal associations. In general, those Swahili who may be considered as upper and middle class are almost entirely from patrician and non-patrician groups of free ancestry and those seen as lower class are of slave ancestry, who find fewer difficulties in making new ties with non-Swahili than do most patricians.

Male slaves and their male descendants became in general urban labourers, of many kinds and degrees of skill and emolument, and small-scale farmers. The sons of former concubines have always generally been accepted as proper patricians even though grudgingly and half-heartedly. Almost all men with any record of slave ancestry have done their best to act according to traditionally proper patrician behaviour, to be accepted as proper Muslims and so devout Swahili. Few have ever been accepted as full patricians, but by living an ordered Muslim Swahili way of life they have been able to retain positions as men of good and stable social position.

Former female slaves and women of slave ancestry have in general been in a different and more difficult situation. 'Emancipation' has the implication of freedom not only from servitude but also of choice and career. But for former slave women and their children (other than the relatively few concubines whose children were legally free in any case), although they might now have had freedom of choice and career there have been extremely few possibilities except to continue as unpaid domestic servants, lowly paid labourers, petty traders or prostitutes.

These occupations have been increasingly devalued in both social esteem and profitability.[18] Unlike male slaves, female domestic slaves had in general been given a status that involved trust and often highly valued responsibilities such as that of nursemaid confidante, the *somo* of patrician girls, who looked after their charges throughout their lives and taught them proper sexual and social behaviour. After abolition ex-slave women lost most of that status and the certainty that went with it. Their former mistresses lost their free domestic labour, and had themselves to lower their own expectations and ranking position; but they had greater opportunities than ex-slave women to gain education and to work in personally responsible and well regarded occupations open to women in the larger and rapidly changing cities such as Mombasa and Dar es Salaam. The necessity to acquire purity by initiation and wedding and to retain it by the appropriate and onerous behaviour of married women was fading as the honour and reputation that it gave husbands and brothers was losing in importance with the decline in their commercial opportunities. They thus pushed down the positions of ex-slave women to the bottom of the social ladder. Many women in Mombasa acted as independent entrepreneurs such as tailors and owners of rentable housing; it is fairly certain that these were women of free ancestry and members of patrician subclans, with wide and effective networks of kinship ties between them.[19] Ex-slave women had none or very few such supportive ties.

Most non-patrician women have held and still hold generally low social position, especially in the patricians' towns; in the commoners' towns their central roles in farming and in the cognatic descent system have protected them from the low and poverty-stricken status that many hold in most patricians' towns. In the latter most women, and especially the majority who are of slave ancestry and so without inherited property of any value, are poor and in continual need of medical and psychological assistance; they lack healthy and safe living conditions and also certainty in their work, expectations and careers. They have several recourses, but in absence of adequate government and town services, their inability to attend mosques and so often to obtain adequate education and save money, probably the most frequent has been the protection of spirits.

The world of formal Islam has remained more clearly associated with men and mosques than has that of women, whose involvement with Islam has always been less immediate or direct. Women have become more closely associated than men with spirit cults, in that the greater ambiguity and uncertainty in their positions has led to their need to dissociate themselves from the world of men and form their own new attachments to different aspects of Divine power, in the form of spirits, an attachment reported from many parts of Africa.[20] It has not been an alternative to formal or orthodox Islam but an addition, and local women at least regard it as an enrichment permitted by God, an aspect of Islam that is theologically and socially legitimate and acceptable.

The religious situation of men has changed by the addition of new practices. One has been the growth of Muslim Sufi brotherhoods, the most popular being the Qadiriyya and the Shadhiliyya, whose members acquire knowledge by self-induced trance, *dhikri*. Membership has not been limited to Swahili, and most members belong to Muslim sub-groups scattered throughout eastern Africa and include poor men whose interests other than religious ones have rarely been those of the Swahili.[21]

There have also been more seemingly secular cultural responses to these changes in men's and women's positions, beginning in the late nineteenth century. Among men, although some women have also participated, it was the appearance of groups known as *beni* (from the English word 'band'), musical and dance groups that present performances or skits in which the members dressed as British officials and other figures of great and virtually unattainable power. Membership has reflected that of the moieties of the patricians' towns; in any town there have typically been rival *beni*, each recruited from a particular moiety, and they have been linked to local football teams and other competitive recreational groups. The most famous have been the *beni* known as Kingi and Scotchi, which paraded in full English and Scottish military attire with brass instruments and bagpipes respectively. *Beni* have not been limited to the Swahili towns but spread as far inland as the eastern Congo, and like the Sufi brotherhoods have not been limited to Swahili. Women have had counterparts in dance and singing groups, the most famous being the *lelemama* of Mombasa. In the later part of the twentieth century *taarab* musical groups based largely on Arab and Indian musical forms have become immensely popular as performers at weddings and other occasions (now with large bands and electric magnification), and including regular programmes on television and radio.[22]

These men's and women's groups have often been taken as copies of and protests against colonial rule and external influences. They are, more importantly, means of acquiring new statuses, skills and prestige in rapidly developing social systems, and their political role is also important. They are the more modern equivalents of nineteenth-century and earlier changes introduced by Hadrami and other religious innovators of those periods.

The Place of Spirits

The belief in spirits may well have been part of Swahili religion for many centuries, but the possession of women by spirits seems only to have become widespread throughout the coastal towns since the middle years of the nineteenth century, and more particularly since the abolition of slavery. Men are also possessed but women form the majority.

Swahili distinguish two main categories of spirits, the *mizimu* and the *majini*. The former are considered more African, the latter more Arabian.[23] The former are associated mainly with locality and the ancestors who have lived there.[24] They are found throughout the commoners' towns, where they are given 'incense' (in the form of money) and other small offerings[25] by anyone wishing to open a field in their localities; the new farmer is thus made into a quasi-descendant of those who originally vivicated the piece of land or water and so acquire a mystical tie with those who already own it, their use of it being merely that of tenant. *Mizimu* do not possess people although they may make them ill.

The *majini* are found also in the patricians' towns, can travel long distances, are infinite in number and are linked more closely to the ultimate sources of power, God and to a lesser extent Satan.[26] They were created by God from fire, lived in Paradise with their leader Iblis, were driven out, and roam the earth among the living. Those who have learned Arabic and accepted Islam are good; those who have not done so are evil. They may cohabit and marry with humans and have children with them so long as proper rules of ranking are followed. They are known mainly for their powers of possession, a close personal relationship with the living that with their sexual and marital relationships places them on the same moral and social level: both are God's creatures and both can teach the other knowledge, either by possession by spirits or by the living teaching them Islam, a symbolic exchange similar to the material exchanges of commerce.

The *majini* include those known as *pepo, shaitani, subiani* and *rohani*, and others of less importance. *Mapepo*, each of which has its own personal name and powers, are not confined to any one place, are limitless in number, and move about the streets and into houses (but not into mosques). They possess the living by mounting them as though horses or by sitting on their heads as though chairs; there is a strong sexual component in the 'seizing' of living women by male spirits. A doctor, male or female, can either exorcise (*punga*) the spirit, periodically appease it with gifts, or initiate the woman concerned into a spirit-association of those possessed by the same spirit (who then becomes their guest). A doctor, *mganga*, has the knowledge of divination by which he or she can recognize the identity of a given spirit; a man who controls a spirit association is more usually termed *fundi*, a master-craftsman. The word for a spirit association is *chama*, (pl. *vyama*) the word also used for a coven of witches.[27]

Mashaitani are evil and dangerous and possess mainly women of slave ancestry. The *marohani* are male and female, usually the former, and found mostly in the larger towns where they become the spirit-spouses of high ranking women and men. A *rohani* spirit is usually a member of a non-Swahili ethnic group that in the past was in a trading relationship with the Swahili and some *marohani* are spirits of Christian Europeans.[28]

There is a spatial distinction among the various kinds of spirits. *Mizimu* are tied to localities considered as their own. A person wishing to cultivate there offers incense to them to be permitted to live and work there as though a descendant of the *mizimu* concerned, who thus become quasi-ancestors. Most *mapepo* are associated with settlements, both those occupied today and with ruined ones where occurred disastrous events, and with the sea, that is with mercantile activity and with Islam that came across the ocean. Often ancient ruins contain evidence of spirit-related activities such as the burning of incense, or their marking out by flags and textiles. The mihrabs of abandoned mosques are particularly favoured.

The *mashaitani*, on the other hand, are associated with the bushland and the interior whence came non-Muslim slaves, and so with barbarous creatures, and if they become visible they assume non-human appearances. The *rohani* spirits are associated almost entirely with patricians' towns and by their ethnic identities with the main local and overseas trading partners with whom marriage was always acceptable. The spirits do not merely replicate the social/asocial world of today but also represent the morally ambiguous aspects of the Swahili mercantile past.[29]

It is said that spirits possess living people, but it is more accurate to say that the latter are possessed voluntarily as an act of will. It is the ambiguity and uncertainty of the status of Swahili women, whether of free or slave ancestries, that lie at the heart of the matter.[30] By being possesed and under protection of a spirit, a women controls her own body and its purity and is thereby in greater control of her own fate as she is now the partner of a morally and ofen sexually more powerful male.

The pattern of possession is a representation of the society, its certainties and ambiguities in the roles of its members. It provides a cognitive map of the hoped for future of those whose roles are uncertain in the ever-changing network of social relations that forms Swahili society. This is done by the giving of knowledge to those (mostly women) who are possessed by particular spirits. By being given knowledge, their status is heightened and given certainty. A woman typically either selects a possessor because her kin, friends or associates (in terms of ethnicity, place of origin, occupation or residence) are adherents of a particular spirit, or she may select a new spirit of her own, one whose teaching will help her acquire a more clearly defined individual identity.

Women possessed by the same spirit typically join an association (*chama*) of its adherents. The women of an association may be neighbours, kins-women, of different ranks, of free or slave ancestry, or linked by occupation. They are usually organized by those members of higher rank who act as patrons for the others and thereby gain authority similar to that acquired by male patrons by their control of their trading clients. Their main activities include dancing and singing songs associated with spirit power, that give the members a recognized social standing.[31] They are concerned largely with finding work and lodging, medical treatment, education, recreation, and building a sense of identity and common purpose among women who in the 'outside' world may lack these things. Most associations are short-lived and limited to particular towns, and a town may have many associations at a given time and yet none at another,[32] linked to factors such as the provision of government and other medical services, of affordable housing, of employ-ment, and of fashions in clothing and songs.[33] An essential element in this process is that of the 'master' who will help a woman through his control of a particular spirit. Most masters are men, who may be perceived as analog-ous to the mosque leaders of Islamic practice.

These cults are a source of knowledge, even though the more devout patricians and religious leaders often denigrate knowledge from spirits as false, even as evil and Satanic, deceiving the enlightened and drawing them away from ordered civilization and back to a barbarian African past. Such suspicion is always present in the minds of older patrician men, who see their erstwhile authority eroded and who often maintain that a woman may easily be seduced by a powerful male spirit who becomes a lover or even husband. Since both may easily breach proper marriage rules the woman and her kin group are thereby polluted, although the marriage of a woman with a *rohani* spirit observes these rules and does not lead to pollution.

A problem arises in the identities of the spirits who throng the streets of a town, as it is questionable whether they are part of a town's *umma* or not. The *mashaitani* are especially open to question, because they wish to control good people for their own ends. There is here a difficulty: a male *shaitani* will try to control, even seduce or marry, a righteous woman; but sinful women may pretend to be so seduced whereas in reality they wish to acquire the power given to them by a *shaitani* to harm other women. *Mashaitani* have perverted what was once good in them, yet they have 'doctors' who claim to be good themselves and attempt only to save innocent women from evil. Members of a town's elite have doubts about them: if they are really so good how do they recognize a *shaitani* spirit as a cause of possession? The doctor will say that a good person can communicate safely with a *shaitani*. These arguments and doubts are a central part of competition for power within a town. Part of this ambiguity is also that *mashaitani*, especially, are *washenzi*, 'barbarian' and 'African', and live mainly in the bushlands around the towns. The women possessed by them tend therefore to be considered *washenzi* and 'African' themselves, of slave origins of which paradoxically they may now be proud. These views are central to conflicts between rich and poor or between urban and rural, whether women or men.

The organization of spirit cults is an image of the former system of patron–client relations in commerce, labour employment, and trade in food and other commodities, including religious teaching. The relations are between the almost entirely male spirits, who are powerful visitors, yet although powerful are guests, and the mostly women members, who are the hosts; the 'masters' are go-betweens. The relationships are typically in terms of kinship, marriage and sexuality. Spirits ride, mount and have sexual relations with those whom they visit; in the case of *marohani* they are stated directly to be husbands as guests visiting their wives. In both possession and marriage the patron, the husband or lover who is male, is considered a guest of the client, who is a bride or a possessed woman. At a wedding the husband is a guest from another house who is invited to go alone into the house and room of the bride. They symbolically exchange items of clothing, of food, of jewels and of aromatic fragrances.[34] A client asks a patron to accept him or her into the latter's *jamaa* network and so to become the host and so patron and protector of the client, the guest. Swahili regard the process of spirit possession in much the same way: as we have mentioned, possession is a voluntary act by the possessed, the client and usually a woman; a client may voluntarily ask a patron for his patronage and then play a subservient role. Patronage, marriage and possession have similar patterns of interpersonal relations, as might be expected in a mercantile society.

As with relations between living persons, both sides have power to break off the relationships when they wish. A spirit can merely leave a women whom he has possessed, and a woman may cease to offer incense and other offerings, as a wife may cease to cook for her husband. Possessor and possessed are partners in exchange – healing and security for offerings – one or the other having temporary power only at any one time.

These patterns of religious behaviour are attempts to make an ordered, secure and foreseeable life according to the will of God. By joining a spirit association women go through a ritual transformation of both their immediate social environment and of their personalities, from downtrodden non-persons without protectors to spiritually empowered persons with some degree of control over their own lives. These women are not creating a new order of society as revolutionaries[35] nor are they forming a new and divisive class system even though rank (both traditional rank and modern class) and behavioural differences are recognized in most associations. Internal authority tends to be exercised by patrician women, women assumed to be of modesty and awareness of shame, whereas the bulk of members are of slave ancestry and both poor and reputedly rough in behaviour. This is regarded as a basic distinction of rank, the contemporary reproducing the traditional.

They are attempting to make a single community out of historically disparate ranks, ethnicities, and degrees of education. The internal organization of the associations, controlled by masters and led by wealthy or powerful women of free ancestry, represents traditional continuity. Members try to re-acquire security and certainty within an insecure world by going back to what today appears to have been one of order under God, rather than one of disarray under secular non-Swahili politicians.

Not all these women's associations are centred upon spirit possession but are dance and music groups.[36] Their dancing is of the many and ever-changing dances of which the most famous has been that called *lelemama*, and others traditionally performed at weddings. They are competitive between the women of rival moieties of a particular town, as is also found with men's dance and sports teams. They establish an internal ranking and sense of order to the otherwise largely amorphous category of women: as with the men's *beni*, their leaders assume roles of British and other external political and social women of authority, with names such as Queeni.

Pollution and Evil

Moral pollution, unlike purity that is centred on the houses and orderliness, is thought to be widespread outside houses and without order, and bestowed on or willingly learned by those wishing to bring it to others, who can in turn learn antidotes from specialist doctors. This process differs from spirit possession in that the living are involved in polluting others. The evil practitioners include the witch (*mwanga*), who has innate powers to harm others and who eats the bodies and despoils the graves of others, and the sorcerer (*mchawi*, *mrogi* or *mlozi*) who can only use material 'medicines' and poisons to harm others.[37]

It is virtually certain that most people – if any – do not actually practice evil in these ways: what is important are the beliefs that people do so. It is the relationships between practitioner and victim that are the most significant factor, whether they are related or unrelated, in bitter competition or not. A believed coven of witches is referred to by the term *chama*, as is also a spirit association. Its basic connotation here is that of a closed body, usually of women, exercising forms of hitherto hidden and forbidden power hitherto held by men, and wishing to undermine male authority by eating children of their husbands' lineages. Men and women are reinventing women, men in the case of covens while women are 're-inventing' themselves as independent of male authority without trying to reform traditional thought and moral concepts. Another form of *chama* has been that of a body of African zombies controlled by Arabs, a notion that is a memory of slavery and of the otherwise inexplicable wealth of Arab slave owners.[38]

These and other beliefs are indirectly linked as perversions of Islam and moral order placed within the contexts of external barbarism and pollution and of the opposition between Africa and Islam, of *mila* and *dini*. In the past caravans and trading ships were associated with outside dangers and protected by forms of Islamic magic by caravan leaders and ships' captains,[39] and all Swahili sailing craft are so protected today.

The set of beliefs in what may be called magic and the mystical is widely associated with the Swahili and are part of the identity given them by others. The Swahili have been seen as commercially powerful and wealthy people who adhere to a religion different from that of other East Africans, a religion that was literate and associated with the world outside Africa, with the Zanzibar Sultanate, with control over Africans who were taken as slaves, with the introduction of textiles and firearms, both objects with important social and political implications. The Swahili have personified power over the physically and spiritually defenceless.

The Swahili coast has long been seen as a place not only of Islam but also of mystical powers that can pervert the normal everyday world of non-Muslim African societies.[40] For the remainder of East Africa the Swahili coast has been a place of mercantile, military, and of both orthodox and perverted mystical powers. On the coast itself patricians have exercised a cultural and religious hegemony; this hegemony has been dispersed far more widely in the interior but in contrary and inverted idioms of Islamic magic and control of 'African' spirits. It has reflected their commercial and moral roles as cultural mediators, believed possessors of secret knowledge linked both to Africa and to Asia while living on the boundary between them.

The Representations and Manifestations of Uungwana

How has Swahili civilization been conceptualized and represented both to the Swahili and other members of coastal society? How have the Swahili made their changing civilization to be experienced, respected, admired and desired? The Swahili patricians have often been portrayed – caricatured would be a better word – as being filled with nostalgia and clinging to the memory of past glories. This is a view of arrogance, ignorance and condescension, as well as of the wish of many Omani and Hadrami families to absorb Swahili civilization as their own, a form of colonialist appropriation. They have copied many of the outward forms of Swahili behaviour, such as their weddings. But they do not truly participate in Swahili civilization – and the Swahili patricians have done their best to deny them participation – and their weddings, for example, copied from those of the patricians, fail to appreciate their symbolism of purity and beauty, substituting mainly commercial splendour.[41]

At the same time Swahili have taken from and adapted elements of other cultures, especially those with which they have traded, ever since their coming into being as merchants, meanwhile carefully retaining the central strength of their own civilization. The objects introduced, adopted and adapted have included clothing, such as the Omani black veil, the *buibui* in the nineteenth century, and ever new patterns of *khanga* in recent decades from India,[42] Europe and China; porcelain from China, Japan, Holland and Portugal; forms of furnishings and household ornaments from India during the nineteenth century when India came to control Zanzibar as an outpost of Indian finance houses; cuisines from India and Asia; cosmetics and perfumes from India and Europe; films and video tapes from India, Japan and America; music and song from Arabia and India; household and commercial tools and machines and technological knowledge from Europe. Some patterns have been virtually forced upon the Swahili in various ways and by various agencies (for example, tourism); others have been gladly taken because of fashion, especially by women as arbiters of purity and so of moral order, to ensure the continuance of what they see as their own societal tradition.

The relationship between fashion and tradition has been central to this everchanging yet persistent and ideally unchangeable set of social relations that compose Swahili society. Throughout their history the Swahili have accepted continual immigration of groups from outside, mostly from Arabia, and have extended their patronage to new clients within Africa; they also forcibly absorbed many from the interior as slaves whose cultures were in part accepted. Some of these processes have involved both new forms of exchange – of goods, of labour, of moral precepts – and also new kinds of visual or material objects that are given value as representing the origins of those involved in the new relationships. The cultures of Asia and elsewhere that have affected the Swahili have been represented by new objects in Swahili culture; and non-Swahili clients within Africa have valued items that represent their Swahili patrons.

The position of Swahili women, at any time in the past or today and irrespective of their ranks, has been one of ambiguity, of ever-changing statuses during their lifetimes. The increase in recent years of women's education, both Muslim and western, has strengthened their social position. The many ambiguities, uncertainties and domestic problems that face this society are focused upon the women; among patrician women upon the purity of their bodies and behaviour and on the houses in which they are given rights of residence. The objects placed and used within these houses are associated with the residential rights of women: the treasures imported from China, such as porcelain, are decommoditicized, demasculinized and feminized as no longer being goods of commercial exchange and the responsibility of men. Other objects from 'outside' are more obviously so: women's clothing, cosmetics and fragrances, domestic utensils and ornaments. Even modern videos, widely viewed everywhere both publicly and domestically, appeal mainly to younger and unmarried women. All these objects of 'global' origins represent in one way or another areas of contradiction and conflict, and of domestic or political independence of women from the authority of men. For example, the adoption of the black veil[43] had clear reference to the politically and culturally unwelcome influence of the Zanzibar Sultanate.[44] The khanga is a piece of clothing of great sexual ambiguity with many layers of meaning within its Swahili mottos;[45] the videos have been received with great doubt and dislike, even fear, as their messages are thought by many older people to threaten the virginity of unmarried daughters.[46]

The most threatening of all late twentieth-century forms of globalization is mass tourism, the nadir of neocolonialism.[47] During the colonial period there were a few places on the coast, such as Malindi, where there were hotels and beach property for Europeans; they had little effect on local people and were then accepted tolerantly. Since the Second World War the situation has changed with the advent of mass tourism from Europe, America and Japan. The coast has suffered vast numbers of culturally illiterate foreigners staying in the many hotels built in the last decades by foreign and local elite entrepreneurs selling Swahili culture and the Swahili landscape. The Swahili themselves have had little say or profit in this commerce, which has affected them negatively and insultingly and introduced new forms of entertainment, drug selling, prostitution, criminal violence, and callous financial and moral exploitation, almost all by non-Swahili. What does come to the Swahili goes generally to marginal members of the towns concerned, has brought about a new category or subclass of young and uneducated men unconcerned with Swahili civilization of which they are ignorant, and has increased the isolation of the Swahili from the development of the rest of their own countries, whose GNP is increased at the expense of their own coastal citizens. The Swahili, as throughout history, remain between Africa and the outside world.

10

Constructing the Mercantile Landscape

Uungwana haugai, bora ni ndarama 'gentle birth is not enough, best is money'
Swahili proverb (Taylor, *African Apharisms or Saws from Swahili-land*
(1891))

To many observers Swahili society has been and remains one difficult of
definition, of ambiguities in internal statuses, and of everchanging and often
confused ethnic composition. Its role has been mediatory; it has features of
both Africa and Asia and is situated on the geographical and cultural
boundary between them, and remains a *tertium quid* that faces both ways
and contains many contradictions within itself.

Any socially attributed identity, whether in terms of ethnicity (that typically appealed to in the Swahili case) or any other, has no permanence. It is
merely a name or term, an idiom or representation of role, used to describe a
person or group in relationship to the wider society. It is an attribute, not an
innate quality, and is changeable or renewable. We are essentially discussing
power that is mercurial in its ownership, its forms and its use.

Identity is also a relative notion that depends upon the observer as much
as on the observed. The identity of the Swahili represent a classic case of a
society constantly redefining itself, through myth and tradition, in language
and dress, names and genealogy, in response to the demands of the observer
– be they Asian or African traders, European or Arab overlords, or western
tourists. At some periods very few have been known as 'Swahili', as in
the later periods of Omani and then European colonization when the ruling
elite was 'Arab'; today many of direct Arab ancestry underplay that identity
and become 'Swahili' instead, thereby stressing an African identity in
the postcolonial world. Nowadays the present society is reworking the
past in order to create new identities, using archaeology and modern historical research, in the same way that nineteenth-century society drew upon
Arabic literature to generate a very different identity. If we look back as
early as the eleventh century, the same process was in operation – this

time to create a Persian identity. Bahram of Mtambwe Mkuu was as little Persian as the nineteenth-century Lamu patricians were Arab, but their identities were forged in the political and social relations of the time.

In these shifting sands of identity, it is the physical which remains constant, and throughout this book we have noticed how important the landscape is to the Swahili – it is like a remembered chronicle which is passed down through the generations, having been learnt by rote. Thus the tombs of founders are visited on an annual basis or the town is encircled in New Year ceremonies. Fumo Liongo may have numerous versions of his supposed poetry extant, but anyone questioning his former existence is shown his tomb outside Kipini. The subclans of the settlements may change their names, but their number is constant, and the archaeological evidence suggests this is because there are fixed numbers of gateways into a settlement or its centre. This is the social landscape of the Swahili, and it forms the link between the past and present.

The Swahili were merchants first and foremost, and created around their communities another form of landscape, a mercantile one, in which they could prosper. The core of this was the town, and at the heart of this was the stone house, with its own rituals, purity and symbolism, that contributed so much to patrician identity. Such houses have served this function, certainly since the fourteenth century, and their role evolved through their timber-and-mud-walled predecessors. The house was also the location for the most important actions of the merchants, by sexual procreation to perpetuate their lineages and by the exchange of commodities to perpetuate their status. The goods that they obtained and retained from their overseas guests were not for common use, but for display as status objects; the houses were museums for these items, whether placed in the wall niches or as cloths pegged to the walls.

The Swahili merchants could live in this manner because they controlled a wider landscape. First they had to obtain food to live on, and here they were lucky. The coastal region is productive, with rainfall that is reliable, at least in comparison with most of Africa, and most soils, based upon eroded coral reefs, fertile. Added to this is the maritime environment, with reefs teeming with fish and shellfish to be freely collected from the creeks and shoals. Most towns could easily support themselves; in some cases the townsmen left their houses, and travelled by boat to their fields for the growing season, in others field slaves were used to operate them. Many of the trading towns lay at the centre of rural conurbations of smaller towns, villages and fields, that supplied these foodstuffs.

Secondly they had to obtain the trading commodities that their merchant-guests had travelled many hundreds or even thousands of miles to obtain from them. As well as passing on the objects from overseas or the interior, the Swahili merchants presided over what can only be described as an industrial complex. Swahili towns were a hive of craftsmen, making silks and textiles, leather shoes, boats, metalwares, beads and jewelry, to name just a few that we can name from the ethnographic or archaeological evidence. Some of this they retained for themselves, but most were for onward exchange to their clients living in the countryside around the conurbations or across the Indian Ocean.

It was these clients, non-Muslim farmers, pastoralists and hunters who were vital for the security of the towns and were often called upon to defend them, as the historical sources make clear. But they were also the suppliers of vital trading commodities such as ivory and skins and in early centuries slaves as well. They were bound into the system through their dependence on Swahili Islam and Islamic protective magic, and through their participation in a shared sacred kingship (especially along the Mrima coast). They also benefited from the craftwares – especially cloth – that came out of the Swahili towns. What is interesting is that the structure of the relations between Swahili patron and hinterland client has remained, even though one client may be replaced by another through the movements of peoples and the exchange of commodities largely replaced by labour. Identities may change but the landscape and its networks persist.

In this book we have traced the history of a society in detail for 2000 years, in which a cluster of Swahili patricians were able to ensure their economic well-being and security until the very recent past. They have been at the head of an unusual society, one comprising a string of settlements along a 1000-mile coastline, with relatively small territory of its own on which to rely. They have had no secure political base in the sense of being a single polity. They have lacked political power with which to control the trade on which they have depended. They have never formed a landed aristocracy able to acquire tenants and vassals to support them in return for rights in land.

They have had to balance predatory enemies and commercial rivals by various means. These have included their centuries-old knowledge of the international trade and what they see as divinely-bestowed knowledge and skills at organizing and running efficient ports-of-trade. During much of their history they have suffered forms of colonial overlordship by others – Arab, Portuguese and other European – but have been able to maintain their commercial position by their monopoly of this knowledge and associated skills. They have strengthened their position by maintaining close interclan links up and down the coast and effective patron–client networks into the hinterland and interior.

They have been Muslim and literate, with cultural hegemony over a wide region and with wider links with Islamic societies elsewhere with whom they have been members of a single *umma*, the worldwide Islamic community. They have been widely credited with forms of powerful magic and mystical powers. These factors have provided them with information about trading partners in both Asia and the African interior, and their mastery of financing the trade has contributed to their knowledge that they have kept to themselves as a basis of their mercantile position. Although in the end they have lost their economic mastery, this took place only in the face of greatly superior political and military power in the hands of the Zanzibar Sultanate and the later European colonial powers.

A particular problem has been for the Swahili to maintain a distinct identity on which their hegemony has so largely depended. They have formed a Janus society, facing towards both the interior and the Indian Ocean, with themselves in an uncertain area between them. As middlemen they have had to distinguish themselves from both their Asian and African partners. They live in Africa, yet have held slaves from the interior: they are neither Asian nor wish to be African and so of the same ancestry as their slaves. They have had to construct an identity different from all other groups of the coast, including not only slaves but also the Omani and Hadrami Arab settlers, and the numerous non-Swahili peoples living just behind the coastline. Identities are socially constructed and can be changed, exchanged, bought, sold and discarded. The Swahili have done all these things at various times and in various places.

The most obvious and most effective identity for this purpose was, and remains, an ethnic one. 'Ethnicity' derives from a perceived origin, whether in their own country or outside it, yet ethnic definitions and boundaries are everywhere uncertain. They have had to ensure and to retain their exclusivity as against other groups (which has often meant attributing to other groups identities different from those claimed by those groups themselves). And among themselves each competitive subclan and lineage had also to ensure and retain its own exclusivity against its rivals. Both have been carried out largely in the idiom of ethnicity and ethnic origins, within an overall structure of hierarchical differences. Their religion, their clothing, cuisine, language and general worldview have roots in both Africa and Asia. Much in everyday life reflects these paradoxes: the importance of intrigue and backbiting, the traditional snobbery of the society and its emphasis on nuances of courteous behaviour and pedigree, its definitions of good and evil and the ways of coping with the latter.

The identities of the several elements of Swahili society have changed their positions relative to one another over many centuries. This process has been referred to by the several forms of Arabization, Swahilization, modernization, globalization, colonization, indigenization and other terms that mean little except when placed in detailed contexts at specific periods. In a sense the overall structure of this society may have changed relatively little over past centuries, but the identities of persons and groups that have played roles and established their own niches within it have done so in terms of these various processes.

During much of the nineteenth century those with or trying to possess hegemony or power claimed to be 'Arabs' by origins and genealogy. During the twentieth century Mijikenda and many other non-Swahili neighbours often tried to gain Swahili identity as wealthy people, but few succeeded. During the nineteenth century many Omani colonists attempted to make their children 'Swahili' so as to claim land and commercial advantages by marrying Swahili women, but most were refused. Today many of formerly claimed Arabian origin assert that there are really no Swahili 'patricians' and that they are equally members of the traditional Swahili elite: this fits with the wider pan-African political wish to be 'indigenous' rather than immigrant colonists.

In this book, we have reviewed Swahili society as a single ongoing entity whose *raison d'être* has been to act as commercial and cultural intermediary in the long-distance trade between eastern Africa and Asia and beyond. Few societies in the world have lasted as long as that of the Swahili, and few have retained the same basic forms and institutions. It has never been isolated from the remainder of Africa or from Asia; and facing in both directions, it has both taken ideas and items of cultural behaviour from both places and also given others to them. Yet it has formed and kept its own civilization based on exchange between its constituent groups and between those of a wider system of trading networks of both Africa and Asia. We have asked and attempted to answer how it has done this.

To what extent has Swahili civilization been determined by its having been a mercantile one? Here we should define the salient features of this civilization that mark it off from neighbouring societies, and compare them to mercantile societies elsewhere. An important question is whether we see the Swahili towns as representing a certain kind of port-of-trade, each at the centre of its own particular network of mercantile ties, obligations and responsibilities; and if so, to what extent is the Swahili system the same as others elsewhere? Or has it been something *sui generis*, due to its specific ecological, historical and cultural contents? It might appear reasonable to see the Swahili case as one of 'state formation' leading to certain periods of colonialist domination and exploitation, and to place the various kinds of ports-of-trade in a single historical developmental sequence: perhaps first as coastal settlements occasionally trading with visitors from overseas, then a local kingdom's outpost as that kingdom tries to control the trade, and then the metropolitan outpost as the metropolitan country tries in turn to take over the trade for itself. This pattern does not fit the Swahili, whose society seems to develop a number of quite distinctive features which we can list as follows:

1   The Swahili have been merchants in a trade that has involved people of many countries, languages, towns, cultures, ethnic origins and relationships. The Swahili have made agreements, alliances and contracts with these many partners, each Swahili settlement ensuring their own particular ties of trust and interdependence with their own partners. These mercantile ties have been cemented by intermarriage and by various kinds of fictive kinship and marital alliance such as concubinage. The merchants have formed a minority of the total society that has included more farmers and fishermen, and formerly slaves, than actual merchants.

2   They are at the heart of an *oikumene* of several complementary parts: at the centre are their settlements and landscape, then the hinterland intermediary groups of close allies; and at its edges the trading partners both of the interior and across the ocean, who trade with each other through the Swahili merchants. The latter are dependent upon their different sets of partners who are themselves in turn dependent on the Swahili at the centre of the entire system of exchange. As merchants, they never formed a single polity nor, until the establishment of the Zanzibar Sultanate, were they effectively controlled by politically superior powers.

3   The society has comprised several ranks each locally defined in terms of 'ethnic' origins, *ad hoc* definitions of identity. The patricians have always formed a minority elite which has held cultural hegemony over others, mainly non-patrician groups, formerly the slaves, more recent immigrants from Arabia and the interior of Africa, all of whom have become members of this single Swahili society. Patrician unilineal descent groups have been rigorously exclusive, and protective of their rights in many forms of material and immaterial property; their use of both endogamous and exogamous marriages has been a necessary and successful strategy. The use of slavery permitted grain and mangrove production for export, enabling patricians to control much of the means of production on the coast itself. The process of private ownership lies at the heart of rights in property (houses), piety (mosques) and purity (women and houses). Without the legal institution of *waqf* the Swahili mercantile economy could never have worked as it has done.

4   The patricians have not been landed aristocrats even though they have owned plantations for export crops. They have been merchants, and even their kings were merchants (as were the sultans of Zanzibar). They have never transformed their wealth into land but into conspicuous consumption, piety and charity (a form of exchange by redistribution). Even so, they were able during slavery to enter the petty trade of local markets by permitting their more trusted slaves to carry on trading pursuits (gold- and silver-smithing, sandal making, signing on as dhow

crews and so on, and often sending their female slaves into prostitution and sharing their income). Meanwhile they could demonstrate their own wealth and piety to one another.

5   At the basis of patrician exclusivity are claims to high-status ancestry, the purity of women and houses, and the honour and reputation of the men. Men face the moral pollution of commerce and the town; women, especially firstborn daughters, acquire purity within their pure houses. The men have been the controllers of mercantile and political matters, and the women have played the complementary role of acquiring purity and exercising domestic authority. There is a balance between the 'dominant' patrilineal descent line and the submerged line of women, one dealing in material commerce and the international world of Islam, and the other dealing in the mystical quality of purity and connected with spirit possession.

6   Adherence to a religion of wide acceptance and literacy but different from those of the local neighbouring peoples, has been crucial.

7   With the importance of hierarchy and ancestry has gone that of nuances of sumptuary behaviour in housing, clothing, bodily fashion and adornment, scholarship, cuisine, elegance and prestigious consumption, to be admired and emulated, so as to distinguish themselves from their African neighbours who lacked these signs of 'civilization' and 'urbanity'.

Postscript: The Witu Incident

If there was any point in the Swahili's long history which represents a watershed, it was dawn on 26 October 1890.[1] A small naval force under Admiral Fremantle and 950 British soldiers had landed near Kipini, and proceeded inland, destroying four villages en route, reaching Witu, a defended enclave in the forests behind the Lamu archipelago. The seven-pound field guns failed to breach the heavy wooden gates, so explosives were used and an entry was soon breached. The attackers found the town empty, apart from a few wounded slaves. The British set about 'to utterly wreck and destroy the town and its defenses': they flattened the stone house, and royal court, also burning the longest and reputedly the best version of the *History of Pate*. The bronze guns now guard the front entrance to Lamu museum, while Witu is little more than a bus stop between Garsen and Lamu.

The sack of Witu was one of numerous incidents, in which British and others established their colonial authority, and which led to the destruction of past proud cultures; in Africa, the list includes more famous and notorious examples such as Benin or Bulawayo. But the Witu incident is one of considerable interest for Swahili historians and its consequences are still apparent today.

Plate 10.1   *The tomb of Ahmed bin Fumoluti al-Nabahani, also known by his throne name 'simba', the founder of Witu, who died there in 1888, shortly before the town was destroyed by the British in 1890. The inscription is noteworthy as the first recorded use of Kiswahili on an epitaph, written in Arabic script (photo Mark Horton).*

After the Battle of Shela in 1812, a conflict between the Omani supported forces of Lamu and those of Pate, the defeated Nabahani ruling clan of Pate established themselves in the mainland region of Ozi, on the Tana River. They built a small settlement at Kau, then moved further inland to Witu around 1862, under their leader Sultan Ahmed bin Fumolati.

The Pate Swahili set about creating a new mercantile landscape around the new town of Witu, using all the well-known strategies that they had employed for centuries in the Lamu archipelago. They built what was in effect a large town some considerable distance inland; an eyewitness of 1867 estimated a population of 45,000. Sultan Ahmed took the title Mwenyemui ('master of the town') and set up a model Swahili town government, complete with a council of patricians who had come with him from Pate as well as from Lamu. There were also sharifs, and office-holders such as *qadi* and *walimu*. Most of the population were ex-slaves and fugitives, who lived in the town or surrounding villages and had an obligation of military service. Sultan Ahmed also had his own slaves, some of whom were allocated to other patricians. The villages around had their own patrician governors, and there many of the refugees were encouraged to settle; they took their wives from the neighbouring Pokomo and Boni, as the

Swahili patricians remained endogamous. The Witu Swahili maintained equal relationships with the pastoralist Oromo, to whom they supplied guns and gained military protection in return. Around Witu the lands were farmed with a wide range of crops, and cattle were kept; within Witu itself, there were craftsmen such as woodworkers and smiths. Trade in forest products was an important part of the economy and ivory (obtained from the Boni and Oromo) became an important export, using routes to the coast.

The plan of Witu itself is not known, but it had a palisade, a gateway that was so narrow that only one person could pass at a time, and it was surrounded by forest. It cannot have been unlike an immense *kaya* or sacred settlement. The speed with which the Pate patricians were able to set up this new town in the remote forest is remarkable, and illustrates how active and effective were their economic and religious networks with the mainland. Witu continued to grow, with its reputation for efficient and fair government as well as for providing a refuge for escaped slaves.

This Swahili utopia was soon drawn into the politics of the Scramble for Africa. Witu was creating a problem for the slave owners of Arab-influenced Lamu, by raiding their slaves and then selling them back to their owners. The first British visit to Witu was in 1885, when the Lamu vice consul Haggard (the brother of the more famous Rider Haggard) concluded that the place should be destroyed, as it was clearly having a detrimental effect on British relations with the Zanzibar Arabs. The Germans had other ideas and from their first visit to Witu in 1875 attempted to promote Witu. Eventually in 1885, the Denhardt brothers made a treaty with Ahmed; in exchange for a grant of land to the German settlers, Ahmed was offered German protection. This was recognized in the first Anglo-German agreement of 1886, as covering the mainland area between Kipini and Kiwayuu island. Witu was seen as the way into Africa, gaining access to Uganda and beyond. The Germans set up a Witu Company to trade their new concession, a canal was dug at the mouth of the Tana, a Post Office was set up in Lamu and even postage stamps were issued in the name of the Swahililand Sultanate. It lasted until 1890, when during the Berlin Conference Witu was exchanged for Heligoland, a small island in the North Sea held by the British. The Witu Sultanate passed to the British and the Germans effectively gave up their ambitions to colonize the Nile headwaters.

With the German claims relinquished on Witu, the British looked for a pretext to destroy it. This came in September 1890, when a number of German settlers were killed near Witu and Fremantle's expedition was dispatched to destroy the town. Fumo Bakari (Ahmed's successor as Sultan) was poisoned shortly afterwards and his successor Fumo Omari exiled to Zanzibar in 1894. The British (and the Imperial British East Africa

Company's agents) recognized puppet rulers of Pate until 1922, when the Sultanate was formally abolished.

Witu represented the last genuine Swahili town, with its independent sultan and patricians, drawn from a history that goes back to the early towns of the Lamu archipelago such as Shanga, Manda and Pate. With its ending in 1890, this historical link was finally broken, and with it, the sense of an independent and indigenous Swahili identity. It was in the British interest, in their relations with the Omanis in Zanzibar, to deny the very existence of this surviving early polity. For if it existed, then on what valid basis were their treaties with the Arab State of Zanzibar? If the Swahili were no more than Arab colonists of an earlier generation, then this would in a curious way legitimize British relations with the *parvenu* Arabs of Zanzibar. So with the burning of Witu went the destruction of the historical legacy of a remarkable mercantile and African civilization, whose activities played a significant part in the economies of both Africa and Eurasia for the best part of two millennia.

Notes

Introduction

1 See Pearson 1998, Walterstein 1974–89, Abu-Lughod 1989, Chaudhuri 1985. Wolf 1982 mentions the Swahili, but the two pages of superficial reference turn out not to be to the Swahili but to nineteenth-century Zanzibari Arabs; nothing is said of actual Swahili society from the viewpoint of the Swahili themselves, nor of their reactions to capitalist exploitation. The book is written from a Eurocentric position, with the 'peoples without history' still at the periphery rather than at their own centre. An example of the contrary approach is Horden and Purcell 2000 who provide an excellent 'post-Braudelian' methodology, as originally expressed in Braudel 1972–3, that moves away from the restraints of world history to provide a refreshing account of Mediterranean civilization.

1 The Swahili Coast

1 Dates throughout this book are expressed in terms of the Christian or common era, and those before are suffixed B C E. Where historical sources or inscriptions provide Islamic dates they have been converted using Freeman-Grenville 1977.
2 General accounts of the Indian Ocean *oikumene* include those by Chaudhuri 1985, 1990; P. D. Curtin, 1984. The accounts of the position within that *oikumene* of the Asian mercantile societies that were for long in contact with the Swahili, and their own internal forms of trade and organization, include those by Pearson 1988, 1998; Tracy 1990, 1991; Das Gupta and Pearson 1987; Clarence-Smith 1989.
3 A good example of the dialogue between the traditional interpretation of the past in face of the archaeological evidence is Wilding 1987, where the local historical community was invited to comment on and interpret the early mosques that had just been found at Shanga.
4 The Swahili face both east and west, north and south, in different situations and periods. Although geographical terms of umland, foreland and hinterland

for the areas surrounding them provide some clarification (Pearson 1998, p. 67, 75ff), we prefer to use the term hinterland to indicate the landward area immediately west of the Swahili towns, and the interior to refer to the more distant regions, whether reached by sea, river, caravan route, road or railway. See also Datoo 1975.

5   Tibbetts 1971 provides a detailed account of how the monsoons were used in the late fifteenth century.

6   Datoo 1970, 1974; Horton 1987b; Kirk 1962; Sheriff 1981. For a modern eyewitness account of the journey from western Asia, see Villiers 1940.

7   Prins 1965.

8   Cassanelli 1986, 1987.

9   Trimingham 1975; Wansbrough 1970. There is no detailed compendium of Arabic sources translated into English covering the coast; Freeman-Grenville 1962b gives a selection of his translations of some of the more useful accounts. Other compilations (in French translation) are Devic 1883; Ferrand 1913; Guillain 1856. Other sources missed in these compilations include Idrisi and al-Jahiz (Lewis 1974), al-Biruni (Levtzion and Hopkins 1981), the Hudud al-Alam (Minorsky 1937), Yaqut (Trimingham 1964, 1975), Buzurg ibn Sharhriyar (Freeman-Grenville 1981) and Ibn Majid (Tibbetts 1971). For the two key texts of al-Ma'sudi and of Ibn Battuta, we have relied upon the authorative translations of Pellat 1962 and Gibb 1962. For a discussion of Chinese sources see especially Duyvendak 1949; Hirth and Rockhill 1911; Shen 1995; Snow 1988; Wheatley 1975.

10 The definition of these pirates depends very much on the viewpoint of the historical source consulted – as anti-colonial fighters or those seeking fortunes outside a European colonial order. See Strandes 1961, 128–133; Turton 1970, for the Turkish and Egyptian incursions. J. M. Gray, 1962, for Europeans, Flint 1963 for the Egyptian attacks on the east coast itself. The most notorious of all pirates, Captain Kidd, also sailed in these waters and is reputed to have buried his treasure on Pemba island.

11 Gray 1950, 1958; Pearson 1998; Strandes 1961; Axelson 1973. For Portuguese sources relating to East Africa, Theal 1890–1903 and Baxter and Da Silva Rego 1962–71; many key early texts of explorers and missionaries are found translated in Freeman-Grenville 1962b. See also Jenson 1973.

12 Cooper 1980, p. 55 observes that the Zanzibar state was 'less an effective institution than a nodal point in a widespread network of commercial relationships'. Accounts of the nineteenth-century sultanate of Zanzibar and its role in the wider ocean *oikumene* are numerous: accounts of outsiders of the period, despite their frequent racist bias, contain useful observers' accounts, while those by insiders have not been published, most being in Arabic. Those that we have consulted include: Bateman 1901; Baumann 1891; Burton and Speke 1858; Burton 1872; Craster 1913; Dale 1920; Dammann 1929; Decken 1869–73; Drocopoli 1914; Elliot 1925/6; Elton 1874; Fitzgerald 1898; Fraser, Tozer and Christie 1871; Ingrams 1931; Kersten 1867–79; Krapf 1860; Lyne 1905; Mac-Donald 1897; New 1873; Pearce 1920; Révoil 1885; Ruete 1886; Sulivan 1873; Voeltzkow 1923; Younghusband 1910. Modern accounts by Swahili and

non-Swahili historians of Zanzibar include: Austen 1971; Flint 1963; Iliffe 1979; Sheriff 1987; Nicholls 1971; Bennett 1978; Cooper 1980; J. M. Gray 1962, 1963; Sheriff and Ferguson 1991; essays in Guennec-Coppens and Caplan 1991, and in Cour Grandmaison and Crozon 1998.

13   Fabian 1968; Hinnebusch 1996; Shariff 1973; Whiteley 1969; Swahili dictionaries also represent the history of the language and its regional dialects which have been 'standardized' on that spoken in Zanzibar, with its strong Arabic influence; compare Johnson 1939 with Krapf 1882 and Sacleux 1939.

14   Arens 1975; Eastman 1971; Mazrui and Shariff 1994.

15   Chittick 1977a, p. 218.

16   Middleton and Campbell 1965; Prins 1967; Zanzibar Government 1953, 1958, 1960.

17   Wansbrough 1970, p. 92; Tolmacheva 1976.

18   Trimingham 1975, p. 136, quoting Ibn Sa'id, Bast al-Ard.

19   Gibb 1962, p. 379. A clue to the identification of Ibn Battuta's Sawahil is that the area supplied Mombasa with grain. This could have been the Lamu area to the north, but is more likely to have been Mrima coast and Pemba island; the latter was the major supplier of foodstuffs for Mombasa. Curiously the Portuguese did not use the term Swahili in any of their writings, preferring the term 'Moor', sometimes differentiating between black Moors and white Moors, the former indigenous or at least long-settled and the latter recently immigrant.

20   Quoted in Burton 1872, vol. 2, p. 481; the Swahili of Pate town are described as 'a people sprung from a mixture of the Galla negroes with the Arabs etc'.

21   Certain clans in some of the older centres, such as Pate and Siyu, use 'Swahilini' as a clan or descent group term. This may hint at an ancient usage, predating the Omani arrival, and possibly supporting Ibn Battuta's reference to the Swahili as a valid term; Prins 1967, p. 82. There is no customary Bantu word USwahili for the Land of the Swahili, an indication that they have never formed a single state or polity.

22   Including, for example, Middleton (1961, p. 8) while working in Zanzibar on the eve of independence. The issue was still sensitive to the Zanzibar government in the mid-1980s. When Horton tried to issue a press release entitled 'early Swahili settlement found on Zanzibar' this was corrected to 'Shirazi' by the then permanent secretary.

23   Prins 1967 Salim 1973, 1976.

24   Some non-Swahili coastal peoples, such as the Pokomo, Mijikenda, Digo, Zaramo and Yao, are Muslims or partly Muslim, but do not speak Kiswahili; they are not included as Swahili even though there is some intermarriage and so ties of personal kinship and affinity; Parkin 1970, 1985. Islam spread into these groups comparatively recently.

25   It is on this point that there has been much confusion in past accounts, in that they have typically been analysed as virtually independent entities rather than as being complementary, and thus their roles have not been easily comprehensible.

26   Middleton 1992 provides much detail on the patricians of the northern coast. This study has been criticized as characterizing all Swahili society

through the opinions of a few Lamu-based patricians. We do not accept this, as they (and not only they) believe they form the social and ideological core of Swahili society and that book examined a much wider range of Swahili civilization.

27 The Arab elite of nineteenth-century Zanzibar did so regard themselves in the sense that the wealthier plantation owners built themselves rural mansions on their plantations in which to spend time for pleasure, especially during the hot season when Zanzibar City itself became unpleasant and the sultans moved to their summer palaces. Patricians did often build small temporary houses for the same reasons outside the towns, but these were never the large palaces and county mansions as were built by the Zanzibar Arabs; Ingrams 1931, 209ff; see Horton (forthcoming) for architectural survey.

28 Each town contains different clusters of patrician groups, for example those in Lamu also being represented by kin and subclans in many other towns, while those of Mombasa or Kilwa are scarcely represented in the northern towns; Middleton 1992, p. 94; Prins 1971, pp. 20–1. For a discussion of Swahili regional autonomy, Parkin 1994.

29 The Kinamte are often credited with the introduction to East Africa of the coconut palm; the Famao are said to be descended from three sets of foreign sailors who settled on the coast, one from China, another from Portugal, the third from Arabia; see el-Zein 1974; Romero 1985.

30 Middleton 1976.

31 Swartz 1978; Knysh 1999.

32 See chapter 3; Middleton 1992, 30ff.

33 The original inhabitants of Zanzibar island are known as the WaHadimu, a name at times said to mean 'slaves' but probably meaning 'protected' or 'tributary' as they maintained their freedom in return for tributary payments under their own rulers who made alliances with the Zanzibar sultans. They (and the waTumbatu) had their own rulers until the late nineteenth century; J. M. Gray 1977; Goldman 1995; Middleton 1961.

34 Grottanelli 1955a; Declich 1987; Cassanelli 1982, 1986, 1987, Cerulli 1922; Lewis 1965; Turton 1975; Prins 1960.

35 Slavery was abolished under the British in 1895 in Zanzibar and Tanganyika, 1904 in Somaliland and 1907 in Kenya. The literature on emancipation is very large, but see especially Cooper 1980; Curtin 1986a, Curtin 1986b; Herlehy and Morton 1988; Mbotela 1956.

36 Arens 1975, 1979, 1987; Hino 1968a, 1968b, 1971; Lary and Wright 1971; Parkin 1972.

37 Bang 1999; Bujra 1971; Nicholls 1971, ch. 5; Sheriff 1987; Yalden-Thompson 1958.

38 Outside observers typically assume that Omani and Hadrami are 'Swahili', especially since most have become wealthy and well-educated and because they themselves claim to belong to the coast and are thus 'Swahili'. However, their main clans and lineages are quite distinct from those of the patricians proper and they are never given the title *waungwana*, or belong to Swahili civilization, *ustaarabu*. They include most local retailers and are divided into

clans, subclans, and lineages and many categories defined by rank, occupation and wealth.

39 Ottenheimer 1984, 1985; Ottenheimer and Ottenheimer 1994; Shepherd 1977.

40 Lofchie 1965; Middleton and Campbell 1965; also Salim 1970, 1972.

41 Among the non-Muslim communities, the Hindus are the most numerous, but there are also Roman Catholic Goans; Delf 1963; Mangat 1969; Seidenberg 1996.

42 Middleton 1961, 52ff; Cooper 1980.

43 For example, many of the revolutionary leaders in Zanzibar after 1964 were from these categories and socially and economically they have frequently been in competition with former slaves, *wazalia*, as unskilled labourers and squatters. They are typically confused with *wazalia* by outsiders as being 'Swahili', but this is not so.

44 In a small number of cases Europeans and Indians have attempted to become Swahili, through residence and conversion to Islam. European women who marry Swahili men, become Muslims and take new names, have been respected and at least partially accepted into Swahili society.

45 The small communities of Chinese fishermen have collected bêche-de-mer, a Chinese delicacy, for export, from the early twentieth century onwards. Some, such as those in southern Pemba, retain their own identity and community. However in one case, a Chinese collector settled on Chovayi island in the Bajun islands, took a Swahili name, became a Muslim and even underwent circumcision at an old age, in a bid to gain local acceptance; he died about 1963; see Snow 1988, pp. 56, 190.

46 This has been achieved in some cases by resisting the visit of any outsider to the community. The island of Tumbatu is well known for this attitude, both during colonial times as well as the present; Kirkman 1964.

47 Salim 1970, 1972.

2 Origins

1 Vogel 1997 provides up-to-date general surveys of the region and the languages spoken. See especially chapters on eastern African advanced foragers, eastern and southern-central Iron Age, and African languages. See also Ehret 1974, 1998; Ehret and Posnansky 1982; Horton 1997b; Phillipson 1977, 1985; Sinclair 1991; Sutton 1990.

2 Ehret 1974.

3 The present-day hunter-gatherers of the Kenyan coast are all living in forest environments, although the Dahalo live very close to the sea; Heine 1982; Nurse 1986; Prins 1963; Stiles 1981; also Champion 1922; Salkeld 1905; Stephen 1978; Tucker 1969; Werner 1913. For the archaeological evidence for the Late Stone Age at Kilwa, see a brief line in Chittick 1974, vol. 1, p. 255, where Middle Stone Age material was also reported in more detail. For Zanzibar, Chami and Wafula 1999.

4 Dewar and Wright 1993. Some of the linguistic reconstructions suggests that the Austronesians first settled the coast before moving to Madagascar, to account for early Bantu loan words. In light of the new discoveries that point to the maritime skills of the Early Iron Age populations (see below), and the earliest evidence in the pollen record that the first clearances took place in south-east Madagascar, the possibility of a Bantu-speaking Early Iron Age population on Madagascar should be considered.

5 Crawford 1984; Grottanelli 1947; Hornell 1934; Macdonald 1992; Wigboldus 1996b. The present-day distribution of outrigger canoes (*ngalawa*) extends northwards from Madagascar to the area around Malindi, and this may be indicative of the primary area of contact using a southern oceanic route.

6 Möhlig 1982; Also Nurse 1983a, 1983b, 1983c; Nurse and Hinnebusch 1993; Shariff 1973;

7 For an example of the imperial historians who were keen in promoting this view see Coupland 1938, 1939; some work published by colonial administrators nonetheless contain much value, e.g. Ingrams 1931; Pearce 1920. Stigand 1913. One such colony has been claimed at Manda in Chittick 1984; see Horton 1984, 1986 for a different view of this evidence. Allen 1993, pp. 1–19 is a useful review of the history of the argument.

8 Ingrams 1931, pp. 41–58 for the fullest of these imaginary accounts. Kirkman 1964 was one of the first to question the historical veracity of this history.

9 Reade 1996.

10 Barnett 1999, p. 69. Wigboldus 1996a, 1996b.

11 Meyer, Todd and Beck 1991; Schmidt et al. 1992; Chami 1994.

12 Some have gone so far as to claim that Punt and the Classical port of Opone (the site of Ras Hafun, on the east coast of northern Somalia) are somehow philologically related. This is most unlikely. For the best assessment of the evidence for Punt and early Egyptian trade with East Africa in general see Phillips 1997.

13 Zarins 1996.

14 The faience bead came from Nakuru; L. Leakey 1931, p. 201. At Ngorongoro, excavations of burial cairns produced pierced cowries, nacre disc heads and marine gastropods, of coastal origin, but 500 km from the sea; M. D. Leakey 1966.

15 Ray 1995 for an overview. The sequence of the Mediterranean ceramics is well documented at the south Indian port of Arikamedu, on the south-east coast of India, which from about 250 BCE was an important entrepôt for indigenous local trade between the western Indian Ocean and the Bay of Bengal. Around 100 BCE, small quantities of Mediterranean amphorae appear at Arikamedu, and this would seem to date the beginning of Red Sea trade – not directly with Arikamedu – but within the western Indian Ocean. The commodities were then exchanged more widely using local networks. As these Mediterranean commodities reached the coasts of India, so it is likely that they also reached the East African coast from around 100 BCE. A major change seems to have taken place during the early part of the first century, which affected both India and East Africa. The quantity of Mediterranean pottery at Arikamedu increases

significantly, and is represented by the Roman finewares such as Arretine ware. Arikamedu continued to be an Indian port but now linked into a much more formal trading network, which supplied the Roman world with spices and textiles. This formal network extended to East Africa as well, in order to procure ivory for the Mediterranean; Begley and De Puma 1991; Horton 1997a.

16 Whitcomb and Johnson 1979, 1982.

17 Turner and Cribb 1996, but see Macdowall 1996, for re-examination of these coin hoards and local stratigraphy to suggest that the short lived duration, which was once believed, has been overstated and that the international trade continued through the second and third centuries.

18 Chittick 1976b, 1977b, 1979. Chittick did not live to complete the excavations or to publish them in detail, but see Smith and Wright 1988 for a study of the Hafun ceramics.

19 Stern 1987.

20 Horton 1996b, pp. 446–8 provides a list of stray classical finds from east and southern Africa.

21 Chami and Msemwa 1997; Chami 1998, 1999a.

22 Harding 1960. The location of these beads is not known, so it is difficult to reassess them.

23 Juma 1996.

24 Sinclair 1991. For Fukuchani, see Horton (forthcoming).

25 Casson 1989; Huntingford 1980 for an earlier translation. Stevenson 1932.

26 Horton 1996b, pp. 415–53. Horton 1990.

27 The timetable can be reconstructed from the known pattern of winds. In July there is a northerly wind in the Red Sea and by September a westerly wind in the Gulf of Aden enabling the ships to catch the north-east monsoon down the African coast in October. The return voyage would begin at any time between May and September, reaching the Gulf of Aden to catch the prevailing easterly in October, which then blows northerly in the Red Sea during October and November – the round trip taking a minimum of fifteen months; Casson 1989.

28 McCrindle 1897, pp. 37–40.

29 The following word *oratoi* was amended in an earlier edition to *Peiratai* (lit. pirates) and more recently into *arotai*, which was translated as farmer, but means more a labourer or dockworker. The most recent view suggests that *oratoi* can be retained and translated as visible, simply meaning that people one sees were big-bodied. If the inhabitants were indeed 'very large', this would rule out local hunter-gatherers, and most likely agriculturalists as well; tall stature is normally associated (and this continues to this day) with pastoralist groups. However, if the coast was inhabited by such pastoralists they seem to have been involved in a complex maritime and fishing culture, which would seem unlikely; Vansina 1997.

30 Chami 1998.

31 Soper 1967a, 1967b.

32 However these two dates were stratigraphically above a dated sample with a fourth/sixth-century date.

33 It is fair to say that this threefold classification has not been accepted by all archaeologists.

34 Chami 1999c.

35 The redating of the Early Iron Age makes sense of another problem in African archaeology. It has long been recognized that the Early Iron Age ceramics found along the Indian Ocean coast of southern Africa bear a very close resemblance to the eastern African ceramics, and that the farming communities must have moved extremely rapidly from north to south, with very little time to change their pottery styles. The 'type' site in the south is Matola, close to the Mozambique coast, which has a first-century radiocarbon date, while other sites of the Matola tradition have radiocarbon dates which are contemporary. A longer East African sequence would help in resolving this ambiguity. Several of the early sites in the south lie adjacent to the coast (e.g. St Lucia Lake sites, Mzonjani, Enkwazini, Maputo University Campus and Zitundo) and exploited maritime environments, and it is just possible that the eastern component of the Early Iron Age could spread south by boat and not overland as is normally thought; Chami 1999b; Hall 1987 for overview and references.

36 Horton 1996a, ch. 12; at Shanga where the ceramics have been counted and studied in particular detail, 41 types have been grouped into four sequential phases labelled A to D according to their stratigraphic position. A developmental sequence can be shown which follows these phases. The basal ceramics – those of phase A – were those of the inhabitants who founded the community around 760.

37 Chittick 1961, 1974, 1984; Abungu 1990; Kirkman 1966; Allibert 1990; Wright 1984, 1992. For material from the eleventh century onwards see especially Allibert, Argant and Argant 1983; Sassoon 1980; Wright 1992.

38 Phillipson 1979; other comparisons were made in particular with the 'group C' pottery, collected in the Usambaras and from excavations at Kaya Singwaya; Abungu 1990; Mutoro 1987; Soper 1967a. In the absence of any other designation, these ceramics, common to both the coast and the interior, were labelled Tana tradition, on account of the first recognition by Phillipson of the connection from his finds at Wenje.

39 Collett 1985. Part of the problem was that ceramics from Early Iron Age sites of the second century were compared to poorly excavated (and dated) material from Manda – comparing assemblages over 800 years apart. Iron Age ceramics were seen to have a single progression in the region, and the ceramics contemporary with the Swahili sites, including Maore ware and Gatung'anga ware, looked quite different to Tana tradition pottery. A case was therefore made (Horton 1990) to link Tana tradition pottery to early pastoralist communities, which by implication would have seen a 'northern' origin for the Swahili, beyond the tsetse infected coastal zone which extended as far north as the Lamu archipelago. There were some grounds for comparison with the pottery produced by these pastoralists, who produced simple open vessels, with incised decoration, often using triangular or criss-cross patterns; Bower 1973; Bower et al. 1977; Collett and Robertshaw 1983.

40 These pastoralist sites were far into the interior, the closest being near Mount Kenya – the source of the river Tana, and dated to the late first millennium BCE.

Here was a possible route to the coast, and while no pastoralist sites have yet been located along this route, the presence of a small group of southern Cushitic speakers still living in the Tana Delta, one of the sites proposed for Rhapta in Ptolemy's *Geography*, did provide some indication that pastoralists did once live along this section of the coast. See Horton 1990 for an extreme statement of this hypothesis.

41 Chami 1994; Haaland 1994; Helm 2000; LaViolette et al. 1989; Schmidt et al 1992. Radiocarbon-dated hinterland sites include Misasa, Dakawa, Kiwangwa and Masuguru (Tanzania), and Mgombani, Chombo and Mteza (Kenya) all with reliable sixth- to tenth-century dates.

42 Chami 1994; Richard Helm's survey of Kenyan coastal hinterland identified 60 sites and his excavations sampled five, spanning Early Iron Age and Tana tradition phases, while his study of some 100,000 sherds made extensive use of multivariate statistics; Helm 2000.

43 Chami 1994; proposed the term Early Iron Working (EIW) for the Early Iron Age and triangular incised ware (TIW) for the Tana tradition pottery. Whilst TIW is descriptively accurate for some of the material, many of the sherds are not decorated with triangular designs, whilst this terminology does not allow for a continuous coastal ceramic tradition, with material that is later, but derivative of the earlier ceramics.

44 Nurse 1982, 1983a; Nurse and Hinnebusch 1993. The proponents of the 'pastoralist' model of Swahili origins (Allen 1993) had a real difficulty in that spoken Swahili has negligible traces of Eastern or Southern Cushitic, which would certainly be expected. If the proto-Swahili once spoke a Cushitic (or even a Nilotic) language, then many more words would have survived in the language than have actually done.

45 Horton (forthcoming).

46 Chittick 1966b; Horton and Clark 1985; A. M. Juma (pers. comm).

47 Chami 1994; Chittick 1975a; LaViolette et al. 1989.

48 Horton 1984; Lamu Ginners, Kipungani, Kiunga, Kiunga Mwina island are the main sites.

49 Examples are Ungwana, Lamu, Pate, Manda and Mbui. Manda has produced a fifth-century radiocarbon date, but the excavator was at the time uninterested in the early levels of the site and dismissed it; Chittick 1967, 1984, p. 67; Horton 1996a, pp. 23–5; Wilson and Omar 1997.

50 Allibert 1990; Chittick 1974, pp. 28–9; Radimilahy 1998; Wright 1984.

51 Duarte 1993; Sinclair 1982, 1987, pp. 86–91, 1991.

52 Chittick 1969b. The sherds (which were not published) are in the British Institute in Nairobi.

3 The Acceptance of Islam

1 Esmail 1975.

2 Freeman-Grenville and Martin 1973, pp. 107, 121; Flury 1922.

3 Chittick 1974, vol. 1, p. 61; Chittick 1984, p. 60; Garlake 1966.

4   Freeman-Grenville 1962b, p. 14; Pellat 1962.

5   Freeman-Greville 1981, p. 35.

6   Trimingham 1964, p. 17, 1975, pp. 122, 135.

7   Gibb 1962, p. 379; Freeman-Grenville 1962b, pp. 27–32.

8   Allen 1993; Kusimba 1999; Nurse and Spear 1985.

9   Various traditions in the Lamu archipelago give the account of the expeditions to East Africa of Abdul Malik, or of his generals, around 696 (AH 77). Some state that his successors as Caliph, al-Mansur and Harun al-Rashid, also conquered East Africa. A list of towns is sometimes given, but several of these are of recent origin and it is likely that these traditions were concocted as part of the Arabization of the coast during the Zanzibar Sultanate; Stigand 1913, pp. 6, 29–30; Hichens 1938, p. 9; Pouwels 1987, p. 55; Hersi 1977; Prins 1967; Tolmacheva 1979. The *Kitab al-Zanuj* or *Book of Zeng* (for the only published version in Italian translation see Cerulli 1957) claims that a Syrian army came to East Africa under Amir Musa ibn Umar to settlements which had accepted Islam during the Caliphate of Umar ibn Khattab.

10 Horton 1996a, ch. 10; Horton 1991.

11 Horton 1996a, ch. 18; H. W. Brown, 1992; 1993.

12 For example the coins minted in Multan, North-West India, which still recognized the Fatimid Caliph in Cairo; Lowick 1983.

13 Freeman-Grenville 1957, 1978a, 1993.

14 The first mosque at Shanga rested on natural sand, but overlay a burnt-out tree stump, that might have been part of an earlier focus of religious activity. Another possible late eighth-century mosque might be inferred from the alignment of Str. 281, located a little way from the centre of the site; Horton 1996a, p. 117.

15 Horton (forthcoming).

16 A. M. Juma (pers. comm.).

17 Sinclair 1987, pp. 87–9.

18 Rogers 1976, p. 130. An account of the cemetery will be published in Horton (forthcoming). Two of the earliest burials were accompanied with incense burners.

19 Wilkinson 1981; Ricks 1970, p. 348 claims evidence that Africans were resident in Siraf during the tenth century.

20 Translated in Freeman-Grenville 1962b, p. 89.

21 Freeman-Grenville 1962b; Strong 1895, p. 35.

22 This could mean that the mosque had a kibla or mihrab.

23 Chittick 1969c; Freeman-Grenville 1962b, p. 221.

24 Pearce 1920, pp. 29–30. Middleton 1992, pp. 30–5, for a fuller analysis of this myth.

25 Pouwels 1987, p. 220; Sacleux 1909, pp. 15–16.

26 Chittick 1965, p. 292, 1974. Allen 1993 thought that the confusion between Shiraz and Shungwaya (a putative homeland of coastal peoples) in some of the traditions – all recorded in the nineteenth and twentieth centuries – as evidence for the 'northern origin'. However such links may not be very old, and are due to the conflation of different traditions. Shungwaya is first mentioned (and shown) on the Dutch map of Linschoten and Langran of 1596, as Jungaya; Van

Linschoten collected his information concerning East Africa in 1583–91, but the account of his voyages do not mention Shungwaya; Freeman-Grenville 1962b, pp. 144–5.

27   Chittick 1984, pp. 217–20

28   Wheatley 1975, p. 104, citing the Song Annals of 1071, which recorded a visit of East Africans to the Chinese court, and also noted that they minted coins in their home country in gold, silver and copper; Hirth and Rockhill 1911, p. 127.

29   Horton, Brown and Oddy 1986. Freeman-Grenville 1986, 1993. The context of the house is that it was built of timber, over recently reclaimed land along the foreshore of the island with dumped pottery dating to c.1000–50.

30   Chittick 1966b; silver coins have also been found at Mafia, as has an imitation Fatimid dinar of the same type that made up some of the Mtambwe gold coins.

31   Freeman-Grenville 1992; Saad 1979.

32   Freeman-Grenville 1962b, p. 136. Shi'ites do not recognise the authority of the Caliphate but instead that authority to lead the faithful descends directly through Fatima, Muhammed's daughter and the wife of Ali. After the murder of Ali in 660 his followers recognized his sons Hasan and Husain, as Imams, leaders who were able to pass on Prophet's revelations. In mainstream Shi'ism, there were twelve Imams in total, passing from father to son, until the twelfth, Muhammed, disappeared in Samarra in 878. Revelation could not be completed until his return, and so this group, known as the Twelvers, cannot accept any further claims to hereditary leadership until the twelfth Imam returns; Sourdel 1983.

33   Freeman-Grenville 1978b, quoting one Portuguese missionary, Fr. Joao dos Santos, who noted that the inhabitants of the coast, 'follow a sect of the Persians, based upon the interpretation of the law of Muhammed made by Ali, and which differs considerably from the sect of the Turks, for whom Umar is the interpreter of the opposite opinion'.

34   Pouwels 1987, pp. 32–7 collected traditions regarding a possible early Shirazi presence in the Lamu archipelago.

35   Flury 1922. For the Siraf connection see Lowick 1985; Whitehouse 1978. In the Swahili *History of Kilwa*, the Shirazi founders are accompanied by Musa bin Amrani, the Bedouin (i.e. a Badys, as mentioned by De Barros). The *Book of Zeng*, a late nineteenth-century source, states that a tribe, known as the Hatami, a section of the Banu Amrani, under a certain Amir Musa bin Umar was sent by the Umayyad Caliph, Abdu'l Malik, taught religion to the people of Mogadishu and Kilwa, and built the fortress at Kilwa. This must be another version of the same tradition, given an 'Arab' interpretation much later; Pouwels 1978, p. 397.

36   Horton forthcoming; Kirkman 1975.

37   The Zaidites, who broke off from the main Shi'ite group with their own concept of Caliphate leadership, followed Zaid ibn Ali, a grandson of Husain, who led a short-lived revolt against the Umayyads in Kufa around 740; they came to live in the Yemen.

38   Freeman-Grenville 1962b, p. 83.

39   Allen 1993, p. 24 also proposed a Zaidite connection for the Shanga Muslims, but was not prepared to accept the clear archaeological evidence for Islam at

Shanga during the eighth century, preferring to date their arrival in the tenth century, after the Zaidites were well established in the Yemen.

40 As described by al-Hamdani; Toll 1968, ch. 46. Jetzer 1981 on the evidence for terracotta coin moulds.

41 Freeman-Grenville 1962b, pp. 83–4

42 Horton 1996a, p. 402; stage F in the development of the site. Mogadishu is most likely to date from the eleventh or early twelfth century; see Jama 1996. Sinclair 1991, differing from the views of Chittick 1982. Mogadishu was first mentioned by Ibn Sa'id (early thirteenth century) and described by Yaqut (*c.*1224) with a republican government like that found at Barawa (Trimingham 1964, pp. 5–6). See also Alpers 1983.

43 The Seveners, often known as the Isma'ilis, held there to be only seven legitimate Imams, the seventh having disappeared in 765, and his return would portend the Millennium. The Isma'ilis were able to found breakaway states in Syria, in Bahrain (the Carmathians), and in Tunisia in 916. The Tunisian Isma'ilis, known as the Fatimids, spread to Sicily and later to Cairo in 968.

44 There was a very large population of East African slaves living in lower Iraq in the ninth century; some certainly became Muslims, including the ruler of the famous Zanj revolt (868–89), Ali ibn Muhammed, who embraced confused Shi'ite and Kharijite doctrines. For twelve years the Zanj maintained a substantial area beyond the control of the Caliphate, defeated several armies sent against them, and even constructed fortresses. Their defeat in 889 led to the massacre of large numbers of them, but some may have escaped and a few could have returned to East Africa which others were involved in establishing the Carmathian movement, which developed in the same region in the aftermath of the Zanj revolt; Popovic 1976.

45 Pouwels 1974; De Barros gives twelve chiefs, but the government was historically based on seven plus seven clans, again a reflection of the seven brothers; it is unclear why De Barros is also inconsistent on the point of seven brothers and twelve chiefs.

46 Wilkinson 1981 proposes that they may have been Kharijite, but there is no trace of Kharijite influence on the northern coast.

47 McKay 1975, p. 26, quoting correspondance of C. P. Rigby on the acquisition of Zanzibar by the Arabs.

48 Allen 1993, p. 180.

49 Kharijite is the broad term given to those who claim that there should be 'no decision but God's' or that matters should be decided entirely on Quranic authority where necessary supplemented by tradition passed down from Muhammed. The state's administrative and political decisions (such as on rules of succession) were totally on Islamic principles. The Islamic community was a 'community of saints' and that any misdemeanour should be punished by death or banishment. In extreme form this provided for the murder of corrupt leaders (and the Kharijites later claimed this as the justification for the murder of Uthman, the third Caliph), the massacre of non-Muslims and in some cases, such as by the extreme Azraqites, the killing of Muslims who did not follow the Kharijite principles.

50 Badger 1871, p. 18; Schacht 1964, Wilkinson 1975, p. 101. The campaign against the Julanda brothers (who may not have been Kharijite, but keen to maintain their local tribal authority) by al-Hajjaj b. Yusuf, the governor of Iraq, was probably in 705.

51 Cerulli 1957; Gray 1958b.

52 Translation is that of Trimingham 1975, p. 130, from Pellat 1962, p. 1, sec. 112.

53 Much of this would have been known by al-Mas'udi, as the Cretan Emirate was still functioning during his lifetime. In the early part of the ninth century, there were a series of revolts against the Umayyad Emir of Spain, Hakam (796–822), mainly by the converted indigenous population, known as the *muwalladun*. These were suppressed with great brutality, but a sizable group were expelled; some went to Fez, and others moved around the Mediterranean, eventually arriving in Alexandria in 813. By this time they seem to have acquired ships and were raiding islands in the Aegean. Probably in 824, an expedition of 40 ships under ibn Hafs landed in Crete, with little resistance, and established a semi-independent emirate which lasted for 140 years. The Cretan Emir was Sunni and held a marginal allegance to the Abbasid Caliphate (for example by placing the Caliph's name on the Emirate's coins), and it seems that the Muslims were fairly rapidly assimilated into the local population; Christides 1984. Very little of the Muslim presence on Crete has survived, for archaeological and numismatic evidence see Miles 1975; Miles and Warren 1972.

54 Wilkinson 1981; Risso 1986, pp. 1–15.

55 Wilkinson 1979, 1981.

56 Trimingham 1975, pp. 129–36; Freeman-Grenville 1988, for the unlikely suggestion that it was located in the Comores, Shepherd 1982, a view also accepted by Allen 1993.

57 Kirkman 1959 identifed the later stone town at Ras Mkumbuu; for the earlier site on the hill see Horton (forthcoming). The research at Chwaka is ongoing; LaViolette 1999; LaViolette and Fleisher 1995.

58 In most mosques the mihrab, or prayer niche, whose original function was to indicate the *qibla* line, developed elaborate ornamentation and often became a deep recess, into which the imam leading the prayers would pray. This does not fit in with Ibadi teachings and their mihrabs are very plain and do not project beyond the thickness of the wall – because everyone is considered equal in the eyes of God – and the practice of the Iman leading the prayers was not followed, except in the case of the one elected Iman in Muscat. The shallow recess emphasized this important theological point and was a trait also found in ninteenth-century Zanzibari mosques, where there was a sizable Ibadi community.

59 It may be significant that no coins have been found at Ras Mkumbuu, even though there are levels contemporary with Mtambwe Mkuu.

60 Wilkinson 1981, 1989.

61 Chittick 1966a, p. 30.

62 Referred to as Shanga, most probably not the town in the Lamu archipelago.

63 Wilkinson 1989, pp. 136–43.

64 Yaqut, writing before 1224, reported that the Sultan of Pemba was an Arab who had recently emigrated from Kufa, suggesting that these doctrines (strongly present in Kufa) had spread to Pemba as well; Trimingham 1975, p. 135.

65 Chittick 1965; Freeman-Grenville 1962a. MH has benefited from long discussions with John Wilkinson concerning the Ibadi dimension to Kilwa's history.

66 The distinction is that sharifs descended via al-Hasan, and sayyids via al-Husain, the two sons of Ali. By the eleventh century, these descendants were Sunni rather than Shi'ite.

67 Cerulli 1957, p. 18; Pouwels 1978. Chittick 1982, p. 49 quotes the Yemeni author, Ibn al-Mujawir (writing in *c*.1232) that the Banu Majid were forced from the Mundhiriyya district of the Yemen in 1159, and one group went to Mogadishu, another to Zeila, and a third to Zafar. Hersi 1977.

68 Martin 1974, pp. 371–4; Saad 1979, pp. 184–91.

69 Pouwels 1978, pp. 225, 396–400; Prins 1967, pp. 82–3.

70 Hasan bin Sulaiman, who was ruling when Ibn Battuta visited Kilwa not only minted copper coins, but also gold coins, where he assumes titles that were in use at the time in Rasulid Yemen; H. W. Brown 1991. The rulers of Mogadishu also begin minting coins around this time; Freeman-Grenville 1963b.

71 Martin 1974, pp. 377–90.

72 Pouwels 1987, pp. 63–72.

73 Kusimba 1999, p. 110, describing one of the Mtwapa burials; Kirkman 1963, p. 11 for a possible non-Muslim burial at Gedi.

74 One of the best known examples is the site of Mbaraki on Mombasa island, where the mosque was recently rebuilt partly to reduce the influence of the spirits; Sassoon 1982. For a discussion of spirits, see chapter 9; Alpers 1984; Swantz 1966, 1970.

75 Horton 1996a, p. 200 for stratified incense burners at Shanga, found among the collapsed rubble of the Friday Mosque. Richard Wilding 1973 found many incense burners during his survey of the tombs on the northern Kenyan coast, and two were also found in the 'house' at Dondo. It is also quite normal to find small offerings (such as plastic, rags, glass bottles), which are often very recent, in ruined mihrab recesses.

4 *The Swahili Coast and the Indian Ocean World*

1 Whitehouse 1996; Whitehouse and Williamson 1975.

2 Whitehouse 1974; Wilkinson 1979; Williamson 1974.

3 Discussed in Wilkinson 1981, pp. 279–81.

4 Popovic 1976. The restoration and extension of the irrigation system is attributed to the time of al-Hajjaj at the beginning of the eighth century; Trimingham 1975, pp. 116–18. The main source for the Zanj in Iraq is Tabari, *Ta'rikh* III, 1747–87 and 1834–2103.

5 Lewis 1974, vol. ii, p. 212.

6 Horton 1996a, p. 367, in levels dating *c.* 750–850; Chittick 1984, p. 209.

7 Hodges and Whitehouse 1983, pp. 103–22, 129.

8   Tampoe 1989.
9   Horton 1996a, pp. 414–16; Ricks 1970.
10 Freeman-Grenville 1962b, p. 16.
11 Ricks 1970, fn. 32 provides a useful discussion of the references.
12 Whitehouse 1968, 1971, 1974, 1979; Wilding 1977; Horton 1996a, pp. 271–
    310 for a list of imports found on East African sites of this period.
13 Williamson 1974. Recent excavations by the British Museum on the site has
    discovered more sherds.
14 Morrison 1984, p. 164.
15 Horton 1987b.
16 Chittick 1966d, no. 6. Chittick 1984, p. 213. Horton 1996a, 373; Horton,
    Brown and Oddy 1986.
17 Summers 1969.
18 Oddy 1984.
19 Sinclair 1987.
20 Freeman-Grenville 1962b, p. 15, 1981, p. 38, 1993.
21 Lamm 1929, vol. i, p. 511.
22 C. Kusimba pers. comm.
23 Goitein 1973. While there is no direct evidence that Jewish merchants sailed to
    East Africa, they were dealing in ivory, crystal and ambergris in Aden and Kish;
    Goitein 1966, p. 339, 1967.
24 For example, pottery from the Yemen appears earlier on in the northern ports,
    such as Mogadishu, and is rare on Pemba island; there is much more Indian
    pottery on Tumbatu than from other sites during the fourteenth century. The
    detailed study of these patterns holds up the prospect of quite detailed analysis
    of trade patterns.
25 Trimingham 1975, p. 125.
26 Lewis vol. ii, 1974, 120; Ricks 1970, pp. 352–7. Whitehouse 1976; Williamson
    1973. The competition between Aden and Kish at this time seems to have been
    over the control of the African trade; Goitein 1954.
27 Morgan 1991.
28 Barnet 1997.
29 Freeman-Grenville 1962b, p. 91; Sutton 1997 for a discussion of Kilwa's
    supposed control of the gold trade.
30 H. W. Brown 1991.
31 Dols 1977.
32 It bears the inscription, in Portuguese: The most high Prince and mighty
    Lord Dom Manuel I ordered the making from the gold and tribute of Kilwa,
    completed in 1506.
33 Baxter and Da Silva Rego, 1962–71, vol. viii, pp. 344–5.
34 Pearson 1998, pp. 48, 101–4. For Barbosa and Pires, their accounts are
    reprinted in Freeman-Grenville 1962b, pp. 124–34; Alpers 1976.
35 Axelson 1973; Newitt 1978; Pearson 1998, pp. 129–54; Strandes 1961.
36 Day 1987, pp. 1–38.
37 Pearson 1998, pp. 84–100 is an excellent modern account; for the sources see
    Baxter and Da Silva Rego 1962–71; Theal 1898–1903.

38 Risso 1986.
39 J. M. Gray, 1957, pp. 1–22, 1962; Sheriff 1987, pp. 15–24; Akinola 1968. For the Portuguese period, Boxer and Azevedo 1960.
40 Allen 1974b; Hichens 1939.
41 Sheriff 1987, p. 37; Martin and Ryan 1977 calculate a higher figure of 4000 in the decades from 1770. See also Nicholls 1971.
42 Alpers 1970, 1992; P. D. Curtin 1981; Freeman-Grenville 1965b; Sheriff 1987, pp. 41–8.
43 Bennett and Brooks 1965; Bhacker 1992.
44 Shayt 1992.
45 The sultans were the largest plantation owners; Cooper 1977; Lovejoy 1983, p. 223.
46 The myths of Kilwa had told how the original immigrant princes acquired and legimated their own power precisely by marrying the daughters of the indigenous rulers they found along the coast. The Swahili were not going to repeat those events with themselves in the losing position. Middleton 1992, p. 34.
47 Middleton 1961, p. 52.
48 Anderson 1954; Bang 1999; Hirsch 1998; Purpura 1997; in Zanzibar the Chief Justice, who was British, sat with the sultans' Islamic judges and local assessors to administer both Islamic and British law.
49 Bennett 1971; Hahner-Herzog 1990; Page 1974.
50 The literature on the caravan trade is substantial; Alpers 1969a, 1969b; Beachey 1962, 1967, 1976; B. Brown 1971; Cummings 1973, 1985; Lamden 1963; Lamphear 1970.
51 For the ivory trade, see Ylvisaker 1982.
52 It is difficult to obtain figures to demonstrate this impoverishment in detail, as it was not accompanied by that of Zanzibar itself: export figures for the entire coast did not show any marked decline; Nicholls 1971; Sheriff 1987.
53 Ylvisaker 1979; see also chapter 10 below.
54 For details on these developments, Cooper 1977, 1980, 1987; also Middleton 1961.
55 Martin and Martin 1978; McMaster 1966.

5 *The Trading System of the Swahili Coast*

1 Freeman-Grenville 1981, p. 31.
2 Duyvendak 1949, pp. 13–14.
3 Freeman-Grenville 1981, p. 66
4 Yakut, translation Trimingham 1964, p. 6.
5 Gibb 1962, p. 379
6 Horton 1996a, p. 60
7 Allen 1979a, p. 11; Middleton 1992, pp. 63–4.
8 Garlake 1973, p. 132
9 Horton 1984, p. 310.

10 The basic studies of East African coins are, H. W. Brown, 1992, 1993; Freeman-Grenville 1957, 1963b, 1978a, 1986; Walker 1936.

11 H. W. Brown 1993; Horton 1996a.

12 Brown 1991

13 H. W. Hirth and Rockhill 1911.

14 Horton 1996a, pp. 375–7.

15 The is also one copper coin of Muhammed bin Ali, known from Zanzibar, who is also represented in silver at Mtambwe.

16 The Mtambwe hoard included three imitation Fatimid dinars; a further one is known from a surface find at Kisimani Mafia. A hoard of ten dinars has also been found in Diego Suaraz harbour in Madagascar (but remains unpublished). None of these are 'crusader copies', nor of Yemeni origin, and local production should be considered for these coins, using an illegible and garbled script.

17 Freeman-Grenville 1962b, p. 40.

18 Freeman-Grenville 1962b, pp. 107–8; Strandes 1961, p. 284.

19 Freeman-Grenville 1962b, p. 140 n.20.

20 Day 1987, pp. 34, 69.

21 Strandes 1961, p. 287.

22 Freeman-Grenville 1962b, pp. 107–8.

23 The Australian coins come from Marchinbar island, and included Dutch coins, the latest being 1784, suggesting that they reached there in the later eighteenth century. A genuine medieval deposition can be suggested for a coin of Daud bin Sulaiman from al-Ballid, near Salalah, and for a small group of coins from Julfar; Hansman 1985.

24 Herbert 1984; The Kilwa coins which have been analysed are almost pure copper, and not alloys, and were made of local metal. It was probably the same for gold. However silver is very rare in sub-Saharan Africa, and Islamic silver dirhams were probably melted down. This would explain why the silver coins are so small and rare, but were nonetheless needed in a trimetallic currency.

25 Horton 1987a, 1987b, 1994.

26 Prins 1982, p. 90, 1984; Gilbert 1998.

27 Freeman-Grenville 1962b, pp. 106–7, 138–9.

28 Axelson 1998, p. 37. While the literature has focused on the *mtepe*, outrigger boats, as are mentioned by Ibn al-Mujawir as sailing between Kilwa and Aden, must also have been important; Trimingham 1975. This is the first reference to the use of the mariner's compass in local boats; it was however in use in the Indian Ocean by the end of the eleventh century, although, given the clear skies, celestial navigation was always more important. Houvani 1995.

29 For example dentate ware from the Comores, dating to the ninth century, found at Shanga; Horton 1996a, p. 254. The pottery also suggests emerging regional style; Horton 1994.

30 Abungu 1990; Abungu and Mutoro 1993; Fawcett and LaViolette 1990.

31 Chami 1994; Helm 2000.

32 Ylvisaker 1979, 1982 for the Lamu area in the eighteenth and nineteenth centuries; also Turton 1975. For the hinterland of Malindi; Champion 1967;

Hamilton 1920–1; Johnstone 1902; Kirkman 1983b. On the hunting groups: Champion 1922; Stiles 1981; Tucker 1969.

33 Freeman-Grenville 1962b, pp. 141, 150.

34 Burton 1872, vol. i, pp. 299, described the attack on the Omani troops in 1840, when the Wagunya (Katwa) 'charged in a firm line, brandishing spear heads like those of the Wamasai, a cubit long, and shouted as they waved their standards, wooden hoops hung round with the dried and stuffed spoils of men. The Arabs fled with such precipitation…' He adds details of how the trophies were obtained using a lanyard, the victim being preferably still alive.

35 Turton 1975; Wilding 1988.

36 The linguistic evidence suggests that the Segeju (most likely the Mossegejos of the Portuguese sources) arrived from the north, as Highland Bantu speaking pastoralists, who may have come into contact with cattle and camel keepers in southern Somalia, on their way to the coast; Nurse 1982. Allen's 1984 hypothesis involves a controversial reading of the traditions.

37 Schmidt 1989.

38 Connah 1996, p. 91; Sutton 1987; A. Reid pers. comm.

39 Freeman-Grenville 1963a, pp. 153–4; Sheriff 1975.

40 Sinclair 1987.

41 Hall 1987 is the best general account. Glass beads provide a good indicator for an Indian Ocean connection, but because of the nature of African soils, can easily intrude into early levels; many of the early dates which have been claimed may well be suspect as the beads are typologically similar to later types. Glass beads are rare on coastal sites until 1000; thereafter 'trade-wind' beads are ubiquitous; Sinclair 1987, p. 150. There was probably trade before 800, but its recognition remains difficult.

42 Voigt 1983.

43 Huffman 1996, pp. 175–91.

44 These bracelets are often thought of as for local use, but they were probably exported as well; al-Ma'sudi notes the export of ivory bracelets to India.

45 Denbow 1986.

46 Specialist traders may have been involved – at least this is one explanation for the very curious traditions of origin of the Lemba, who claim a confused past in southern Arabia. The Yao may have been another such group of specialist traders.

47 Levtzion and Hopkins 1981, p. 58.

48 Garlake 1973, Huffman 1996, pp. 125–74.

49 Sutton 1997.

50 Garlake 1973, plates ix, x and xii show most of what has survived. In addition, there were reports of over 30,000 glass beads.

51 Sinclair 1987, pp. 91–7.

52 The Portuguese 'town' of Sofala has been partly covered by the sea. The early Sofala of the historical sources may have been located further south in the region of Chibuene/Inhambane.

53 Hall 1987, p. 118.
54 Beach 1994, pp. 97–108
55 Fagan 1969, pp. 102–6, 135–45.
56 Pearson 1998, p. 103.
57 E. J. Brown 1980; Gray and Birmingham 1970; Roberts 1968.
58 Low 1963.
59 There were many efforts by colonial administrations to find substitutes: elephant, zebra, giraffe and others were tried but were unsuccessful (except for in the Belgian Congo where elephants were successfully trained and used for lumber work until Congo independence).
60 Mainly Kamba, Luyia, Luo, Nyamwezi, Yao, Sukuma and Swahili slaves. See Cummings 1973, 1985; Lamden 1963.
61 Abdy 1924. See below, chapter 7.
62 Chagga chiefs had these intermediaries at their various courts in the late nineteenth century; Sally Falk Moore, pers. comm.
63 There is useful material on this process, although not always clearly linked to the patron–client networks. See, for example, Parkin 1972, 1989; Willis 1993; Cooper 1987.
64 Some Swahili and non-Swahili interior traders brought caravans to Pangani; Glassman 1995.
65 The guest-rooms or *sabule* were used for these visitors. The daughters remained with their children in their natal houses and did not follow their husbands to Arabia.
66 Some of these towns exist today as 'Swahili' towns; European 'explorers', traders, and missionaries of the period had perforce to use the help and shelter of coastal caravans and the hospitality of local Zanzibar-linked potentates. Some places, such as Tabora, later became important Christian mission stations where local rulers saw the advantage of encouraging missionaries to remain as educators and, probably more important, as de facto representatives of European administrations after Zanzibar lost its power in the interior to the British and Germans.
67 There has been little study of this phenomenon: almost all records were written in Gujerati and neither easily available nor translated into English, and the histories of trade have been strongly Eurocentric; Salvadori 1997.
68 Many colonial game wardens throughout the twentieth century were also Baluchi and small Baluchi quarters were found in many of the district headquarters of the region.
69 It took a long time for metal coinage to be acceptable inland, for example by caravan porters who would be paid wages in it, as there was nothing they could do with it other than make it into body ornaments; Cummings 1973.
70 This should not be exaggerated: sellers and buyers were at that time almost entirely Omani Arabs, and it would seem doubtful that clan and lineage links between the many Omani families did not enter somewhere into these transactions. But our evidence is inadequate.

71   The later situations in Mozambique would indicate that the Portuguese took on the previous roles of the Swahili whom they ousted from that region. Despite the very great mass of archival data from Mozambique, we know of no records that might throw more light on this ultimately ethnic question; Newitt 1995.

72   el-Zein 1974, p. 38.

73   Except for mangrove poles which were stored in the open near the jetties (as they still are), and slaves who were kept in safety on the mainland; a large enclosure for the storage of slaves survives at Bagamoyo.

74   Transactions in the Lamu food market in the late 1980s varied as to whether seller and buyer were Gikuyu or Swahili, and whether (rarely) they were in any way related. Prices demanded and given varied with these factors.

75   There is a large literature on nineteenth- and twentieth-century Mombasa: among other sources see especially Cooper 1987; Hayle 1999; Kindy 1972; Russel 1981; Salin 1973, 1976; Silberman Strobel 1979; Swartz 1991, ch. 2; Willis 1993; Wilson 1961.

76   Kopytoff 1986.

77   Appadurai 1986.

78   The exceptions were those considered to be 'enclaved' and removed from exchange by having to be given to rulers as forms of tribute, such as the 'royal' parts of hunted animals that symbolized royal power.

79   Cloth has other qualities. An innate one is that it rarely lasts very long unless carefully treated and tended, so that its age and the age of its possession may increase its value as an indicator of the cultural inheritance of its owners (whether wearers or museum keepers); Appadurai 1986.

80   In the late nineteenth century Arab and French traders worked at Kilwa to obtain slaves for export to the then French-owned Mascarene Islands; the currency used was Indian; Freeman-Grenville 1965b.

81   In the manumission, the manumitter was in a sense indebted to the ex-slave who had indirectly bestowed him with moral credit.

6   *The Urban Landscape*

1   Urbanism has often been defined in terms of cultural features that it possesses, often ending up as 'laundry lists' of traits, such as population concentrations, craft specializations, public architecture, trade, taxation and writing; on such criteria few cities in pre-colonial sub-Saharan Africa would qualify (McIntosh 1998). A more useful approach is to consider the cultural context, for example Wheatley 1972 or Lapidus 1969 for the oriental or Islamic city. An Islamic city is defined by possession of a mosque, baths and a central market. 'Traditional' Swahili towns have a mosque, but rarely a food market and never baths. They are *sui generis*. For African urbanism, see McIntosh 1998; for a critique of the Swahili 'City State' and Hankansson see Sinclair 2000.

2   Urbanity is intimately linked to *ustaarabu*, usually translated as 'civilization' and often taken as meaning the quality of being Arab; the word comes from

the root verb *-staarabu*, to gain understanding or wisdom from long residence.

3   Destruction is normally in bushland areas, by large animals, developers or farmers. Pate, which once had many stone houses, has been almost cleared for building stones by the present inhabitants.

4   Aldrick 1990; Allen 1979a, 1979b; Brown 1985, p. 175; Horton 1996a, pp. 26–61.

5   Allen 1979a; Garlake 1966; Ghaidan 1976; Kirkman 1963, 1973; Wilson 1979b, 1982.

6   Some of the early Shanga stone houses also had thatch over their flat roofs, suggesting that there was an intermediate stage. Some stone houses in Pate still have thatch on their flat roofs, apparently to keep the house cool and control the run-off of the heavy rains.

7   Horton 1993. Donley-Reid 1990 takes an alternative view.

8   Horton 1996a, pp. 38–40; Meffert 1980.

9   Ottenheimer 1984

10   Révoil 1885; Wilson 1982. These settlement forms are very similar to the *Raya* settlements of the Mijikenda and there may be a link between them; Horton 1987a; Mutoro 1987; Weyner 1915.

11   Allen 1993, p. 222. We are grateful to Stéphane Pradines for his results from Gedi.

12   Middleton (1992: 55 ff) suggested Stone-town and Country-town, the former a translation of *miji ya mawe*, (lit. towns of stone). This terminology is confusing, as it excludes towns before stone architecture became widespread in the fourteenth century, while some towns built of stone (for example Nungwi in northern Zanzibar) do not operate as 'stone towns', but are more like the country towns. Our revised terminology stresses the owners of the settlements, rather than their general characteristics. Although Middleton's original terms were clearly stated to refer to their functions and occupants and not to their physical appearance, many critics have failed to comprehend that qualification. More importantly, either category of town may over time take on the functions and composition of the other, a fact that can be dealt with more easily with this new terminology.

13   Allen 1973, 1974a, 1979a; Donley 1982, 1984, 1987; Donley-Reid 1990; Ghaidan 1975, 1976; Middleton 1992, ch. 3.

14   Pouwels 1987, pp. 63–8.

15   Wilson 1979a; el-Zein 1974: p. 133, for an account of the two cemeteries of Lamu town and burial by clan affiliation.

16   The house of Habib Swaleh, the famous Lamu saint and reformer which has been preserved as a place of pilgrimage from the early twentieth century and follows the 'Bajuni' plan.

17   Three examples of stone houses with central passageways, at Dondo, Mvuleni and Fukuchani, have Portuguese associations, and the plan may have arisen from contact with early European settlers. The Mvuleni and Fukuchani houses are defended with a perimeter wall and loopholes for muskets, and the most likely explanation is that they were Portuguese farms but built by Swahili craftsmen.

18   J. W. T. Allen, 1981; Glassman 1995.

19   Much less archaelogical research has been undertaken on these towns as they have not been seen in the past as typically Swahili. This is wrong, and these towns are as much part of the economy and society as the more famous stone towns; Middleton 1961 on the commoners' towns of Zanzibar and Pemba, Caplan 1975, 1982 on Mafia; Goldman 1995 on Pemba.

20   For example Nungwi at the northern tip of Zanzibar or the 'towns' on the Micheweni peninsula – Micheweni, Shumba, Wingwi, Maziwa Ngombe and Kiuyu on Pemba. An exception is the very interesting town of Kojani which lies on a small peninsular jutting out into the sea, a typical location for a patricians' town. Little modern research has taken place there except for unpublished work by P. A. Lienhardt and a brief report in Middleton 1961, p. 56.

21   Uroa is of some interest, because when Freeman-Grenville visited in the 1950s, he commented that it was a village built of mud and thatch; Freeman-Grenville 1957.

22   Allen 1981b; Kusimba 1999, pp. 121–4; Wilson 1982.

23   Wilson 1978, 1980.

24   Horton and Mudida 1993.

25   Kusimba 1996, pp. 707–11.

26   Regional differences in the character of towns may also be important; Horton 1994.

27   Prins 1956–8, 1965, 1967, 1971; Caplan 1975; Swartz 1991; Middleton 1961, 1992. Anthropologists have tried to offer definitions that may be used for comparative purposes, but other writers appear to have little or no interest in these matters.

28   For example, the congregational mosque of the town of Lamu stands in a street, Teremkoni 'place of descending' from the dunes behind the town to the sea-front, which is the only named street out of many except for the *msita wa mui*, 'the street of the town', the main street of shops running the length of the town's one street behind the seafront. Other streets are not named.

29   In a sense different from the more conventional anthropological one, which refers to marriage divisions. The word 'deme' has been used in place of moiety but demes, at least in Lamu, are distinct entities, as we explain in chapter 8. Middleton 1992, p. 81; Prins 1971.

30   The word *mkao* (lit. community of joint residence) is sometimes heard for *mtaa*.

31   Swahili poetry is a central part of contemporary social action, and of the remembered past, and forms an important part of modern electioneering. The literature on Swahili poetry is large, but see especially, Abdulaziz 1977; J. W. T. Allen, 1971; Farsi 1958; Ingrams 1931, p. 392; Knappert 1967, 1979; Shariff 1973, 1988; Scheven 1981; Velten 1907; Whiteley 1958.

32   el-Zein 1974, ch. 7; Glassman 1995; Gray 1955; Hirschberg 1974; Middleton 1992.

33   Glassman 1995; Gray 1955.

34   el-Zein 1974; Middleton 1992, p. 77.

35   Middleton 1961, pp. 17, 34; as long ago discussed for the Nuer of the Sudan; Evans-Pritchard 1940.

36 For Lamu, Allen 1974b; for Siyu, H. Brown 1985, p. 130, 1988; Eastman and Topan 1966.

37 Including the central courtyard of a house, the workspace of a garage, and also an airfield.

38 This is a plural form, the singular *jengo* rarely being used; there are many words for different kinds of building and these are in general use instead.

39 Middleton 1961, p. 21. Caplan 1975; Goldman 1995.

40 The English word 'farming' does not give a true picture of the Swahili activity of producing vegetable foods, which is done more by what in English is called 'gardening'. The growing of crops in 'fields' *makonde* is very different; Nabhany 1985.

41 This word is used also for plantations. It is also used throughout East Africa for any kind of field or productive plot, but for the Swahili it has very specific reference.

42 Despite its importance, there are rather few accounts of Swahili land tenure and use; Middleton 1961; Caplan 1975. For earlier colonial reports, J. M. Gray, 1956; Great Britain 1933–4; McGeagh and Addis 1934; Pakenham 1945.

43 This situation has changed markedly in the last several decades, especially in Zanzibar, but there is little published on the matter, that is concerned with wider social implications rather than narrow legal ones.

44 Although in Pate the patricians have preferred sorghum; see below.

45 Middleton 1961.

46 Allen 1974a, p. 128; Fitzgerald 1898, p. 392.

47 The frequency of bread ovens (known as *mofa*) from excavated sites suggests that bread made from sorghum flour was the staple in the pre-sixteenth-century period, and that the practice at Pate is a survival of this tradition; for Chinese accounts of flour cakes, Freeman-Grenville 1962b, p. 21.

48 There is a large literature on Swahili slavery; see especially Cooper 1973, 1977, 1980; Akinola 1972, 1987; Lodhi 1973; Sheriff 1987; Nicholls 1971; Lovejoy 1983; Curtin 1983; Manning 1990; Miers and Kopytoff 1977; Austen 1989; Hutchinson 1874, Eastman 1988b. Others are listed in Middleton 1992, p. 204. Patricians were the principal owners and traders until the founding of the Zanzibar sultanate, whose economy was also based on the institution (as was Oman itself). Sheriff has argued that the numbers of exported slaves have been exaggerated, and his figures are acceptable. Even so, the drain on African humanity over the centuries was enormous. Although there remain many doubts as to the provenance of slaves and of slave trading from one period to another, the central and especially the southern areas of the interior became increasingly important in the ever wider and ever more brutal trade of nineteenth-century Zanzibar, which virtually destroyed many of the economies and societies of the interior.

49 Cooper 1980; Middleton 1961, p. 43.

50 Never those given to free women or taken from the members of the Prophet's family, but rather those extolling virtues such as obedience or devoted work.

51 There is often published a set of photographs from the Lamu Museum of 'women of Lamu' dressed in elaborate clothing and jewellery. These were

slaves, dressed up by their mistresses, who themselves would never have agreed to be photographed.

52 Concubines, *suria*, pl. *masuria*, the prefix indicating someone of formally recognized status, were women who were given their own small houses by their owners; their children were legitimate and they would normally be given their freedom at the birth of their first child, although they would usually continue as concubines to the same men and were often inherited by the latters' brothers or even sons.

53 This is our own term in this context, and we think it is a useful development of the ideas in Middleton 1972; Horne 1984, see also Datoo 1975.

54 This list is not comprehensive, and we could perhaps include other conurbations, such as those of the Comoro Islands or of northern Madagascar.

55 A remnant of this is the Zanzibar government's cattle ranch, on the mainland to the north of Bagamoyo, which was established after the Union as a political gesture.

7   Social Networks

1 A main difficulty in this analysis is the nomenclature for the many social groups found in the Swahili towns, the clustering of which and the usage of kinship terms is peculiar to each. This is not a 'full' account but merely enough information to help explicate Swahili mercantile practice. The most useful accounts are those by Prins 1956–8; Caplan 1969, 1975; Swartz 1991; Middleton 1992, ch. 4. Landberg 1977, ch. 5. Our knowledge of details of social organization is limited to the twentieth century: we can probably assume that they have remained relatively unchanged in the same way as other organizational features such as types of settlement and forms of exchange.

2 Knysh 1999, p. 215 for detailed documentary evidence for Hadrami in Arabia itself covering several centuries, which is so far lacking among the Swahili. The suspected theft of many precious Swahili family papers by European scholars has made such research difficult in East Africa.

3 In addition there have been and are still made certain assumptions not based on actual behaviour but on outmoded and simplistic views of the nature of descent and kinship. The most persistent has been the unfounded view that the Swahili have at one time or other, and also today, reckoned descent matrilineally: this view appears to be both a misinterpretation of some items of behaviour and also a vestige of outmoded evolutionist thinking; Middleton 1992, p. 99.

4 The Swahili word is *nasaba*, used preferably to refer to those from Arabia. An African genealogy is rarely called *nasaba*, which has the implication of 'good' or 'gentle' ancestry.

5 Although in recent years many people of slave ancestry have produced long genealogies, typically going back to great kings of the interior.

6 Many writers have disliked these terms, others have used them indiscriminately and incorrectly, and others have simply denied their existence altogether.

7 Omani and Hadrami immigrants recognize far more subclans and lineages, including those classed as Ghafiria, Hinawia, Besa, and the royal Busaidi and Yarubi; Ingrams 1931, p. 194; Yalden-Thompson 1958.

8 See Evans-Pritchard 1940; I. M. Lewis 1955.

9 There is a very considerable literature on Mombasa, see especially Berg 1968; also DeBlij 1968; Hinawy 1964, 1970; Janmohamed 1976; Kindy 1972; Silberman 1950; Stren 1970; Swartz 1991.

10 Berg 1968; Strobel 1979; Swartz 1991, p. 32.

11 Middleton 1961; Caplan 1969, 1975.

12 As is typical of patrilineal descent systems. However, some writers have mistaken this as indicating matriliny; Middleton 1992, p. 99; Shepherd 1977, 1987.

13 Middleton 1961, p. 52; Arens and Arens 1978; Busaidy 1958; Goldman 1995.

14 Prins 1956–8; Swartz 1991, p. 64. Properly the kin terms used by patricians possess plural forms that differ according to the ages or ranks of the speaker and the person addressed, whereas these plural forms are rarely used by non-patricians; and these days with their general loss of overall seniority in the society at large they are rarely used by patricians themselves; Middleton 1992, p. 213.

15 Middleton 1992, p. 143.

16 Landberg 1977, p. 11; Moreau 1941, 1944; Pedler 1940; Middleton 1992, p. 111; Abdy 1924.

17 The term was also used between the Swahili rulers of Vumba and non-Swahili dependent groups during an interregnum when former political ties had yet to be reaffirmed; Baker 1949.

18 Tanner 1962, 1964.

19 See Middleton 1961; Middleton 1992, ch. 5; Guennec-Coppens 1987; L. Holy 1985.

20 The term has as plural *masuria*, the prefix denoting a formally recognized social status. Concubines were mostly educated women who had adopted Islam and could acquire a reputable status in the town at large; Strobel 1979, p. 48.

21 Lambert 1962–3.

22 Hollis 1900; McKay 1975, pp. 68–70.

23 Ottenheimer 1984, 1985; Shepherd 1977.

24 Sheriff and Ferguson 1991, pp. 109–87. 'Colonial rule' is there held to have begun with the British and German presence in Zanzibar, and overrule by the earlier Omani rulers of the Zanzibar Sultanate, when a different system of hierarchy obtained, is not so considered.

25 Allen 1993, pp. 198–9; McKay 1975, p. 69.

26 There are a number of studies of land tenure and property, often undertaken for the Zanzibar government; see especially, J. M. Gray 1956; Middleton 1961; Pakenham 1945; Singer 1996.

27 For example, rights in a coconut palm do not give rights to the soil in which it grows, which may be held by others. The Afro-Shirazi slogan, used by squatters towards Omani-Arab plantation owners, was 'the trees are yours, the land is ours'.

28 The *Minhaj et Talibin*, the standard work on Islamic law used among the Swahili and others of the East African coast, states 'Any Muslim can own land in a Muslim country by vivicating it if the land has never been vivicated before or that it was inhabited during the time of Jahilia but it has been left to go to waste'; Middleton 1961, p. 75.

29 It is important to stress that we are here referring to Swahili legal and moral rules only, and we are aware that these patterns may or may not be found among other Muslim peoples.

30 A few have sold houses to Europeans, who stand outside the local ranking system.

31 Anderson 1954, pp. 93–4; Lienhardt 1996.

32 Middleton 1992, p. 135 uses the English term 'entail', but 'trust' is more accurate.

33 Anderson 1954, pp. 93–4; Lienhardt 1966, 1996.

34 Bang 1999. This was the situation under British protectorate administration: the Commissioners in Zanzibar City had jurisdiction over the Kenyan coast, formally under control of the Zanzibar Sultanate. The present situation is uncertain. In recent years the commissioners have proved skilful and effective in preventing the independent governments of Kenya and Tanzania from proclaiming *waqf* property for governmental and private enterprise. They have been unable to do so in the case of non-*waqf* property, to the detriment of local citizens whose family lands have been taken from them in large numbers and without compensation by new elites.

35 Lienhardt 1959.

36 Lienhardt 1996.

37 The main literature on gender issues include, Caplan 1976, 1982, 1989; Eastman 1984, 1988a; Guennec-Coppens 1983; Hirsch 1998; Lambek 1983; Landberg 1986; Mbughuni 1982; Mirza and Strobel 1989; Romero 1987; Tanner 1962, 1964.

38 Western writers tend to refer to gender merely in terms of definitions used in the West, and often of what it is thought ideal gender relations ought to be.

39 Eastman 1984 incorrectly refers to *mwanamke* as female slave, and as opposed to *mngwana*, a patrician: the terms are non-comparable except in the crudest sense.

40 Middleton 1992, p. 129. Women who own houses are widely found throughout Swahili society but are not patricians: indeed, an early account by New 1873 on which many references are based refers clearly to non-patrician marriages.

41 Caplan 1989.

42 Among the non-patrician residents, the Bajuni mostly possess patrilineal descent groups. Hadrami and Omani Arab communities are composed of corporate patrilineal lineages. Families of slave ancestry in some cases remain so closely linked to the lineages of their former patrician owners as often virtually to be subsumed as members. But most are poor, with few permanent items of property, and form matrifocal and matrifilial clusters that are not corporate and exist structurally on the periphery of their particular towns' society. Some writers have claimed that these families are matrilineal. But they lack corpo-

rateness and the claim is mistaken: matrifiliation is not matriliny; Middleton 1992, p. 100.

43 Part of the misunderstanding appears to be due to confusion between descent and lineality. Every person claims descent from both his or her father's side and his or her mother's side, and on both sides may recognize direct lines of descent, one through men only and the other through women only. The terms patrilineal and matrilineal refer properly only to whichever line is selected to be corporate and so accounted permanent and with exclusive rights in its own property and offices.

44 This is the convention of tanistry, by which a successor to authority is chosen before his predecessor's death.

45 A firstborn patrician daughter is expected both to have personal ability and also a reputation for sexual morality: she must be a virgin at marriage and if notorious for promiscuity may not be counted as a suitable bride.

46 In both cases she married another cousin, but he was not confirmed as lineage head, only as a husband.

47 We plead ignorance here, as neither of us has worked with Omani or Hadrami families, and the published work of others in the domestic domain appears somewhat unreliable.

48 Very much higher in some impoverished areas, such as the smaller settlements of Pate island; Bujra 1968, 1975.

8 *Governance*

1 Sultanates continued on the Comores until the early twentieth century; the last paramount sultan, Sultan Said Ali, died in 1916, although his descendants have been involved in politics from time to time. The last legitimate Sultan of Witu, Fumo Omari, was deposed by the British and exiled to Zanzibar in November 1894, and a puppet sultan, Omari Madi, installed. He lived into the 1920s, and with his death, which went practically unnoticed, there was no attempt to revive the Witu/Pate Sultanate; Ylvisaker 1979, p. 163. The last Sultan of Zanzibar, Jamshid bin Abdullah, by no means a traditional Swahili ruler, was deposed in the Revolution of January 1964, and now lives in a modest house in Southsea, near Portsmouth, England. His former royal palace in Zanzibar has been turned into a museum and tourist attraction.

2 Most are translated in Freeman-Grenville 1962b; also J. M. Gray, 1951–2, (n.d.); Harries 1977; Hitchens 1938, 1940; Hollis 1900; Lambert 1953; Prins 1958; Stamboul 1951; Tolmacheva 1993; Velten 1907; Werner 1914. There are several unpublished manuscripts on microfilm in the Library of the University of Dar es Salaam, and an incomplete duplicate set in the School of Oriental and African Studies, London, collected by the late J. W. T. Allen.

3 The only published accounts of the demes appear to be in Prins 1967, p. 46, 1971 and Middleton 1992, p. 81, which come to somewhat different conclusions.

4 In his account of *beni* associations in Lamu, Ranger 1975, p. 25, mentions a famous Bwana Zena, implying that he was a patron of one association linked with his deme; presumably there was an opposite patron, Bwana Suud, for the other.

5 Allen 1976; Boyd 1978; Sassoon 1975. For chairs, Allen 1989.

6 Freeman-Grenville 1965a; Stigand 1913, pp. 29–102; Tolmacheva 1993; Werner 1914.

7 Risso 1986 provides a good account of the Omani background; also Kirkman 1983a.

8 Chittick 1969a.

9 Chittick 1969a, p. 319, claimed that 'it is doubtful whether anything useful can be deduced from these dreary catalogues. The mythical stories (mainly in the Stigand version) on the other hand have appeal and literary merit; it is good to know that they are being edited as tales for children.'

10 Freeman-Grenville 1962b, p. 269; Prins 1967, pp. 92–4

11 Even during the Nabahani period, there were bitter disputes. which tend to be glossed over in the *History*. For example during the visit of Smee and Hardy in 1811, quoted by Burton 1872, pp. ii, 475, 'we had already learnt that from our pilots and others who had visited us on board that the place was distracted by civil dissentions; the sooltanship being claimed by two cousins whose respective adherents occupying the same town occasioned by their contentions a continual sense of confusion.' Freeman-Grenville 1962b, pp. 272–3 for the Stigand version of these events. On the Pate *siwa* see Allen 1972, 1976; Sassoon 1975. On the French *siwa*, J. Moulier (pers. comm.).

12 Freeman-Grenville 1962b, p. 160. The Friar went on to visit the ruler of Faza at the other end of the island, a much less important town, but found him with long trailing robes, and on his head a striped turban of damasked silken cloth, and carrying a long Turkish scimitar. On the Portuguese encounter with Swahili see Horton 1998.

13 The Friday mosque at Shanga was burnt down when the site was abandoned, and while this could have been accidental, some kind of military action as recorded as having taken place in the *History of Pate* is as likely.

14 Monclaro a Portuguese missionary who visited Pate in 1569, noted that 'its Moorish priest was the chief of all the coast'. Freeman-Grenville 1962b, p. 142.

15 Horton and Blurton 1988.

16 Allen 1982a, 1993, pp. 193–212.

17 A date of 1050 would possibly tie in with the 'arrival' of the Arabs oppressed by the king of al-Hasa, either Carmathians or the Harthi; see chapter 3.

18 Berg 1968; Berg and Walter 1968; Prins 1967, p. 102.

19 Swartz 1991, p. 53 for a different view.

20 A term not used until immediately after the Second World War when political parties were established in Kenya; before then they were usually grouped by the pejorative term waNyika, 'people of the arid lands behind the coast'; Prins 1952.

21 The most useful accounts of Mombasa as a polity include those by Berg 1968; Cooper 1977; Prins 1967, p. 102; Swartz 1978, 1991; Willis 1993. See also Gray 1947; Harries 1959.

22 Boxer and Azevedo 1960; Freeman-Grenville 1980, pp. xii–xvii.

23 Kirkman 1983b.

24 When the Portuguese returned they found 'one old man called Faquevalle' who was apparently a member of the ruling family, and was made governor. During the events of 1727–8, the leader of the Three was Sh. bin Ahmed el-Malindi, who was probably descended from the early ruling family; J. M. Gray, 1957, pp. 5–7.

25 The accounts of the Mombasa system of government are confusing for several reasons: the continual interference from outside Arab groups, the Busaidi of Zanzibar and the Mazrui of Mombasa and neighbouring towns in particular; the decline in commercial importance of the Swahili merchants as patrons, and the demography of the city with the decline of the Swahili themselves into a small minority of its inhabitants; the twentieth-century establishment of a more 'modern' system by the British; and the even greater outside control exerted by the independent government of Kenya; Swartz 1991, p. 30. See also Hinawy 1970; Kindy 1972; Emery 1833; Owen 1833.

26 There are problems in identifying Ozi today, as three archaeological sites, whose original names have been lost, lie close together to the east of the river Tana; Kirkman 1966 (who made up the three names of Mwana, Shaka and Ungwana); Allen 1982b; Freeman-Grenville 1966b, p. 253.

27 Shungwaya is a mythical place of origin of some Swahili clans, somewhere 'in the north'. Allen 1993 is mainly devoted to rewriting Swahili history in terms that assume that Shungwaya actually existed. His advocacy for its reality, somewhere in the region of the Lamu archipelago, has met with disdain by most professional historians doubtful of his work as an academic amateur. The main criticism that can be levelled against Allen is that he takes myth as history (hardly a severe failing in the context of his time). In this book we have avoided the issue as being at present, and perhaps forever, unprovable. For other discussions of Shungwaya, Allen 1983, 1984; Cashmore 1961; Champion 1967; Chittick 1976a; Grottanelli 1955b; Morton 1973, 1977; Prins 1972; Spear 1974a, 1978; Willis 1993. For the linguistic arguments, see Hinnebusch 1976; Nurse and Spear 1985.

28 There are many interpretations of the Fumo Liongo myth. See among others Rozenstroch 1984; Werner 1915, 1926/8, 1933; Steere 1870; Harries 1962; Knappert 1967, 1970, 1979; Klein-Arendt 1986; Chiraghdin 1973; Mbele 1976; Shariff 1987; Willis 1986; also Middleton 1992, 29f.

29 Of which the most eccentric is that he was a Christian prince; Knappert 1979, p. 68.

30 Kirkman 1966, p. 10.

31 Axelson 1998, pp. 46–7; Freeman-Grenville 1962b, pp. 54–5. For Malindi in general see Martin 1973.

32 Baker 1949; Dickson 1917, 1921; Hollis 1900; Lambert 1957, 1958a, 1958b; McKay 1975; Prins 1967, p. 94; Robinson 1939.

33 This was supplied by Pate according to Vumba traditions.

34 This last is a widespread feature among kingships in Africa.

35 W. T. Brown 1971; Feierman 1974. Glassman 1995.

36   The account of Mtoro bin Mwinyi Bakari dealing with Bagamogo is the clearest; J. W. T. Allen 1981; see also Baker 1941; Glassman 1995; Harries 1965; J. de V. Allen 1981a; Prins 1967, pp. 94–8.

37   Freeman-Grenville and Martin 1973, p. 118; Sassoon 1966.

38   Ingrams 1931, pp. 153–9. For archaeological evidence from Pujini, LaViolette 1998, 2000.

39   J. M. Gray 1959–60, 1977; Ingrams 1931, pp. 147–53; Pearce 1920, pp. 171–3; Prins 1967, pp. 97–8.

40   An independent royal line continued on Tumbatu until around 1856, but very little is known about it; Prins 1967, p. 97.

41   Middleton 1961, p. 17.

42   Formerly among the Hadimu of Unguja by the local ruler, the *mwenye mkuu*, and since the demise of this and similar rulers elsewhere, by the central government. On Zanzibar and Pemba traditional government has been largely superceded by the organization imposed by the government party, the CCM, and where the branch chairman and secretary have assumed leadership of the community.

43   His description of Mogadishu is a puzzle as, 100 years earlier, Yakut described a system of town government like that at Barawa; Freeman-Grenville 1962b, pp. 28–31; Trimingham 1964, p. 5.

44   Chittick 1969c, 1974; Freeman-Grenville 1962a, 1962b, pp. 34–49, 91–3, 221–6; Strong 1895.

45   Chittick preferred this house to have been lived in by the 'factor', an office holder not mentioned in any historical sources.

46   See chapter 3. The Portuguese version gives the name of the father of Ali, the supposed founder of the Shirazi dynasty as Hócen, which most closely approximates to Husain, while the Arabic version gives his father as Hasan, but the founder of the dynasty as Ali bin al-Husain bin Ali.

47   This view differs from Saad 1979, who made the mistaken assumption that the coin-producing rulers must have immediately preceded the Mahdali dynasty.

48   The *History of Tumbatu* was lost in a house fire around 1934, and we have only a brief precis of it left; Ingrams 1931, 144.

49   The Ahdali was different to the Mahdali as Martin makes clear: both Pouwels and Chittick assume them to be the same. The Awali may first have come to Pate (at least this is what their genealogies and histories record) and one version gives the name as Seyyid Abubarkari Masela bin Ahmed. Hadrami sources suggest that they came to East Africa during the fourteenth and fifteenth centuries. They continued to live in Pate but another group moved to Vumba (possibly from Tumbatu) in the seventeenth or eighteenth century where, as we have seen, they came to rule the Vumba polity.

50   Pearce 1920, p. 250.

51   Askew 1999.

52   In many African states, 'queen mothers' are not the actual royal mothers but senior women of kingly lineages who have special responsibilities for women's disputes and who remain socially 'male'.

53   Middleton 1992, p. 44.

54   Huffman 1980, 1996.

55 Pellat 1962; incomplete translation of the East African sections in Freeman-Grenville 1962b, pp. 14–17.
56 Freeman-Grenville 1959. Pellat 1962, pp. 848, 871.
57 Allen 1993, p. 136.
58 Guillain 1856, i, p. 190, translation by MH.
59 B. Lewis, 1974, ii, pp. 117–18.

9 *Knowledge, Purity and Power*

1 We refer to 'Swahili religion' not to separate it from Islam but merely to view Swahili religious thought and behaviour as a single whole unique to the Swahili. We are not claiming that features of Swahili religion are either unorthodox or orthodox in Islam, or are or are not acceptable to Muslim scholars and theologians everywhere. What we discuss comprises that told to us by both Swahili scholars and by those 'ordinary' Swahili who try to learn of the world and of their place within it.
2 Many Muslims and others have denied that the *mila* should be or can be part of orthodox Islam. This view appears to be that of many fundamentalist groups but goes seemingly against both the Qu'ran and everyday practice in most of the Islamic world.
3 Pouwels 1987, p. 196.
4 This knowledge is often known as *uganga*, the knowledge of a religious doctor, including that of natural remedies for sickness; Hirschberg 1974.
5 A main distinction is between knowledge of *dunia*, that comes from inside Swahili society and is temporary, and sacred knowledge that comes from beyond the local and the present and is true in the everlasting sense; also D. Parkin 1985.
6 B. G. Martin, 1971; Pouwels 1987; Bang 1999, for accounts of Swahili and Arab historians and theologians.
7 Nabhany 1979; Prins 1965.
8 There is a large literature on the actual marriages themselves and their symbolism; Middleton 1992, ch. 5; Guennec-Coppens 1980, 1983, 1987; Shepherd 1977; Donley 1979, 1984; P. R. Curtin, 1984; Lambert 1965; Strobel 1975; Werner and Hitchens 1934; Ottenheimer 1984; Fichtner 1995. Allen 1973, 1979a provides evidence for the connection between the decoration in plaster (and formerly cut coral) of the *zidaka* niches in the stone houses and the marriage ceremony.
9 In the past a house was kept pure by a senior free woman or a trusted female slave of the lineage who was also responsible for the ritual preparation of a girl for her wedding as a pure and virginal bride. See Middleton 1992, 143f.
10 There are however many women reputed for their scholarship, from which they may acquire even greater purity than that of most women.
11 Middleton 1992, p. 179.
12 Bates 1965; Brantley 1981; Middleton 1965; Freeman-Grenville 1963; Glassman 1995; Raum 1965; Smith 1976.

13 This was also the period when Indian metal currency was being brought into wide use throughout East Africa. Hadrami traders could make use of it without the need for the former non-monetary exchange between fictive kin, patrons and clients.

14 el-Zein 1974, ch. 3; Lienhardt 1959; Middleton 1992, p. 169; Pouwels 1987, ch. 8.

15 Sheriff 1995. The houses, while arranged along narrow streets, are often outward looking with verandas and windows, and have large central stairs. Those of the Old Town of Mombasa are also very different from traditional Swahili architecture, with strong Indian and Arab influences. It is possible to define a distinctive 'Zanzibar style' of architecture which evolved during the mid-nineteenth century.

16 Even the sultans themselves often claimed, at least for public consumption, that they also were 'Swahili' as one of us (JM) was told in 1958 at an audience with His Highness Seyyid Khalifa ibn Harub.

17 For example many became civil servants under the British; Bang 1999.

18 The position of prostitutes has varied immensely, depending mainly on their status before the abolition of slavery; that of slave prostitutes in Zanzibar City and Mombasa was very low, and they had to return much of their earnings to their owners. After abolition, however, many women of free ancestry had to become prostitutes simply in order to live, especially those deserted by their husbands and left with small children. These women have rarely suffered obloquy, and have been able to practise their work in order to save money for a dwelling and for education of their children without public disapproval; Bujra 1975; Strobel 1979.

19 Strobel 1979; Mirza and Strobel 1989.

20 Beattie and Middleton 1969; Boddy 1989; Lambek 1981, 1988, 1993; Lewis 1966b, 1971.

21 For references to the brotherhoods see Middleton 1992, p. 170; Nimtz 1980; Pouwels 1987; Trimingham 1964, p. 93.

22 For *beni*; Lambert 1962–3; Ranger 1975; for *taarab* see Askew 1997, 1999; Fichtner 1995.

23 The plural prefix for the former is *mi-*, denoting only marginal human status; that for the latter is *ma-*, denoting a defined status or higher rank.

24 The spirits linked closely to ancestors are also known as *koma*.

25 The uses of incense, aloe wood, sandalwood and other fragrances play an important part in Swahili life: they both represent material objects of value and also protect the living from mystical dangers around them.

26 There is a large, scattered and unorganized body of writings on Swahili spirit cults. Problems include the wide variety of spirits believed to exist and to harm or possess human beings; the generally short-lived existence of cults associated with them; and the widespread disapproval of the more devout mosque leaders who hold that spirits originate in Africa and so are barbarous, even though still creatures of God. Accounts include Giles 1987, 1989; Lambek 1993; Strobel 1979; Caplan 1997; R. F. Gray 1969; Gomm 1975; Ingrams 1931, ch. 42; I. M. Lewis 1966b, 1971, Lienhardt 1968; also Middleton 1992, 170ff; Skene 1917.

27 The word *chama* is also used for a *deme*, as a group of people linked for common achievement of government, for a dance group or any form of voluntary association or non-business company.

28 Middleton 1992, p. 174.

29 This organization of spirits is that found in most patricians' towns; but there are many variant classifications, typically using the same terms but with different references; R. F. Gray 1969.

30 Caplan 1997; Middleton 1992, Nisula 1999, p. 170.

31 Strobel 1979; Askew 1997, 1999; Caplan 1997; Giles 1987.

32 Strobel 1979 described those she found in Mombasa before 1975, but none were found there in the late 1980s; and most of the cults described by Giles 1987 no longer exist, although others have come to take their place. There appear to be no detailed published accounts of the social statuses of association members of various roles; they are typically referred to merely as 'women'.

33 Nisula 1999 on Zanzibar City.

34 Middleton 1992, ch. 6.

35 Some accounts see them in this light, presumably an attempt by the writers to ennoble them in western eyes. They hardly need to be patronized in this way: they are noble enough in themselves.

36 For *lelemama* see Strobel 1979, ch. 6, p. 15; Giles 1987; Fargion 1998; Middleton 1992, 141ff.

37 Ingrams 1931, pp. 455–77; Parkin 1979, 1985; Middleton 1992, p. 181.

38 Ingrams 1931, p. 467. It is widely believed that at dawn may be seen silent lines of grey-faced and chained men escorted by their Arab masters.

39 Cummings 1973, 1985; Glassman 1995, ch. 2; Prins 1969, 1984.

40 Pemba, in particular, has had and still has the reputation as a place of magic and evil power. People still go there from elsewhere to learn them. Lienhardt 1968, writes of similar beliefs on the Ngao coast that are found also in many of the Hadimu towns of Zanzibar Island.

41 Middleton 1992, p. 150.

42 Amory 1985; Linnehuhr 1997; Schmidt and Beck 1993; Volker 1992.

43 In recent years also coloured, as can be seen in Zanzibar City. Slave women did not normally wear black veils but rather body coverings of coarse black cloth, *kaniki*: the distinction between free and slave was retained until the universal adoption of the black veil obliterated one distinction between free and slave.

44 There were still in 1990 many Swahili towns where women remained unveiled except at the first view of visiting strangers; examples include Pate and Siyu towns, and Kojani island.

45 Middleton 1992, p. 141.

46 Fuglesang 1993.

47 Peak 1989; Staszak 1969.

10 Constructing the Mercantile Landscape

1 Ylvisaker 1979.

Bibliography

Abdulaziz, M. H. (1977) *Muyaka: Nineteenth Century Swahili Popular Poetry*. Nairobi: East Africa Publishing House.

Abdy, D. C. (1924) 'Notes on *utani* and other Bondei customs'. *Man* 24, pp. 165–6.

Abungu, G. H. O. (1990) Communities on the River Tana, Kenya: An Archaeological Study of Relations Between the Delta and the River Basin, AD 700–1890. Unpublished Ph.D. thesis, University of Cambridge.

Abungu, G. H. O. and Mutoro, H. W. (1993) 'Coast-interior settlements and social relations in the Kenya coastal hinterland'. In T. Shaw, P. Sinclair, B. Andah and A. Okpoko (eds), *The Archaeology of Africa: Food, Metals and Towns*. London: Routledge, pp. 694–704.

Abu Lughod, Janet (1989) *Before European Hegemony: The World System AD 1250–1350*. Oxford: Oxford University Press.

Akinola, G. A. (1968) 'The Mazrui of Mombasa'. *Tarikh* 2, 3, pp. 26–40.

Akinola, G. A. (1972) 'Slavery and slave revolts in the Sultanate of Zanzibar in the 19th century'. *Journal of the Historical Society of Nigeria* 6, pp. 215–28.

Aldrick, J. (1990) 'The nineteenth-century carved wooden doors of the East African coast'. *Azania* 25, pp. 1–18.

Allen, J. de V. (1972) *Lamu (notes on material culture)*. Privately published.

Allen, J. de V. (1973) 'Swahili ornament: A study of the decoration of the eighteenth century plaster work and carved doors of the Lamu region'. *Art and Archaeology Research Papers* 3, pp. 1–14; 4, pp. 87–92.

Allen, J. de V. (1974a) 'Swahili culture reconsidered. Some historical implications of the material culture of the northern Kenyan coast in the eighteenth and nineteenth centuries'. *Azania* 9, pp. 105–38.

Allen, J. de V. (1974b) *Lamu Town, A Guide*. Mombasa: Rodwell Press.

Allen, J. de V. (1976) 'The *siwas* of Pate and Lamu: two antique sideblown horns from the Swahili Coast'. *Art and Archaeology Research Papers* 9, pp. 38–47.

Allen, J. de V. (1977) *Al-Inkishafi – Catechism of a Soul, by Sayyid Abdalla bin Ali bin Nasir*. Nairobi: East African Literature Bureau.

Allen, J. de V. (1979a) 'The Swahili house: cultural and ritual concepts underlying its plan and structure'. In J. de V. Allen and T. H. Wilson, *Swahili Houses and Tombs of the Coast of Kenya*. London: Art and Archaeology Research Papers, pp. 1–32.

Allen, J. de V. (1979b) 'Siyu in the eighteenth and nineteenth centuries'. *Transafrican Journal of History* 8, 2, pp. 1–35.
Allen, J. de V. (1981a) 'The Swahili world of Mtoro bin Mwinyi Bakari'. In J. W. T. Allen (ed.), *The Customs of the Swahili People*. Berkeley: University of California Press, pp. 211–30.
Allen, J. de V. (1981b) 'Swahili culture and the nature of East Coast settlement'. *International Journal of African Historical Studies* 14, pp. 306–34.
Allen, J. de V. (1982a) 'The "Shirazi" problem in East African coastal history'. *Paideuma* 28, pp. 9–28.
Allen, J. de V. (1982b) 'The names of the Tana Delta sites'. *Azania* 17, pp. 165–72.
Allen, J. de V. (1983) 'Shungwaya, the Mijikenda and the traditions'. *International Journal of African Historical Studies* 16, pp. 455–85.
Allen, J. de V. (1984) 'Shungwaya, the Segeju and Somali history'. In T. Labahn (ed.), *Archaeology and History, Proceedings of the Second International Congress of Somali Studies, 1983*. Hamburg: Buske, pp. 35–72.
Allen, J. de V. (1989) 'The *Kiti Cha Enzi* and other Swahili Chairs'. *African Arts* 22, 3, pp. 54–62.
Allen, J. de V. (1993) *Swahili Origins: Swahili Culture and the Shungwaya Phenomenon*. London: James Currey.
Allen, J. de V. and T. H. Wilson (eds) (1982) 'From Zinj to Zanzibar: Studies in History, Trade, and Society on the Eastern Coast of Africa' *Paideuma* 28.
Allen, J. W. T. (1971) *Tendi: Six Examples of a Swahili Classical Verse Form*. Nairobi: Heinemann.
Allen, J. W. T. (ed.) (1981) *The Customs of the Swahili People: The Desturi za Waswahili of Mtoro bin Mwinyi Bakari and Other Persons*. Berkeley: University of California Press.
Allibert, C. (1990) 'Le site de Dembeni (Mayotte, Archipel des Comores)'. *Études Océan Indien* 11, pp. 63–172.
Allibert, C., Argant, A. and Argant, J. (1983) 'Le site de Bagamoyo (Mayotte, Archipel des Comoro)'. *Études Océan Indien* 2, pp. 5–40.
Alpers, E. A. (1967) *The East African Slave Trade*. Dar es Salaam: The Historical Association of Tanzania.
Alpers, E. A. (1969a) 'The coast and the caravan trade'. In I. N. Kimambo and A. J. Temu (eds), *A History of Tanzania*. Nairobi: East African Publishing House, pp. 35–56.
Alpers, E. A. (1969b) 'Trade, state, and society among the Yao in the 19th century'. *Journal of African History* 10, 3, p. 417.
Alpers, E. A. (1970) 'The French slave trade in East Africa (1721–1810)'. *Cahiers d'Etudes Africanes* 10, 37, pp. 80–124.
Alpers, E. A. (1975) *Ivory and Slaves in East Central Africa: Changing Patterns of International Trade to the Late Nineteenth Century*. London: Heinemann.
Alpers, E. A. (1976) 'Gujarat and the trade of East Africa c.1500–1800'. *International Journal of African Historical Studies* 9, 1, pp. 22–45.
Alpers, E. A. (1983) 'Muqdisho in the nineteenth century: a regional perspective'. *Journal of African History* 24, pp. 441–59.

Alpers, E. A. (1984) 'Ordinary household chores: Ritual and power in a 19th-century Swahili women's spirit possession cult'. *International Journal of African Historical Studies* 17, 4, pp. 677–702.

Alpers, E. A. (1992) 'The ivory trade in Africa: an historical overview'. In D. H. Ross, (ed.), *Elephant: The Animal and its Ivory in African Culture*. Los Angeles: Fowler Museum, pp. 349–63.

Amory, D. P. (1985) The Kanga Cloth and Swahili Society: Mke in Nguo. Unpublished paper, Program in African Languages, Yale University.

Anderson, J. N. D. (1954) *Islamic Law in Africa*. London: HMSO (Reprinted Cass, 1970).

Appadurai, Arjun (ed.) (1986) *The Social Life of Things: Commodities in Cultural Perspective*. Cambridge: Cambridge University Press.

Arens, W. (1975) 'The Waswahili: The social history of an ethnic group'. *Africa* 45, 4, pp. 426–38.

Arens, W. (1979) *On the Frontiers of Change: Mto wa Mbu, Tanzania*. Ann Arbor: University of Michigan Press.

Arens, W. (1987) 'Mto wa Mbu: A rural polyethnic community in Tanzania'. In I. Kopytoff (ed.), *The African Frontier: The Reproduction of Traditional African Societies*. Bloomington: Indiana University Press, pp. 242–54.

Arens, W. and Arens, D. A. (1978) 'Kinship and marriage in a polyethnic community'. *Africa* 48, pp. 149–60.

Askew, K. (1997) Performing the Nation: Swahili Musical Performance and the Production of Tanzanian National Culture. Unpublished Ph.D. Dissertation, Harvard University.

Askew, K. (1999) 'Female circles and male lines: gender dynamics along the Swahili coast'. *Africa Today* 46, 3/4, pp. 67–102.

Austen, R. A. (1971) 'Patterns of development in 19th century East Africa'. *International Journal of African Historical Studies* 46, pp. 645–57.

Austen, R. A. (1989) 'The nineteenth century Islamic slave trade from East Africa (Swahili and Red Sea Coasts): A tentative census'. In G. Clarence-Smith (ed.), *The Economics of the Indian Ocean Slave Trade in the Nineteenth Century*. London: Frank Cass, pp.21–44.

Axelson, E. (1973) *The Portuguese in South-East Africa 1488–1600*. Johannesburg: Struik.

Axelson, E. (1998) *Vasco de Gama: The Dairy of his Travels through African Waters 1497–99*. Somerset West (RSA): Stephan Phillips.

Badger, G. P. (1871) *History of the Imâns and Sayyids of 'Omân from AD 661–1856*. London: Hakluyt Society.

Baker, E. C. (1941) 'Notes on the Shirazi of East Africa'. *Tanganyika Notes and Records* 11, pp. 1–10.

Baker, E. C. (1949) 'Notes on the history of the Wasegeju'. *Tanganyika Notes and Records* 27, pp. 16–41.

Bang, Anne K. (1999) Intellectuals and Civil Servants: Early 20th century Zanzibar 'Ulama' and the colonial state. Unpublished paper, African Studies Association, Philadelphia.

Barnet, P. (1997) *Images in Ivory: Precious Objects of the Gothic Age*. Princeton: Detroit Institute for Arts, Princeton University Press.

Barnett, T. (1999) *The Emergence of Food Production in Ethiopia*. Oxford: British Archaeological Reports no. 763.

Bateman, G. W. (1901) *Zanzibar Tales told by Natives of the East Coast of Africa*. Chicago: Saalfield.

Bates, M. L. (1965) 'Tanganyika: Changes in African life, 1918–1945'. In V. Harlow and E. M. Chilver (eds), *History of East Africa*, vol. II. Oxford: Clarendon Press, pp. 625–40.

Baumann, O. (1891) *Usambara und seine Nachgebiete*. Berlin: Reimer.

Baxter, T. W. and Da Silva Rego, A. (1962–71) *Documents on the Portuguese in Mozambique and Central Africa*. Lisbon and Salisbury (8 vols).

Beach, D. (1994) *The Shona and their Neighbours*. Oxford: Blackwell Publishers (Peoples of Africa).

Beachey, R. W. (1962) 'The arms trade in East Africa in the late nineteenth century'. *Journal of African History* 3, pp. 451–67.

Beachey, R. W. (1967) 'The East African ivory trade in the nineteenth century'. *Journal of African History* 8, pp. 269–90.

Beachey, R. W. (1976) *The Slave Trade of Eastern Africa*. London: Rex Collings.

Beattie, J. and Middleton, J. (eds) (1969) *Spirit Mediumship and Society in Africa*. London: Routledge and Kegan Paul.

Begley, V. and De Puma, R. (1991) *Rome and India: The Ancient Sea Trade*. Madison: Wisconsin University Press.

Bennett, N. R. (1971) *Mirambo of Tanzania, ?1840–1884*. New York: Oxford University Press.

Bennett, N. R. (1978) *A History of the Arab State of Zanzibar*. London: Methuen.

Bennett, N. R. (ed.) (1968) *Leadership in Eastern Africa: Six Political Biographies*. Boston: Boston University Press.

Bennett, N. R. and Brooks, G. E. (1965) *New England Merchants in Africa*. Boston: Boston University Press.

Berg, F. J. (1968) 'The Swahili community of Mombasa 1500–1900'. *Journal of African History* 9, 1, pp. 35–56.

Berg, F. and Walter, B. (1968) 'Mosques, population and urban development in Mombasa'. *Hadith* 1, pp. 47–100.

Bhacker, M. R. (1992) *Trade and Empire in Muscat and Zanzibar: Roots of British Domination*. London: Routledge.

Boddy, Janice (1989) *Wombs and Alien Spirits: Women, Men, and the Zar Cult in Northern Sudan*. Madison: University of Wisconsin Press.

Bower, J. R. F. (1973) 'Seronera: excavations at a stone bowl site in the Serengeti National Park, Tanzania'. *Azania* 8, pp. 71–104.

Bower, J. R. F., Nelson, C. M., Waibel, A. F. and Wandibba, S. (1977) 'The University of Massachusetts Later Stone Age/Pastoral "Neolithic" comparative study in central Kenya: an overview'. *Azania* 12, pp. 119–46.

Boxer, C. R. and de Azevedo, C. (1960) *Fort Jesus and the Portuguese in Mombasa, 1593–1729*. London: Hollis and Carter.

Boyd, A. (1978) 'The musical instruments of Lamu'. *Kenya Past and Present* 9, pp. 3–8.

Brantley, C. (1981) *The Giriama and Colonial Resistance in Kenya, 1800–1920*. Berkeley: University of California Press.

Braudel, F. (1972–3) *The Mediterranean and the Mediterranean World in the Age of Phillip II*. London: Collins.

Brown, B. (1971) 'Muslim influence in trade and politics in the Lake Tanganyika region'. *International Journal of African Historical Studies* 4, 6, pp. 617–30.

Brown, E. J. (1980) Traditional Blacksmiths and Metalworking in Kenya. Unpublished Ph.D. thesis, Edinburgh University.

Brown, H. (1985) History of Siyu: The Development and Decline of a Swahili Town on the Northern Kenyan Coast. Unpublished Ph.D. thesis, Indiana University.

Brown, H. (1988) 'Siyu: town of the craftsmen'. *Azania* 23, pp. 101–13.

Brown, H. W. (1991) 'Three Kilwa gold coins'. *Azania* 26, pp. 1–4.

Brown, H. W. (1992) 'Early Muslim coinage in East Africa: the evidence from Shanga'. *Numismatic Chronicle*, pp. 83–7.

Brown, H. W. (1993) 'Coins of East Africa: an introductory survey'. *Yarmouk Numismatics* 5, pp. 9–16.

Brown, W. T. (1971) A Pre-colonial History of Bagamoyo: Aspects of the Growth of an East African Coastal Town. Unpublished Ph.D. thesis, Boston University.

Bujra, A. S. (1971) *The Politics of Stratification: A Study of Political Change in a South Arabian Town*. Oxford: Clarendon Press.

Bujra, J. (1968) An Anthropological Study of Political Action in a Bajuni Village in Kenya. Unpublished Ph.D. thesis, University of London.

Bujra, J. (1975) 'Production, property, prostitution: Sexual politics in Atu'. *Cahiers d'Etudes Africaines* 12, pp. 13–39.

Burton, R. and Speke, J. H. (1858) 'A coasting voyage from Mombasa to Pangani'. *Journal of the Royal Geographical Society* 20.

Burton, R. F. (1872) *Zanzibar: City, Island and Coast*. London: Tinsley Bros (2 vols).

Busaidy, Hamed bin Saleh El-(1958) *Ndoa na Talaka (Marriage and Divorce)*. Nairobi: East African Literature Bureau.

Caplan, P. A. (1968) 'Sheikh Mbarak bin Rashid bin Salim el- Mazrui'. In Bennett (1968).

Caplan, P. A. (1969) 'Cognatic descent groups on Mafia Island, Tanzania'. *Man* 4, 3, pp. 419–31.

Caplan, P. A. (1975) *Choice and Constraint in a Swahili Community: Property, Hierarchy, and Cognatic Descent on the East African Coast*. Oxford: Oxford University Press.

Caplan, P. A. (1976) 'Boys' circumcision and girls' puberty rites among the Swahili of Mafia Island, Tanzania'. *Africa* 46, 1, pp. 21–33.

Caplan, P. A. (1982) 'Gender, ideology, and modes of production on the East Coast of Africa'. *Paideuma* 28, pp. 29–43.

Caplan, P. A. (1989) 'Perceptions of gender stratification'. *Africa* 59, 2, pp. 196–208.

Caplan, P. A. (1997) *African Voices, African Lives: Personal Narratives from the Swahili Village*. London: Routledge.

Cashmore, T. H. R. (1961) 'Notes on the chronology of the Wanika'. *Tanganyika Notes and Records* 57, pp. 153–72.

Cassanelli, L. V. (1982) *The Shaping of Somali Society.* Philadelphia: University of Pennsylvania Press.

Cassanelli, L. V. (1986) 'Society and culture in the riverine region of southern Somalia'. In K. Loughran, J. Loughran, J. W. Johnson and S. Samatar (eds), *Somalia in Word and Image.* Bloomington: Indiana University Press, pp. 67–95.

Cassanelli, L. V. (1987) 'Social construction on the Somali frontier: Bantu former slave communities in the nineteenth century'. In I. Kopytoff (ed.), *The African Frontier: The Reproduction of Traditional African Societies.* Bloomington: Indiana University Press, pp. 216–38.

Casson, L. (1989) *The Periplus Maris Erythraei. Text with Introduction, Translation and Commentary.* Princeton: Princeton University Press.

Cerulli, E. (1922) 'The Watta: A low caste of hunters'. *Harvard African Studies* 3, pp. 200–14.

Cerulli, E. (1957) *Somalia: Scritti Vari, Editi ed Inediti.* Rome: Curia dell'Administrazione Fuduciaria Italiana dell Somalia (3 vols).

Chami, F. (1994) *The Tanzanian Coast in the First Millennium AD: An Archaeology of the Iron-Working, Farming Communities.* Uppsala: Societies Archaeologica Upsaliensis, Studies in African Archaeology 7.

Chami, F. (1999a) 'Roman Beads from the Rafiji Delta, Tanzania. First incontrovertible archaeological link with the Periplus'. *Current Anthropology* 40, 2, pp. 237–41.

Chami, F. (1999b) 'Graeco-Roman trade link and the Bantu migration theory'. *Anthropos* 94, 1–3, pp. 205–15.

Chami, F. (1999c) 'Mafia island in the Early Iron Age and its relationship with the Mainland'. *Azania* 34.

Chami, F. A. (1998) 'A review of Swahili archaeology'. *African Archaeological Review* 15, 3, pp. 199–218.

Chami, F. A. and Msemwa, P. J. (1997) 'A new look at culture and trade on the Azanian coast'. *Current Anthropology* 38, pp. 673–7.

Chami, F. A. and Wafula, G. (1999) 'Zanzibar in the Aqualithic and Early Roman periods'. *Muita* 8, pp. 1-14.

Champion, A. M. (1922) 'Notes on the Wasanye'. *Journal of the East Africa and Uganda Natural History Society* 17, pp. 21–4.

Champion, A. M. (1967) *The Agiryama of Kenya.* London: Royal Anthropological Institute.

Chaudhuri, K. N. (1985) *Trade and Civilization in the Indian Ocean: An Economic History from the Rise of Islam to 1750.* Cambridge: Cambridge University Press.

Chaudhuri, K. N. (1990) *Asia Before Europe.* Cambridge: Cambridge University Press.

Chiragdin, S. (1960) 'Maisha ya Sheikh Mbaruk bin Rashid al- Mazrui'. *Swahili* 31, pp. 150–79.

Chiragdin, S. (1973) *Utenzi wa Fumo Liyongo by Muhammed Kijumwa.* Dar es Salaam.

Chittick, H. N. (1961) *Kisimani Mafia. Excavations at an Islamic Settlement on the East African Coast.* Dar es Salaam: Antiquities Division Occasional Paper no. 1.

Chittick, H. N. (1965) 'The "Shirazi" colonisation of East Africa'. *Journal of African History* 6, pp. 275–94.

Chittick, H. N. (1966a) 'Kilwa, a preliminary report'. *Azania* 1, pp. 1–37.

Chittick, H. N. (1966b) 'Report on the excavations at Kisimani Mafia and Kua'. *Tanzania Antiquities Report for 1964.* Dar es Salaam, pp. 15–16.

Chittick, H. N. (1966c) 'Unguja Ukuu: the earliest imported pottery and an Abbasid dinar'. *Azania* 1, pp. 161–3.

Chittick, H. N. (1966d) 'Six early coins from near Tanga'. *Azania* 1, pp. 156–7.

Chittick, H. N. (1967) 'Discoveries in the Lamu Archipelago'. *Azania* 2, pp. 37–67.

Chittick, H. N. (1969a) 'A new look at the History of Pate'. *Journal of African History* 10, pp. 375–91.

Chittick, H. N. (1969b) 'An archaeological reconnaissance of the southern Somali coast'. *Azania* 4, pp. 115–30.

Chittick, H. N. (1969c) 'The early history of Kilwa Kivinje'. *Azania* 4, pp. 153–8.

Chittick, H. N. (1974) *Kilwa. An Islamic Trading City on the East African Coast.* Nairobi: British Institute in Eastern Africa, memoir 5 (2 vols).

Chittick, H. N. (1975a) 'An early salt-working site on the Tanzanian coast'. *Azania* 10, pp. 151–3.

Chittick, H. N. (1975b) 'The peopling of the East African coast'. In H. N. Chittick and R. I. Rotberg (eds), *East Africa and the Orient.* New York: Africana, pp. 16–43.

Chittick, H. N. (1976a) 'The Book of the Zenj and the Mijikenda'. *International Journal of African Historical Studies* 9, pp. 68–73.

Chittick, H. N. (1976b) 'An archaeological reconnaissance in the Horn: the British Somali Expedition 1975' *Azania* 11, pp. 117–33.

Chittick, H. N. (1977a) 'The East Coast, Madagascar and the Indian Ocean'. In R. Oliver (ed.), *Cambridge History of Africa Vol. 3.* Cambridge: Cambridge University Press, pp. 183–231.

Chittick, H. N. (1977b) 'Pre-Islamic trade ports of the Horn'. In R. E. Leakey and B. A. Ogot (eds), *Proceedings of the 8th Panafrican Congress of Prehistory and Quaternary Studies.* Nairobi: National Museums of Kenya. pp. 364–6.

Chittick, H. N. (1979) 'Early ports in the Horn of Africa'. *International Journal of Nautical Archaeology* 8, 4, pp. 273–7.

Chittick, H. N. (1982) 'Medieval Mogadishu'. *Paideuma* 28, pp. 45–62.

Chittick, H. N. (1984) *Manda: Excavations at an Island Port on the Kenya Coast.* Nairobi: British Institute in Eastern Africa, memoir 9.

Chittick, H. N. and R. I. Rotberg (eds) (1975) *East Africa and the Orient.* New York: Africana Press.

Christides, Vassilios (1984) *The Conquest of Crete by the Arabs (ca. 824). A Turning Point in the Struggle between Byzantium and Islam.* Athens: University Athens.

Clarence-Smith, G. (ed.) (1989) *The Economics of the Indian Ocean Slave Trade in the Nineteenth Century.* London: Cass.

Collett, D. P. (1985) The Spread of Early Iron-Producing Communities in Eastern and Southern Africa. Unpublished Ph.D. thesis, University of Cambridge.

Collett, D. P. and Robertshaw, P. (1983) 'Pottery traditions of early pastoral communities in Kenya'. *Azania* 18, pp. 107–25.

Connah, G. (1996) *Kibiro: The Salt of Bunyoro Past and Present*. London: British Institute in Eastern Africa.

Cooper, F. (1973) 'The treatment of slaves on the Kenya coast in the nineteenth century'. *Kenya Historical Review* 1, pp. 87–107.

Cooper, F. (1977) *Plantation Slavery on the East Coast of Africa*. New Haven: Yale University Press.

Cooper, F. (1980) *From Slaves to Squatters: Plantation Labor and Agriculture in Zanzibar and Coastal Kenya, 1890–1925*. New Haven: Yale University Press.

Cooper, F. (1987) *On the African Waterfront: Urban Disorder and the Transformation of Work in Colonial Mombasa*. New Haven: Yale University Press.

Coupland, R. (1938) *East Africa and its Invaders*. Oxford: Clarendon Press.

Coupland, R. (1939) *The Exploitation of East Africa*. London: Faber and Faber.

Cour Grandmaison, Colette Le and Crozon, Ariel (eds) (1998) *Zanzibar Aujourd'hui*. Paris: Karthala.

Craster, J. E. E. (1913) *Pemba, The Spice Island of Zanzibar*. London: Unwin.

Crawford, R. D. (1984) 'Domestic fowl'. In I. L. Mason (ed.), *Evolution of Domesticated Animals*. London and New York: Longmans, pp. 298–310.

Cummings, Robert (1973) 'A note on the history of caravan porters in East Africa'. *Kenya Historical Review* 1, 2, pp. 109–38.

Cummings, Robert (1985) 'Wage labor in Kenya in the nineteenth century'. In C. Coquery-Vidrovich and P. E. Lovejoy (eds), *The Workers of African Trade*. Beverly Hills and London: Sage Publications, pp. 193–208.

Curtin, P. D. (1981) 'African enterprise in the mangrove trade: the case of Lamu'. *African Economic History* 10, pp. 23–33.

Curtin, P. D. (1984) *Cross-Cultural Trade in World History*. Cambridge: Cambridge University Press.

Curtin, P. R. (1982) 'The Sacred Meadows: A case study of "Historyland" vs. "Anthropologyland"'. *History in Africa* 9, pp. 337–46.

Curtin, P. R. (1983) 'Laboratory for the oral history of slavery: The island of Lamu on the Kenya coast'. *American Historical Review* 88, 4, pp. 858–82.

Curtin, P. R. (1984) 'Lamu weddings as an example of social and economic change'. *Cahiers d'Etudes Africaines* 24, pp. 131–55.

Curtin, P. R. (1986a) '"Where have all the slaves gone?": Emancipation and post-emancipation in Lamu, Kenya'. *Journal of African History* 27, pp. 497–512.

Curtin, P. R. (1986b) 'Lamu and the suppression of the slave trade'. *Slavery and Abolition* 7, 2, pp. 148–59.

Dale, G. (1920) *The Peoples of Zanzibar*. London: UMCA.

Dammann, E. (1929) *Beitrage aus arabischen Quellen zur Kenntnis des negerischen Afrikas*. Bordesholm: Nolke.

Das Gupta, A. and Pearson M. N. (eds) (1987) *India and the Indian Ocean 1500–1800*. Calcutta and New York: Oxford University Press.

Datoo, B. A. (1970) 'Misconceptions about the use of monsoons by dhows in East African waters'. *East African Geographical Review* 8, pp. 1–10.

Datoo, B. A. (1974) 'Influence of monsoons on movements of dhows along the East African coast'. *East African Geographical Review* 12, pp. 23–33.

Datoo, B. A. (1975) *Port Development in East Africa*. Nairobi: East African Literature Bureau.

Day, J. (1987) *The Medieval Market Economy*. Oxford: Blackwell Publishers.

DeBlij, H. (1968) *Mombasa, an African City*. Evanston: Northwestern University Press.

Decken, C. C. von der (1869–73) *Reisen in Ostafrika* (ed., O. Kersten). Leipzig and Heidelberg.

Declich, Francesca (1987) 'I Goscia della regione del medio Giuba nella Somalia Meridionale: Un gruppo etnico di origine bantu'. *Africa* (Roma) 42, 4, pp. 570–99.

Delf, G. (1963) *Asians in East Africa*. London: Oxford University Press.

Denbow, J. (1986) 'A new look at the later prehistory of the Kalahari'. *Journal of African History* 27, pp. 3–29.

Devic, L. M. (1883) *Le Pays des Zandjs ou la côte orientale d'Afrique au moyen-âge*. Amsterdam: Oriental Press.

Dewar, R. and Wright, H. T. (1993) 'The culture history of Madagascar'. *Journal of World Prehistory* 7, 4, pp. 417–66.

Dickson, T. A. (1917) 'Notes on the Segeju'. *Journal of the East Africa and Uganda Natural History Society* 11, pp. 167–8.

Dickson, T. A. (1921) 'The regalia of the Wa-Vumba'. *Man* 21, pp. 33–5.

Dols, M. (1977) *The Black Death in the Middle East*. Princeton: Princeton University Press.

Donley, L. W. (1979) 'Eighteenth-century Lamu weddings'. *Kenya Past and Present* 11, pp. 3–11.

Donley, L. W. (1982) 'House power: Swahili space and symbolic markers'. In I. Hodder (ed.), *Symbolic and Structural Archaeology*. Cambridge: Cambridge University Press, pp. 63–73.

Donley, L. W. (1984) The Social Uses of Swahili Space and Objects. Unpublished Ph.D. thesis, University of Cambridge.

Donley, L. W. (1987): 'Life in the Swahili town house reveals the symbolic meaning of spaces and artefact assemblages'. *African Archaeological Review* 5, pp. 181–92.

Donley-Reid, L. W. (1990) 'A structuring structure: the Swahili house'. In S. Kent (ed.), *Domestic Architecture and the Use of Space; An Interdisciplinary Cross-Cultural Study*. Cambridge: Cambridge University Press, pp. 114–26.

Drocopoli, I. N. (1914) *Through Jubaland to the Lorian Swamp*. London: Seeley Service.

Duarte, R. T. (1993) *Northern Mozambique in the Swahili World*. Stockholm: Central Board of National Antiquities.

Duyvendak, J. J. L. (1949) *China's Discovery of Africa*. London: School of Oriental and African Studies, Occasional Paper.

Eastman, C. M. (1971) 'Who are the Waswahili?'. *Africa* 41, 3, pp. 228–36.

Eastman, C. M. (1984) 'Waungwana na Wanawake: Muslim ethnicity and sexual segregation in coastal Kenya'. *Journal of Multilingual and Multicultural Development* 5, pp. 97–112.

Eastman, C. M. (1988a) 'Women, slaves, and foreigners: African cultural influences and group processes in the formation of northern Swahili coastal society'. *International Journal of African Historical Studies* 21, 1, pp. 1–20.

Eastman, C. M. (1988b) Service (Utumwa) as a Contested Concept of Swahili Social Reality. Unpublished paper, University of Washington.

Eastman, C. M. and Topan, F. M. (1966) 'The Siu: notes on the people and their language'. *Swahili* 36, pp. 222–48.

Ehret, C. (1974) *Ethiopians and East Africans: The Problem of Contacts*. Nairobi: East African Publishing House.

Ehret, C. (1998) *An African Classical Age*. Charlottesville: University of Virginia Press.

Ehret, C. and Posnansky, M. (eds) (1982) *The Archaeological and Linguistic Reconstruction of African History*. Berkeley: University of California Press.

Elliot, J. A. G. (1925/6) 'A visit to the Bajun Islands'. *Journal of the Asiatic Society* 25, pp. 10–22, 147–63, 245–63, 338–58.

Elton, J. F. (1874) 'On the coast country of East Africa south of Zanzibar'. *Journal of the Royal Geographical Society* 44, pp. 227–52.

El-Zein, A. H. M. (1974) *The Sacred Meadows: A Structural Analysis of Religious Symbolism in an East African Town*. Evanston: Northwestern University Press.

Emery, J. (1833): 'Short account of Mombasa and the neighbouring coast of Africa'. *Journal of the Royal Geographical Society* 3, pp. 280–3.

Esmail, Z. (1975) 'Towards a history of Islam in East Africa'. *Kenya Historical Review* 3, pp. 147–58.

Evans-Pritchard, E. E. (1940) *The Nuer*. Oxford: Clarendon Press.

Fabian, Johannes (1968) *Language and Colonial Power: The Appropriation of Swahili in the Former Belgian Congo, 1880–1938*. Cambridge: Cambridge University Press.

Fagan, B. M. (1969) 'Excavations at Ingombe Ilede 1960–2'. In B. Fagan, D. W. Phillipson and S. C. H. Daniels (eds), *Iron Age Cultures in Zambia*, vol. 2. London: Chatto & Windus, pp. 51–161.

Fargion, Janet T. (1998) 'La musique et la danse: la taarab'. In Cour Grandmaison and Crozon (1998), pp. 275–87.

Farsi, S. S. (1958) *Swahili Sayings from Zanzibar*. Nairobi: East African Literature Bureau (2 vols).

Fawcett, W. B. and LaViolette, A. (1990) 'Iron Age settlement around Mkiu, southeastern Tanzania'. *Azania* 25, pp. 19–26.

Feierman, S. (1974) *The Shambaa Kingdom: A History*. Madison: University of Wisconsin Press.

Ferrand, G. (1913) *Relations de Voyages et Textes Géographique Arabes, Persans et Turks relatifs à l'extrême Orient de 8e au 18e Siècles*. Paris.

Fichtner, C. (1995) *Tanz der Geschlechter: Die Hockzeits Performance an der Muslimischen Kuste Ostafricas*. Munster: LIT Verlag.

Fitzgerald, W. W. A. (1898) *Travels in the Coastlands of East Africa and the Islands of Zanzibar and Pemba*. London: Chapman and Hall.

Flint, John (1963) 'The wider background to partition and colonial occupation'. In R. Oliver and G. Mathew (eds), *History of East Africa*, vol. I. London: Clarendon Press, pp. 352–90.

Flury, S. (1922) 'The Kufic inscription of Kizimkazi Mosque, Zanzibar, A. D. 1107'. *Journal of the Royal Asiatic Society* 21, pp. 257–64.

Fraser, H. A., Tozer, Bp. and Christie, J. (1871) *The East African Slave Trade*. London: Harrison.

Freeman-Grenville, G. S. P. (1957) 'Coinage in East Africa before Portuguese times'. *Numismatic Chronicle* (6th Series) 17, pp. 151–79.

Freeman-Grenville, G. S. P. (1959) 'Mediaeval evidences for Swahili'. *Journal of the East African Swahili Committee* 29, pp. 10–23.

Freeman-Grenville, G. S. P. (1962a) *The Medieval History of the Coast of Tanganyika, With Special Reference to Recent Archaeological Discoveries*. London: London University Press.

Freeman-Grenville, G. S. P. (1962b) *The East African Coast. Select Documents from the First to the Earlier Nineteenth Century*. London: Clarendon Press.

Freeman-Grenville, G. S. P. (1963a) 'The Coast, 1498–1840'. In R. Oliver and G. Mathew (eds), *History of East Africa*, vol. I. Oxford: Clarendon Press, pp. 129–63.

Freeman-Grenville, G. S. P. (1963b) 'Coins from Mogadishu, c.1300 to c.1700'. *Numismatic Chronicle*, pp. 179–200.

Freeman-Grenville, G. S. P. (1963c) 'The German sphere, 1884–98'. In R. Oliver and G. Mathew (eds), *Oxford History of East Africa*, vol. 1. London: Clarendon Press, pp. 433–53.

Freeman-Grenville, G. S. P. (1965a) Habari za Pate: *History of Pate*, by Muhammad bin Bwana Mkuu al-Nabhani, revised and enlarged by Muhammad bin Fumo Omari al-Nabhani Bwana Kitini. Unpublished paper.

Freeman-Grenville, G. S. P. (1965b) *The French at Kilwa Island*. Oxford: Clarendon Press.

Freeman-Grenville, G. S. P. (1977) *The Muslim and Christian Calendars: Being Tables for the Conversion of Muslim and Christian Dates from the Hijra to the Year A.D. 2000*. London: Rex Collings (2nd edition).

Freeman-Grenville, G. S. P. (1978a) 'Numismatic evidence for chronology at Kilwa'. *Numismatic Chronicle* (7th series), pp. 191–6.

Freeman-Grenville, G. S. P. (1978b) 'Shi'i rulers at Kilwa'. *Numismatic Chronicle* (7th series), pp. 187–90.

Freeman-Grenville, G. S. P. (ed. and trans.) (1980) *The Mombasa Rising Against the Portuguese, 1631, From Sworn Evidence*. London: British Academy and Oxford University Press.

Freeman-Grenville, G. S. P. (1981) *The Book of the Wonders of India by Captain Buzurg ibn Shahriyar of Ramhormuz*. London and The Hague: East West Publications.

Freeman-Grenville, G. S. P. (1986) 'A find of silver pieces at Mtambwe Mkuu, Pemba Island, Zanzibar, Tanzania'. *Antiquaries Journal* 66, pp. 372–4.

Freeman-Grenville, G. S. P. (1988) 'The early spread of Islam in East Africa; some problems'. African History Seminar SOAS, 16 November 1988.

Freeman-Grenville, G. S. P. (1992) 'A new look at the *Chrónica dos Reyes de Quiloa* following recent archaeological discoveries'. Symposium on Maritime Routes and Associated Networks, Sagres, Portugal, 28 April–1 May 1992.

Freeman-Grenville, G. S. P. (1993) 'Apropos the gold of Sofala'. In O. Hulac and M. Mendel (eds), *Threefold Wisdom – Islam, the Arab World and Africa*. Prague: Academy of Sciences of the Czech Republic, Oriental Institute, pp. 89–106.

Freeman-Grenville, G. S. P. and Martin, B. G. (1973) 'A preliminary list of the Arabic inscriptions on the East African coast'. *Journal of the Royal Asiatic Society* pt 2, pp. 98–122.

Fuglesang, Minou (1993) *Veils and Videos: Female Youth Culture on the Kenyan Coast*. Stockholm: University of Stockholm.

Garlake, P. (1966) *The Early Islamic Architecture of the East African Coast*. Nairobi and Oxford: British Institute in Eastern Africa, memoir 1.

Garlake, P. (1973) *Great Zimbabwe*. London: Thames and Hudson.

Ghaidan, U. (1975) *Lamu: A Study of the Swahili Town*. Nairobi: East African Literature Bureau.

Ghaidan, U. (1976) *Lamu, a Study in Conservation*. Nairobi: East African Literature Bureau.

Gibb, H. A. R. (1962) *The Travels of Ibn Battuta 1325–54. Vol. 2*. London: Hakluyt Society Series, vol. 110.

Gilbert, E. (1998) 'The *Mtepe*: regional trade and the late survival of sewn ships in East African waters'. *International Journal of Nautical Archaeology* 27, 1, pp. 43–50.

Giles, L. (1987) 'Possession cults on the Swahili coast: a re-examination of theories of marginality'. *Africa* 57, 2, pp. 234–58.

Giles, L. (1989) Spirit Possession on the Swahili Coast: Peripheral Cults or Primary Texts. Unpublished Ph.D. thesis, University of Texas at Austin.

Glassman, Jonathon (1995) *Feasts and Riot: Revelry, Rebellion, and Popular Consciousness on the Swahili Coast, 1856–1888*. London: James Currey.

Goitein, S. D. (1954) 'Two eye-witness reports on an expedition of the king of Kish (Qais) against Aden'. *Bulletin of the School of Oriental and African Studies* 16, pp. 247–547.

Goitein, S. D. (1966) *Studies in Islamic History and Institutions*. Leiden: E. J. Brill.

Goitein, S. D. (1967) *A Mediterranean Society. The Jewish Communities of the Arab World as Portrayed in the Documents of the Cairo Geniza*. Berkeley and Los Angeles: University of California Press.

Goitein, S. D. (1973) *Letters of Medieval Jewish Traders*. Princeton: Princeton University Press.

Goldman, H. (1995) A Comparative Study of Swahili in Two Rural Communities in Pemba, Zanzibar, Tanzania. Unpublished Ph.D. dissertation, New York University.

Gomm, R. (1975) 'Bargaining from weakness: Possession on the south Kenya coast'. *Man* 10, 4, pp. 530–43.

Gray, J. M. (1947) 'Rezende's description of East Africa in 1634'. *Tanganyika Notes and Records* 23, pp. 2–29.

Gray, J. M. (1950) 'Portuguese records relating to the Wasegeju'. *Tanganyika Notes and Records* 29, pp. 85–97.

Gray, J. M. (1951–2) 'A history of Kilwa'. *Tanganyika Notes and Records* 31, pp. 1–28; 32, pp. 11–37.

Gray, J. M. (1955) 'Nairuz or Siku ya Mwaka'. *Tanganyika Notes and Records* 38, pp. 1–22.

Gray, J. M. (1956) *Report on the Inquiry into Claims to Certain Land at or near Ngezi, Vitongoji, in the Mudiria of Chake Chake, in the District of Pemba.* Zanzibar: Government Printer.

Gray, J. M. (1957) *The British in Mombasa.* London: Macmillan.

Gray, J. M. (1958a) *Early Portuguese Missionaries in East Africa.* London: Macmillan.

Gray, J. M. (1958b) Notes on Ras Mkumbuu. Typescript held in Zanzibar Archives.

Gray, J. M. (1959–60) 'Zanzibar local histories'. *Swahili* 30, pp. 24–50; 31, pp. 111–39.

Gray, J. M. (1962) *A History of Zanzibar from the Middle Ages to 1856.* London: Oxford University Press.

Gray, J. M. (1963) 'Zanzibar and the coastal belt, 1840–1884'. In R. Oliver and G. Mathew (eds), *History of East Africa*, vol. I. Oxford: Clarendon Press, pp. 212–51.

Gray, J. M. (1977) 'The Hadimu and Tumbatu of Zanzibar'. *Tanganyika Notes and Records* 81/82, pp. 135–53.

Gray, J. M. (n.d.) *Chronicles of Zanzibar.* Zanzibar Museum (Government Printer).

Gray, J. R. and Birmingham, D. (eds) (1970) *Pre-colonial African Trade.* London: Oxford University Press.

Gray, R. F. (1969) 'The Shetani cult among the Segeju of Tanzania'. In J. Beattie and J. Middleton (eds), *Spirit Mediumship and Society in Africa.* London: Routledge and Kegan Paul, pp. 171–87.

Great Britain (1933–4) *Kenya Land Commission: Evidence.* Nairobi: Government Printer.

Grottanelli, V. L. (1947) 'Asiatic influences on Somali culture'. *Ethnos* 4, pp. 153–81.

Grottanelli, V. L. (1955a) *Pescatori dell'Oceano Indiano.* Rome: Cremonese.

Grottanelli, V. L. (1955b) 'A lost African metropolis'. In J. Lucas (ed.), *Afrikanische Studien.* Berlin: Akademie Verlag, pp. 231–42.

Guennec-Coppens, F. Le (1980) *Wedding Customs in Lamu.* Lamu: Lamu Society.

Guennec-Coppens, F. Le (1983) *Les Femmes Voilées de Lamu, Kenya: Variations culturelles et dynamiques sociales.* Paris: Editions Recherches sur les Civilisations.

Guennec-Coppens, F. Le (1987) 'L'Instabilité conjugale et ses conséquences dans la société swahili de Lamu (Kenya)'. In D. Parkin and D. Nyamwaya (eds), *Transformations of African Marriages.* Manchester: Manchester University Press, pp. 233–46.

Guennec-Coppens, F. Le and Caplan, P. (eds) (1991) *Les Swahili entre Afrique et Arabie.* Paris: Karthala.

Guillain, M. (1856) *Documents sur l'Histoire, la Géographie, et la Commerce de l'Afrique Orientale.* Paris: Bertrand (3 vols).

Haaland, R. (1994). 'Dakawa: an Early Iron Age site in the Tanzanian hinterland'. *Azania* 29–30, pp. 238–47.

Hahner-Herzog, I. (1990) *Tippu Tip und der Elfenbeinhandel in Ost- under Zentral-Afrika im 19. Jahrhundert*. Munchen: Tuduv-Verlag.

Hall, M. (1987) *The Changing Past: Farmers, Kings and Traders in Southern Africa, 200–1860*. Cape Town and Johannesburg: David Philip.

Hamilton, R. W. (1920–1) 'Land tenure among the Bantu Wanyika of East Africa'. *Journal of the Africa Society* 20, pp. 13–18.

Hansman, J. (1985) *Julfar, an Arabian port, its Settlement and Far Eastern Trade from the 14th Century to the 18th Century*. London: Royal Asiatic Society, Prize Publication Fund XXII.

Harding, J. (1960) 'Two Frankish beads from the coast of Tanganyika'. *Medieval Archaeology* 4, pp. 126–7.

Harries, L. (1959) 'Swahili traditions of Mombasa'. *Afrika und Ubersee* 43, 2, pp. 81–105.

Harries, L. (1962) *Swahili Poetry*. Oxford: Clarendon Press.

Harries, L. (ed. and trans.) (1965) *Swahili Prose Texts: A Selection from the Material Collected by Carl Velten from 1893 to 1896*. London: Oxford University Press.

Harries, L. (ed. and trans.) (1977). *The Swahili Chronicle of Ngazija by Said Bakari bin Sultan Ahmed*. Madison: University of Wisconsin Press.

Heine, B. (1982) 'Language and history of the Boni'. In B. Heine (ed.), *Recent German Research on Africa: Language and Culture*. Tubingen: Institute for Scientific Cooperation, pp. 106–14.

Helm, R. (2000) Conflicting Histories: The Archaeology of Ironworking, Farming Communities in the Central and Southern Coast Region of Kenya. Unpublished Ph.D. University of Bristol.

Herbert, E. (1984) *Red Gold of Africa*. Wisconsin: University of Wisconsin Press.

Herlehy, Thomas and Morton, Rodger F. (1988) 'A coastal ex-slave community in the regional and colonial economy of Kenya: the WaMisheni of Rabai, 1880–1963'. In Suzanne Miers and Richard Roberts, (eds) *The End of Slavery in Africa* Madison: University of Wisconsin Press, pp. 254–81.

Hersi, A. A. (1977) The Arab Factor in Somali History: The Origins and the Development of Arab Enterprise and Cultural Influences in the Somali Peninsula. Unpublished Ph.D. thesis, University of California at Los Angeles.

Hichens, W. (1938) 'Lamu Chronicle (Khabari Lamu)'. *Bantu Studies* 12, pp. 3–33.

Hichens, W. (ed.) (1939) *Al-Inkishafi: The Soul's Awakening*. London: Sheldon Press.

Hichens, W. (1940) *Diwani ya Muyaka bin Haji Al-Ghassaniy*. Johannesburg: University of the Witwatersrand Press.

Hinawy, Mbarak Ali (1964) 'Notes on customs in Mombasa'. *Swahili* 34, 1, pp. 17–35.

Hinawy, Mbarak Ali (1970) *Ali Al-Akida and Fort Jesus, Mombasa*. Nairobi: East African Literature Bureau (2nd edition).

Hinnebusch, T. J. (1976) 'The Shungwaya hypothesis: a linguistic reappraisal'. In J. T. Gallogher (ed.), *East African Culture History.* Syracuse: Syracuse University Program in Eastern African Studies.

Hinnebusch, T. J. (1996) 'What kind of language is Swahili?' *Afrikanische Arbeit-spapiere* 47, pp. 73–95.

Hino, S. (1968a) 'Social stratification of a Swahili town'. *Kyoto African Studies* 2.

Hino, S. (1968b) 'The occupational differentiation of an African town'. *Kyoto African Studies* 2.

Hino, S. (1971) 'Neighbourhood groups in an African urban society: Social relations and consciousness of the Swahili people of Ijiji, a small town of Tanzania, East Africa'. *Kyoto African Studies* 6.

Hirsch, Susan (1998) *Pronouncing and Persevering: Gender and the Discourses of Disputing in an African Islamic Court.* Chicago: University of Chicago Press.

Hirschberg, W. (1974) 'Der Suaheli-Kalender an der Ostkuste Afrikas'. In *In Memoriam Antonio Jorge Dias I*, Lisbon: Junta de Investigacoes Cientificas do Ultramar, pp. 215–28.

Hirth, F. and Rockhill, W. W. (1911) *Chau Ju-Kua: His Work on the Chinese and Arab Trade in the Twelfth and Thirteenth Centuries, Entitled Chu-yan-chi.* St Petersburg.

Hitti, P. K. (1970) *History of the Arabs.* London: Macmillan (10th edition).

Hodges, R. and Whitehouse, D. (1983) *Mohammed and Charlemagne and the Origins of Europe.* London: Duckworth.

Hollis, A. C. (1900) 'Notes on the history of Vumba, East Africa'. *Journal of the Royal Anthropological Institute* 30, pp. 275–300.

Holy, L. (1985) 'Power, agnation and marriage in the Middle East'. In R. Fardon (ed) *Power and Knowledge.* Edinburgh: Scottish Academic Press, pp. 103-25.

Horden, P. and Purcell, N. (2000) *The Corrupting Sea.* Oxford: Blackwell Publishers.

Horne, D. L. (1984) Mode of Production in the Social and Economic History of Kilwa to 1884. Unpublished Ph.D. thesis, University of California at Los Angeles.

Hornell, J. (1934) 'Indonesian influences on East African culture'. *Journal of the Royal Anthropological Institute* 37, pp. 305–32.

Horton, M. C. (1984) The Early Settlement of the Northern Swahili Coast. Unpublished Ph.D. thesis, University of Cambridge.

Horton, M. C. (1986) 'Asiatic colonization of the East African coast: the Manda evidence'. *Journal of the Royal Asiatic Society* pt 2, pp. 201–13.

Horton, M. C. (1987a) 'Early Muslim trading settlements on the East African coast: new evidence from Shanga'. *Antiquaries Journal* 67 pt 2, pp. 290–323.

Horton, M. C. (1987b) 'The Swahili corridor'. *Scientific American* 257, 3, pp. 86–93.

Horton, M. C. (1990) 'The *Periplus* and East Africa'. *Azania* 25, pp. 95–9.

Horton, M. C. (1991) 'Primitive Islam and architecture in East Africa'. *Muqarnas* 8, pp. 103–16.

Horton, M. C. (1993) 'Swahili architecture, space and social structure'. In M. Parker-Pearson and C. Richards (eds.), *Architecture and Order.* London: Routledge.

Horton, M. C. (1994) 'Closing the corridor: archaeological and architectural evidence for emerging Swahili regional autonomy'. In D. Parkin (ed.) *Continuity and Autonomy in Swahili Communities*. London: SOAS, pp. 15-21.

Horton, M. C. (1996a) *Shanga. The Archaeology of a Muslim Trading Community on the Coast of East Africa*. London: British Institute in Eastern Africa.

Horton, M. C. (1996b) 'Early maritime trade and settlement along the coasts of East Africa'. In J. Reade, ed., (1996), pp. 439–60.

Horton, M. C. (1997a) 'Mare Nostrum – a new archaeology in the Indian Ocean'. *Antiquity* 71, pp. 753–55.

Horton, M. C. (1997b) 'Archaeology and Prehistory: East Africa'. In J. Middleton (ed.), *Encyclopedia of Africa South of the Sahara*, vol. 1. New York: Seibner's Sons, pp. 90–5.

Horton, M. C. (1998) 'The Portugese encounter, with the Swahili towns of the East African Coast'. In J. Hallett and C. Amaral (eds) *Cultures of the Indian Ocean*. Lisbon: Comissão Nacional para as Comemoracões dos Descobrim entos Portugeses, pp. 373-84.

Horton, M. C. (forthcoming) *Zanzibar and Pemba: Archaeological Investigations of an Indian Ocean Archipelago*. London: British Institute in Eastern Africa.

Horton, M. C., Brown, H. W. and Oddy, W. A (1986) 'The Mtambwe hoard'. *Azania* 21, pp. 115–23.

Horton, M. C. and Blurton T. R. (1988) '"Indian" Metalwork in East Africa: the bronze lion statuette from Shanga'. *Antiquity* 62, 234, pp. 11–23.

Horton M. C. and Clark, C. M. (1985) *Zanzibar Archaeological Survey 1984-5*. Zanzibar: Ministry of Information Culture and Sports.

Horton, M. C. and Mudida, N. (1993) 'Exploitation of marine resources: evidence for the origins of the Swahili communities of East Africa'. In T. Shaw, P. Sinclair, B. Andah and A. Okpoko (eds), *The Archaeology of Africa: Food, Metals and Towns*. London: Routledge, pp. 673–93.

Hourani, G. F. (1995) *Arab Seafaring in Indian Ocean in Ancient and Early Medieval Times*. Princeton: Princeton University Press (revised and expanded edition).

Hoyle, E. (1999) 'Port concentration, inter-port competition and revitalization: the case of Mombasa, Kenya'. Maritime Policy Management 26, pp. 161-74.

Huffman, T. N. (1980) 'Archaeology and ethnohistory of the African Iron Age'. *Annual Review of Anthropology* 11, pp. 133–50.

Huffman, T. N. (1996) *Snakes and Crocodiles. Power and Symbolism in Ancient Zimbabwe*. Johannesburg: University of Witwatersrand Press.

Huntingford, G. W. B. (ed.) (1980) *The Periplus of the Erythraean Sea*. London: The Hakluyt Society.

Hutchinson, E. (1874) *The Slave Trade of East Africa*. London: Sampson Low.

Iliffe, J. A. (1979) *Modern History of Tanganyika*. Cambridge: Cambridge University Press.

Ingrams, W. H. (1931) *Zanzibar: Its History and its People*. London: Witherby.

Jama, A. O. (1996) *The Origins and Development of Mogadishu AD 1000-1850*. Uppsala: University of Uppsala.

Janmohamed, K. K. (1976) 'Ethnicity in an urban setting: A case study of Mombasa'. *Hadith* 6, pp. 186–206.

Jenson, J. R. (1973) *Journal and Letter Book of Nicholas Buckeridge, 1651–1654*. Minneapolis: University of Minnesota Press.

Jetzer, J. C. (1981) 'Terracotta coin moulds'. *Numismatics International Bulletin* 15, 11.

Johnson, F. (1939) *A Standard Swahili-English Dictionary*. Oxford: Oxford University Press.

Johnstone, H. B. (1902) 'Notes on the customs of the tribes occupying Mombasa sub-district'. *Journal of the Royal Anthropological Institute* 32, pp. 263–72.

Juma, A. M. (1996) 'The Swahili societies and the Mediterranean world: pottery of the late Roman period from Zanzibar'. *Antiquity* 70, pp. 148–54.

Kersten, O. (1869–79) *Baron Carl Claus von der Deckens Reisen in Ostafrika in den Jahren 1859 bis 1861*. Leipzig: Winter'sche.

Kindy, H. (1972) *Life and Politics in Mombasa*. Nairobi: East African Literature Bureau.

Kirk, W. (1962) 'The north-east monsoon and some aspects of African history'. *Journal of African History* 3, 2, pp. 263–7.

Kirkman, J. S. (1954) *The Arab City of Gedi: Excavations at the Great Mosque, Architecture and Finds*. London: Oxford University Press.

Kirkman, J. S. (1959) 'Excavations at Ras Mkumbuu on the island of Pemba'. *Tanganyika Notes and Records* 53, pp. 161–78.

Kirkman, J. S. (1963) *Gedi, The Palace*. The Hague: Mouton.

Kirkman, J. S. (1964) *Men and Monuments on the East African Coast*. London: Lutterworth.

Kirkman, J. S. (1966) *Ungwana on the Tana*. The Hague: Mouton.

Kirkman, J. S. (1973) Gedi: the houses and the walls. Typescript, Fort Jesus Museum, Mombasa.

Kirkman, J. S. (1975) 'Some conclusions from archaeological excavations on the coast of Kenya 1948–1966'. In H. N. Chittick and R. I. Rotberg (eds), *East Africa and the Orient*. New York: Africana, pp. 226–47.

Kirkman, J. S. (1983a) 'The early history of Oman in East Africa'. *Journal of Oman Studies* 6, pt 1, pp. 41–58.

Kirkman, J. S. (1983b) 'The Muzungulos of Mombasa'. *International Journal of African Historical Studies* 16, 1, pp. 73–82.

Klein-Arendt, Reinhard (1986) 'Liongo Fumo: Eine ostafrikanische Sagengestalt aus der Sicht der Swahili und der Pokomo'. *Afrikanische Arbeitspapiere, Schriftenreihe des Kölner Institut für Afrikanistik* 8, pp. 57–86.

Knappert, J. (1967) *Traditional Swahili Poetry: An Investigation into the Concepts of East African Islam as Reflected in the Utenzi Literature*. Leiden: Brill.

Knappert, J. (1970) *Myths and Legends of the Swahili*. London: Heinemann.

Knappert, J. (1979) *Four Centuries of Swahili Verse*. London: Heinemann.

Knysh, Alexander (1999) 'The Sada in history: A critical essay on Hadrami historiography'. *Journal of the Royal Asiatic Society* (3rd series) 9, 2, pp. 215–22.

Kopytoff, Igor (1986) 'The cultural biography of things: commodization as process'. In Arjun Appadurai (ed.), *The Social Life of Things: Commodities in Cultural Perspective*, Cambridge: Cambridge University Press, pp. 64–94.

Krapf, J. L. (1860) *Travels, Researches and Missionary Labours during an Eighteen Years' Residence in Eastern Africa*. London.

Krapf, J. L. (1882) *A Dictionary of the Swahili Language*. London: Trubner & Co. (reprint 1969, New York).

Kusimba, C. M. (1996) 'Spatial organisation at Swahili archaeological sites in Kenya'. In G. Pwiti and R. Soper (eds), *Papers of the 10th Conference of the Pan African Association of Prehistory and Related Subjects*. Harare: University of Zimbabwe, pp. 703–14.

Kusimba, C. M. (1999) *The Rise and Fall of Swahili States*. Walnut Creek: Altamira Press.

Lambek, M. (1981) *Human Spirits: A Cultural Account of Trance in Mayotte*. New York: Cambridge University Press.

Lambek, M. (1983) 'Virgin marriage and the autonomy of women in Mayotte'. *Signs* 9, pp. 269–83.

Lambek, M. (1988) 'Spirit possession/spirit succession: aspects of social continuity among Malagasy speakers in Mayotte'. *American Ethnologist* 15, 4, pp. 710–31.

Lambek, Michael (1993) *Knowledge and Practice in Mayotte: Local Discourses of Islam, Sorcery, and Spirit Possession*. Toronto: University of Toronto Press.

Lambert, H. E. (1953) 'The taking of Tumbe town'. *Journal of the East African Swahili Committee* 23, pp. 36–45.

Lambert, H. E. (1957) *Ki-Vumba: A Dialect of the Southern Swahili Coast*. Kampala: East African Swahili Committee.

Lambert, H. E. (1958a) *Chi-Chifundi: A Dialect of the Southern Swahili Coast*. Kampala: East African Swahili Committee.

Lambert, H. E. (1958b) *Chi-Jomvu and Kingare: Subdialects of Mombasa*. Kampala: East African Swahili Committee.

Lambert, H. E. (1962–3) 'The Beni dance songs'. *Swahili* 33, pp. 18–21.

Lambert, H. E. (1965) 'Some initiation songs of the southern Kenya coast'. *Swahili* 35, 1, pp. 49–67.

Lamden, S. C. (1963) 'Some aspects of porterage in East Africa'. *Tanganyika Notes and Records* 61, pp. 158–9.

Lamm, C. J. (1929) *Mittelarterliche Gläser und Steinchnittarbeiten aus dem nachen Osten*. Berlin: Dietrich Reimer/Ernst Vohsen (2 vols).

Lamphear, J. (1970) 'The Kamba and the northern Mrima coast'. In R. Gray and D. Birmingham (eds), *Pre-colonial African Trade*. London: Oxford University Press, pp. 76–102.

Landberg, P. W. (1977) Kinship and Community in a Tanzania Coastal Village (East Africa). Unpublished Ph.D. thesis, University of California at Davis.

Landberg, P. W. (1986) 'Widows and divorced women in Swahili society'. In B. Potash (ed.), *Widows in African Societies*. Stanford: Stanford University Press, pp. 107–30.

Lapidus, I. (1969) 'Muslim cities and Islamic societies'. In I. Lapidus (ed.), *Middle Eastern Cities*. Berkeley and Los Angeles: University of California Press.

Lary, P. and Wright, M. (1971) 'Swahili settlements in northern Zambia and Malawi'. *International Journal of African Historical Studies* 4, pp. 547–74.

Bibliography

Laviolette, A. (1998) Preliminary Report, Archaeological Investigations at Pujini (HAJX) and Chwaka (JxHL) Pemba 1997. MSS in Zanzibar Museum and Archives.

LaViolette, A. (1999) Preliminary Report, Archaeological Investigations at Chwaka (JxH1) Pemba. mss in Zanzibar Museum and Archives.

LaViolette, A. (2000) 'Swahili Archaeology on Pemba Island, Tanzania: Pujini, Bandari ya Faraji, and Chwaka, 1997-98'. *Nyame Akuma* 53, pp. 50-63.

LaViolette, A. and Fleisher, J. (1995) 'Reconnaissance of sites bearing Triangular Incised Ware (Tana Tradition) on Pemba Island, Tanzania'. *Nyame Akuma* 44, pp. 59–65.

LaViolette, A., Fawcett, W. and Schmidt, P. (1989) 'The Coast and the hinterland: University of Dar es Salaam Field Schools 1987–88'. *Nyame Akuma* 32, pp. 38–46.

Leakey, L. (1931) *The Stone Age Cultures of Kenya Colony*. Cambridge: Cambridge University Press.

Leakey, M. D. (1966) 'Excavations in the Burial Mounds of Ngorongoro Crater'. *Tanzania Notes and Records*, pp. 123–35.

Levtzion, N. and Hopkins J. F. P. (1981) *Corpus of Early Arabic Sources for West African History*. Cambridge: Cambridge University Press.

Lewis, B. (1974) *Islam: from the Prophet Mohammed to the Capture of Constantinople*. London: Macmillan (2 vols).

Lewis, I. M. (1955) *The Peoples of the Horn of Africa*. London: International African Institute.

Lewis, I. M. (1965) *The Modern History of Somaliland*. London: Weidenfeld & Nicholson.

Lewis, I. M. (1966a) *Islam in Tropical Africa*. Oxford: International African Institute.

Lewis, I. M. (1966b) 'Spirit possession and deprivation cults'. *Man* 1, pp. 307–29.

Lewis, I. M. (1971) *Ecstatic Religion*. Harmondsworth: Penguin.

Lienhardt, P. A. (1959) 'The Mosque College of Lamu and its social background'. *Tanganyika Notes and Records* 53.

Lienhardt, P. A. (1966) 'A controversy over Islamic custom in Kilwa Kivinje, Tanzania'. In Lewis (1966a), pp. 374–86.

Lienhardt, P. A. (1968) *The Medicine Man: Swifa ya Nguvumali, by Hasani bin Ismael*. Oxford: Clarendon Press.

Lienhardt, P. A. (1996) 'Family waqf in Zanzibar'. *Journal of the Anthropological Society of Oxford* 27, 2, pp. 96–106.

Linnehuhr, Elisabeth (1997) 'Kanga: Popular cloth with messages'. In Karin Barber (ed.), *Readings in African Popular Culture*. London: Oxford University Press for International African Institute & James Currey, pp. 138–41.

Lodhi, A. (1973) *The Institution of Slavery in Zanzibar and Pemba*. Uppsala: Scandinavian Institute of African Studies.

Lofchie, M. F. (1965) *Zanzibar: Background to Revolution*. London: Oxford University Press.

Lovejoy, Paul E. (1983) *Transformations in Slavery: A History of Slavery in Africa*. Cambridge: Cambridge University Press.

Low, D. A. (1963) 'The northern interior, 1840–84'. In R. Oliver and G. Mathew (eds), *History of East Africa*, vol. 1. London: Clarendon Press, pp. 297–351.

Lowick, N. M. (1983) 'Fatimid coins of Multan'. *Numismatic Digest* (Journal of the Indian Institute of Research in Numismatic Studies) 7 pts, I/II, pp. 62–9.

Lowick, N. M. (1985) *Siraf: The Coins and Monumental Inscriptions*. London: British Institute of Persian Studies, Siraf Fascicule 15.

Lyne, R. N. (1905) *Zanzibar in Contemporary Times*. London: Hurst and Blackett.

Macdonald, K. C. (1992) 'The domestic chicken (*Gallus gallus*) in sub-Saharan Africa: a background to its introduction and its osteological differentiation from indigenous fowls (Numidinae and *Francolinus* sp.)'. *Journal of Archaeological Science* 19, pp. 303–18.

MacDonald, J. R. L. (1897) *Soldiering and Surveying in British East Africa, 1891–1894*. London: Arnold.

Macdowall, D. W. (1996) 'Gazetteer of Roman artefacts'. In H. P. Ray and J-F Salles (eds) *Early Maritime Contact in the Indian Ocean*. New Delhi: Manohar, pp. 79–96.

Mangat, J. S. (1969) *A History of the Asians in East Africa*. London: Clarendon Press.

Manning, P. (1990) *Slavery and African Life. Occidental, Oriental and African Slave Trades*. Cambridge: Cambridge University Press, African Studies Series 57.

Martin, B. G. (1971) 'Notes on some members of the learned class of Zanzibar and East Africa in the nineteenth century'. *African Historical Studies* 4, 3, pp. 525–45.

Martin, B. G. (1974) 'Arab migrations to East Africa in medieval times'. *International Journal of African Historical Studies* 7, pp. 367–90.

Martin, E. B. (1973) *The History of Malindi*. Nairobi: East African Literature Bureau.

Martin, E. B. and Martin, C. P. (1978) *Cargoes of the East. The Ports, Trade and Cultures of the Arabian Seas and the Western Indian Ocean*. London: Elm Tree Books.

Martin, E. B. and Ryan, T. C. I. (1977) 'A quantitative assessment of the Arab slave trade of East Africa, 1770–1896'. *Kenya Historical Review* 5, pp. 71–91.

Mazrui, A. M and Shariff, I. N. (1994) *The Swahili*. Trenton: Africa World Press.

Mbele, Joseph L. (1976) 'The identity of the hero in the Liyongo epic'. *Research in African Literature* 17, 4, pp. 470.

Mbotela, J. J. (1956) *The Freeing of the Slaves in East Africa*. London: Evans.

Mbughuni, P. (1982) 'The image of women in Kiswahili prose fiction'. *Kiswahili* 49, pp. 15–24.

McCrindle, J. W. (1897) *The Christian Topography of Cosmas, an Egyptian Monk*. London: Hakluyt Society.

McGeagh, W. R. and Addis, W. (1934) *Review of the Systems of Land Tenure in Zanzibar and Pemba*. Zanzibar: Government Printer.

McIntosh, R. J. (1998) 'Western representations of urbanism and invisible African towns'. In S. K. McIntosh (ed.), *Pathways to Complexity: An African Perspective*. Cambridge: Cambridge University Press.

McKay, W. F. (1975) A Pre-Colonial History of the Southern Kenya Coast. Unpublished Ph.D. thesis, Boston University.

McMaster, D. N. (1966) 'The ocean-going dhow trade to East Africa'. *East African Geographical Review* 4, pp. 13–24.

Meffert, E. F. (1980) *Hydrothermal Comfort in Lamu Town*. Nairobi: University of Nairobi, Department of Architecture, Paper no. 6.

Meyer, C., Todd, J. M. and Beck, C. W. (1991) 'From Zanzibar to Zagros: a copal pendant from Eshnunna'. *Journal of Near Eastern Studies* 50, pp. 289–98.

Middleton, J. (1961) *Land Tenure in Zanzibar*. London: HMSO (Colonial Research Studies no. 23).

Middleton, J. (1965) 'Kenya: changes in African life, 1912–1945'. In V. Harlow and E. M. Chilver (eds), *History of East Africa*, vol. II. Oxford: Clarendon Press, pp. 333–94.

Middleton, J. (1972) 'Patterns of settlement in Zanzibar'. In P. J. Ucko, R. Tringham and D. Dimbleby (eds) *Man, Settlement, and Urbanism*. London: Duckworth, pp. 285–92.

Middleton, J. (1976) 'The immigrant communities (3): The Arabs of the East African coast'. In D. A. Low and A. Smith (eds), *History of East Africa*, vol. III. Oxford: Clarendon Press, pp. 489–507.

Middleton, J. (1992) *The World of the Swahili*. New Haven and London: Yale University Press.

Middleton, J. (1997) 'The delicacy of ethnography'. *Ethnos* 62, pp. 127-36.

Middleton, J. and Campbell, J. (1965) *Zanzibar, its History and Politics*. London: Oxford University Press.

Miers, Suzanne and Kopytoff, Igor (eds) (1977) *Slavery in Africa: Historical and Anthropological Perspectives*. Madison: University of Wisconsin Press.

Miles, G. C. (1975) 'Excavations at Ag. Prtros, Herakleion'. *Proceedings of the Third International Cretological Congress*, vol. 3, pp. 225–30.

Miles, G. C. and Warren, P. M. (1972) 'An Arab building at Knossos'. *Annual of the British School of Athens* 67, pp. 285–96.

Minorsky, V. (1937) *Hudud al-Alam: Translation and Commentary*. London: Luzac.

Mirza, S. and Strobel, M. (1989) *Three Swahili Women*. Bloomington: Indiana University Press.

Möhlig, W. J. G. (1982) 'Field studies in comparative dialect research on Kenya Swahili dialects'. In B. Heine (ed.), *Recent German Research on African Language and Culture*. Tübingen: Institute for Scientific Cooperation, pp. 54–61.

Moreau, R. E. (1941) 'The joking relationship (utani) in Tanganyika'. *Tanganyika Notes and Records* 12, pp. 1–10.

Moreau, R. E. (1944) 'Joking relationships in Tanganyika'. *Africa* 14, pp. 386–400.

Morgan, P. (1991) 'New thoughts on old Hormuz: Chinese ceramics in the Hormuz region in the thirteenth and fourteenth centuries'. *Iran* 29, pp. 67–84.

Morrison, H. M. (1984) 'The glass'. In H. N. Chittick, *Manda. Excavations at an Island Port on the Kenya Coast*. Nairobi: British Institute in Eastern Africa, memoir 8, pp. 181–90.

Morton, R. F. (1973) 'The Shungwaya myth of Mijikenda origins, a problem of late nineteenth-century Kenya coastal history'. *International Journal of African Historical Studies* 5, pp. 397–423.

Morton, R. F. (1977) 'New evidence regarding the Shungwaya myth of Mijikenda origins'. *International Journal of African Historical Studies* 10, 4, pp. 628–43.

Mutoro, H. W. (1987) An Archaeological Study of the Mijikenda *Kaya* Settlements on the Hinterland of the Kenya Coast. Unpublished Ph.D. thesis, University of California at Los Angeles.

Nabhany, A. Sh. (1979) *Sambo ya Kiwandeo (The Ship of Lamu Island)*. Leiden: Afrika Studiecentrum.

Nabhany, A. Sh. (1985) *Umbuji wa Mnazi*. Nairobi: East African Publishing House.

New, C. (1873) *Life, Wanderings and Labours in Eastern Africa*. London: Hodder and Stoughton.

Newitt, M. (1978) 'The southern Swahili coast in the first century of European expansion'. *Azania* 13, pp. 111–26.

Newitt, M. (1995) *A History of Mozambique*. Bloomington: Indiana University Press.

Nicholls, C. S. (1971) *The Swahili Coast: Politics, Diplomacy, and Trade on the East African Littoral, 1798–1856*. London: Allen and Unwin.

Nimtz, A. H. (1980) *Islam and Politics in East Africa*. Minneapolis: University of Minnesota Press.

Nisula, T. (1999) *Everyday Spirit and Medical Interventions: Ethnographic and Historical Seula Notes on Therapeutic Conventions in Zanzibar Town*. Helsinki: Suomen Antropologiner.

Nurse, D. (1982) 'Segeju and Daisu: a case study of evidence from oral traditions and comparative linguistics'. *History in Africa* 9, pp. 175–208.

Nurse, D. (1983a) 'A linguistic reconsideration of Swahili origins'. *Azania* 18, pp. 127–50.

Nurse, D. (1983b) 'History from linguistics: the case of the Tana river'. *History in Africa* 10, pp. 207–38.

Nurse, D. (1983c) 'On dating Swahili'. *Études Océan Indien* 2, pp. 59–72.

Nurse, D. (1986) 'Reconstruction of Dahalo history through evidence from loan-words'. *Sprache und Geschichte in Afrika* 7, 2, pp. 267–305.

Nurse, D. and Hinnebusch, T. (1993) *Swahili and Sabaki*. Berkeley: University of California Press.

Nurse, D. and Spear, T. (1985) *The Swahili. Reconstructing the History and Language of an African Society, 800–1500*. Philadelphia: Pennsylvania University Press.

Oddy, W. A. (1984) 'Gold in the southern African Iron Age'. *Gold Bulletin* 17, 2, pp. 70–8.

Ottenheimer, M. (1984) 'Matrilocal residence and nonsororal polygyny: a case from the Comoro Islands'. *Journal of Anthropological Research* 35, pp. 328–35.

Ottenheimer, M. (1985) *Marriage in Domoni: Husbands and Wives in an Indian Ocean Community*. Prospect Heights: Waveland Press.

Ottenheimer, M. and Ottenheimer, H. (1994) *Historical Dictionary of the Comoro Islands*. London: Methuen.

Owen, W. F. W. (1833) *Narrative of Voyages to Explore the Shores of Africa, Arabia, and Madagascar*. London: Bentley (2 vols).

Page, M. E. (1974) 'The Maniema hordes of Tippu Tip'. *International Journal of African Historical Studies* 7.

Pakenham, R. H. W. (1945) *Land Tenure among the Wahadimu at Chwaka, Zanzibar Island.* Zanzibar: Government Printer.

Parkin, D. (1970) 'Politics of ritual syncretism: Islam among the non-Muslim Giriama of Kenya'. *Africa* 40, 3, pp. 217–33.

Parkin, D. (1972) *Palms, Wine, and Witnesses.* San Francisco: Chandler.

Parkin, D. (1979) 'Straightening the paths from wilderness: a case of divinatory speech'. *Journal of the Anthropological Society of Oxford* 10, pp. 147–60.

Parkin, D. (1985) 'Entitling evil: Muslims and non-Muslims in coastal Kenya'. In D. Parkin (ed.), *The Anthropology of Evil.* Oxford: Blackwell, pp. 224–43.

Parkin, D. (1985) 'Controlling the u-turn of knowledge'. In R. Fardon (ed.) *Power and Knowledge.* Edinburgh: Scottish Academic Press, pp. 49–60.

Parkin, D. (1989) *The Sacred Void.* Cambridge: Cambridge University Press.

Parkin, D. (ed) (1994) *Continuity and Autonomy in Swahili Communities.* London: SOAS.

Peak, R. (1989) 'Swahili stratification and tourism in Malindi Old Town, Kenya'. *Africa* 59, 2, pp. 209–20.

Pearce, F. B. (1920) *Zanzibar: The Island Metropolis of Eastern Africa.* London: T. Fisher Unwin.

Pearson, M. N. (1988) 'Brokers in West Indian port cities: The role in servicing foreign merchants'. *Modern Asian Studies* 22, 3, pp. 461 ff.

Pearson, M. N. (1998) *Port Cities and Intruders: The Swahili Coast, India, and Portugal in the Early Modern Era.* Baltimore: Johns Hopkins (World History African Studies).

Pedler, F. J. (1940) 'Joking relationship in East Africa'. *Africa* 13, pp. 170–3.

Pellat, C. (1962) *Mujuj al-Dhahab wa-Ma'adin al-Jauhar of al- Mas'udi* (text and translation by C. Barbier de Meynard and P. de Courteille, *Les Prairies d'or*, revised edition) Paris: Societie Asiatique.

Phillips, J. (1997) 'Punt and Aksum: Egypt and Horn of Africa'. *Journal of African History* 38, pp. 423–57.

Phillipson, D. W. (1977) *The Later Prehistory of Eastern and Southern Africa.* London: Heinemann.

Phillipson, D. W. (1979) 'Some Iron Age sites in the lower Tana valley'. *Azania* 14, pp. 155–60.

Phillipson, D. W. (1985) *African Archaeology.* Cambridge: Cambridge University Press.

Piggott, D. (1941) 'Mafia – its history and traditions by Amur Umar Sa'adi'. *Tanganyika Notes and Records* 12, pp. 23–7.

Popovic, A. (1976) *La Révolte des esclaves en Iraq au III/IX siècle.* Paris: Paul Guethner.

Pouwels, R. L. (1974) 'Tenth-century settlement of the East African coast: the case for Qarmatian/Isma'ili connections'. *Azania* 9, pp. 65–74.

Pouwels, R. L. (1978) 'The medieval foundations of East African Islam'. *International Journal of African Historical Studies* 9, pp. 201–27, 393–405.

Pouwels, R. L. (1987) *Horn and Crescent. Cultural Change and Traditional Islam on the East African Coast, 800–1900.* Cambridge: Cambridge University Press.

Prins, A. H. J. (1952) *The Coastal Tribes of the North-Eastern Bantu*. London: International African Institute.

Prins, A. H. J. (1956–8) 'An analysis of Swahili kinship terminology'. *Journal of the East African Swahili Committee* 26, pp. 20–8; 28, pp. 9–16.

Prins, A. H. J. (1958) 'On Swahili historiography'. *Journal of the East African Swahili Committee* 28, pp. 26–40.

Prins, A. H. J. (1960) 'The Somaliland Bantu'. *Bulletin of the International Committee on Urgent Anthropological and Ethnological Research* 3, pp. 28–31.

Prins, A. H. J. (1963) 'The didemic diarchic Boni'. *Journal of the Royal Anthropological Institute* 93, pp. 174–86.

Prins, A. H. J. (1965) *Sailing from Lamu: A Study of Maritime Culture in Islamic East Africa*. Assen: Van Gorcum.

Prins, A. H. J. (1967) *The Swahili-Speaking Peoples of the East African Coast*. London: International African Institute (revised edition).

Prins, A. H. J. (1969) 'Islamic maritime magic: a ship's charm from Lamu'. In H. Greshat and H. Jungraithmayr (eds), *Wort und Religion*. Stuttgart: Evangelischen Missionsverlag.

Prins, A. H. J. (1971) *Didemic Lamu, Social Stratification and Spatial Structure in a Muslim Maritime Town*. Groningen: Instituut voor Culturele Antropologie der Rijksuniversiteit.

Prins, A. H. J. (1972) 'The Shungwaya problem: Traditional history and cultural likeness in Bantu Northeast Africa'. *Anthropos* 67, pp. 9–35.

Prins, A. H. J. (1982) 'The Mtepe of Lamu, Mombasa and the Zanzibar sea'. *Paideuma* 28, pp. 85–100.

Prins, A. H. J. (1984) *Watching the Seaside: Essays on Maritime Anthropology*. Groningen: Rijksuniversiteit Groningen.

Purpura, A. (1997) Knowledge and Agency: the Social Relations of Islamic Expertise in Zanzibar Town. Unpublished PhD thesis, City University of New York.

Radimilahy, C. (1998) *Mahilaka*. Uppsala: University of Uppsala.

Ranger, T. O. (1975) *Dance and Society in Eastern Africa 1890–1970: The Beni Ngoma*. London: Heinemann.

Raum, O. F. (1965) 'German East Africa: Changes in African tribal life under German administration, 1892–1914'. In V. Harlow and E. M. Chilver (eds), *History of East Africa*, vol. II. Oxford: Clarendon Press, pp. 163–208.

Ray, H. P. (1995) 'A resurvey of Roman contacts with the East'. In M-F Boussac and J-F Salles (eds), *Athens, Aden and Arikamedu*. New Delhi: Manohar, pp. 75–95.

Reade, J. (ed.) (1996) *The Indian Ocean in Antiquity*. London: Kegan Paul International.

Révoil, C. (1885) 'Voyage chez les Benadirs, les Çomalis et les Bayouns en 1882 et 1883'. *La Tour du Monde* 49, pp. 1–80; 50, pp. 129–208.

Ricks, T. M. (1970) 'Persian Gulf seafaring and East Africa, ninth-twelfth centuries'. *African Historical Studies* 3, 2, pp. 339–57.

Risso, P. (1986) *Oman and Muscat, an Early Modern History*. London: Croom Helm.

Roberts, A. (ed.) (1968) *Tanzania before 1900*. Nairobi: East African Literature Bureau.

Robinson, A. E. (1939) 'The Shirazi colonisation of East Africa: Vumba'. *Tanganyika Notes and Records* 7, pp. 92–112.

Rogers, M. (1976) *The Spread of Islam*. Oxford: Elsevier- Phaidon.

Romero, P. (1985) 'Generations of strangers: the Kore of Lamu'. *International Journal of African Historical Studies* 18, pp. 455–72.

Romero, P. (1987) 'Possible sources for the origin of gold as an economic and social vehicle for women in Lamu (Kenya)'. *Africa* 57, 3, pp. 364–76.

Rozenstroch, M. (1984) Liongo Fumo: Legende et signification politique. Unpublished thesis, University of Paris.

Ruete, E. (1886) *Memories of an Arabian Princess*. New York: Appleton.

Russell, J. (1981) *Communicative Competence in a Minority Group: A Sociolinguistic Study of the Swahili speaking Community of the Old Town, Mombasa*. Leiden: Brill.

Saad, E. (1979) 'Kilwa dynastic historiography: A critical study'. *History in Africa* 6, pp. 177–207.

Sacleux, Ch. (1909) *Grammaire des Dialectes Swahilis*. Paris.

Sacleux, C. (1939) *Dictionnaire Swahili-Français*. Paris: Institute d'Ethnologie.

Salim, A. I. (1970) 'The movement for Mwambao or coast autonomy in Kenya 1956–63', *Hadith* 2, pp. 212–28.

Salim, A. I. (1972) 'Early Arab-Swahili political protest in colonial Kenya'. *Hadith* 4, pp. 71–84.

Salim, A. I. (1973) *The Swahili-Speaking Peoples of Kenya's Coast, 1895–1945*. Nairobi: East African Publishing House.

Salim, A. I. (1976) '"Native or Non-Native"? The problem of identity and the social stratification of the Arab Swahili of Kenya'. *Hadith* 6, pp. 65–85.

Salkeld, R. E. (1905) 'Notes on the Boni hunters of Jubaland'. *Man* 94, 168–70.

Salvadori, C. (1997) *Two Indian Travellers: East Africa 1902–1905*. Mombasa: Friends of Fort Jesus.

Sassoon, H. (1966) *Guide to the ruins at Kunduchi*. Dar es Salaam: National Culture and Antquities Division.

Sassoon, H. (1975) *The Siwas of Lamu*. Nairobi: Lamu Society.

Sassoon, H. (1980) 'Excavations at the site of early Mombasa'. *Azania* 15, pp. 1–42.

Sassoon, H. (1982) 'Mbaraki Pillar and related ruins on Mombasa Island'. *Kenya Past and Present* 14, pp. 26–34.

Schacht, J. (1964) 'Review of *The Medieval History of the Coast of Tanganyika* by G. S. P. Freeman-Grenville'. *Bibliotheca Orientalis* 21, p. 111.

Scheven, A. (1981) *Swahili Proverbs*. Washington: University Press of America.

Schmidt, E. and Beck, R-M. (1993) 'Leso: Spiegel islamischer Frauenkultur in Mombasa'. In H. Forkl (ed.), *Die Garten des Islam*. Stuttgart and London.

Schmidt, P. R. (1989) 'Early exploitation and settlement in the Usambara Mountains'. In A. C. Hamilton and R. Bensted-Smith, *Forest Conservation in the East Usambara Mountains Tanzania*. Gland and Cambridge: IUCN Tropical Forest Programme, pp. 75–8.

Schmidt, P. R., Karoma, N. J., LaViolette, A., Fawcett, W. B., Mabulla, A. Z., Rutabanzibwa, L. N. and Saanane, C. M. (1992) *Archaeological Investigations in the Vicinity of Mkiu, Kisarawe District, Tanzania.* Dar es Salaam: Archaeological Contributions of the University of Dar es Salaam, Occasional Paper no. 1.

Seidenberg, D. A. (1996) *Merchant Adventurers. The World of East African Asians 1750–1985.* New Delhi: New Age Publishers.

Shariff, I. N. (1973) 'Waswahili and their language: Some misconceptions'. *Kiswahili* 43, pp. 67–75.

Shariff, I. N. (1987) The Identity and Faith of Fumo Liyongo. Unpublished paper to African Studies Association, Denver.

Shariff, I. N. (1988) *Tungo zetu: Msingi wa Mashairi na Tungo Nyinginezo.* Trenton: Red Sea Press.

Shayt, D. A. (1992) 'The material culture of ivory outside Africa'. In D. H. Ross (ed.), *Elephant: The Animal and its Ivory in African Culture.* Los Angeles: Fowler Museum, pp. 367–81.

Shen, J. (1995) 'New thoughts on the use of Chinese documents in the reconstruction of Swahili history'. *History in Africa* 22, pp. 349–58.

Shepherd, G. M. (1977) 'Two marriage forms in the Comoro Islands; an investigation'. *Africa* 47, 4, pp. 344–59.

Shepherd, G. M. (1982) 'The making of the Swahili: A view from the southern end of the East African coast'. *Paideuma* 28, pp. 129–48.

Shepherd, G. M. (1987) 'Rank, gender, and homosexuality: Mombasa as a key to understanding sexual options'. In P. Caplan (ed.), *The Cultural Construction of Sexuality.* London: Tavistock Publications, pp. 240–70.

Sheriff, A. M. H. (1975) 'Trade and underdevelopment: economic history of the East African coast from the 1st to the 15th century'. *Hadith* 5, pp. 1–23.

Sheriff, A. M. H. (1981) 'The East African coast and its role in maritime trade'. In G. Mokhtar (ed.), *Unesco General History of Africa,* vol. 2. London: Heinemann, pp. 551–67.

Sheriff, A. M. H. (1987) *Slaves, Spices and Ivory in Zanzibar.* London: James Currey.

Sheriff, A. M. H. (ed.) (1995) *The History and Conservation of the Zanzibar Stone Town.* London: James Currey.

Sheriff, A. M. H. and Ferguson, E. (eds) (1991) *Zanzibar under Colonial Rule.* London: James Currey.

Silberman, L. (1950) 'The social survey of the Old Town of Mombasa'. *Journal of African Administration* 2, pp. 14–21.

Sinclair, P. J. J. (1982) 'Chibuene – an early trading site in southern Mozambique'. *Paideuma* 28, pp. 149–64.

Sinclair, P. J. J. (1987) *Space Time and Social Formation: A Territorial Approach to the Archaeology and Anthropology of Zimbabwe and Mozambique c.0–1700 AD.* Uppsala: Societas Archaeologica Upsaliensis.

Sinclair, P. J. J. (1991) 'Archaeology in eastern Africa: an overview of current chronological issues'. *Journal of African History* 32, pp. 179–219.

Sinclair, P. J. J and Håkanssan, T. (2000) 'The Swahili: City-State culture'. In M.H. Hansen (ed.) *A Comparative Study of Thirty City-State Cultures.* Copenhagen: Royal Danish Academy of Sciences and Letters, pp. 463–82.

Singer, Shambie (1996) 'An investigation of land tenure in Zanzibar shamba land'. *Anthropos* 91, pp. 457–71.

Skene, R. (1917) 'Arab and Swahili dances and ceremonies'. *Journal of the Royal Anthropological Institute* 47, pp. 413–34.

Smith, A. (1976) 'The end of the Arab Sultanate: Zanzibar 1945–1964'. In D. A. Low and A. Smith (eds), *History of East Africa*, vol. III. Oxford: Clarendon Press, pp. 196–211.

Smith, M. C. and Wright, H. T. (1988) 'The ceramics from Ras Hafun in Somalia: notes on a classical maritime site'. *Azania* 23, pp. 115–41.

Snow, P. (1988) *The Star Raft. China's Encounter with Africa*. London: Weidenfeld & Nicholson.

Soper, R. C. (1967a) 'Iron Age sites in north-eastern Tanzania'. *Azania* 2, pp. 19–36.

Soper, R. C. (1967b) 'Kwale: An early Iron Age site in south- eastern Kenya'. *Azania* 2, pp. 1–18.

Sourdel, D. (1983) *Medieval Islam*. London: Routledge & Kegan Paul (English edition).

Spear, T. T. (1974a) 'Traditional myths and linguistic analysis: Singwaya revisited'. *History in Africa* 4, pp. 229–46.

Spear, T. T. (1974b) 'Traditional myths and historian's myths: variation on the Singwaya theme of Mijikenda origins'. *History in Africa* 1, pp. 67–84.

Spear, T. T. (1978) *The Kaya Complex*. Nairobi: Kenya Literature Bureau.

Stamboul, Omari bin (1951) 'An early history of Mombasa and Tanga'. *Tanganyika Notes and Records* 31, pp. 32–6.

Staszak, Jean-Francois (1969) 'L'ouverture economique et la tourisme: zones franches et villages-clubs'. In Cour Grandmaison and Crozon, eds, (1969), pp. 169–87.

Steere, E. (1870) *Swahili Tales, as Told by the Natives of Zanzibar*. London: Bell and Daldy.

Stephen, H. (1978) Hunting and Gathering as a Strategic Adaptation: The Case of the Boni of Lamu District, Kenya. Unpublished Ph.D. thesis, Boston University.

Stern, E. (1987) 'Early glass from Heis on the north Somali coast'. *Annales des 10 éme Congrés par l'Historie du Verre, Madrid, 1985*, pp. 23–36.

Stevenson, E. L. (1932) *The Geography of Claudius Ptolemy*. New York: New York Public Library.

Stigand, C. (1913) *The Land of Zinj: Being an Account of British East Africa, its Ancient History and Present Inhabitants*. London: Constable.

Stiles, D. (1981) 'Hunters of the northern East African coast: origins and historical processes'. *Africa* 51, 4, pp. 848–62.

Strandes, J. (1961) *The Portuguese Period in East Africa* (trans. and ed. J. F. Wallwork and J. S. Kirkman). Nairobi: East African Literature Bureau.

Stren, R. (1970) 'Factional politics and central control in Mombasa, 1960–69'. *Canadian Journal of African Studies* 4, 1, pp. 33–56.

Strobel, M. (1975) 'Women's wedding celebrations in Mombasa, Kenya'. *African Studies Review* 18, 3, pp. 35–45.

Strobel, M. (1979) *Muslim Women in Mombasa 1890–1975*. New Haven: Yale University Press.

Strong, S. A. (1895) 'The history of Kilwa'. *Journal of the Royal Asiatic Society* 27, pp. 385–430.

Sulivan, G. L. (1873) *Dhow Chasing in Zanzibar Waters*. London: Sampson Low.

Summers, R. (1969) *Ancient Mining in Rhodesia*. Salisbury: National Museum of Rhodesia, memoir 3.

Sutton, J. E. G. (1987) 'Hyrax Hill and the Sirikwa: new excavations on site II'. *Azania* 22, pp. 1–36.

Sutton, J. E. G. (1990) *A Thousand Years of East Africa*. Nairobi: British Institute in Eastern Africa.

Sutton, J. E. G. (1997) 'The African lords of the international gold trade before the Black Death: al-Hasan bin Sulaiman of Kilwa and Mansur Musa of Mali'. *Antiquaries Journal* 77, pp. 221–42.

Swantz, M-L. (1966) Religious and Magical Rites of the Bantu Women in Tanzania. Unpublished paper, Dar es Salaam.

Swantz, M-L. (1970) *Ritual and Symbol in Transitional Zaramo Society: With Special Reference to Women*. Uppsala: Gleerup-Lund (Studia Missionalia Uppsaliensia 16).

Swartz, Marc J. (1978) 'Religious courts, community and ethnicity among the Swahili of Mombasa: An historical study of social boundaries'. *Africa* 49, pp. 29–41.

Swartz, Marc J. (1991) *The Way the World Is. Cultural Processes and Social Relations among the Mombasa Swahili*. Berkeley: University of California Press.

Tampoe, M. (1989) *Maritime Trade between China and the West*. Oxford: British Archaeological Reports, Int. Series 555.

Tanner, R. E. S. (1962) 'Relationships between the sexes in a coastal Islamic society: Pangani District, Tanganyika'. *African Studies* 21, 2, pp. 70–82.

Tanner, R. E. S. (1964) 'Cousin marriage in the Afro-Arab community of Mombasa, Kenya'. *Africa* 34, 2, pp. 127–38.

Taylor, W. E. (1891) *African Aphorisms or Saws from Swahili-land*. London: Sheldon Press.

Theal, G. M. (1890–1903) *Records of South-Eastern Africa*. Cape Town: Government Printer of Cape Colony. Cape Town: Government Printer of Cape Colony (9 vols).

Tibbetts, G. R. (1971) *Arab Navigation in the Indian Ocean before the Coming of the Portuguese*. London: Royal Asiatic Society.

Toll, C. (1968) *Kitab al-jauharatain al'atiqatain al-ma'i'atain min al-safra' walbaida'* by al-Hamdani. Uppsala: Studia Semitica Upsaliensia I.

Tolmacheva, M. (1976) 'The origin of the name "Swahili"'. *Tanganyika Notes and Records* 77–8, pp. 27–37.

Tolmacheva, M. (1979) '"They came from Damascus in Syria": a note on traditional Lamu historiography'. *International Journal of African Historical Studies* 12, pp. 259–69.

Tolmacheva, M. (1993) *The Pate Chronicle: Edited and Translated from mss 177, 321 & 358 of the Library of the University of Dar es Salaam*. Ann Arbor: Michigan State University Press.

Tracy, James D. (1990) *The Rise of Merchant Empires: Long-distance Trade in the Early Modern World* 1350–1750. Cambridge: Cambridge University Press.

Tracy, James D. (1991) *The Political Economy of Merchant Empires*. Cambridge: Cambridge University Press.

Trimingham, J. S. (1964) *Islam in East Africa*. London: Clarendon Press.

Trimingham, J. S. (1975) 'The Arab geographers and the East African coast'. In H. N. Chittick and R. I. Rotberg (eds), *East Africa and the Orient*. New York: Africana, pp. 115–46, 272–83.

Tucker, A. N. (1969) 'Sanye and Boni'. In H. J. Grashat and H. Jungraithmayr (eds), *Wort und Religion*. Stuttgart: Evangelischen Missions.

Turner, P. J. and Cribb, J. (1996) 'Numismatic evidence for the Roman trade with ancient India'. In Reade, ed., (1996), pp. 309–19.

Turton, E. R. (1970) 'Kirk and the Egyptian Invasion of East Africa in 1875: A reassessment'. *Journal of African History* 11, 3, pp. 355–70.

Turton, E. R. (1975) 'Bantu, Galla, and Somali migration in the Horn of Africa: A reassessment of the Juba/Tana area'. *Journal of African History* 16, pp. 519–37.

Vansina, J. (1997) 'Slender evidence, weighty consequences: on one word in the *Periplus Maris Erythraei*'. *History in Africa* 24, pp. 393–7.

Velten, C. (1907) *Prosa und Poesie der Suaheli*. Berlin.

Vérin, P. (1986) *The History of Civilisation in North Madagascar*. Rotterdam: Balkema.

Villiers, A. (1940) *Sons of Sinbad*. New York: Scribners.

Voeltzkow, A. (1923) *Witu-Inseln und Zanzibar-Archipel. Reise in Ostafrika in din Jahren 1903–1905*. Stuttgart.

Vogel, J. O. (1997) *Encyclopedia of Precolonial Africa*. Walnut Creek: Altamira Press.

Voigt, E. A. (1983) *Mapungubwe: An Archaeozoological Interpretation of an Iron Age Community*. Pretoria: Transvaal Museum.

Volker, K. (1992) Mapambo: Die Ornamente der Frau. Unpublished master's thesis, Freie Universitat Berlin.

Walker, J. (1936) 'The History of the coinage of the Sultans of Kilwa'. *Numismatic Chronicle*, pp. 43–81.

Wallerstein, Immanual (1974–89) *The Modern World System*. New York: Academic Press. (3 vols).

Walsh, M. (1992) 'Swahili ethnobotany and ethnoarchaeology'. *Azania* 28, pp. 135–6.

Wansbrough, J. (1970) 'Africa and the Arab geographers'. In D. Dalby (ed.), *Language and History in Africa*. London: Cass, pp. 89–101.

Werner, A. (1913) 'A few notes on the Wasanye'. *Man* 13, pp. 199–201.

Werner, A. (1914) 'Swahili history of Pate'. *Journal of the African Society* 14, pp. 148–61, 278–97, 392–413.

Werner, A. (1915) 'The Bantu coast tribes of the East Africa Protectorate'. *Journal of the Royal Anthropological Institute* 45, pp. 326–54.

Werner, A. (1926–8) 'The Swahili saga of Liongo Fumo'. *Bulletin of the School of Oriental and African Studies* 4, pp. 247–55.

Werner, A. (1932) *The Story of Miqdad and Mayasa*. Medstead: Azania Press.

Werner, A. (1933) *Myths and Legends of the Bantu*. London: Harrop.

Werner, A. and Hichens, W. (eds) (1934) *Utendi wa Mwana Kupona (Advice of Mwana Kupona upon the Wifely Duty)*. Medstead: Azania Press.

Werth, E. (1915) *Das Deutsch-ostafrikanische Kustenland*. Berlin: Reimer.

Wheatley, P. (1972) 'The concept of urbanism'. In P. J. Ucko, R. Tringham and G. W. Dimbleby (eds), *Man, Settlement and Urbanism*. London: Duckworth, pp. 601–37.

Wheatley, P. (1975) 'Analecta Sino-Africa Recensa'. In H. N. Chittick and R. I. Rotberg (eds), *East Africa and the Orient*. New York: Africana, pp. 76–114, 284–90.

Whitcomb, D. (1975) 'The archaeology of Oman: a preliminary discussion of the Islamic periods'. *Journal of Oman Studies* 1, pp. 123–57.

Whitcomb, D. and Johnson, J. H. (1979) *Quseir al-Qadim. 1978. Preliminary Report*. Cairo: ARCE.

Whitcomb, D. and Johnson, J. H. (1982) *Quseir al-Qadim 1980 Preliminary Report*. Cairo: ARCE Reports, vol. 7.

Whitehouse, D. (1968) 'Excavations at Siraf, first interim report'. *Iran* 6, pp. 1–22.

Whitehouse, D. (1971) 'Excavations at Siraf, fourth interim report'. *Iran* 9, pp. 1–18.

Whitehouse, D. (1974) 'Excavations at Siraf, sixth interim report'. *Iran* 12, pp. 1–30.

Whitehouse, D. (1976) 'Kish'. *Iran* 14, pp. 146–50.

Whitehouse, D. (1978) 'Siraf: an Islamic city and its rôle in art'. *Storia della Città* 7, pp. 54–8.

Whitehouse, D. (1979) 'Islamic glazed pottery in Iraq and the Persian Gulf: the ninth and tenth centuries'. *Estrado da Annali dell'Intituto Orientale di Napoli* 39 (N.S. 29), fasc. 1, pp. 45–61.

Whitehouse, D. (1996) 'Sasanian maritime activity'. In Reade, ed., (1996), pp. 339–49.

Whitehouse, D. and Williamson, A. (1975) 'Sasanian maritime trade'. *Iran* 11, pp. 29–49.

Whiteley, W. H. (1958) *The Dialects and Verse of Pemba*. Kampala: East African Swahili Committee.

Whiteley, W. H. (1969) *Swahili: The Rise of a National Language*. London: Methuen.

Wigboldus, J. S. (1996a) 'The spread of crops into sub-equatorial Africa during the early Iron Age'. *Azania* 29–30, pp. 75–88.

Wigboldus, J. S. (1996b) 'Early presence of African millets near the Indian Ocean'. In Reade, ed., (1996), pp. 75–88.

Wilding, R. (1973) A report on archaeological fieldwork on the northern Kenyan Coast, 1971–1973. Typescript held in British Institute in Eastern Africa Library.

Wilding, R. (1977) The Ceramics of the Lamu Archipelago. Unpublished Ph.D. thesis, University of Nairobi.

Wilding, R. (1987) *The Shanga Panel. Proceedings of Meeting to Discuss the Findings of the Archaeological Excavations at Shanga, Pate Island, Kenya*. Coast Museum Studies, occasional paper 1.

Wilding, R. (1988) *The Shorefolk; Aspects of the Early Development of Swahili Communities.* Mombasa: Fort Jesus, occasional paper 2.

Wilkinson, J. C. (1975) 'The Julanda of Oman'. *Journal of Oman Studies* 1, pp. 97–108.

Wilkinson, J. C. (1979) 'Suhar (Sohar) in the early Islamic period: the written evidence'. Proceedings of the Fourth International Conference of South Asian Archaeology, Naples.

Wilkinson, J. C. (1981) 'Oman and East Africa: new light on early Kilwan history from the Omani sources'. *International Journal of African Historical Studies* 14, 2, pp. 272–305.

Wilkinson, J. C. (1989) 'The Omani and Ibadi background to the Kilwah Sirah: the demise of Oman as a political and religious force in the Indian Ocean in the 6th/12th century'. In A. K. Irvine, R. B. Serjeant and G. R. Smith (eds), *A Miscellany of Middle Eastern Articles in Memoriam Thomas Muir Johnstone 1924–1983.* London: Longmans, pp. 131–48.

Williamson, A. (1973) 'Hurmuz and the trade of the Gulf in the 14th and 15th centuries'. *Proceedings of the Seminar for Arabian Studies* 3, pp. 52–68.

Williamson, A. (1974) 'Harvard archaeological survey of Oman, 1973, III – Sohar and the sea trade of Oman in the tenth century'. *Proceedings of the Seminar for Arabian Studies* 4, pp. 78–95.

Willis, J. (1986) Fumo-Liongo: a confusion of histories. Unpublished paper, School of Oriental and African Studies.

Willis, J. (1993) *Mombasa, the Swahili and the Making of the Mijikenda.* Oxford: Clarendon Press.

Wilson, G. (1961) 'Mombasa – a modern colonial municipality'. In A. W. Southall (ed.), *Social Change in Modern Africa*, London: Oxford University Press and International African Institute, pp. 98–112.

Wilson, T. H. (1978) *The Monumental Architecture and Archaeology North of the Tana River.* Nairobi: National Museums of Kenya.

Wilson, T. H. (1979a) 'Swahili funerary architecture of the North Kenya coast'. In J. de V. Allen and T. H. Wilson, *Swahili Houses and Tombs.* London: Art and Archaeology Research Papers, pp. 33–46.

Wilson, T. H. (1979b) 'Takwa, an ancient Swahili settlement of the Lamu archipelago'. *Kenya Past and Present* 10, pp. 6–16.

Wilson, T. H. (1980) *The Monumental Architecture and Archaeology of the Central and Southern Kenya Coast.* Nairobi: National Museums of Kenya.

Wilson, T. H. (1982) 'Spatial analysis and settlement patterns on the East African coast'. *Paideuma* 28, pp. 201–20.

Wilson, T. H. and Omar, A. L. (1997) 'Archaeological investigations at Pate'. *Azania* 32, pp. 31–76.

Wolf, E. (1982) *Europe and the Peoples without History.* Berkeley: University of California Press.

Wright, H. T. (1984) 'Early Seafarers of the Comoro Islands: the Dembeni phase of the IX-Xth centuries'. *Azania* 19, pp. 13–59.

Wright, H. T. (1992) 'Early Islam, oceanic trade and town development on Nzwani: the Comorian archipelago in the XIth-XVth Centuries'. *Azania* 28, pp. 81–128.

Yalden-Thompson, (1958) A Paper on the Oman Arabs in Zanzibar Protectorate. Zanzibar. Unpublished paper.

Ylvisaker, M. (1979) *Lamu in the Nineteenth Century: Land, Trade and Politics.* Boston: African Studies Centre, Boston University.

Ylvisaker, M. (1982) 'The ivory trade in the Lamu area'. *Paideuma* 28, pp. 221–31.

Younghusband, E. (1910) *Glimpses of East Africa and Zanzibar.* London: Longmans.

Zanzibar Government (1949) *Zanzibar Guide.* Zanzibar: Government Printer (2nd edition).

Zanzibar Government (1953) *Notes on the Census of the Zanzibar Protectorate 1948.* Zanzibar, Government Printer.

Zanzibar Government (1958) *The Report of the Supervisor of Elections on the Elections in Zanzibar, 1957.* Zanzibar: Government Printer.

Zanzibar Government (1960) *Report on the Census of the Population of Zanzibar Protectorate (Taken on the Night of the 19th and 20th March, 1958).* Zanzibar: Government Printer.

Zarins, J. (1996) 'Obsidian in the larger context of Predynastic/Archaic Egyptian Red Sea trade'. In Reade, ed. (1996), pp. 89–106.

Index

Index